AUTHOR	DE GRAMONT. S.	CLASS No.	944.03
TITLE	Epitaph for kings.	BOOK No.	
			86901239

This book must be returned on or before the date shown above
LANCASHIRE COUNTY LIBRARY
C

EPITAPH FOR KINGS

MARIE ANTOINETTE STAG-HUNTING
By Le Brun

EPITAPH FOR KINGS

BY

SANCHE DE GRAMONT

ILLUSTRATED

HAMISH HAMILTON

LONDON

First published in Great Britain, 1968
by Hamish Hamilton Ltd
90 Great Russell Street London WC1
Copyright © 1967 by Sanche de Gramont

SBN 241 01604 5

Printed in Great Britain by Butler and Tanner Ltd
Frome and London

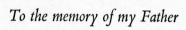

To the memory of my Father

NOTE ON MONEY

I⊤ is awkward to try to compare the eighteenth-century French livre and today's English pound. For one thing, prices in a rural economy do not follow the same pattern as in a highly industrialized economy. Food in eighteenth-century France was relatively cheap, but manufactured goods and colonial products like coffee and tea were dear. A wig could cost as much as a cow. For the sake of convenience, while underlining the approximate nature of the comparison, one can say that after the reform of 1726, which fixed the value of the gold louis at 24 livres (in other words, 8 ounces of gold were worth 740 livres), the French livre had roughly the purchasing power of about twelve shillings today. There are 20 sous in a livre, 3 livres in an écu (crown), and 10 livres in a pistol.

CONTENTS

LIST OF ILLUSTRATIONS

Let's talk of graves, of worms and epitaphs;
Make dust our paper and with rainy eyes
Write sorrow on the bosom of the earth,
Let's choose executors and talk of wills:
And yet not so, for what can we bequeath
Save our deposed bodies to the ground?
Our lands, our lives and all are Bolingbroke's,
And nothing can we call our own but death
And that small model of the barren earth
Which serves as paste and cover to our bones.
For God's sake, let us sit upon the ground
And tell sad stories of the death of kings:

—RICHARD II,
Act III, Scene ii

INTRODUCTION

> *Pray consider, sirs, that I neither blame nor approve*
> *—I relate.*
>
> —TALLEYRAND

> *Certain Greeks, hoping to advertise how clever*
> *they are, have tried to account for the flooding of*
> *the Nile in three different ways. Two of the ex-*
> *planations are not worth dwelling upon, beyond*
> *a bare mention of what they are: one is that the*
> *etesian winds cause the water to rise by checking*
> *the flow of the current toward the sea ... the second*
> *explanation is less rational, being somewhat, if I*
> *may so put it, of a legendary character: it is that*
> *the Nile exhibits its remarkable characteristics be-*
> *cause it flows from the Ocean, the stream of which*
> *encircles the world. The third theory is much the*
> *most plausible, but at the same time furthest from*
> *the truth: according to this, the water of the Nile*
> *comes from melting snow—but as it flows from*
> *Lybia through Ethiopia into Egypt, that is from a*
> *very hot into a cooler climate, how could it possibly*
> *originate in snow? Obviously this view is as worth-*
> *less as the other two. . . . If, after criticizing these*
> *theories, I must express an opinion myself about a*
> *matter so obscure as to why the Nile floods in*
> *summer, I would say (to put the whole thing in the*
> *fewest words) that during winter the sun is driven*
> *out of his course by storms toward the upper part*
> *of Lybia. It stands to reason that the country nearest*
> *to, and most directly under the sun should be most*
> *short of water, and that the streams which feed the*
> *rivers in that neighbourhood should most readily*
> *dry up.*
>
> —HERODOTUS

WHEN A KING of France died, his doctors performed ✓ a fearsomely thorough autopsy. The body was cut open from the throat to the hips. The heart and intestines were removed and embalmed like a pharaoh's. The other organs were studied for signs of tumours and the cranium was opened so that the brain could be examined. The body was then embalmed and placed in a double coffin, the inner one lead and the outer one walnut or oak.

This book attempts, in a less clinical manner, to perform an autopsy on French society before the Revolution of 1789, which usually goes under the name of *ancien régime*. The events of 1789 are seen, not as the start of a revolutionary era, but as the end of the longest continuous form of government in French history, 800 years of unbroken dynastic succession. The monarchy achieved its great task, the creation of the French nation, and then ceased to function. In the eighteenth century, with which the greater part of this book is concerned, a revolution became necessary because all avenues of peaceful change were obstructed.

The monarchy had survived far graver crises than the one which threatened it on the eve of the Revolution: in the Hundred Years' War, the king was captured and entire provinces fell into English hands; in the fourteenth century, the Paris Mayor, Etienne Marcel, ✓ led a revolt which forced Charles V to flee his capital; in the fifteenth century, an impotent dauphin had to be rescued by Joan of Arc; in the sixteenth century, the wars of religion lapsed into a long civil strife with massacres of Protestants as sanguinary as any Revolutionary terror; in the seventeenth century, the *fronde des princes* made an eleven-year-old Louis XIV flee Paris at night to escape assas- ✓ sination by his own nobility. The Revolution, in the beginning, was no more than a less menacing *fronde*.

When Louis XIV died in 1715, the French monarchy was the strongest in Europe, the one least threatened by internal strife, and ✓ yet it was the first to be toppled. Seventy-seven years later, Louis XVI was decapitated, and the magic chain of royal succession was severed. In a relatively short time, absolute monarchy proved that it had neither the strength to crush the forces which threatened it nor the flexibility to assimilate them. It was frozen in its inadequacies. It could not continue as it was, and it could not change. The Revolution was conducted against a regime already soft with decay. On one hand, like the centenarian writer Fontenelle, who died 'from an incapacity to continue to exist,' it had come to the end of its natural life span. On the other, like an ageing gladiator facing a freed slave armed with trident and net, it had to be put to death.

How and why did the *ancien régime* decline? In trying to answer these questions I have steered a middle course between two conflicting historical theories. The first is Carlyle's belief that history is 'the essence of innumerable biographies,' which would lay much of the blame at the satin-shod feet of Louis XV and Louis XVI, or their wives and mistresses, favourites and ministers, confessors and valets. But weaker kings survived more desperate times. The second is Tolstoi's conviction that men are the puppets of circumstance, in which case one would have to concede that the carriage of French monarchy would have overturned no matter who the coachman and postilions had been. This cannot be demonstrated, for history, unlike the story of the lady or the tiger, offers only one ending. Events abolish options. It is pointless to wonder what would have happened in 1789 if France had had a strong instead of a weak king, or if Marie Antoinette had been thrifty and retiring instead of a meddlesome spendthrift. This is not analysis, it is wishful thinking. It is impossible to prove that an event like the French Revolution might have been avoided given a different set of participants or circumstances for the simple reason that history presents us with a successful revolution. It is equally impossible to prove that the French Revolution was inevitable in the particular form that it took, since we cannot know what the result of the options would have been. This is the double shell of history. One can no more demonstrate that a given situation might have had a different outcome than one can demonstrate that its result was preordained. There are no lessons to be drawn from the *fait accompli* of events—such as affirming that reforms are vain because they were attempted and failed, or that harshness in kings is preferable to indecision. The lessons are elsewhere, in the minute inspection of the mechanism and articulation of events. Mathematicians are given data which will lead to the answer. In historical writing the method is reversed: the answer is known but the data must be sought. Events do not cast shadows into the future, but into the past.

This fitting of data to a foreknown conclusion can lead to two dangerous temptations, that of the historian-prosecutor and that of the single cause. Most French historians since the Revolution have been caught in a cycle of apologetics. One generation blackens the *ancien régime* to whitewash the Revolution, and the next weeps for the monarchy and laments the evils of Republicanism. The *ancien régime* and the Revolution become defendants in a never-ending trial prosecuted by the great historians, who are often conditioned by the period in which they are writing. Adolphe Thiers, chafing under the Bourbon Restoration of the early nineteenth century, described the Revolution as a deliverance in order to brand the Restoration as a new oppression. A few years later, Jules Michelet, with a lyric gift unencumbered by accuracy, created the folk-myth of the Revolution. He invented a mystique patterned on the monarchy's own theory of divine right. The Revolution was a Day of Judgment, the oppressed people rose up to replace 'Tyranny in the name of Grace.' The Revolution was a sacred act of patriotism. It had saved France. Michelet's misty incantations do not rest on historical evidence. They are their own romantic justification. 'I beg you to come look at this defeated people,' he writes, 'a poor Job surrounded by false friends. . . . Behold his pained and silent gaze at the king. What does this gaze say? "O King, you whom I made my God, before whom I erected my altar, whom I asked for salvation when I was at death's door, you my hope and you my love. . . . What? Did you feel nothing?"'

The next cycle came in the second half of the nineteenth century, when historians were disillusioned by the rapid succession of unstable regimes and the violence of French political life. They traced the nation's misfortunes to the Revolution. Outstanding among these pyrrhic chroniclers were Ernest Renan, who termed the execution of Louis XVI the suicide of France, and Hippolyte Taine, who mourned the lost classicism of the eighteenth century and the advent of government-by-street-riot. In their view, the cataclysm of the Revolution was not heroic, as Michelet had imagined, but chaotic. The old institutions had been destroyed and the abhorrent vacuum had not been filled.

Among contemporary historians, the prosecution and defence has continued along political lines. Socialist and Marxist historians from Jean Jaurés to Albert Mathiez and Albert Soboul have defended the thesis of a bourgeois Revolution, essentially a struggle between landed property and moneyed capitalism. The ambitious and wealthy bourgeoisie overthrew the clergy and nobility. This view has the merit of dissipating a great many myths connected with the Revolution, such as the theory of a sudden popular uprising against the king, but its case depends too completely on the inevitability of the class struggle and on the oppression of the bourgeoisie by the two privileged orders. The ranks of the nobility and the clergy were in fact open to the bourgeoisie during most of the *ancien régime*, and the wealthy middle class was more concerned with joining the privileged orders than with overthrowing them.

Right-wing historians writing under the shadow of monarchist movements of the twenties and thirties like the *Action Française* hearkened back to the *douceur de vivre* of the *ancien régime* and conjured up an only slightly flawed Eden. Nostalgia for that supreme father figure, the king, led Frantz Funck-Brentano to argue that sealed letters (arbitrary arrests on the king's written order) were humane and benevolent, an expression of the monarch's patriarchal function in caring for his errant children. Regret for the corporate state and a distaste for the rule of public opinion made Pierre Gaxotte attempt a rehabilitation of Louis XV. He wrote of a monarch so enlightened and a France so prosperous and liberal that one is left wondering incredulously how the Revolution could have begun fifteen years after his death.

One of the few major French historians who did not try to weave the cloth of history into preconceived designs was Alexis de Tocqueville, who in his dispassionate study *The Old Regime and the Revolution* made some points which should have guided subsequent writers. He saw that the Revolution was not an isolated moment in history, but rather, 'the complement of a long labour, an abrupt and violent end to the work of ten generations. If it had not taken place, the old social structure would still have collapsed everywhere, here sooner, here later; except that it would have continued to crumble piecemeal instead of collapsing all at once.' Tocqueville also saw that the Revolution came first in France because France was better off than most other European countries. Wherever vigorous medieval institutions still prevailed, they could not be abolished. Awareness of exploitation exists only at a certain level. A small landowner, with an investment to protect and his crop to get out, is more sensitive to unfair taxes than a serf whose livelihood, however wretched, is guaranteed by the lord. Feudalism never inspired more hatred than at the moment when it was about to disappear. Tocqueville also observed, through the devouring flames of the Revolution, the continuity of some monarchic institutions—administrative centralization, the preponderance of Paris over the provinces, guarantees for civil servants, the multiplicity (but not the venality) of offices. No regime annihilates its predecessor. There is always a legacy.

The temptation of the single cause antedates the historian-prosecutor. It appears in the writing of émigré nobles who, refusing to consider the complexity of the events which had sent them into exile, preferred to attribute them to a mysterious plot. The Revolution was the work of the Freemasons, who infiltrated every level of government and conspired to overthrow the monarch; it was the work of the king's cousin, the diabolical duc d'Orléans, who hoped to replace Louis XVI and paid the mob to riot; it was the work of the English, bent on vengeance after the loss of the American colonies—messages had been intercepted proving English involvement, and the English ambassador had been seen paying off street mobs. These legends die hard, especially if they contain a drop of truth diluted with gallons of rumour and conjecture. Contemporary historians like Bernard Faÿe are still shaking the spectre of Freemasonry and Orléanist plots at their readers.

The single cause is an attractive and orderly explanation. Once chosen, evidence that contradicts it is ignored while supporting arguments are amplified. Some writers, like Roustan and Louis Madelin, blame the Revolution on the eighteenth-century philosophes. Others, including Lord Acton and the duc de Castries, see the example of the American Revolution as the essential cause. Still others attribute the decline of the *ancien régime* more or less exclusively to economic forces, lack of leadership, the misery of the peasants, the ambition of the bourgeoisie, the bad example of the upper clergy, the decline of the nobility, the intellectual ferment in Europe, the irreverence of Voltaire, the high price of bread, Rousseau's *Social Contract*, the banishment of the Jesuits, Parlement's long opposition to the crown, military defeats, unfavourable peace negotiations, and other reasons. All have their importance in the pattern of decline, none is the single cause.

Decline, like mould, was invisible. At court, on the battlefield, in the private preoccupations of kings, in the government response to a plague in the provinces, in the appropriation of army commissions and bishoprics by the aristocracy, in the execution of a criminal, in a provincial riot, in the failure of kings to observe their own ceremonies, in the social origins of mistresses and the nationality of queens. Even the first wave of men who overthrew the *ancien régime*, like Lafayette and Mirabeau, remained faithful examples of its disorders and contradictions. They put to death a society with which they were still obsessed and were soon relieved by a second, cold-eyed generation of revolutionaries.

The path of decline is strewn with clues—food, fashions, sexual habits, garden styles, popular books—everything from a conversation between the queen and her page to the applause received by a play or the carved wooden figures sold at county fairs. The disintegration of a society with a 725-year life span and a 75-year death agony is a total experience. The smallest detail can be relevant. As Jean Giraudoux wrote in *Tiger at the Gates*: 'It is by their way of sneezing or of wearing down their heels that a condemned people can be recognized.'

The source material on the monarchy's decline in eighteenth-century France is overwhelming. The problem is one of an embarrassment of riches. There is little virtue in saying that nothing in this book is invented. It is merely a tribute to a regime's obsession with chronicling its own demise. The writer needs no recourse to imagined conversations, the secret thoughts of persons long in their graves, famous sayings that were never said (like *'après moi le déluge'*), or plausible but unverifiable details to brighten a narrative ('as she rode off in her carriage, Marie Antoinette sighed and remembered the last delicious moments she had spent with Fersen,' is one example I recently came across). Eighteenth-century France is a banquet of documentation. Was there ever a period, apart from our own, which described itself in such detail? At every level of society, a need was felt to consign the era to paper. Thanks to the administrative centralization under Louis XIV, provincial records were scrupulously kept. Ministers kept minutes of their meetings. The reports of police agents and informers on Paris life have been preserved, as have the reports of foreign ambassadors to their sovereigns. In the absence of mass media, there was correspondence. Nowhere is the tone of the Regency more precisely caught than in the voluminous letters of Louis XIV's sister-in-law, the Palatine Princess, to her German friends and relatives. It is also in the letters of Marie Antoinette to her mother, her brother, and her friends that the best understanding of that much-maligned queen's character can be found.

And what are memoirs if not correspondence with oneself? Much of the light in the Age of Enlightenment was cast by an army of private scribes whose only common denominator was a passion for recording what it saw and heard. In its ranks are to be found the loftiest and humblest subjects of the kingdom: from Louis XVI, who kept an exact if arid account of his daily occupations, to a peasant named Pierre Prion, who wrote what he called a 'chronologette' of his village of Aubais, near Nîmes, from 1744 to 1759. Other memoir-ists include members of the government, like the marquis d'Argen-son, Minister of Foreign affairs under Louis XV; courtiers like the duc de Lauzun, the duc de Croÿ, the baroness d'Oberkirch, and that matchless European gadabout, the prince de Ligne, who was so much at home in eighteenth-century society that he claimed never to have known a day of unhappiness; attendants to the royal family, like the marquis de Calvière, a page of Louis XV, or the indiscreet Madame Campan, one of Marie Antoinette's maids; soldiers like the maréchal de Saxe, priests like the abbé de Véri, booksellers like S. P. Hardy, lawyers like Edmond-Jean-François-Barbier, journalists like J. Cruppi, writers like Jean-François Marmontel, and a hundred others. The memoirs are generally tendentious, often badly written, and sometimes suspect (the nineteenth-century 'discoveries' by the abbé Soulavie of memoirs by the duc de Richelieu and others have been exposed as a fraud, and the memoirs of Madame de Pompa-dour's maid, Madame du Hausset, are considered at least partly apocryphal); but they are almost always illuminating.

A writer exploring past centuries cannot, as Ulysses wished, feed the shadows blood to bring them back to life and question them. What he can do is listen to the French eighteenth century's many voices, which ring in the ears like the surf in a seashell, alive, arrest-ing, and present.

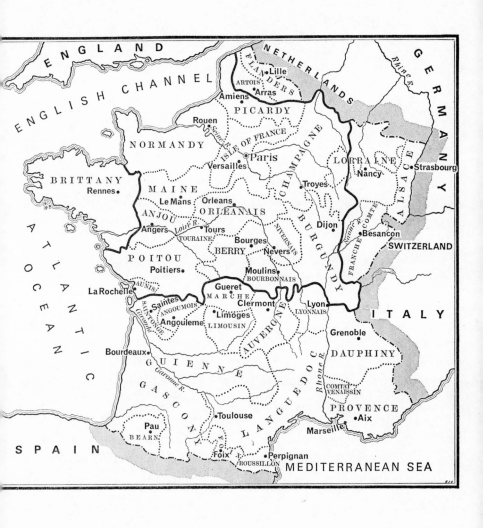

EPITAPH FOR KINGS

I

THE EIGHTH SACRAMENT

France created an eighth sacrament which could only be administered in Reims—the sacrament of royalty.

—ERNEST RENAN

My son, remember that the monarchy is nothing more than a public office, and that you will have to turn in very exact accounts when you die.

—LOUIS LE GROS TO THE FUTURE LOUIS VII

THROUGHOUT THE vicissitudes of their history, the French have maintained a mystical faith in their own ordained superiority and that of their country. France is the product of 'an intelligent foresight,' Napoleon believed. The order and regularity of its rivers, its protected harbours, its generous coastline, the fertile valleys that link its provinces, its temperate climate, and its rich soil, are viewed as evidence of divine favouritism. In the same way, the French see their language as the best language. In 1784, Antoine de Rivarol won the Berlin Academy's prize for his 'Essay on the Universality of the French Language.' He called it 'the human language' and said that 'French syntax is incorruptible —what is not clear is not French.' As for other languages, he said it was preferable to bore in French than to divert in English, while Italian was the tongue of a country 'which had provided buffoons to all of Europe.' For Voltaire, French was 'the language of Europe,' which it indeed threatened to become. Its subtlety disguised as logical precision made it the language of diplomats, its capacity for innuendo the language of courtiers. Long after the decline of France's army, her syntax continued to sweep Europe, conquering minds with a natural order of thought that began with a subject, continued with a verb, and ended with a predicate. The French character was a felicitous blend of virtue, intelligence, and valour. French kings became saints (it took longer for subjects of humble extraction—Joan of Arc was not canonized until 1920). French soldiers were feared for what the Italians called *la furia francese*. French writers of any reputation were enticed to foreign courts with generous subsidies. The French made a virtue even of their faults. Factionalism, already observed by Julius Caesar, who wrote that 'in Gaul, not only all the cantons and all the cities, but all the families are divided into rival factions,' became the mark of a proud, individualistic people; avarice became thrift, the wool stocking under the mattress, the result of prudence and hard work.

The French monarchy was the supreme monarchy. Anyone, anywhere in Europe, who referred to 'the king,' meant of course the king of France. Louis XIV refused to be grouped with other kings under the term 'Their Majesties,' because, he said, there might be deduced 'an equality which does not exist.' Michel Suriano, the Venetian ambassador to Paris, reported in 1562 that 'by unanimous consentment of all peoples, the kingdom of France has always been recognized as the first and most excellent kingdom in Christianity, as much for its dignity and power as for the absolute authority of he who governs it . . . it is the oldest kingdom, having begun not much later than 400 years after the birth of Christ . . . and it was the first to embrace the Christian religion . . . which won for its sovereign the title of eldest daughter of the church.'

The Venetian shrewdly listed the three reasons for the unique character of the French monarchy—its power, its absolutism, and its divine origin. The power had regularly increased, so that in the early eighteenth century, the French army was the mightiest, the French king was the richest, and France was the most populated country in Europe, with 19 million subjects, compared with 5 million in England, and 2 million in Prussia. If the French king caught a chill, the rest of Europe shivered. For what was the rest of Europe? England, having imported a German prince as sovereign, was torn by internal dissension. The Austrian empire was an archipelago of operetta principalities strung from the North Sea to the Danube. Spain, still feeling the effects of its long war against the Moors, had accepted as its sovereign the grandson of Louis XIV. Italy was a league of trading counters. Russia was a Tartar desert with a window on Europe (Peter the Great, hungry for the improvements of Western civilization, visited France in 1721, and learned about quartering and the boot, which he adapted to his own needs). Prussia was a tiny giant, eager to seize a destiny beyond its means.

Absolutism gave the French monarchy a special patina of perfection. The sovereign was the owner of this kingdom. For centuries, taxes were considered an emergency measure in time of war because the normal expense of government was met by the income from the king's domains. Countries like England, where Parliament could curb the king's authority, or Austria, where the nobility shared royal power, were held in contempt by Louis XIV, who said that 'the subjection of a monarch to the law of his people is the last calamity which can befall a gentleman of our rank.' Absolutism came to be considered an essential condition of the monarchy. 'Sovereignty,' wrote the jurist Le Bret in 1632, 'is no more divisible than the geometrical point.' In no way did it depend on the personal qualities of the monarch, and another jurist wrote that 'as evil as a prince may be, the revolt of his subjects is always infinitely criminal.' The idea that absolutism was the ideal form of monarchy went unchallenged in France until the eighteenth century. The abbé Dubois, minister under the Regency that followed the death of Louis XIV in 1715, wrote that 'if you associate your subjects to the rule, to what dangers would France not be exposed? In countries where two powers act together, such as England and Hungary, you have only trouble and discussions, whereas peace reigns wherever an absolute government can overrule the bold will of the people.' The French king, although absolute, was not despotic, for he had to respect fundamental laws concerning justice, property rights and his own succession. Divine right established a tautology between absolutism and justice, since the king was morally responsible to God.

Finally, it was the miraculous origin of the French monarchy which set it above others. The historical fraud which established the miracle reaches back to the invasion of Gaul by a fearsome Rhineland tribe called the Franks, after the death of the Roman Emperor Aurelian in the year 275. Dyed red hair swept over their foreheads, thick tufts on their cheeks, their bodies adorned with seaweed and auroch horns, the Franks charged the Roman legions with axes and bloodcurdling cries and became known as 'those of blood and fire.' They venerated a family said to descend from a marine deity. One of its members was Merovée, the king-warrior who led his tribe at the battle of the Catalaunian Fields in 451, where Attila the Scourge of God was defeated by a coalition of Gauls, Franks, and Romans.

It was Merovée's grandson, Clovis, who began the work of French unification. He became master of the Franks and ended Roman influence in Gaul by defeating the Roman legions at Soissons in 486. The advantages of unification had been demonstrated by the Romans—national justice was stronger and more equitable than tribal justice; roads, bridges, and a common currency favoured trade and travel. But the Romans had abandoned Gaul with the time of national kings still distant, and the gap was filled by a second unifying force, the church. Priests replaced proconsuls, frightened populations grouped around churches, and monasteries became repositories of the written tradition.

Clovis was a cruel, vengeful, superstitious opportunist—he murdered relatives to consolidate his power, axed a disobedient soldier in the back, and prayed to pagan gods for victory on the battlefield. He had, however, married the Burgundian Christian Princess Clotilda, and in 496, his army threatened with extinction by the Alemanni despite appeals to his own gods, he promised to become a convert to his wife's faith if he were victorious. No sooner had he spoken (according to the only surviving contemporary chronicle, by Grégoire de Tours) than the Alemanni turned tail.

Clovis was baptized in 498 or 499 (no one is quite sure) by Saint Rémi, the bishop of Reims, along with 3,000 of his men. The ferocious, long-haired king of the barbarians, standing waist-deep in the bathtub-sized baptismal font, bowed his head to receive the holy oil as the future saint said: 'Humble yourself, Sicambrian; adore what you have burned, burn what you have adored.' The moment is climactic in the foundation of France. It sealed the pact between crown and mitre which made the French ruler a king by divine right and an intermediary of God. It guaranteed the survival of Christianity, for at the end of the fifth century Clovis was the only Christian chief of state in the Western world. Clovis' baptism founded the first Christian state on the ruins of the Roman Empire and made France the eldest daughter of the church.

The miracle was an afterthought, propagated, if not invented, four centuries later by the Archbishop of Reims, Hincmar, in his hagiography of Saint Rémi. Describing Clovis' baptism, Hincmar wrote that as Rémi prayed, a dove 'whiter than snow' appeared, bearing in its beak a phial of chrism (a mixture of oil and aromatic balm) with which he anointed the king of the Franks. This was divine investiture for a fact. Clovis had been anointed like the kings of the Old Testament, directly by God. As the legend developed and the miracle became accepted, it took on the dual aspect of baptism and coronation. Beginning in the twelfth century, French kings were regularly crowned at Reims, in a re-enactment of the miraculous baptism-coronation of Clovis. They were anointed with what was purported to be the very flask which had been carried down from the heavens in the dove's beak—a narrow-necked glass phial as big as a fig, encased in a dove-shaped reliquary with coral beak and feet, itself reposing in a gold, jewel-studded box. On coronation days the phial, or Holy Ampulla, was placed on the cathedral's main altar and opened with great pomp. A particle of the mysterious substance it still contained, a reddish sediment, was removed with a gold needle and blended with the holy oil dabbed onto the king's forehead, chest, and back. (In 1793, a member of the Convention named Ruhl smashed the Holy Ampulla against the pedestal of an equestrian statue of Louis XV.)

For 700 years the mystical pre-eminence of divine-right monarchy in France rested on the legend of the heavenly dove. The French sovereign was the Very Christian King. In medieval literature he was often called 'the Sergeant of God.' He corresponded to the archetypal figure of the king-priest and the king-magician. The pope was elected by cardinals, whereas the king needed no go-betweens— his power came directly from on high. Every gesture and act of the king's daily routine thus was lifted to a liturgical level, of which the artifices of eighteenth-century court etiquette are an elaboration. With repeated telling, the legend was embellished by accessory miracles. Clovis' emblem was a toad, but an angel appeared to Clotilda and told her that her husband's strength would increase in battle if he adopted the stylized cross or trident known as the fleur-de-lys. Thus, even the royal standard had a divine origin.

The king himself became a miracle-worker. The ability to heal, visible evidence of each coronation's supernatural nature, was first mentioned in twelfth-century texts. In 1579 a writer named Etienne Forcatel traced the power to Clovis, who had cured a scrofulous equerry named Lancinet, 'whose room was filled with a dazzling light.' The healing of the scrofulous became a part of the coronation ceremony. Hundreds, and sometimes thousands, of men and women with distended necks (scrofula is a tuberculosis of the lymph glands) waited in rows outside Reims cathedral, from which the king emerged in a cloth-of-gold coat to trace a sign of the cross from forehead to chin and across the cheeks of each one, saying: 'God heal you, the king touches you.' Afterwards, to make sure he did not catch their disease, the king washed his hands three times—in vinegar, plain water, and orange water. Other courts made timid attempts to imitate the French king's power to heal—the Danish king was at one time said to heal epileptics while the Hungarian king's speciality was jaundice—but their thaumaturgy did not take. In France, the curative powers of the monarch were taken so seriously that medical treatises advised that if all else failed, the scrofulous should be 'sent to be touched and blessed by the king.' There was widespread belief in the effectiveness of the royal cure, although it was equally accepted that the king could not cure everyone. Many who were not helped the first time hopefully returned. Persisting illness cast doubt on the patient's faith, not the king's power. Healing the scrofulous was an inoffensive and perhaps even useful collective delusion, free, available to all, and far safer than many remedies then on the market. Louis XIV, who knew his job, touched the scrofulous on most major religious holidays, sometimes as often as eight times a year.

But here, as in all else, the decline was felt. During the reign of Louis XV, the marquis d'Argenson came across a man who claimed to have been cured by the king's touch. He had a certificate of cure drawn up, signed, notarized, and sent to Versailles. Alas, his zeal was not appreciated, and an icy reply came back that no one doubted the king's ability to heal. To seek evidence for a dogma is already to suspect it. Worse, on three different occasions—in 1739, 1740, and 1744—Louis XV was kept by his confessor from healing the scrofulous. Since he had publicly exhibited a new mistress just before a religious holiday, he was not in the required state of grace. This repeated failure to perform one of the few remaining duties which placed the king in contact with his people was damaging evidence that the king-magician was incapacitated.

The final particularity of the French monarchy that the miracle of the dove helps explain is the Salic Law, which prohibits the female line of the royal family from ruling. England had her Elizabeth, Russia her Catherine, and Austria her Maria Theresa, while France had only regencies in which an infant king's mother was powerful, like Ann of Austria or Catherine de Medici, or reigns in which

LOUIS XIV CURING THE SCROFULOUS
By Jouvenet

LOUIS XIV PLAYING BILLIARDS
Engraving by Trouvain

Showing the Appartement, 1694, the Third Room. From Left to Right: Monsieur, The Duc de Vendôme, The Comte de Toulouse, M. de Chamillart, The King, The Comte d'Armagnac and The Duc de Chartres

mistresses like Madame de Maintenon or Madame de Pompadour gained power. The Salic Law, originally a Frankish penal code which declared that daughters could not inherit land (probably because they could not bear arms to defend it), was deformed to prohibit the succession of the female line. In the Middle Ages, this prohibition was explained in terms of the monarchy's sacred nature. The French king, inheritor of the Holy Ampulla, had priestly functions no woman could assume.

A fifteenth-century writer, Jean Charlier de Gerson, explained: 'The Holy Ampulla was brought by an angel to Saint Rémi so that Clovis and his successors could be anointed with the holy oil of chrism. By virtue of this sacrosanct union, the king of Franks, can, by his mere touch, heal those suffering from a certain infirmity. A woman is not judged capable of doing this, since women are forbidden the administration of the sacraments, and even, at certain times, admission to churches' (this last reflecting the idea of woman as periodically unclean).

Clovis, although he unknowingly laid the foundation for the miraculous origin of the French monarchy, did not contribute to making the French nation, but to dividing it, for the territory he had conquered was carved up by his four sons at his death. The basic principles of dynastic succession still had to be established: that the kingdom was indivisible, that kings could be chosen from the same family rather than elected, and that a king could confer the right of succession on his son. The three centuries of rule under the Merovingian *rois fainéants* (do-nothing kings) was a long intermission of disunity and stagnation. It was in one sense the sign of a vigorous people that such kings were replaced. The Carolingians, who took the crown from the *rois fainéants* in the eighth century, were royal officials, unrelated to deities, but they needed no lineage. Men like Charles Martel (Charles the Hammer), who stopped the Arab invasion at Poitiers in 732, and his grandson, Charlemagne, who eclipsed Clovis as a legendary hero, are their own ancestors. The Carolingian 'palace revolution' was sanctioned by Pope Stephen II, who recognized Charles Martel's son, Pepin the Short, in 754, thereby placing the power of the church behind the new dynasty.

The kingdom continued to be regarded as an inheritance to be divided among a ruler's sons. Charlemagne's empire was dismembered at the treaty of Verdun in 843 into three faltering kingdoms. Out of the fragmentation and disorder of the Carolingian dynasty emerged the complex web of feudal commitments. Power lay with the great fiefs: Normandy, Brittany, Flanders, Anjou, Burgundy, Aquitaine, Toulouse, and Champagne. As central authority crumbled, isolated lords found safety in retrenchment, attachment to the land, and the austere security of their fortified castles. The essential human equation was protection in exchange for suzerainty. What you could defend was yours. In the midst of lawlessness, chivalry was devised, basically as a method for regulating violence. (The American cowboy is probably history's closest counterpart to the feudal knight—a man alone, who must rely on his own strength and courage in the absence of law and order, who is always armed, unfailingly courteous to women, kind to his horse, and ruthless with enemies.) What influence crown and church still had fostered peace and order—the truce of God suspended fighting from Wednesday night until Monday morning, and on religious holidays.

From this anarchical and hostile collection of fiefs there arose the dominant feudal house of Robert the Strong, which owned vast domains in France's heartland. Robert the Strong, Count of Anjou and Blois, contested the Carolingian claim to the crown in the ninth century and won the clergy's support. For more than a century, the crown changed hands between the Carolingians and his family. Then, in 987, Hugh Capet, the great-grandson of Robert the Strong, was elected king by the nobles and had the good sense to have his son crowned while he was still alive, thereby establishing the principle of dynastic succession. The warrior-king argued that 'if I were killed in battle, there might be quarrelling among the lords, the evil might tyrannize the meek, and the people might fall into captivity.'

The reign of Hugh Capet, from 987 to 996, begins the longest unbroken dynastic rule the Western world has ever known. The Capetians gave fourteen kings to France, and were succeeded in 1328 by the related Valois branch (descended from a younger son of the Capetian king Philippe III the Bold), which provided thirteen kings and was relayed in 1589 by the Bourbon branch (descended from a younger son of the Capetian king Saint Louis), which was overthrown in 1792 after providing five kings. Three branches of the same house gave France thirty-two kings, who ruled without interruption for 805 years—an impressive longevity record in view of what followed: the Republic to which the 1789 Revolution gave birth was a seven-year period of gestation for France's next dynasty, the Napoleonic, which lasted fifteen years. The Bourbons returned for an inconclusive Restoration, two kings and another fifteen years, which was followed by the eighteen-year constitutional monarchy of the Orléans branch of the Bourbon house. The ephemeral Second Republic of 1848 gave way to a Second Empire in 1852 and a Third Republic in 1871, which achieved intimations of immortality by lasting until World War II. The parliamentary anarchy of the post-war Fourth Republic led to its replacement by General de Gaulle's Fifth Republic in 1958. Opinion is divided as to whether this fifth attempt to give France a republican government will outlive its founder.

The Capetian kings made the French nation. Hugh Capet at the outset governed a few scattered parishes and counties, some 400 square miles around Paris which roughly correspond to the province of Ile de France. The ruler's authority extended no further—if he travelled outside the area he risked being ransomed or murdered. In the rest of the country there were as many codes of law as there were fiefs, 150 different currencies, and a dozen languages, such as Normand, Picard, Frankish, Provençal, and Basque. The formidable drama of national unity was essentially a struggle between the king and the feudal lords, who were at the start his equals. Eight centuries of French history are in large part concerned with the patient erosion of feudal prerogatives and the slow accretion of national territory. First, the principle of succession had to be established. The practice of electing the king's son during the king's lifetime became a formality. In the twelfth century Philippe-Auguste was the first king to dispense with the formality and make the monarchy completely hereditary. The principle of an elected king also withered away. The oath of the early kings was: 'I, made king by the mercy of God and the election of the people.' After Philippe–Auguste, there was a transitional phase in which the idea of election co-existed with the idea of heredity. At the coronation, the archbishop said: 'Lord, multiply your gifts on this your servant, who with humble devotion we elect to the kingdom . . .' Then, addressing himself directly to the king, he added: '. . . keep the state long, for it has been kept until now by your father, through hereditary right.' In the final stage, the suggestion that the king was elected disappeared entirely from coronation ceremonies.

The early kings were property-owners. France was the enclosure they owned and could defend, just as today Norman landowners still surround their gardens with six-foot-high walls, and die happy if they can bequeath their children some extra parcel of land they have been able to acquire—the orchard to the east, the pasture at the edge of the forest. So it was the business of each king to increase his property, like a dowry to the nation. The acquired pieces were stitched to France in various ways—by conquest, purchase, negotiation, or marriage. Normandy was won from England in 1204; Brittany was annexed in 1547; François I conquered Bresse in 1535; Henry IV brought in the Béarn and Navarre; the Thirty Years' War won the northeastern bishoprics of Toul, Metz, and Verdun; the Treaty of Westphalia gave France Alsace, and the Peace of the Pyrenees Artois, Roussillon, and Flanders; in 1662 Louis XIV bought three North Atlantic forts, including Dunkirk, from Charles II of England for 5 million pounds; in 1679 he conquered Franche-Comté and other Flemish cities; and in 1681 he 'annexed' the city of Strasbourg. Louis XV acquired Lorraine as a result of his marriage and Corsica in a barter with the Republic of Genoa. When the monarchy fell, it was, curiously enough, under a king who had not increased France's territory, as if the inherited mission which Philippe-Auguste had recommended to his sons, 'the patient increase of the kingdom,' was over.

The territorial gains of French kings diminished the feudal lords. These miniature monarchs gradually lost the right to keep their own armies, mint their own currency, levy their own taxes and customs duties, and keep slaves. With the church and the Third Estate as its allies, the monarchy domesticated the mighty lords, dangerous rivals to its own authority, who became a warrior caste at its service. The age of 'sweet suzerainty' vanished, the age which the court-paddocked eighteenth-century nobility would evoke with nostalgia, 'good old days' when the dungeons were full and the granaries were empty, when the population of the fief had to repair to the castle to avoid murder by marauding bands, when the lord himself slept with his horse in his room so he would not be caught by surprise, when the coat of mail was kept ready in wood coffers filled with bran, and castle walls were decorated with crossbows, swords, and halberds. Above all, the age when the king was a lord elected by his peers.

As the kingdom was formed, its subjects naturally fell into three orders—the priests (clergy), warriors (nobility), and all other subjects, from the poorest peasant to the richest banker, who were designated under the vague and inclusive term of Third Estate. The monarchy's ally in its quarrels with the nobles and the church was the Third Estate, just as in chess the pawns defend the king against the threatening knights and bishops. There was an identity of interests between king and commoner—to end the abuses of feudalism. In the fourteenth century kings began convening assemblies of the three orders, or estates, known as Estates General, when they needed national support against some external threat or when they sought the alliance of the Third Estate and the church against the nobility. The Third Estate had few rights and was not powerful enough to oppose the policies of the monarchy. Its only aim was relief from the exploitation of the nobility. It was glad to help the king reduce the power of the nobles. At the Estates General of 1614, such extravagant demands of the nobility as a 1,000-crown fine for anyone who addressed a commoner as 'sir' were blocked by the coalition of king and Third Estate.

Thus, France was made, thanks to the piecemeal accumulation of land, the subjugation of the feudal nobility, and the alliance of the king and the Third Estate. But all three of these instruments of unity carried within them seeds of the monarchy's decline. The confused way the nation had been gathered seriously limited the king's power. Provinces and cities accepted becoming a part of France as long as they could keep a large measure of autonomy and a number of privileges. The free city of Bayonne paid no tax on tobacco and the free province of Provence was exempted from duties on the sale of oil. The province of Franche-Comté had its own tax system. Cities in Alsace annexed in 1648 continued to swear allegiance to the German empire for thirty years after they had become French. Navarre continued to be a distinct kingdom after it had rallied France. The king was a duke in Brittany and a count in Provence. Every province, every city, had its own laws based on custom, so that Voltaire wrote that 'in France, a man changes laws as often as relay horses.' Taxes varied from place to place. Major cities like Paris and Beauvais did not pay the *taille*, a tax on income. There were still under Louis XVI cities where royal troops could not enter, and expressions such as 'Norman nation' and 'Breton nation' were commonly used. This was the dilemma of the *ancien régime*: an absolute ruler, whose authority derived from God, but who was so hamstrung by the network of special interests and privileges and the resistance to centralization that he could not impose national legislation or a fair method of taxation. Louis XIV created the intendancies in a laudable attempt to impose a single administrative

structure in France, but the correspondence of the intendants to their
government are filled with examples of local resistance to their
efforts, particularly when it came to taxes. Thus, Napoleon, after the
Revolution, could still refer to 'this mottled France, lacking administrative or legal unity, more an accumulation of twenty kingdoms
than a single state.' France under the *ancien régime* was still patched
with enclaves. The price of unification was administrative confusion, a country impossible to govern except by expedient, a sum
of particularisms refractory to change. The monarchy developed
under this double phenomenon of ever-greater centralization and
ever-resisting regional particularism.

As the state settled into its corporate structure, there was increasing resistance to royal interference in guild matters. The masters of
the 124 guilds or corporations kept the membership low and were
hostile to innovations. It took surgeons hundreds of years to become
disaffiliated from the guild of barbers, where tradition had placed
them. The makers of gingerbread were allowed by their guild to
sell it only in certain shapes. The king was powerless to persuade
artisans to take up new crafts, and thus created royal workshops—
Sèvres for porcelain, Aubusson for tapestry, Baccarat for glass.

The nobility, although diminished, remained fractious. The pattern of the monarchy is not one of the people rising against the
king but of the nobility making periodic efforts to regain its lost
grandeur. The nobility was progressively deprived of political power
in an attempt to make it a harmless class of privileged servants of the
crown. In other European countries the emphasis was on service to
the nation. The English nobility was not exempt from taxation and
maintained no feudal privileges, but it provided statesmen and sat in
the Lords. Conversely, Englishmen were knighted for service to the
state, so that the class remained vigorous and politically effective. It
was a law-abiding class that made the base of English power 'a
federation of country houses.' But while the English nobility had
power without privileges, the French nobility had privileges without
power. The best-known noble families were gradually forced to
adopt the profession of courtier, or king's parasite; the old noble
families which were not at court tended their provincial estates and
obtained army commissions for their sons, but a few acceded to
important political posts. Moreover, nobles suffered a loss of status,
or derogation, if they entered most forms of business or industry
(overseas commerce, mining and glass-making were allowed). It was

under François I that families began to aspire to recognition at the glittering Renaissance court and hunger for invitations to hunts and balls. This was proof that unity had been achieved, an acknowledgment of the king's supremacy, and the invention of a system perfected by Louis XIV to keep the nobility content and inoffensive by doling out artificial honours.

The nobility's existence became more glamorous as the court's magnificence increased, but the glamour masked a sense of futility. Like sediment at the bottom of a glass, nobiliary privileges remained after the services which justified them had vanished. The nobility's virtual tax exemption dated from the days of its great military contributions, which were all but over in the eighteenth century. Noble landowners continued to demand a toll at river crossings and roads, which went back to the times when they kept up the roads and bridges, now maintained by the state. Lords continued to collect field rent, every twelfth sheaf of the crop, every fourth barrel of wine, and subjected tenants to an imaginative array of other demands, from fixing the chapel steeple to beating the pond for frogs which disturbed the sleep of the lady of the manor. The lord insisted on daily reminders of his superiority. Tenants had to doff their hats. He had a special pew in church, the right to a square weathercock (a reminder of the feudal banner), the right to carry a sword, to paint his coat of arms on his carriage door, and, if his family could pass the test of the court genealogist and trace its noble origins to the fourteenth century, the right to be presented at court. Great lords became great beggars, dependent for the pursuit of an expensive life at court on the king's favour, and too busy paying attendance on the monarch for other pursuits. Montesquieu, although he believed that a strong nobility was necessary to curb the despotism of the monarch, was disheartened by the tame species the court produced. 'A great lord,' he wrote, 'is a man who sees the king, speaks to ministers, and has ancestors, debts, and a pension.' His characteristics are 'ambition with laziness, servility with pride, the desire to enrich himself without working, an aversion for the truth, contempt for the duties of the citizen, fear of the Prince's virtue, complaisance for his weaknesses. . . .' Perhaps Talleyrand's nostalgic phrase that 'whoever has not known the *ancien régime* has not known the sweetness of life' referred to that time of privilege without responsibility, when a courtier could participate in the most exquisitely refined society the Western world has produced with the help of a royal pension, a titular abbey, or some other lucrative but undemanding office.

The French Revolution, which abruptly ended the *douceur de vivre* of the *ancien régime*, was not a popular uprising against the king but the result of a long struggle between the reform-minded monarchy and a reactionary nobility defending its privileges, which wore the monarchy down to such a point of ineffectiveness that fresh forces, the forces of the Revolution, were brought into play to over-throw the reactionary establishment. At first the Revolution was royalist (Robespierre himself was royalist in 1789). It was only after Louis XVI's pathetic blunders and panicky betrayal that he was tried and put to death, three and a half years after the 'great days' of 1789. As feudalism had given rise to a feudal, or sword, nobility, the creation of a centralized state gave rise to an administrative, or robe, nobility. These were prosperous bourgeois who had become noble through membership in various Parlements and councils (the Parle-ments were not legislative chambers in the English sense but tribunals with judiciary functions). Under the reigns of Louis XV and Louis XVI, the old sword nobility and the more recent robe nobility formed a conservative alliance which successfully blocked nearly all the monarchy's attempts to adapt to social change, thereby preparing the way for a revolution whose victims they were to be. There was also a liberal nobility which supported the ideas of the Enlightenment, fought in the American War of Independence, joined Masonic lodges, and welcomed the Revolution when it came. Louis de Noailles, who commanded a regiment in the American war, explained that 'I believed that the Revolution was inevitable, and that we could control it; carried beyond the limits I had foreseen, I thought it was better to follow it than be crushed by it.' He fled to America, but his father, mother, grandmother, wife, and mother-in-law were guillotined.

The third linchpin in the making of monarchic France, the alliance of the king and the Third Estate, also had unforeseen results. The Third Estate helped the crown subdue defiant lords and dis-regard the claims of the clergy. This did not mean that the three orders assembled in Estates General were in any sense a parliament. The king generally summoned them when he was sure of an alliance between the Third Estate and one of the other two orders against the third. In exchange for the support of the Third Estate, the king promised order at home and glory abroad, not a share in the government. In England the nation was formed by a successful alliance of the three orders against the king, which led to Simon de Montfort's Assembly in 1265, thirty-seven years before the first Estates General were summoned. In France, the national spirit developed as a part of, not against, absolute monarchy.

National unity was forged thanks to the unwritten pact between the king and the Third Estate, which reinforced absolution and prevented the development of a French constitutional monarchy. The alliance could have succeeded only if the king had been able to reduce the inequities between the Third Estate and the privileged classes, thereby fulfilling his part in what remained a one-sided arrangement. But reform programmes shattered against the robe-sword coalition. The Third Estate's unrewarded loyalty to the monarch did not allow the Estates General to develop into a regular parliamentary body which would have made the Revolution unnecessary. The Third Estate never struggled for representation. It was more generous than persevering. Its love for the king was noted by many foreign observers. It was the mystic adoration of the king-priest, whose power came from on high, borne on the wings of the dove, as well as gratitude toward the king-warrior, who shielded the nation from its enemies. The Scottish traveller John Moore wrote in 1779 that although 'everything in this kingdom [France] is arranged for the accommodation of the rich and the powerful, and little or no regard is paid to the comfort of citizens of an inferior station,' these very citizens adulate the king. 'The most inconsiderate circumstance which relates to the monarch is of importance; whether he eat too much or too little at dinner; the coat he wears, the horse on which he rides . . . if he happen to be a little indisposed, all Paris, all France is alarmed. . . . At a review, the troops . . . are engrossed in contemplation of their Prince—Have you seen the King?—Look—Ah, there he is. The King is laughing.—Apparently he is pleased.—I am delighted.—Ah, he is coughing.—Did he cough?—Yes, by Gad! And strongly.—I am in despair.' A year before the Revolution, the German writer von Vizine wrote: 'This worthy feeling [love of the monarchy] is inbred in the French. The humblest chimneysweep is transported with joy when he sees his sovereign. He grumbles about taxes but gives his last penny . . . the thing in the French that is worth respecting and imitating is their love for the sovereigns of their country.' It was precisely because the concept of the king as father of the people was so strongly rooted in France that the leaders of the Revolution did not dare submit Louis XVI's death sentence to national ratification, and insisted on carrying out a regicide intended to shock the nation off its knees. 'The Frenchman,' Louis XVI had written, 'is incapable of regicide.'

The leaders of the Revolution knew that in putting Louis XVI to death they were not only killing an individual king but breaking the indispensable chain of succession. The power of the monarchy lay not in the virtues and defects of the men who wore the crown (sometimes over their eyes, Rivarol said) but in its ability to endure. When Henri IV was assassinated in 1610 by the lunatic Ravaillac, his wife, Marie de Médicis, said, 'Alas, the king is dead.' 'In France, Madam, kings do not die,' replied Chancellor Sillery. In the same moment that one king died another reigned. This is, of course, the meaning of the phrase 'The king is dead—long live the king.'

Each king was aware that national unity depended upon his ability to keep the chain of succession intact. This meant having a male heir and averting civil war and revolution. The monarchy was not a form of government which demanded the regular appearance of supermen. It was based, quite to the contrary, on a principle of succession strong enough to withstand the most disastrous reigns, a principle which exalted the virtues of strong monarchs and masked the deficiencies of weak ones. The accident of birth placed men unfit to rule on the throne, but the dynasty went on nonetheless. The family of French kings is not fixed at a steady level of wisdom, courage, and virtue, but rises and falls like the waves of a seismograph. Their only common trait was their ability to reproduce, a passion for the hunt, and disorderly love lives (with the exception of the monogamous Louis XVI). The custom of giving most of them a name based on a characteristic made them wear their qualities and defects like badges. There was a headstrong Louis, a debonair Louis, a Louis that stammered, and a fat Louis. There was a wise Charles, a simple Charles, a bald Charles, a victorious Charles, and an affable Charles. There were long reigns: seventy-two years for Louis XIV and fifty-nine years for Louis XV, and short reigns: François II, the round-cheeked, sickly, fifteen-year-old husband of Mary Stuart, died after a year on the throne. There were sensible kings like Louis XII, who said that he would rather have courtiers laugh at his avarice than the people weep over his prodigality; treacherous, melancholy kings like Charles IX, who ordered the massacre of the Protestants in the sixteenth century; spendthrift kings like Philip the Fair, who arrested the Jews so he could seize their goods; homosexual kings like Henri III, whose *mignons* (darlings) called him Alexander as though he were destined for great things, and who was painted by Van Loo wearing pearl earrings; virile kings like Henri IV, who ruled 'with my arse in the saddle and gun in my fist,' who stopped in the midst of battle to write a love letter, and who embodied favourite French qualities, for he was frivolous, wise, tender, brave, and industrious; superstitious kings, like Louis XI, who surrounded himself with astrologers but nonetheless had the scientific curiosity to pardon a man sentenced to death on condition he serve as guinea pig in a gallstone operation; kings overshadowed by a great minister, as Louis XIII was by Cardinal Richelieu, or by a mistress, as Henri II was by Diane de Poitiers (Henri II, the sportsman king, who was killed in a joust); arrogant, epicurean kings like François I, builder of river castles, weaver of cloth-of-gold tents, collector of Renaissance artists, in whose arms Leonardo da Vinci is said to have died; mad kings, like Charles VI, who gave his kingdom away to Henry V of England. And finally, the most exalted example of the species, the king who so diffused majesty that he was compared to the sun.

II

THE SUN KING

*The Sun was chosen [as a royal emblem] because
the unique quality of the brilliance which surrounds
it, the light it communicates to other heavenly bodies
which compose a kind of Court around it, the just and
even allotment of its light among all the various
tropics of the world, the good it does everywhere,
endlessly producing on all sides life, joy, activity, its
uninterrupted movement despite an always tranquil
appearance, its constant and invariable path, from
which it is never drawn or diverted, is assuredly the
most beautiful and vivid image of a great monarch.*
—Louis XIV, *Mémoires*

*Louis XIV became a stately mummy intended for
future deification thanks to the nostalgia of some, or
for supreme derision thanks to the passionate an-
tagonism of others.*
—Pierre Goubert, *Louis XIV et Vingt Millions
de Français*

LOUIS XIV was born in what seemed a miraculous manner,
twenty-three years after the childless marriage of his parents,
Louis XIII and Ann of Austria. Outliving his son and grandson, he had reason to believe in his own immortality. Or at least in
the immortality of the final, rigid, despotic form he imposed on the
monarchy. And yet the system which he bequeathed his five-year-
old great-grandson in 1715 survived him by only seventy-seven years,
a life span equal to his own. The longest and most glorious of reigns
was finally in the image not of Versailles, monumental, solid, and
enduring, but of the catherine wheels the courtiers watched from the
gardens of the palace, dazzling, costly, and self-consuming. The

brilliance of his reign could not be repeated and its extravagance sapped France's resources. Louis XIV created a style of government which was magnificent, but not transmissible. It is one thing to be awed by the brilliance of his reign, and another to discern the flaws that helped make that brilliance possible.

Louis XIV is at the same time the best-known and the most elusive French king. Few men's lives have been recorded in such detail. We know that he tore the nipples of his wet nurses, which to the Swedish ambassador Grotius was a sign of precocious rapacity; that as a child of two he began to show a pronounced aversion for his father; that Mazarin, the Prime Minister who may have married his widowed mother, made him sleep in threadbare sheets and was stingy with pocket money; that at the age of twelve he translated Caesar from Latin into French. We know from his valet that he generally spent one half-hour of the morning on his close-stool, and from his autopsy that the size of his intestines was unusually large after fifty years of gluttony. We know he ate with his fingers and was fond of peas, that he seldom took baths or read a book, that he wore six-inch heels to make him appear taller than his five feet four inches, that he changed his suits three times a day, and that he was 'filled with a just and singular horror for the inhabitants of Sodom.' We know that he had six different ways of doffing his hat to ladies, grading them like eggs, and that beneath the enamel of his perfect courtesy lay an equally perfect selfishness; when his granddaughter had a miscarriage he complained that it would upset the schedule of his day. We know that Versailles cost 65 million pounds and 227 lives (accidents on the construction site).

We have a day-by-day record of life at court, which was so precisely regulated, wrote Saint-Simon, that even if you were 300 leagues away, you had only to look at your watch and your calendar to know exactly what the king was doing. We know that he made a point of sharing the queen's bed every night, but that she often had occasion to note that his vigour had been expended between other sheets. We know that one mistress, Madame de Montespan, gave him aphrodisiacs made with the excrement of toads, while another, Madame de Maintenon, who became his morganatic wife (and was three years his senior), complained to her confessor when she was in her fifties that 'it would be hard to imagine to what degree husbands extend their demands. With them, one must submit to nearly impossible things.' We know that his health was impaired by the repeated bleedings and purges of his doctors, and that they broke his jaw while pulling out his few remaining rotten teeth when he was forty, which explains the downward-turning mouth and slack jaw of his later portraits. We know he liked to hunt and attend military sieges, to which court painters were summoned so they could catch him in battle dress at the moment of victory. We know that he liked praise better than anything, and are left to ponder why a monarch so powerful needed constantly to be reminded of his greatness. The result was the only art ever developed by the courtiers of Versailles, flattery; if prizes were given for toadying at Versailles, perhaps third prize would go to the fellow who replied, when Louis XIV asked him the time: 'Whatever time Your Majesty desires;' second prize to the king's natural son, the duc du Maine, who told his father after a long military campaign: 'Ah, Sire, I will never learn anything. My tutor grants me a holiday each time you win a victory;' and first prize to the duc d'Antin, Superintendent of Buildings, who placed wedges under the statues at Versailles so that the king would notice they were awry and d'Antin would have the opportunity to praise his perceptiveness.

What is less apparent is how Louis XIV was able so long to mesmerize an entire nation into gratifying his pursuit of personal glory. His worst mistakes had public approval. Everyone applauded when he built Versailles, set out to defeat Holland on a flimsy pretext, and persecuted the Huguenots. By what Louis XIV himself termed 'an extraordinary accident,' the nation was for more than half a century united behind its king. This was partly because he had restored internal order after a century of religious wars. Periods of civil strife make authority desirable, just as periods of authoritarian rule are generally followed by a more relaxed regime. As Voltaire said, 'all was tranquil under his reign.' This was its first merit. The king's personal merit was in being the opposite of a *roi fainéant*. He worked six to eight hours a day, and wrote in his memoirs that he was 'informed of everything, listening to my humblest subjects, knowing at each hour the number and quality of my troops and the conditions of my fortresses, incessantly giving the required orders, treating immediately with foreign ministers, receiving and reading dispatches, personally drafting some of the answers, regulating expenses and receipts of the state, and keeping my affairs more secret than any of my predecessors.' The king also knew how to surround himself with valuable men, an art which he said 'may be learned order. Colbert imposed rigid state controls on commerce and industry and gave France her first planned economy, drafting 150 decrees to standardize the quality of manufactured goods. Concerned with the balance of trade, he established high tariffs to keep out foreign goods and tried to stimulate French exports. He built cities and canals, created industries, and during his tenure the French navy increased from 20 to 267 warships. He created four colonial trade companies, encouraged explorers and colonial expeditions, and had sugar planted in the Caribbean islands. But little of his vigorous administration endured. His navy was sunk, his colonial companies failed, and his mercantilism did not outlast him. Financial order was incompatible with a war economy. Vauban built or improved 333 fortresses, precursors of the Maginot Line, and like it considered impregnable. But Vauban's utility was two-edged; when his fortresses fell into the hands of the enemy his was the unhappy task of proving that they could be breached. He also drafted a tax reform project that he presented to the king, which in its wording seemed to anticipate the famous pamphlet of the abbé Sieyès on the Third Estate. 'There has never been enough consideration for the little people in France,' he wrote in his proposal for a single income tax with no exemptions, 'it is exploited and despised, and yet it is the most considerable part of the population by its number and by the real services it renders the state.' Louis XIV banned the publication of Vauban's proposal, and there was talk of locking him up, but he died before a decision could be reached.

Louvois seemed obsessed with the idea that anyone who dared to oppose the Sun King should be destroyed. He mixed zeal with sycophancy. He urged massive reprisals in the war against the Dutch, telling the maréchal de Boufflers: 'If the enemy burn one of our villages, burn ten of theirs.' But when Louis XIV expressed displeasure at the extent of looting and destruction, he did a swift about-face and wrote to the maréchal de Luxembourg that the king was astonished 'to see the country being looted and exposed to all the violence of the soldiers. You know as well as anyone that this is the best way to ruin the troops and the country. . . . His Majesty has ordered me to tell you that he desires remedies to be taken. . . .' Louvois showed similar eagerness in the persecution of Protestants, and wrote in a directive that 'His Majesty wishes those who refuse religion to be treated with extreme harshness.' But again, when

but not taught.' His best ministers were able, but even more they were dedicated. Colbert continued to serve long after his programme to restore order to the nation's finances had been totally defeated by the expenses of war.

There was nothing original about the Sun King's programme. It was to the letter an implementation of the absolutist charter of his father's great cardinal-minister, Richelieu: 'To ruin the Huguenot party, humble the pride of the lords, reduce all subjects to their duties, and lift his [the king's] name among foreign nations to its proper level.'

Reduce all subjects to their duties

Obsessed with order, Louis XIV made France resemble a tidy room, where every subject could find his proper place by measuring its distance from the king's, and knew what to believe, what was beautiful, what was good, and what was right. Louis XIV even wrote out a mandatory itinerary in twenty-five points for the visit of the Versailles gardens. He seemed to have been born to realize the Cartesian dream of an orderly world, to answer the mathematician-philosopher's wish: 'It is true that the visible world would be more perfect if lands and seas had more ordered shapes . . . If the rains were more regular, the lands more fertile: in a word, if there were not so many monsters and disorders.'

To help eliminate monsters and disorders at home, Louis XIV created the post of Police Lieutenant for the kingdom in 1667. The Police Lieutenant had broad powers in matters of crime, public order, and censorship, and developed a vast network of spies. He bragged that 'when you see three persons chatting in the street, you may be sure that one of them at least is in my pay.' He governed the 'Black Cabinet,' an early form of thought control, which prepared for the king a weekly digest of what his subjects were saying in their private correspondence. A half-serious remark about king or country could lead to imprisonment without trial in the Bastille.

Censorship was enforced thanks to the 'royal privilege' which books required for publication. Fifty of the eighty members of the guild of printers and librarians had their licences revoked under Louis XIV, who reserved the right to create new ones. Teachers were told what to teach. In 1691, the philosophy professors at the University of Paris were warned against 'subversive propositions

. . . such as the one that all prejudices must be disregarded and everything must be doubted before knowledge can be secured.' The Académie Française, created by Richelieu, announced that the language was 'fixed,' and became a vigilant guardian of syntax and the heavy, pompous *style noble*. The greatest writers of the century, Molière, Racine, Corneille, La Fontaine, Boileau, La Bruyère, wrote fatuous, banal compliments to Louis XIV, on whose subsidies they depended. 'Great king,' wrote Boileau, 'if you cease being victorious, I will cease to write.' 'One of his glances,' wrote La Fontaine, 'made me not only satisfied but overwhelmed.' Corneille, having been named 'first dramatic poet of the world' in 1633, and awarded 2,000 pounds, wrote to the king that he would borrow 'a little of your conduct, a little of your courage, and study in you the great art of reigning.'

Parlement, whose right to make public remonstrances against royal decrees was the only tolerated opposition under the *ancien régime,* was silenced by Louis XIV. He ruled in 1673 that protests could only be voiced once the decrees were endorsed, which of course made them useless. Parlement, under Mazarin, had systematically opposed government decrees, going so far as refusing to endorse military expenses in wartime. And the part Parlement played in the *fronde* determined Louis XIV to silence the only form of organized protest left in the nation. Thus, Louis XIV shaped a France where no dissonant note jarred the chorus of adulation, where his 'accredited pens,' his palaces, his courtiers, his official art, and the medals constantly struck to commemorate his life and deeds, all served to glorify his reign.

Was he at the same time insensitive to the needs of his subjects? Not as long as the initiative came from him. He liked to say that he was as much a Frenchman as he was a king, and displayed his concern for the nation's welfare by becoming personally involved in the minutiae of administration. In 1673, he personally ordered the evacuation of a block of houses in Saint-Germain where smallpox had been declared. By giving his attention to such quotidian matters, he fulfilled his role as father of the people. In 1704, he personally ordered that a provincial nobleman guilty of incest be committed to a hospital. In 1708 he ordered an official in the city of Laon to stop cutting down shade trees on the city's outskirts. With such personal touches, the king showed his subjects that he was a tireless worker who knew every inch of his kingdom.

But national interest in matters great and small was heeded only insofar as it coincided with personal glory. In years of famine, Louis XIV decreed that well-off provinces would have to help distress areas. He created the framework of an efficient provincial administration by naming Intendants to supplement the aristocratic and often incompetent provincial governors. But to any suggestion critical of his reign, Louis XIV replied with icy scorn. When his brother, Monsieur, called his attention to the misery in the countryside during the terrible winter of 1709, Louis XIV replied: 'And what if four or five hundred thousand of those scoundrels die, since they are useful for nothing, would France be any the less France?'

Humble the pride of the lords

Louis XIV divorced power and prestige while making himself the sole dispenser of both. He chose his ministers outside the nobility so that they would have no claims to grandeur by birth—Colbert was the son of a draper, Louvois was a third-generation civil servant, and Vauban, who was Commissioner General of Fortifications and maréchal de France, was the son of an impoverished soldier. One of his few ministers recruited from the aristocracy was Arnaud de Pomponne, whom Louis eventually revoked, saying: 'Everythin[g] that passed through his hands lost some of the force and grande[ur] which one must have when executing the orders of a king of Fra[nce] who has not been unsuccessful.' Louis had several ways of illustra[ting] to his ministers that all power must come from him. On[e was] naming them verbally, as though their appointments did not [need] written announcement. Another was a return to the tradi[tion that] ministers are king's servants—Colbert and Louvois had to [perform] such chores as finding lodgings at Versailles for the king's [guests.] The ministers were expected to be grateful enough for t[he honor] of serving the king to pay handsomely for it, just [as at] certain famous restaurants pay for the right to work th[e] ation of large tips. In 1671, when Louis XIV wrote [to Arnaud] de Pomponne to appoint him Secretary for For[eign Affairs, he] advised him that the office would cost 800,000 livr[es. He would pay] 300,000 himself and give Pomponne a promissory [note for the rest] he would have to raise himself. But although th[e right to serve] the king cost a fortune, it was never refused.

The ministers were faithful executors of th[e]

Louis XIV objected to the brutal methods of an Intendant named Marillac, who boasted that he had obtained 30,000 conversions in a single year, Louvois wrote: 'His Majesty has ordered me to let you know that he absolutely wants you to cease all violence . . . even if the violence has produced conversions.' In the second, pious phase of the king's life, the ministers outdid each other in religious devotion. Le Peletier went to vespers each day, and Torcy knew all the psalms by heart.

Conversely, the nobility was stripped of power in exchange for the fool's gold of court life at Versailles. The move to Versailles served three purposes—it was an instrument of propaganda and a permanent exhibit of French splendour, it allowed Louis to escape a capital which he detested, and it domesticated the nobility. The construction of Versailles was a life's work. It was as a young man of thirty that Louis asked the architect Le Vau to draw up plans for enlarging his father's hunting lodge in the wooded plain ten miles from Paris; it was only fourteen years later, in 1682, that he and his court moved there permanently; and it was not until 1710 that the chapel was completed and that Louis, now in his seventies and fixed in the daily habits of majesty, first knelt to pray there. The palace was designed as the antithesis of a feudal castle. The pre-absolutist castles were built in strategically dominant positions, they were difficult of access because of moats and drawbridges, they bristled with turrets, and their few windows were designed more to be fired through than to let in light. Versailles is an emblem of absolutism not only in its grandeur, but in that it is indefensible. The monarchy no longer needed drawbridges and turrets, and replaced them with the longest horizontal frontage of any building in Europe (475 metres) and with hundreds of high, regularly spaced windows. It was open to the public (special carriages, called chamber pots, took Parisians to Versailles and back), and there were as many visitors under Louis XIV as there are today, as many as 6,000 in a single day, who sometimes prevented the king from taking his daily walk. As soon as they entered the courtyard, visitors were met with signs of the king's supremacy, allegorical groups of sculpture which showed a felled eagle (the Austrian empire) and a recumbent lion (the Spanish monarchy).

Paris had been the capital of French kings since the twelfth century. It was the base from which the Capetians had conquered France. It was a natural capital, 'the true heart of the kingdom,' according to Vauban, 'the common mother of the French, the summary of France.' At the same time it was unruly, irreverent, and independent. On five separate occasions from the fourteenth to the seventeenth centuries it had been in open conflict with the king: during Etienne Marcel's bourgeois commune in 1357, the popular insurrection of the Maillotins in 1382, the revolt of the University and the guilds in 1436, the religious-inspired revolt of 1584, and the *fronde* under Louis XIV. With its insurrectional tradition and its enclaves of independent authority, like the Parlement and the University, Paris was naturally odious to the representative of absolute authority. Before Louis XIV, Henri III had said of Paris: 'Oh, bloated and capricious capital, you need to be bled.' The Sun King, although he amnestied the principal *frondeurs*, never amnestied Paris. He preferred to remove himself from what he could not control. He did not, like Peter the Great, who built Saint Petersburg to free Russia from Asian dominance, create an alternate capital. He simply moved to Versailles. But while the palace protected him from the disorders of the capital, it also sealed him off from his people, so that one visitor described Versailles and its court of 10,000 nobles as 'a foreign enclave inside the nation.' However artificial, Versailles was sufficient unto itself, a society so glamorous and exclusive that whatever went on elsewhere could be disregarded.

With the move to Versailles, the tradition of nomadic kings, travelling with their court from one castle to the next, was lost. Louis XIV left Versailles for his secondary residences in the vicinity, Marly, Compiègne, and Fontainebleau, but he saw little of France, and once spent seven years without setting foot in Paris. Louis XV saw only the provinces he had to cross to reach the battlefields of Flanders. Louis XVI rarely visited Paris. When his brother-in-law, the Austrian Emperor Joseph II, came to Versailles in 1777, he told Louis XVI how much he had admired the Invalides. Yes, replied Louis XVI, he would have to go and see it sometime because he had heard it was very interesting. It was finally the Paris mob, marching on Versailles in October, 1789, which ended the century-long divorce between the French king and his capital.

Louis XIV could see no middle ground for his nobility between rebellion and humiliation. He feared another *fronde*. But in summoning the second order of the kingdom to his baroque palace to assume roles in the elaborate game of praise-the-king, he created the new threat of an idle, useless, and totally dependent nobility. After but not taught.' His best ministers were able, but even more they were dedicated. Colbert continued to serve long after his programme to restore order to the nation's finances had been totally defeated by the expenses of war.

There was nothing original about the Sun King's programme. It was to the letter an implementation of the absolutist charter of his father's great cardinal-minister, Richelieu: 'To ruin the Huguenot party, humble the pride of the lords, reduce all subjects to their duties, and lift his [the king's] name among foreign nations to its proper level.'

Reduce all subjects to their duties

Obsessed with order, Louis XIV made France resemble a tidy room, where every subject could find his proper place by measuring its distance from the king's, and knew what to believe, what was beautiful, what was good, and what was right. Louis XIV even wrote out a mandatory itinerary in twenty-five points for the visit of the Versailles gardens. He seemed to have been born to realize the Cartesian dream of an orderly world, to answer the mathematician-philosopher's wish: 'It is true that the visible world would be more perfect if lands and seas had more ordered shapes . . . If the rains were more regular, the lands more fertile: in a word, if there were not so many monsters and disorders.'

To help eliminate monsters and disorders at home, Louis XIV created the post of Police Lieutenant for the kingdom in 1667. The Police Lieutenant had broad powers in matters of crime, public order, and censorship, and developed a vast network of spies. He bragged that 'when you see three persons chatting in the street, you may be sure that one of them at least is in my pay.' He governed the 'Black Cabinet,' an early form of thought control, which prepared for the king a weekly digest of what his subjects were saying in their private correspondence. A half-serious remark about king or country could lead to imprisonment without trial in the Bastille.

Censorship was enforced thanks to the 'royal privilege' which books required for publication. Fifty of the eighty members of the guild of printers and librarians had their licences revoked under Louis XIV, who reserved the right to create new ones. Teachers were told what to teach. In 1691, the philosophy professors at the University of Paris were warned against 'subversive propositions

. . . such as the one that all prejudices must be disregarded and everything must be doubted before knowledge can be secured.' The Académie Française, created by Richelieu, announced that the language was 'fixed,' and became a vigilant guardian of syntax and the heavy, pompous *style noble*. The greatest writers of the century, Molière, Racine, Corneille, La Fontaine, Boileau, La Bruyère, wrote fatuous, banal compliments to Louis XIV, on whose subsidies they depended. 'Great king,' wrote Boileau, 'if you cease being victorious, I will cease to write.' 'One of his glances,' wrote La Fontaine, 'made me not only satisfied but overwhelmed.' Corneille, having been named 'first dramatic poet of the world' in 1633, and awarded 2,000 pounds, wrote to the king that he would borrow 'a little of your conduct, a little of your courage, and study in you the great art of reigning.'

Parlement, whose right to make public remonstrances against royal decrees was the only tolerated opposition under the *ancien régime*, was silenced by Louis XIV. He ruled in 1673 that protests could only be voiced once the decrees were endorsed, which of course made them useless. Parlement, under Mazarin, had systematically opposed government decrees, going so far as refusing to endorse military expenses in wartime. And the part Parlement played in the *fronde* determined Louis XIV to silence the only form of organized protest left in the nation. Thus, Louis XIV shaped a France where no dissonant note jarred the chorus of adulation, where his 'accredited pens,' his palaces, his courtiers, his official art, and the medals constantly struck to commemorate his life and deeds, all served to glorify his reign.

Was he at the same time insensitive to the needs of his subjects? Not as long as the initiative came from him. He liked to say that he was as much a Frenchman as he was a king, and displayed his concern for the nation's welfare by becoming personally involved in the minutiae of administration. In 1673, he personally ordered the evacuation of a block of houses in Saint-Germain where smallpox had been declared. By giving his attention to such quotidian matters, he fulfilled his role as father of the people. In 1704, he personally ordered that a provincial nobleman guilty of incest be committed to a hospital. In 1708 he ordered an official in the city of Laon to stop cutting down shade trees on the city's outskirts. With such personal touches, the king showed his subjects that he was a tireless worker who knew every inch of his kingdom.

But national interest in matters great and small was heeded only insofar as it coincided with personal glory. In years of famine, Louis XIV decreed that well-off provinces would have to help distress areas. He created the framework of an efficient provincial administration by naming Intendants to supplement the aristocratic and often incompetent provincial governors. But to any suggestion critical of his reign, Louis XIV replied with icy scorn. When his brother, Monsieur, called his attention to the misery in the countryside during the terrible winter of 1709, Louis XIV replied: 'And what if four or five hundred thousand of those scoundrels die, since they are useful for nothing, would France be any the less France?' ✓

Humble the pride of the lords

Louis XIV divorced power and prestige while making himself the sole dispenser of both. He chose his ministers outside the nobility so that they would have no claims to grandeur by birth—Colbert was the son of a draper, Louvois was a third-generation civil servant, and Vauban, who was Commissioner General of Fortifications and maréchal de France, was the son of an impoverished soldier. One of his few ministers recruited from the aristocracy was Arnaud de Pomponne, whom Louis eventually revoked, saying: 'Everything that passed through his hands lost some of the force and grandeur which one must have when executing the orders of a king of France ✓ who has not been unsuccessful.' Louis had several ways of illustrating to his ministers that all power must come from him. One was naming them verbally, as though their appointments did not merit a written announcement. Another was a return to the tradition that ministers are king's servants—Colbert and Louvois had to attend to such chores as finding lodgings at Versailles for the king's mistresses. ✓ The ministers were expected to be grateful enough for the privilege of serving the king to pay handsomely for it, just as waiters in certain famous restaurants pay for the right to work there, in expectation of large tips. In 1671, when Louis XIV wrote to the marquis de Pomponne to appoint him Secretary for Foreign Affairs, he advised him that the office would cost 800,000 livres, offering to pay 300,000 himself and give Pomponne a promissory note for the 500,000 he would have to raise himself. But although the honour of serving the king cost a fortune, it was never refused.

The ministers were faithful executors of the Ludovican mania for order. Colbert imposed rigid state controls on commerce and industry and gave France her first planned economy, drafting 150 decrees to standardize the quality of manufactured goods. Concerned with the balance of trade, he established high tariffs to keep out foreign goods and tried to stimulate French exports. He built cities and canals, created industries, and during his tenure the French navy increased from 20 to 267 warships. He created four colonial trade companies, encouraged explorers and colonial expeditions, and had sugar planted in the Caribbean islands. But little of his vigorous administration endured. His navy was sunk, his colonial companies failed, and his mercantilism did not outlast him. Financial order was incompatible with a war economy. Vauban built or improved 333 fortresses, precursors of the Maginot Line, and like it considered impregnable. But Vauban's utility was two-edged; when his fortresses fell into the hands of the enemy his was the unhappy task of proving that they could be breached. He also drafted a tax reform project that he presented to the king, which in its wording seemed to anticipate the famous pamphlet of the abbé Sieyès on the Third Estate. 'There has never been enough consideration for the little people in France,' he wrote in his proposal for a single income tax with no exemptions, 'it is exploited and despised, and yet it is the most considerable part of the population by its number and by the real services it renders the state.' Louis XIV banned the publication of Vauban's proposal, and there was talk of locking him up, but he died before a decision could be reached.

Louvois seemed obsessed with the idea that anyone who dared to oppose the Sun King should be destroyed. He mixed zeal with sycophancy. He urged massive reprisals in the war against the Dutch, telling the maréchal de Boufflers: 'If the enemy burn one of our villages, burn ten of theirs.' But when Louis XIV expressed displeasure at the extent of looting and destruction, he did a swift about-face and wrote to the maréchal de Luxembourg that the king was astonished 'to see the country being looted and exposed to all the violence of the soldiers. You know as well as anyone that this is the best way to ruin the troops and the country. . . . His Majesty has ordered me to tell you that he desires remedies to be taken. . . .' Louvois showed similar eagerness in the persecution of Protestants, and wrote in a directive that 'His Majesty wishes those who refuse his religion to be treated with extreme harshness.' But again, when

Louis XIV objected to the brutal methods of an Intendant named Marillac, who boasted that he had obtained 30,000 conversions in a single year, Louvois wrote: 'His Majesty has ordered me to let you know that he absolutely wants you to cease all violence . . . even if the violence has produced conversions.' In the second, pious phase of the king's life, the ministers outdid each other in religious devotion. Le Peletier went to vespers each day, and Torcy knew all the psalms by heart.

Conversely, the nobility was stripped of power in exchange for the fool's gold of court life at Versailles. The move to Versailles served three purposes—it was an instrument of propaganda and a permanent exhibit of French splendour, it allowed Louis to escape a capital which he detested, and it domesticated the nobility. The construction of Versailles was a life's work. It was as a young man of thirty that Louis asked the architect Le Vau to draw up plans for enlarging his father's hunting lodge in the wooded plain ten miles from Paris; it was only fourteen years later, in 1682, that he and his court moved there permanently; and it was not until 1710 that the chapel was completed and that Louis, now in his seventies and fixed in the daily habits of majesty, first knelt to pray there. The palace was designed as the antithesis of a feudal castle. The pre-absolutist castles were built in strategically dominant positions, they were difficult of access because of moats and drawbridges, they bristled with turrets, and their few windows were designed more to be fired through than to let in light. Versailles is an emblem of absolutism not only in its grandeur, but in that it is indefensible. The monarchy no longer needed drawbridges and turrets, and replaced them with the longest horizontal frontage of any building in Europe (475 metres) and with hundreds of high, regularly spaced windows. It was open to the public (special carriages, called chamber pots, took Parisians to Versailles and back), and there were as many visitors under Louis XIV as there are today, as many as 6,000 in a single day, who sometimes prevented the king from taking his daily walk. As soon as they entered the courtyard, visitors were met with signs of the king's supremacy, allegorical groups of sculpture which showed a felled eagle (the Austrian empire) and a recumbent lion (the Spanish monarchy).

Paris had been the capital of French kings since the twelfth century. It was the base from which the Capetians had conquered France. It was a natural capital, 'the true heart of the kingdom,' according to Vauban, 'the common mother of the French, the summary of France.' At the same time it was unruly, irreverent, and independent. On five separate occasions from the fourteenth to the seventeenth centuries it had been in open conflict with the king: during Etienne Marcel's bourgeois commune in 1357, the popular insurrection of the Maillotins in 1382, the revolt of the University and the guilds in 1436, the religious-inspired revolt of 1584, and the *fronde* under Louis XIV. With its insurrectional tradition and its enclaves of independent authority, like the Parlement and the University, Paris was naturally odious to the representative of absolute authority. Before Louis XIV, Henri III had said of Paris: 'Oh, bloated and capricious capital, you need to be bled.' The Sun King, although he amnestied the principal *frondeurs*, never amnestied Paris. He preferred to remove himself from what he could not control. He did not, like Peter the Great, who built Saint Petersburg to free Russia from Asian dominance, create an alternate capital. He simply moved to Versailles. But while the palace protected him from the disorders of the capital, it also sealed him off from his people, so that one visitor described Versailles and its court of 10,000 nobles as 'a foreign enclave inside the nation.' However artificial, Versailles was sufficient unto itself, a society so glamorous and exclusive that whatever went on elsewhere could be disregarded.

With the move to Versailles, the tradition of nomadic kings, travelling with their court from one castle to the next, was lost. Louis XIV left Versailles for his secondary residences in the vicinity, Marly, Compiègne, and Fontainebleau, but he saw little of France, and once spent seven years without setting foot in Paris. Louis XV saw only the provinces he had to cross to reach the battlefields of Flanders. Louis XVI rarely visited Paris. When his brother-in-law, the Austrian Emperor Joseph II, came to Versailles in 1777, he told Louis XVI how much he had admired the Invalides. Yes, replied Louis XVI, he would have to go and see it sometime because he had heard it was very interesting. It was finally the Paris mob, marching on Versailles in October, 1789, which ended the century-long divorce between the French king and his capital.

Louis XIV could see no middle ground for his nobility between rebellion and humiliation. He feared another *fronde*. But in summoning the second order of the kingdom to his baroque palace to assume roles in the elaborate game of praise-the-king, he created the new threat of an idle, useless, and totally dependent nobility. After his death, the nobility sought to regain political power and became the foe of weaker kings. Nonetheless, it is a measure of Louis' authority that under his reign the descendants of feudal barons who had been the king's equals fought and intrigued for the right to live in the tedious discomfort of Versailles, where they could adore their sovereign. They received in return a rigidly calibrated series of rewards, such as the right to hand the king his shirt in the morning, accompany him on hunts and weekends to Marly, and wear an embroidered blue and red royal jerkin, worthy ancestor of the Legion of Honour.

And yet the fascination of court life persisted, partly because Louis XIV had invented a land of enchantment which was a convincing alternative to real life, and partly because he was the source of patronage. Courtiers spent fortunes to keep up appearances, and the king could be generous with his titled lackeys. Money was the glue that held the court together, and Louis XIV was the first French king to make extravagance a method of government. As soon as he finished Versailles he began Marly. A castle was built for Madame de Montespan, who was out of favour before it was finished. Rivers were diverted and swamps were drained at enormous expense so that the king could be shown taming nature. Luxury enhanced the king's reputation abroad, provided the trappings of divinity at home, and ruined the nobility, which Louis now could harness with his pursestrings. A position of favour at court was eminently negotiable. The king's mistresses made fortunes by collecting commissions from favour seekers. Madame de Montespan got a cut on all the meat sold to Paris butchers. Daquin gave her 2,000 livres for using her influence to have him named first doctor to the king. There was a system of payoffs and kickbacks unrivalled since the corruption of Byzantium, and considered natural enough to be mentioned in official correspondence. The minister Barbézieux wrote the new governor of the Bastille, Monsieur de Saint-Mars, that on top of his 25,000-livres-a-year salary he could count on 'the normal profit to be made on the sums the king provides for the upkeep of the prisoners, which can be considerable.' Certain courtiers were specialized in one type of paid favour. The princesse d'Harcourt could get a courtier invited to one of the king's exclusive weekends at Marly for 2,000 livres. The marquis de Dangeau arranged marriages for a percentage of the dowry. Finally, there were courtiers who made it their business to know what offices were vacant. The duc de

Saint-Simon, when he bought a regiment, paid a 3,500-livres 'fee' to the 'agent' who had told him it was available.

Louis XIV, who prohibited the nobility from dealing in most forms of business under pain of derogation, was the greatest merchant of all, thanks to the venality of offices. The device of selling a judgeship or an army commission like a piece of property went back to the Capetians, and the only attempt to suppress it, under Henri III, was short-lived. But no king had made such an industry of selling offices as Louis XIV. He created hundreds of meaningless posts and made the army top-heavy with officers to milk the wealthy bourgeois who wanted to buy their way into the nobility. For by purchasing a magistrature or a captaincy, which they could (with additional payments) transmit to their heirs, they could also make the magic transition from Third Estate to nobility. In making the monarchy's finances dependent on the creation of new offices, Louis XIV responded to the aspirations of the bourgeoisie, but also swelled the ranks of the robe nobility, a class of clamorous reactionaries with a vested interest in the feudal privileges which they had bought so dearly. The patent letters conferring nobility at a price were revoked nine times during the reign of Louis XIV, and the holders had to buy new ones. The king himself was astonished by the success of the measures. 'Who will buy them?' he asked his Minister of Finance, Desmarets, who wanted to create new offices. 'Your Majesty ignores one of the finest prerogatives of the king of France,' Desmarets replied, 'which is that when a king creates an office God instantly creates a fool to buy it.'

Having deserted the capital and caged the nobility, Louis XIV transformed his day into a public ceremony. Etiquette, which seems to us an absurd magnification of trivia, was the essential machinery of the system. The king's most inconsequential acts had to be given a ritualistic meaning in which the courtiers, divested of power, could share. La Bruyère has described the extent to which it went: 'The great of the nation meet each day at a certain time in a temple called church . . . they form a vast circle at the foot of the altar, standing with their backs to the priest and the holy mysteries, their faces lifted towards their king, who can be seen kneeling at a tribune . . . one cannot help noticing in this usage a sort of subordination; for the people seem to be adoring the prince, who is adoring God.'

The etiquette perfected by Louis XIV altered the function of the monarchy. The primary function of the king became visibility. He had to get up and go to bed in public, and eat in public. Courtiers entitled to the *petites entrées* could watch the king defecate on his *chaise percée*, decorated with mother-of-pearl landscapes, a privilege which shocked the Italian visitor Primi Visconti, who wrote: 'What price does even the most repulsive thing that comes from the king have in this country? It is true that this king is very decent and uses the position out of ceremony rather than necessity.' The simplest act, like bringing Louis XIV a glass of wine, took on the solemnity of the Offertory in a Catholic mass, and involved four servants. A cup-bearer said: 'Drink for the king.' The head cupbearer advanced like an altar boy bearing cruets, with a gold platter under a covered glass and two crystal decanters, one containing water and the other wine. Flanked by two assistants, he brought the tray to the king's table, sampled the wine and water in gold cups, and uncovered the king's glass. The tray was presented, and the king served himself. From Louis XIV on, the French monarch was so continuously on display that Frederick II of Prussia said that if he were king of France he would hire a stand-in.

Louis XIV's great discovery was that he could stylize the essential functions of the monarchy. His public availability was a stylized version of the magistrate-king, the tradition that the humblest subject could appeal directly to the king for justice. This was no longer true, but it was acted out daily by the courtiers who whispered their *placets* to the king as they handed him his shirt or held the candle for him. In the same manner, Louis XIV's trips to the front with his official historian, official painter, official poet, official mistress, and a sampling of courtiers who watched the battle from a safe distance, were a stylized representation of the warrior-king, a corruption of more valorous times when kings had fought in the thick of their troops and been wounded and captured.

Ruin the Huguenot party

The only form of democracy the king had ever practised was the democracy of the bed; as a young man, he accepted the favours of women of humble origins, including 'peasant wenches, gardeners' daughters, and chambermaids.' He was only superficially religious, and his early inclinations were libertine. He once clambered over the rooftops of his castle at Saint-Germain-en-Laye to join a lady. After his marriage to the tiny, pink Spanish Infanta he shocked the pious

55

by glorifying his liaisons and siring nine illegitimate offspring. He caused a scandal by serving as godfather of Molière's first child, when it was rumoured that the playwright had married his own illegitimate daughter. But after these brisk salad days Louis XIV became a reformed sinner under the influence of Madame de Maintenon. Governess of two of the king's bastards by Madame de Montespan, Maintenon waged a patient, laborious campaign to win the king's confidence and affection. She offered a tranquil contrast to Montespan's outbursts and whims and, with a hypocrisy Louis XIV never suspected, convinced him of her selfless devotion to his person. She was a demure, soft-spoken bigot who nobly submitted to the 'painful occasions' which the king's lust demanded, in the name of a higher interest. For she believed that a miracle had placed her on the king's path and in his bed, and that she had a divine mission to guide him in spiritual affairs. Her faith was strong, and her mission was accomplished. At the age of forty-two, Louis XIV renounced the diversity of pleasure and remained faithful to Madame de Maintenon until his death.

A year after discarding his other mistresses Louis made the permanent move to Versailles, which was still a construction site teeming with thousands of workers. And a year after that, the queen died, which gave Madame de Maintenon a clear field. It is virtually certain that Louis XIV secretly married her (she refused to live in sin), and it is probable that the marriage took place the same year as the queen's death. There were unmistakable signs of Madame de Maintenon's new prominence—she remained seated in front of royal princesses; the king took her to see war games at Compiègne and showed her public deference.

Under his morganatic wife's tutelage, Louis took up piety with as much zeal as he had displayed in wenching. In 1684, operas and plays were banned at Versailles during Lent. Courtiers who did not carry out their Easter obligations were scolded. The king made lists of those who talked during mass. He exiled homosexuals, including his own natural son, the fifteen-year-old comte de Vermandois. The war against sin spread beyond the court, and unmarried couples were hunted throughout the kingdom like heretics. A woman charged with 'consoling a Swiss who had lost his wife' was sent to a convent. The court became pious and, wrote Saint-Simon, 'it sweated hypocrisy.' The dauphin, summoning his mistress during Lent, insisted that they both fast because he did not want to commit more than one sin. Monsieur, the king's brother, liked to rub medals of the Holy Virgin over his naked body. 'You cannot convince me,' his wife said, 'that you are honouring the Virgin by promenading her image over those parts which are destined to put an end to virginity.' 'You cannot know the power of the Holy Virgin's relics,' Monsieur replied. 'They care for all the parts which they touch.' Courtiers were ready to appear virtuous if that was the king's desire, and La Bruyère observed that a pious courtier is one who 'under an atheist king, would be an atheist.' Madame de Maintenon was pleased. 'The king's sanctity is each day fortified,' she wrote to her own spiritual adviser, the bishop of Chartres, in 1690. Proof of her growing power was the envy of the king's ministers. 'The great man's old garbage pail,' was what Louvois called her.

The king's piety coincided with the period of his greatest glory. He had extended his borders, built up his navy, conquered colonies, increased foreign trade, and imposed his law on Europe. The orthodoxy of Louis XIV prevailed from his sanctimonious court to all the capitals of Europe, with one infuriating exception in his own country—the Protestants. The motto 'one king, one church' was not a reality as long as 5 per cent of the population of 19 million stubbornly resisted his faith. As a result, Louis XIV spent years demonstrating how to be at the same time a good Catholic and a bad Christian. He was an indifferent theologian. Nor was he trying to please Pope Innocent XI, with whom he was quarrelling, and who disapproved of persecutions and forced conversions. His main motive was preserving religious unity in a country which had in the previous century been victimized by religious dissension. He would not tolerate heresy, and believed that subjecting the Protestants was politically necessary, and would add both to his and God's greater glory. In 1682 an assembly of the clergy had pressed the king to show greater zeal in the matter of the Huguenots. He was encouraged by his Jesuit confessor, his ministers, and Madame de Maintenon. For the last thirty-five years of his reign he carried out a persecution which ranks in history alongside the Spanish expulsion of the Moors and Jews, the Spanish Council of Blood in the Lowlands, and the twentieth-century persecutions of the Armenians and the Jews. It was his Crusade, except that instead of rescuing Jerusalem from the infidels like his saintly ancestor he carried it out against his own people.

The degrees of persecution can be summed up in the year-by-year decrees: 1679—Protestants are prohibited from holding synods; 1680 —Protestant women are barred from the profession of midwife; mixed marriages are banned; 1681—Protestant children may be converted from the age of seven; 1682—illegitimate children of Protestants will be raised as Catholics; 1684—the king's subjects are prohibited from giving charity to Protestant poor and sick; 1685—no Protestant may have Catholic servants; temples that celebrate mixed marriages will be destroyed; Protestant lawyers, doctors, clerks, surgeons, apothecaries, printers, and librarians will not be allowed to exercise their professions; anyone denouncing the export of Protestant capital will be entitled to half.

And finally, also in 1685, the Edict of Nantes, under which Henri IV had granted the Protestants freedom of worship, was revoked, and the terrible years of forced conversion and emigration began. The rationale of persecution is so consistent that measures identical to those enacted by Louis XIV against the Huguenots were again enforced 250 years later in the Nazis' anti-Semitic Nürnberg Decrees for the Protection of the Blood, or *Blutschutzgesetz*—the ban against mixed marriages, the inaccessibility of certain occupations, the ban against hiring servants from outside the persecuted group. The next step in the persecution of the Protestants, as in the twentieth-century persecution of the Jews, was violence. The dragoons sacked entire towns and tortured their populations, hanging men and women by their feet and curing them like hams over burning stacks of wet hay until they recanted their faith, pulling out their body hair, throwing them into fires and down wells, giving them the choice between death and immediate conversion. The Huguenots had to flee France, practise their faith secretly, or recant. From 200,000 to 300,000 escaped to the friendly Protestant nations of England and the Low Countries, and to Brandenburg, soon to become Prussia. Those who remained and met clandestinely were often massacred when they were caught. If Protestants who accepted conversion made posthumous written denials, their bodies were exhumed. If it is true that Louis XIV was not always aware of the harsh measures against the Huguenots, which were sometimes initiated by overzealous officials, it is also true that he showed little curiosity about the methods used to obtain forced conversions.

Louis XIV achieved the all-Catholic France he wanted, or at least the illusion of it. But he also weakened the monarchy. The forced emigration deprived France of hundreds of thousands of diligent subjects. Many Huguenots joined the armies and navies of the allies in the wars against Louis XIV. They formed centres of opposition and published anti-Louis XIV propaganda. Moreover, Louis XIV alienated the Protestant powers of Europe, where he was portrayed as a devouring ogre. Echoes of his infamy reached the New World, and Benjamin Franklin recalled hearing as a youth a sermon in Old South Church, Philadelphia, in which Louis XIV was called 'the persecutor of the people of God.' Finally, Louis XIV helped put the leader of European Protestantism, the Dutch Stadtholder William of Orange, on the English throne. Both Whigs and Tories feared that the Catholic Stuart James II would imitate the French king and try to destroy the Anglican Church. A marriage was arranged between William of Orange and Mary, the eldest daughter of James II. When the English king showed anti-Anglican inclinations, Tories and Whigs appealed to William, who landed in England with 15,000 men in 1688. James II fled to France, and William and Mary occupied the vacant throne in 1689.

With a religious enemy of the French king on its throne, England had an additional reason to form the anti-French alliances which clouded the final years of Louis' reign. Thus, for a variety of reasons, the persecution of the Protestants was a catastrophe for France. Seldom has a purely religious and internal affair had such far-reaching political results.

Having dealt with the Protestants, Louis proceeded to chastise the dissident Catholics who called themselves Jansenists. Any departure from the Catholicism of prayer books and catechisms smacked to him of heresy. The Jansenist programme of a return to personal holiness and the imitation of the life of Christ was highly suspect to Louis XIV. Jansenist contacts in the mid-seventeenth century with former *frondeurs* like the Cardinal de Retz were not forgotten. The royal caretaker of religious purity considered that a convent full of elderly ladies, called Port-Royal, was a danger to the state, and he had it razed in 1710. The remains in the Port-Royal cemetery were disinterred and dumped into paupers' graves. By destroying physical property Louis XIV hoped to eradicate the movement. Instead, he kindled a revival of Jansenism which scorched his successors. With their fanatical faith, and belief in the action of divine grace, the Jansenists would have been the natural enemies of the Enlightenment and the allies of the monarchy against the Philosophes' attacks on the church. But Louis' persecutions turned them into what he accused them of being—a schismatic force that weakened eighteenth-century Catholicism and served as a pretext for Parlement to pick a continuous quarrel with the monarchy. The Jansenist issue, intrinsically so trivial, plagued the entire reign of Louis XV.

The Sun King's last demonstration of religious zeal was to urge Pope Clement XI to condemn an obscure Jansenist tract published forty-two years earlier by a Father Quesnel, called 'New Testament with Moral Reflections.' After some hesitation, the pope in 1713 published the Unigenitus Bull, which condemned 101 propositions in Father Quesnel's book. In proving his orthodoxy, Louis XIV split the French church, part of which refused to accept the Bull. Once again, he left an unresolved issue for his successors to cope with. The Sun King believed that his vigilance as a defender of the faith was insurance for the afterlife. The statement attributed to him shortly before his death is: 'God should not forget what I have done for Him.'

*Lift his name among foreign nations
to its proper level*

Louis XIV preferred only one thing to the enforcement of religious orthodoxy. He died admitting that 'I loved war too much.' His personal reign began with the death of Mazarin in 1661 and lasted fifty-four years, during thirty-one of which he was at war with the rest of Europe. He behaved as though imbued with the message of a sermon he had heard in the church of Saint-Louis when he was ten. Cardinal de Retz praised his ancestor Saint Louis, not for his piety but for his qualities as a warrior. 'Saint Louis sanctified arms by tempering their violence with the laws of Christian discipline,' he said. 'Kings save themselves by giving battle . . . and Saint Louis probably had greater merit because of the orders he gave at the head of his army than because of his prayers. . . .'

Ironically enough, what were perhaps the most important territorial gains of his reign, the Artois and the Roussillon, were obtained in 1659, under Mazarin's tutelage. Under his personal reign, Louis XIV won the Franche-Comté and that part of Flanders which corresponds roughly to the actual Département du Nord, as well as Strasbourg and other important cities, but he lost his claim to Lorraine and Savoie and to French extension to the Rhine, and had to give up the Hudson's Bay territories and Newfoundland. The peculiar character of Louis' wars was that he began by pursuing the traditional policy of the *pré carré*, that is securing France's boundaries against other European powers, but that after his early successes he seemed bent on the gratuitous humiliation of other European powers. The courts of Europe had to be periodically reminded that the French kingdom was the oldest and most powerful. 'The kings of France, hereditary kings,' wrote Louis XIV, '. . . can boast that in the world today, there is without exception no better house, no monarchy so ancient, no greater power, no authority so absolute.' This attitude derived partly from an inflated view of his own position, partly from a lack of understanding of the development of the rest of Europe. To the end of his reign, Louis considered that the Austrian emperor was the illegal successor of Charlemagne and that his power was illusory because he was elected. He did not believe that England was capable of becoming a great power, and he despised the Dutch as a bourgeois Protestant plutocracy, refusing to consider that it was a wealthy commercial nation which could buy allies and boasted the largest fleet in Europe. His ministers commonly referrred to the Dutch as the 'pickpockets of the seven seas,' and 'the horse dealers of Europe.' Conversely, he overestimated Spanish power and continued to consider Spain his principal enemy, not realizing that he had turned all of Europe against him.

His first weapon to curb Europe was money. He bought from the duc de Lorraine his eventual right to that province (which he later lost) and bought Dunkirk from the British. He paid subsidies to Dutch deputies, Polish lords, Irish Catholics, English renegades, and the king of Denmark, in return for which they defended French aims. What he could not buy he conquered. The first major war of his personal reign began in 1672, when a French army under Turenne invaded Holland. Louis XIV did not bother to declare war, and the reason he gave for the surprise attack in placards posted all over Paris was 'the unbearable ingratitude and vanity of the Dutch' (one of their crimes may have been striking a medal which showed five horsemen beneath a sun, with the inscription 'they stopped the sun in the middle of the sky'). The swift French advance and the passage of the Rhine made the Dutch open the dikes and flood the country to prevent its occupation. Many rich merchants sacrificed their gardens and art collections to the waters of the Zuider Zee. At the same time, the Dutch were willing to negotiate and an embassy was sent to Louis in June. One of his peace conditions was that each year the Dutch should send an ambassador to Versailles bearing a medal on which it was engraved that the United Provinces owed their freedom to the Very Christian King. Negotiations were broken off, a European coalition formed against France to help the Dutch, and the war dragged on until the Peace of Nimeguen in 1679. This is generally considered the zenith of Louis' power in Europe. Spain ceded Franche-Comté and her fortresses on France's northern border. Louis XIV, Voltaire later wrote, had dictated the peace terms: 'Victorious from the outset of his reign, never having besieged any fortress without taking it, superior in every way to his united enemies, the terror of Europe for six consecutive years, and finally her arbiter and peacemaker, adding Franche-Comté, Dunkirk, and half of Flanders to his states.' Another way of putting it would be that Louis started an undeclared war against the Dutch for no reason other than they had incurred his personal displeasure, rejected an early peace by making absurd demands, set the pattern of European coalition against France, and that, instead of crushing the Dutch he had to restitute the fortress of Maestricht and rescind Colbert's 1667 tariff on foreign goods. Paris' Saint-Martin gate, ordered to commemorate the French conquest of Holland, was finished just as the last of Louis' troops were pulling out of the Low Countries. At home, all of Colbert's patient improvements and fiscal reforms were upset by the strain of war. In the decade of peace from 1661 to 1671 the king's net income had doubled, but by 1676 there was a deficit of 24 million pounds. Colbert could no longer subsidize French colonies and royal manufactures. Forgotten taxes reappeared and new ones were devised. Colbert, accepting that the king loved war above everything, resigned himself to the hasty expedients of previous ministries.

As arbiter of Europe, Louis tried to impose the constraints of court etiquette on international affairs. His violent reactions to the most trivial slights show that in his mind prestige was a matter of vital importance. Just as a courtier might be exiled for neglecting his devotions, international incidents were multiplied over matters of precedence. When the Spanish ambassador's coach passed in front of the French ambassador's in a London procession in 1661, Louis XIV demanded a formal apology from the Spanish king, his father-in-law, and insisted on the recall of the rash ambassador. When the king of England, a year later, demanded that on 'English seas' foreign vessels should be the first to salute English ships, Louis became so incensed that Charles II gave way. When Louis learned in 1684 that the maritime republic of Genoa was building ships for the Spanish fleet, he sent, instead of a warning or a diplomatic note, his own fleet to bomb Genoa for six days. The Doge, one of whose sacred duties was never to leave the city, personally came to Versailles to humble himself before the great king. In 1686 Louis sent an army into the independent duchy of Savoy to massacre its Protestant citizens, who were charged with helping the Huguenots flee France. Not even the pope was safe from Louis' tantrums. Under Innocent XI, every ambassador except the French had given up claims to diplomatic immunity for their Rome embassies to keep the neighbourhoods from becoming the refuge of whores and gangs of thieves. In 1687 the pope informed Louis XIV that no French ambassador would be received unless he subscribed to the general rule. Louis replied that he had been placed on his throne directly by God 'to give examples to others and not to receive them,' and occupied the papal enclave of Avignon as a reprisal.

Another form of provocation was the policy of *réunions*. Relying on medieval documents and the vague or obscure clauses of recent treaties, Louis claimed the legal right to more than a hundred towns, fiefs, and villages on his northeastern boundary. These unilateral rulings were no more than a continuation of expansionism in peacetime. In September, 1681, 30,000 French troops massed outside the walls of Strasbourg to enforce the Sun King's claims, and made that city capitulate. Once again the aggressive foreign policy of the Very Christian King goaded the rest of Europe into a coalition, called the League of Augsburg, formed in 1686. It was headed by Louis' most tenacious foe, William of Orange, now king of England. The war lasted nine years on four different fronts and exhausted the French economy. The price of wheat quintupled, and in 1693 and 1694 so severe a famine gripped France that in cities the poor ate the innards of slaughtered animals which butchers threw into gutters, and in the countryside they ate roots and grass which they boiled in water. This time Louis was no longer the arbiter of Europe. At the Treaty of Ryswick in 1697 he had to restore all the towns and fortresses acquired through his spurious legal claims. He kept the city of Strasbourg, but lost the rich province of Lorraine. And he suffered a blow to his pride in having to recognize the Protestant Prince William of Orange as William III of England.

For a few years Europe was at peace, and might have remained so

had it not been for the death of the scrofulous and degenerate
Spanish king, Charles II, in 1700. Louis XIV had a valid claim to the
Spanish throne, being the son and husband of Spanish Infantas.
When the king's will was made public, offering the throne to Louis'
grandson, the duc d'Anjou, on condition that he renounce all claims
to ruling France, Louis accepted. Placing his grandson on the
throne of his traditional enemy was a diplomatic victory viewed with
misgivings by the rest of Europe, but it did not automatically mean
another war.

The European powers had reason enough to fear France alone,
not to mention a Franco-Spanish empire. It was up to Louis to prove
that Spain would pursue an independent course, and reassure England, Holland, and Germany that no threat of Franco-Spanish imperialism existed. Instead, he declared in 1701 that the new Spanish
king, Philip V, would keep his rights to the French throne, as would
his descendants. This violation of the Spanish king's will was
coupled with a new affront to the detested Dutch. Spanish fortresses
in the Lowlands were, by agreement, occupied by Dutch garrisons—
French troops moved into the fortresses in the name of the Spanish
king and threw the Dutch out. Europe again was anxious, and Louis
XIV multiplied his gestures of arrogance as though to force another
war. The powerful commercial classes of England and Holland
feared that France would appropriate the lucrative Spanish colonial
trade. Their fears were confirmed when the *Asiento*, the right to
supply African slaves to Spain's American colonies, passed from a
Portuguese to a French company in which Louis XIV himself was a
stockholder. Spain seemed more and more to be governed from
Versailles, and a precautionary Grand Alliance was formed among
the German princes, the Austrian emperor, the Dutch, and the
English king. Louis' final arrogance, when the dethroned Stuart
king, James II, died in 1701, was to recognize his son, James III, as
the legitimate English ruler, repudiating the agreement made at
Ryswick. The angry English reaction against 'the Papist king' made
war inevitable.

In each of his three successive wars against Europe Louis XIV
fared less well. Now he was an old man, worried about saving his
soul, relishing the brittle satisfactions of piety, spending more and
more time with his confessor, going through the paces of his court
performance with the same solemn haughtiness, but mindful perhaps that the world outside Versailles was not as perfectly orches-

Photo: Bibliothèque Nationale

RACINE READING TO LOUIS XIV
An engraving showing an imaginary interview

THE PLAGUE AT MARSEILLES, 1720
An engraving after de Troy

Photo: Bibliothèque Nationale

trated. His great generals were dead, and it was becoming a problem to recruit the huge armies necessary to defeat the combined forces of Europe under two brilliant leaders—John Churchill, Duke of Marlborough, and Prince Eugene of Savoy, who had joined the Austrians after being refused a command by Louis XIV. The chapter headings of the thirteen-year War of Spanish Succession are the names of French defeats. The maréchal de Villeroi was captured in Italy; in 1704, Marlborough threw the French out of Germany at Blenheim, and crushed another French army at Ramillies in 1706; Prince Eugene destroyed a third army at Turin in the same year; in 1707, France was invaded from the south as an allied army reached Provence; in 1708, the French north was invaded, the city of Lille was taken, and Louis XIV's grandson, the duc de Bourgogne, showed at the defeat of Audenarde that he had inherited none of the Bourbon appetite for war—the only order he gave was to retreat; in 1709, the northern village of Malplaquet was the scene of a blood-bath which routed the armies of two maréchaux, Boufflers and Villars. In 1712, the seventy-four-year-old monarch, saddened by the deaths of the duc and duchesse de Bourgogne and their eldest son, all in a single week, his country overrun by allied armies, was a pathetic figure contemplating the desperate last stand of the French monarchy, during which he would sacrifice his life. His advisers wanted him to retreat to Blois, for the enemy was approaching Paris. On July 12 he received his commander-in-chief, the maréchal de Villars, at Marly. Villars was leaving for the decisive battle with the enemy coalition. 'If the battle is lost,' Louis XIV told him, 'write only to me. I will climb on my horse and ride to Paris with your letter in my hand; I know the French; I will bring you 200,000 men, and I will be buried with you beneath the ruins of the monarchy.' Fortunately, such fanciful heroics were unnecessary. On July 24, Villars, after a bold night march on Eugene of Savoy's camp at Denain, attacked and won, while Prince Eugene bit his gloves in helpless rage. At Denain, Villars saved the shreds of the Sun King's imperialism and forced the conclusion of the Treaty of Utrecht. The old conqueror had become an appeaser. All the nostrums of the finance ministers had been exhausted—tax increases, devaluations, high-interest borrowing. The king had sent his gold plate to be melted down and his jewellery to be pawned. He was no longer the living god beyond criticism. In Paris, people recited mournfully: 'Our Father, who art in Versailles, thy name is no longer hallowed, thy kingdom is no longer so great, thy will is no longer done either on earth or on the waters.' At court, Madame de Maintenon shuddered to think that 'there are murmurs at his very door.'

It all led to the rearrangement of Europe in the Treaty of Utrecht, a year before Louis' death. The French king recognized England's Protestant House of Hanover while his grandson, Philip V of Spain, relinquished all claims to the French throne. Savoy and Nice remained the property of the king of Savoy, and Newfoundland and Acadia were lost to the king of England. Finally, the Sun King, who had made such a practice of humiliating the smaller states of Europe, suffered two humiliations himself—he had to promise to expel his guest, James Stuart, from France, and to raze the fortifications of Dunkirk within five months of the treaty signature.

The only successful aspect of Louis' imperialism was not imposed by his armies, but spread unopposed through Europe—the conquering baroque. With an army of artists who obeyed him as faithfully as his generals, Louis XIV gave the world lessons in majesty. Versailles and the secondary residences had satellites in every European country—the garden façade of Hampton Court in England, Sans Souci in Prussia, Het Loo in Holland, Schönbrunn Palace in Austria. Marly was copied by the elector of Mainz, Trianon inspired Pagodenburg near Munich. The royal square and the equestrian statue travelled to Lisbon (Commerce Square), Brussels (Place Royale), Copenhagen (Amalienborg Square), and Vienna (Joseph II Square). The royal portrait, in sabled coronation costume or on horseback in the heat of battle, a speciality of Louis' court painter Hyacinth Rigaud, was adopted by every minor German prince. The theatrical, grandiloquent style of Louis XIV furniture and decoration, in which even tables and chairs were made to trumpet the king's glory, infiltrated every court. The occupation of Europe that French troops failed to achieve was carried out by the French dancing master, the French tutor, the French governess, and the French artists and men of letters who were invited to foreign courts to demonstrate correct taste. Court life as it developed at Versailles, with its posturing, its fussy elegance, its daily regimen of laced and beribboned trivia, and its hieratic monarch, was the centre of a Galilean, not a Catholic universe. It would have been heresy to suggest otherwise.

There were, however, cracks in the classicism. At the same time that the monarchy-sponsored art and thought of the French splendid century paraded across Europe, an underground intellectual move-✓ ment was challenging its orthodoxy. There was no comprehensive programme, but simply a questioning of certain articles of faith, a number of suggested alternatives to seventeenth-century dogmas. Thus, the Enlightenment was not exclusively an eighteenth-century movement, most of its ideas having been first formulated under Louis XIV's long reign. There were muted but persistent voices which urged an examination of doctrine rather than blind respect for the church; respect for natural law rather than faith in divine law; a monarchy founded on the rights of subjects rather than their duties; the consideration of change as salutary rather than dangerous; the need for equality based on law rather than social stratification based on custom. History as fable, religion as hagiography, science as a Cartesian dream, politics as a form of worship, no longer sufficed. In 1678, Richard Simon wrote a critical history of the Old Testament and protested against such terms as 'it has always been taught,' and 'it has always been believed.' Deists, who wanted the heavens anonymous but not empty, began to write long before Voltaire.

Under Louis XIV, two famous churchmen illustrated the coexistence of rival systems of thought. Bossuet, with his bombastic rhetoric, defended religious orthodoxy and the king's persecution of the Protestants, fed Louis' vanity by comparing him to the first Christian emperors, and became a bishop. Fénelon, tutor of the king's grandson, the Duke of Burgundy, favoured a theory of aristocratic government repugnant to the king. In 1699, suspected of Quietism, one of his books was condemned by Innocent XII, and he was banished from court after being attacked by Bossuet. This was for the king a convenient way to separate an influential tutor from his royal pupil. Fénelon had expressed the novel idea that the purpose of a king's rule was to serve his people. The idea was scorned by Louis XIV, who reversed the proposition, but it was accepted sixty years later by Louis XVI, who said that his only aim was to make his people happy. Anti-clerical writers like Toland and empiricists like John Locke laid the groundwork for Diderot's *Encyclopédie*. Locke's *Essay Concerning Human Understanding* was published in 1690, and informed the generations of French thinkers obsessed with Cartesian methodology that there was a visible world which would yield some of its secrets under examination. In art also, the grandiose style of Louis XIV developed into the soft, female sinuousness

of rococo during his reign. Chronologically, Watteau is as much a
Louis XIV as a Regency painter. Much of the interior decoration
done in royal residences during the last fifteen years of Louis' life,
such as the refurbishing of Marly by Pierre Lepautre in 1699, are
full-blown rococo, a reaction against the sumptuous discomfort of
the conquering baroque.

Louis' attempt to freeze history according to his definition of 'one
king, one faith, one law' could not succeed. The one king died in
1715, the one law and the one faith ran the gauntlet of the eighteenth
century, at the end of which the guillotine stood waiting. Louis XIV
left France with more provinces and cities than she had before his
reign, and he also decorated the kingdom. In Paris alone, his reign
is responsible for the Invalides, the Louvre Colonnade, the Tuileries
Garden, the Place des Victoires, the Observatoire, the Val de Grace
Church and the Champs Elysées. He made territorial gains, but
Utrecht returned France to her borders of 1697 and launched the
British Empire. Louvois, who toadyingly told Louis XIV that his
motto should be *Seul Contre Tous*, was accurately predicting a dangerously isolated France. However, it is also significant that after
Louis XIV, France was not invaded until the end of the *ancien
régime*. Again, in his religious policies, Louis XIV did not succeed
in his intentions. In wanting to impose the unity of the church he
provoked a schism. In wanting to regulate ideas, he favoured the
advent of free thought. But the fault must be shared with the
century's theological discord. As his successors found, it was impossible to reconcile the religious factions. Another unforeseen result of
his reign was that in attempting to regulate the order of his succession he returned the Parlement to power. However, it may be
answered that it was not he but the Regent who restored Parlement's
right to remonstrate. His reign had many achievements, it was in a
sense the masterpiece of the *ancien régime*, and one historian has
viewed Louis XIV essentially as an artist, whose art was kingship.
But the great and glorious length of the Sun King's reign, the
magnificence of his court, the intellectual and artistic achievements
imitated by the rest of Europe, the attempts to improve France's
economy and administration, and the early military successes, must
be weighed against the high cost of the absolutist machine.

It was the ideal, abstract, Platonic construction of a single will,
which could not outlast its maker. Under Louis XIV, absolutism
both reached its peak and began its rapid decline. Like a chemist, he

isolated and distilled pure power. He was half Spanish, and there was something hispanic and inquisitional in his passion for piety and state police. He loved war, a voracious mistress. His court was the centre of a civilized world, but it was narcissistic, a school for lackeys, and set a precedent of cliques and favouritism which few French governments since have been able to avoid. He made splendour necessary, but depleted the treasury—there was a 45-million-livres deficit for 1715 and a staggering national debt of 3,000 million livres. He bequeathed his successor two irreconcilable mandates: a tradition of unrivalled extravagance and a fiscal position of chronic bankruptcy.

Louis XIV was one of that race of great men who do not serve the nation they lead but consume it. True statesmanship consists in uniting a nation with the minimum of constraint, not regiments of dragoons. The Sun King died apologizing for his bad example, and asked the infant Louis XV not to imitate his fondness for construction and warfare. Perhaps he realized on his deathbed that he had fitted the nation into a straitjacket which it would throw off once he was gone. One measure of his achievement was expressed by the Sorbonne professor who always began his lectures on the Age of Reason with the words: 'The precise Dangeau wrote on September 1, 1715: "the king died this morning at 8:15." For us, gentlemen, the eighteenth century begins on this day.'

III

THE EIGHT-YEAR CENTURY

The Regency is a century in eight years.
—Duclos, *Chroniques Indiscrètes sur la Régence*

IN AUGUST of 1715, the courtiers who had watched Louis
XIV receive emissaries on his throne, parade through his
gardens on high heels, consume prodigious amounts of food at
one sitting, and don his bedclothes at night were privileged to
attend his final representation: his death. Like everything else he
did, it was conducted publicly and with considerable majesty. The
first attack came on August 10 at Marly as he supervised the place-
ment in his gardens of marble statues imported from Rome. Two
days later he complained of sciatica, and on the 13th he attended his
last formal dinner, retiring thereafter to his bed for an eighteen-day
death scene. The doctors, ignoring the nature of his ailment (a
gangrenous leg), administered their usual placebos—purges, bleed-
ing, baths in asses' milk and in a mixture of Burgundy wine and
aromatic herbs which they swilled in a silver tub. They took his
pulse in turn, according to seniority, and brought Italian musicians
to his bedside to play soothing motets. 'Do you think this can help
me?' Louis XIV asked.

The Sun King put his final moments to good use, telling courtiers
not to weep for him, for, after all, he was mortal. He played his
final role with a bathos that must have been embarrassing for anyone
remembering the harshness of his reign. To his confessor he complained that he was not suffering enough for the expiation of his sins.
But to the cardinals who attended his bedside he said that responsibility for his religious policies was theirs, and that his conscience was
clear before God, since he had only followed their orders. He sat in
a wheel-chair, with his gangrenous leg on a stool, dispensing last-

70

minute advice to the members of his family. 'The king's stead-fastness,' wrote his sister-in-law, the Palatine Princess, 'is beyond description; he is giving orders as though he was going on a trip.' He burned his private papers and gave detailed instructions that his child-successor should be taken to Vincennes after his death. On August 27, his surgeon, Maréchal, operated, cutting into the black-ened flesh as the king cried out: 'Ah, Maréchal, how you are hurting me!' On September 1 he died, and the duc de Bouillon, Grand Chamberlain, changed the black plume in his hat for a white one to proclaim the new king. The following day Maréchal opened the body, removed the heart and intestines, and performed his autopsy. The embalmed body was dropped into a lead casket, which was placed in a thick oak coffin sealed with iron bands. The engraved copper plate nailed onto the oak said: 'This is the body of the very high and very powerful prince Louis XIV, called the great, of the family of the house of Bourbon, king of France and of Navarre, deceased in Versailles the first of September 1715 at the age of 77 years less five days, and born in Saint Germain en Laye September 5, 1638. He reigned 72 years, 3 months, and 18 days.'

Louis XV was five years old. When he sat on the throne, his feet did not touch the ground. Until he reached his majority, at the age of fourteen, France would be governed by a regency, one of those interludes that invariably endanger the monarchy. A regency is a period in which the central figure of the monarchy is absent, a period of momentary freedom from the restraints of absolute authority. It is also a period in which whatever is accomplished may be ques-tioned and repudiated once the new king is crowned, and in which the fragmentation of authority gives rise to factionalism and con-spiracy. It is finally a period of reaction against the previous reign and a period of innovation, a parenthesis between two absolute monarchs.

Louis XIV understood the dangers of a long regency. He lacked confidence in the Regent, his reprobate nephew Philippe d'Orléans, whom he had once called a 'boastful compendium of crimes.' Scandal and calumny seemed to shadow Philippe. He was accused of incestuous relations with his daughter, the duchesse de Berry, and of poisoning Louis XIV's grandson, the duc de Bourgogne. What-ever credit the Sun King gave to the charges against his nephew, he was concerned about leaving the kingdom in the hands of a man with such a tainted reputation.

His concern led him to tamper with the thread of succession, something no French king had ever dared, for it was a betrayal of the dynastic principle. In an attempt to control the monarchy's succession beyond the grave, Louis XIV arranged for his two bastard sons by Madame de Montespan, the duc du Maine and the comte de Toulouse, to inherit the crown. The Sun King's last extravagance was his will, an example of personal absolutism stretched to the point of absurdity. Like a Greek god changing the course of a river, he picked his own successors to show that he was his own dynastic principle. In 1714, by royal decree, the effete, crippled duc du Maine and the ineffectual comte de Toulouse, 'fruit of a double adultery' (since both the king and Madame de Montespan were married when they were born), were made Princes of the Blood in line for the crown after the death of the legitimate successor, the young Louis XV. The purpose of this move was to block Philippe d'Orléans' access to the throne. At about the same time, Louis XIV drafted his will, which stripped Philippe of most of the powers of the Regency in favour of the duc du Maine, who was put in charge of the young king's education and guard. The secret will, with its seven seals, was entrusted to the Paris Parlement and kept in a safe that could be opened only with three keys.

As he lay dying, Louis XIV made a hypocritical attempt to reassure the duc d'Orléans, telling him: 'My nephew, I have made a will in which I have preserved all the rights owed your birth—I have made the dispositions I felt to be wisest—if there is something that is not right it will be changed.' Only the last part of the statement proved true. As soon as Louis XIV had expired Philippe set in motion a coup to invalidate the king's will and regain the power of the Regency. He displayed organization, resoluteness, and decisiveness. The royal bastards, caught off guard by his quickness to act, offered no resistance. Philippe summoned Parlement on September 2. The robed lawyers arrived at the Palace of Justice to find that it was ringed with troops. The king's will was read. It called for a ten-member regency council in which Philippe d'Orléans had only one vote. It offered the nation a Regency without a Regent. Philippe rose to speak. He said that the will's dispositions contradicted the words he had heard from the dying king's lips and were an insult to his birth and his attachment to the crown. He asked that the will be set aside. Without even deliberating or voting, Parlement gave Philippe the Regency by acclamation. Ten days later, on September 12, Louis XV attended his first bed of justice (a session of Parlement at which the king appeared in person) to confirm the decisions. The cannons of the Bastille roared as he entered the capital. Prince Charles de Lorraine, Grand Equerry of France, showed the child-king pieces of the true cross in the Sainte Chapelle. Louis XV took his place in the Palace of Justice on a throne decorated with fleur-de-lys. Prompted by his tutor, the ageing maréchal de Villeroy, he told Philippe: 'Sir, I wish to assure you of my affection—my chancellor will tell you the rest.' Now France had a Regency with a Regent.

It had been wishful thinking on Louis XIV's part to hope that Parlement, a body whose voice he had stifled during his long reign, would rise to defend a measure which no theory of kingship since Byzantium could possibly admit. Awakening as though from a deep sleep to resume its political role, Parlement came to the Regent's defence, though not without coaxing. A deal was made that changed French history. Philippe, to win its support, promised to restore Parlement's traditional right to criticize royal decisions. The passage of his speech which won him unanimous acclamation was: 'Whatever right I may have to hope for the Regency, sirs, I may assure you that I will deserve it by my zeal at the service of the king and my love for the public good, particularly while I am aided by your advice and your wise remonstrances.' The great victor of the day was not Philippe but Parlement, which had recovered its right to remonstrate, avenged itself on Louis XIV by setting aside his will, and become the Regent's creditor.

The Paris Parlement and the twelve Parlements of provincial France had nothing in common with the English parliaments. They were not legislative assemblies, but tribunals, sovereign courts which rendered justice in the name of the king. The Paris Parlement, by far the most powerful because it claimed jurisdiction over roughly half the kingdom, boasted direct descendance from the informal assemblies called Marzfelds which had been held under the Frankish kings. Invoking some nebulous, pre-monarchical, unwritten constitution, Parlement claimed the right to register the laws of the kingdom, since it had to pass judgment on those who broke them. This was at first a pure formality. A royal decree would be drafted, sealed, and sent to Parlement to be inscribed in a book of laws. But it gradually became a political weapon, for the right to register laws implied the right to refuse to register them. Created as instruments

73

of the king's pleasure, Parlements gradually came to consider themselves the voice of the nation and the guardians of legality against
the whims of kings. The refusal to register laws and the practice of
written remonstrances which held up royal decisions became the
only form of political opposition under the *ancien régime*.

At the same time that Parlement began to insist that only with its
stamp of approval could the royal will become the public will, the
method of recruitment in its ranks changed. In the early days, its
members were named by the king, but in the sixteenth century seats
on the tribunals went up for sale as the venality of offices spread.
One bought a judgeship, just as today seats are bought on the stock
exchange. A seat on the Paris Parlement could cost as much as
500,000 or 700,000 livres (most were less expensive) and was a valuable investment. Thus, a narrow and powerful caste was formed,
which, under the guise of the public good, defended its own interests. A small group of men owned French justice, which helps to
explain the corruption and snail's pace of eighteenth-century courts.
Meting out justice was good business, and the members of Parlement
often became rich men who made up the core of the gown nobility
and transmitted their office to their sons like physical property. A
member of the Nicolaï family occupied the seat of First President of
the Court of Audits without interruption from 1506 until the reign
of Louis XVI. The interests of Parlement were those of wealthy
landowners, attached to their purchased prerogatives and obsessed,
just as the court aristocracy was, with the preservation of their
privileges. The twelve provincial Parlements imitated Paris. As
Henri IV told Dubernet of the Bordeaux Parlement in 1608: 'Who
wins a trial at Bordeaux? Whoever has the thickest wallet.' Parlement accomplished the feat of enlisting the support of public opinion
for a completely reactionary programme which tried to scuttle every
royal reform. From the sixteenth century to the French Revolution,
there is not a single enlightened measure it did not oppose, from tax
increases to repulse an invader, to the creation of the Académie
Française.

As judges, they opposed judicial reforms which threatened to do
away with some of their abusive practices, such as the 'spices,' a
mandatory gift of money which a petitioner had to offer the judges
who had heard his case. As landlords, they opposed the abolition of
serfdom, and the end of forced labour for public works projects. As
tax-exempt members of the robe nobility they opposed tax reforms.

They were against the dissolution of the equally narrow-minded guilds because the guilds were always involved in litigation and were thus a good source of revenue. Their mentality was absurdly restrictive. In 1758 the Intendant of Paris ordered pigeons to be kept indoors because they were eating grain that had just been planted. Parlement voided the ordinance on the grounds that the Intendant had exceeded his authority.

Even so, since it was the only body which dared oppose the crown, Parlement projected a popular image. It published its remonstrances, full of windy rhetoric about the reign of despots, which were widely read and helped to obscure real issues. The orators of Parlement were compared to Cicero and Demosthenes. In 1756, a third-generation lawyer at the Paris Parlement, Edmond-Jean François Barbier, noted that 'the remonstrances of Parlement presented to the king on August 22 are being sold to the public. They are perfectly well written and contain strong maxims against royal authority which impress the public.' Voltaire, who saw through the popular image, said that citizens who supported Parlement were 'flies who took the side of spiders.'

Louis XIV had silenced Parlement but had done nothing to change it, so that when the Regent restored it to power it immediately took up its ancient role as a special-interests lobby dedicated to undermining royal authority. From the Regency to the Revolution, Parlement and the king conducted a running quarrel. This is the most tedious chapter of the monarchy's decline, but it is also the one in which the monarchy's prestige and honest efforts towards reform were constantly beaten down by the legalistic tricks and harassment of the gentlemen of the robe. Philippe d'Orléans did not have to wait long before Parlement availed itself of the right to remonstrate he had so generously handed it. In May, 1716, Parlement remonstrated against a decree re-establishing the post office superintendent. Philippe had recourse to the old methods of intimidation. When Parlement refused to register a royal decree, a bed of justice was held, during which the king personally told the lawyers that he wanted to be obeyed. Before the Regency, the king's presence had been enough. But now that Philippe had handicapped his own authority by resurrecting a strong Parlement, he needed new methods to subject it. In 1720, he exiled the Paris Parlement *en masse* to the nearby town of Pontoise. This was an escalation of reprisal methods to force obedience to the king's will. Thus the Regency went full circle from restoring Parlement to power to devising new measures to curb it. The cycle of remonstrances, beds of justice and exile continued under Louis XV and Louis XVI with fastidious regularity. Each time the king scored a point the lawyers bounced back with a net of legal objections to ensnare the monarchy. Towards the end of his reign an exasperated Louis XV abolished Parlements altogether in what amounted to a *coup d'état*, but his youthful successor, uncertain in the ways of power, reinstalled them. The result of Philippe d'Orléans' Faustian pact with Parlement was a chronic problem with which the monarchy was unable to cope successfully and which contributed to its downfall.

From the first day of his caretaker rule, Philippe placed the Regency under the sign of repudiation of Louis XIV. By invalidating his will, he bore out Louis XIV's own prophecy that a dead king can achieve no more than the humblest of his subjects. He carried this repudiation into many other areas, like the buyer of a house who completely redecorates every room so that it shows no traces of the previous owner's taste. Louis XIV had specified that his young successor was to move to the château de Vincennes while Versailles was aired out, and then return to the palace. But the Regent, who longed for the turbulent pleasures of the capital, argued that the Vincennes climate was too harsh for Louis XV's delicate health and moved the royal family to Paris. The courtiers packed their bags and returned to the boredom of their provincial castles, the town of Versailles suffered from unemployment, and the palace became an uninhabited tourist attraction. Instead of pursuing the Sun King's religious persecutions, Philippe practised religious tolerance. He exiled Louis XIV's sanctimonious Jesuit confessor, Father Tellier, and amnestied the Protestants. He named the Jansenist archbishop of Paris, Cardinal de Noailles, chairman of his 'council of conscience,' a sort of ministry of religious affairs. Instead of maintaining a police state, one of Philippe's first decisions was to free a number of Bastille prisoners who were victims of sealed letters; among them was the seventy-year-old marquis d'Arenberg, who had spent eleven years in the fortress for helping a Jansenist leader to escape France. Instead of pursuing an imperialist foreign policy, Philippe strove to keep the peace. For the first time in her history, absolutist, Catholic France was allied with her hereditary enemy, parliamentary, Protestant England. Instead of humiliating the nobility, Philippe gave the lords their first taste of power in more than a century. Louis XIV's small and devoted group of Secretaries of State gave way to a hydra-headed government apparatus of councils, each of which was largely staffed from the ranks of the old court nobility, with men better known for their manners than their sagacity—there was a Council of Regency, which eventually grew to have twenty-six members, and Councils of Conscience, Foreign Affairs, War, Navy, Finances, Commerce, and the Interior. 'Frenchmen,' commented a pamphleteer, 'fear not events sinister, our Regent has seventy ministers.'

In a very short time, under the Regent's tutelage, the monarchy moved towards less autocratic, more flexible positions. With the barrier of the court removed, the rulers of the nation were less isolated from their people. The Regent was an anti-despot, a man for his time. As his reign was a period of transition, so was he a figure of transition, reflecting at the same time the superstitions of the seventeenth century and the questioning irreverence and human-ism of the eighteenth century. Philippe d'Orléans, forty-one when he became Regent in 1715, was a short, plump, puffy-cheeked, red-faced man who had been almost blinded in one eye during a game of tennis, and who liked to be told that he resembled his ancestor Henri IV. He was a professed atheist who read Rabelais inside a Bible bind-ing at midnight mass at Versailles and who liked to hold orgies on such religious holidays as Good Friday. But although he did not believe in God, he did believe in the devil, and spent long hours in the stone quarries of Vaugirard trying to conjure up his presence. He sought out the advice of soothsayers. His German mother wrote in 1707: 'A madman in Paris believes he can make an angel appear in a chimney; to amuse himself, my son seeks the madman out, and among other impertinences, asks him how much longer the king will live.' But he was also drawn to science and had a chemistry laboratory where it was rumoured that he manufactured undetect-able poisons. The best argument against the charge that he poisoned members of the royal family in order to reign himself is that Louis XV survived him. He was in some ways a man of great taste and intelligence, while in others he showed an almost barbaric coarseness. He had the artistic temperament of a Renaissance prince and the morals of a tomcat. He acted in the plays of Racine and Molière. He composed the music for an opera that was performed be-fore Louis XIV. He collaborated with the Regency's official painter, Antoine Watteau, on the costumes and sets of several plays. He was himself a gifted painter and engraver, and published an edition of

Daphnis and Chloe with his own illustrations. He was said to have painted nude studies of his daughter, the duchesse de Berry. He was against censorship, and ordered the reprinting of books suppressed by Louis XIV, such as Fénelon's *Telemachus*. He protected artists, even those who insulted him, and enjoyed having scurrilous pamphlets about him read aloud. A pamphleteer was once brought before him. 'Do you believe what you write?' he asked. The pamphleteer replied that he did. 'If you had said you did not I would have had you locked up,' said the Regent. There were limits, however, and Philippe sentenced a pamphleteer named Voltaire to an eleven-month period of meditation in the Bastille. Voltaire, twenty-two and convinced that scandal was the best fuel for a literary career, had put the Regent's alleged incest to verse. In addition, he bragged to a police spy that he knew the name of the clinic in Auteuil where the duchesse de Berry was about to give birth secretly to her father's child. In 1718, however, when Voltaire's first play, *Oedipus*, was performed, the Regent rewarded him with a pension. Voltaire said that while he was grateful to Philippe for subsidizing his board he hoped he would no longer furnish his lodging.

The Regent orchestrated a revolution in manners. It was not so much a passage from virtue to debauchery as one from hypocrisy to candour. The courtiers of Louis XIV practised their vices in hiding. The Regency exulted in its excesses. Philippe proclaimed his loathing of those who were 'devils abroad and saints at home.' He encouraged the reaction against the bluestocking sanctimoniousness of the previous reign. In 1716 he inaugurated the Opera balls, where for 6 livres a head, a society that was the antithesis of the Versailles court could mingle behind masks and disguises that abolished social distinctions. The ballroom was so successful that an annex was built in the Louvre. Regency style meant sheer muslin dresses with plunging necklines, described as 'adorned indecency' (women pencilled blue veins on their busts to make their skins seem whiter); curvilinear furniture, with light woods and marquetry; the festive canvases of Watteau, which succeeded the solemn, ermine-enveloped ostentation of Rigaud's royal portraits as official art; and the disparagement of conventional morality.

'All that one reads in the Bible about the excesses of Sodom and Gomorrah does not even come close to the life led in Paris,' wrote the Palatine Princess. 'Out of nine young men who were dining the other day with my grandson the duc de Chartres, seven had the

French sickness.' Women succeeded in matching the men. Mademoiselle de Blois taught her talking parrot to say 'Madam, kiss my arse.' Madame de Pramenoux expressed her interest in budding industry by asking to visit a factory so that she could measure the male workers' instruments. Monsieur de Gacé had his wife sent to a convent because she had danced in the nude in mixed company. The Princess of Würtemburg shared her bed with her fifteen-year-old son. The abbess of Montbuisson swore by 'the fourteen bastards I have borne.'

In a society where debauchery was fashionable the Regent was the trend-setter. As he explained it, anyone who worked as hard as he did was entitled to an occasional binge. 'From six in the morning until nightfall,' he said, 'I am constrained to prolonged and tiring labours; if I did not amuse myself a little afterwards I could not bear it, I would die of melancholy.' Accordingly, after a full day's work, during which he drank nothing stronger than hot chocolate, he retired to his silk-upholstered private apartments in the Palais-Royal with a chosen company called the *roués* (a word derived from the torture of the *roue*, or wheel, and designating anyone worthy of such torture). The *roués* were chosen for their capacity to drink, tell off-colour stories, and join in the evening's entertainment without flinching. Female guests were a mixture of whores, starlets from the Opera, and ladies of condition who happened to be the *roués'* mistresses. The Regent's parties took place behind locked doors guarded by forty servants chosen for their great size, who had orders not to interrupt him under any condition. No servants were allowed inside. The guests prepared their own meals in a small kitchen where all the utensils were solid silver. The Regent invented dishes like carp roe with crayfish sauce and haunch of venison soaked in madeira on orange slices. Dom Pérignon champagne and Tokay wine waited on ice in gold-rimmed hanapers. The Regent was famous for downing half a dozen bottles at a sitting. As the evening wore on there were various forms of amusement. Sometimes a cardboard crown was placed on the Regent's head and the assembly shouted 'Long live the king.' Sometimes La Fare, one of the most diligent rakes, projected with a magic lantern of his own invention slides that showed extravagant positions of lovemaking (perhaps the first 'blue' movies). Sometimes Madame de Tencin, a classics scholar who had done research into the orgies of past civilizations, brought in nude dancers from the Opera to enact mythological scenes. After the show, the guests were left to their own devices. On one occasion, the Regent put out the lights, and a few minutes later threw open a cupboard full of lighted candles, with results that everyone thought hilarious.

In his determined, systematic debauchery, the Regent seemed to be making up for the long years of false piety under Louis XIV. Thanks to his suppers, the descriptions of which were embellished by pamphleteers, the Regency is remembered mainly as a period of scarlet sinning which outdid the Romans. In fact, the Regent had the triple virtue of sinning with candour, keeping his private life separate from public affairs, and never picking, among his many mistresses, a favourite who would assume a political role. He had a Rabelaisian nature. He 'swore like a pagan,' his mother said, and insulted his ministers. His diplomatic code was based on obscenities —a mild example is the code word for Jesuits, which was hemorrhoids. But he was loyal to his friends, generous with his enemies, and his mother acknowledged that his nature was 'like a dove's, without venom.'

The real significance of the Regency, however, is not to be found in its lax morals, but in the failure of the changes attempted by the Regent. In a first phase, the Regency moved away from the absolutism of Louis XIV and tried to impose a number of reforms. But the reforms weakened the regime, and Philippe had to reverse his field and return to the policies of Louis XIV.

The experiment of restoring the nobility to power had to be abandoned after three years. The lords had been weaned from affairs of state too long. In some cases they were plainly incompetent. The maréchal de Villars, head of the war council, was asked to read one of his reports but could not decipher his own handwriting. The duc de Noailles, head of the finance council, liked to come to meetings without his files so that no one could challenge what he was saying.

The lords showed more inclination for affairs of rank and precedence than for governing the nation. Their great victory came in 1717, when Parlement broke Louis XIV's decree making the duc du Maine and the comte de Toulouse royal princes. But aside from the 'reduction of the royal bastards,' there was little they agreed on, and, according to the marquis d'Argenson, 'the councils degenerated into a real bear garden. No one got along, there were disputes and delays, and the only result was confusion and anarchy.' In 1718, the councils were disbanded, and the Regent resurrected 'the five kings,' the

Chancellor and the four Secretaries of State who had governed France under Louis XIV. Real power, however, was increasingly in the hands of one ambitious man. The Regency, after its half-hearted attempt at group government with its 'seventy ministers,' ended with the familiar crutch of weak kings, a cardinal-prime minister in the tradition of Richelieu and Mazarin.

The rise to power of Guillaume Dubois, the son of a provincial pharmacist, is a study in a kind of *arrivisme* peculiarly common to eighteenth-century France, which belies the theory that social classes were frozen and that the corridors of power were inaccessible to men of humble origin. Dubois was bright enough to win a scholarship to study in Paris. The superior of the college recommended him for a position as assistant tutor in the household of the duc d'Orléans. He began exercising his influence on the future Regent when Philippe was a boy of twelve. Despite his abbot's tonsure, he was an atheist and a cynic, and he taught Philippe that virtue and religion are the masks of power. Hostile biographers show him at night in side streets recruiting ladies of easy virtue for his young ward, and, later, during the Regency, participating in the suppers of the *roués*. Although he was certainly unscrupulous enough to pander for the Regent and carry out other unsavoury chores, he was personally an abstemious man whose obsessive ambition excluded other pursuits. His is a classic case of overcompensation. The aristocracy made fun of this ferret-faced little man with his unhealthy, leaden complexion and his blond wig which was a parody of elegance. He had been 'born in the mud.' As a result, he was insatiable for honours, and worked tirelessly to deserve them.

The Regent made Dubois a Councillor of State in 1715, but it was not until a year later that he was able to prove his astuteness. In July, 1716, he was sent on a mysterious mission to Holland, posing as an expert in rare books. He stayed at the Nassau Arms in the Hague and browsed in libraries. But he found time for secret meetings with the Earl of Stanhope, the British Secretary of State, who also happened to be in the Hague. They negotiated the future of Europe while pretending to examine a first edition of the *Imitation of Christ*. Dubois described the negotiations in a 170-page report he sent the Regent. He managed to turn France's impoverished position into an advantage. 'You cannot know the strength of a nation on the edge of bankruptcy,' he told Stanhope. An agreement was reached which was to become, in January, 1717, the Triple Alliance of

France, England, and Holland. The English king was granted his
ancient appellation, 'King of England, France, and Ireland;'
Philippe promised to exile Anne Stuart's brother, the Jacobite pretender, who had been given asylum and support in France; Holland
obtained posthumous revenge on the Sun King by insisting that it
be referred to as 'a great power;' the Regent agreed to destroy the
French fortifications of Mardyck, which had been built under the
pretence of repairing a canal after the Dunkirk fortifications had
been razed according to the Treaty of Utrecht. By conceding these
points, Philippe won the peace and reversed the foreign policy of the
previous reign, which had been based on alliance with Spain. He
was accused of appeasement by courtiers who still heard the trumpets
of battle at the very mention of England, but he gave Europe its only
interval of peace in the eighteenth century, a twenty-three-year
breathing spell that lasted until the War of the Austrian Succession in
1740 once again made enemies of England and France. The treaty
delighted the Regent, who wrote Dubois that he had saved France.
The seven-year-old Louis XV is reported to have said: 'I did not
believe abbots could be so useful.' The maréchal d'Huxelles, head of
the Foreign Affairs Council, was so outraged by the new policy that
he refused to sign the treaty until he had been threatened with
dismissal. A year later, the councils were disbanded and Dubois was
named Minister of Foreign Affairs.

Although the alliance with England kept Europe relatively peaceful, it resulted in a plot to overthrow Philippe. The Regency, however, was an era when every programme failed, even plots to overthrow it. This particular plot was hatched by the grandson of
Louis XIV, who had become Philip V of Spain, and his minister,
Cardinal Alberoni, the son of an Italian gardener. The plan was to
kidnap the Regent, lock him up in a Spanish fortress, and proclaim
Philip V Regent of France. The Spanish ambassador to the French
court, Cellamare, enlisted discontented courtiers like the duc and
duchesse du Maine, whom the Regent had stripped of power and
titles. It was a very confused affair, more comic than menacing, full
of secret midnight meetings and messages so cryptic that not even
the conspirators understood them. Thanks to the indiscretions of
a brothel owner, two couriers were arrested with compromising
papers. The Spanish embassy was ringed with musketeers and
searched. The Regent had caught about a dozen of France's highest-
born courtiers in the act of treason, but he went along with the

opéra-bouffe aspects of the plot and behaved without harshness. The duc du Maine and his midget wife were exiled to provincial fortresses, and a handful of other courtiers were imprisoned. Ambassador Cellamare was deported. Just at this time, December, 1718, England declared war on Spain, and France had to join her new ally in the fray. Louis XIV had fought a long and costly war to secure his grandson on the Spanish throne. Now, five years after his death, it was Bourbon against Bourbon as the troops of Louis XV crossed the Pyrenees to fight the armies of his uncle. The war was a series of ironies. The Regent had some difficulty finding a general to lead his expeditionary force and finally appointed the Duke of Berwick, a naturalized French mercenary. He was the bastard son of James II and thus the brother of the Jacobite pretender the Spanish were supporting, as well as a Spanish grandee and a personal friend of the Spanish king. Philip V believed that if he showed himself on the battlefield, the French troops would acclaim him as their rightful monarch. Instead, the French task force helped the English destroy their only rival on the high seas, the Spanish navy, and Philip V had no choice but to make the peace of 1720, which ended forever Spain's expansionist dreams.

Having settled France's foreign policy problems, Dubois turned to religious affairs, not to serve God but to emulate his idol, Cardinal Richelieu. He asked his secretaries to draw up a list of every title and honour Richelieu had ever won, so that he would know what to ask for himself. In his obsession with the cardinal's hat, he persuaded Philippe to reverse the liberal religious policies of the Regency's early years. In church affairs, the Regent was a disinterested observer who never concealed his atheism. When prelates came to him for favours, he would reply politely: 'I am not of your parish.' His daughter Louise Adelaïde had taken the veil and signed her letters 'bride of our lord Jesus Christ,' to which he replied: 'I fear that I am not on very good terms with my son-in-law.' He was inclined towards tolerance and wanted the kingdom's various religious factions to make their peace. But no sooner had he ordered a stop to the persecution of Jansenists and honoured their leader, the Cardinal de Noailles, than the Jansenists began harassing their old enemies, the Jesuits, and reopened the quarrel of the Unigenitus Bull. In December, 1715, the University of Paris joined the dispute, refusing to recognize the Bull. Jansenists freed from prison or returned from exile resumed interrupted litigation before friendly courts. Noailles tried to prevent Jesuits from preaching and hearing confessions. He also opposed the Regent's liberal measures towards the persecuted Huguenots. Philippe made an honest attempt to reconcile the factions, even going so far as to preside at theological conferences. He was the advocate of reason against fanaticism. He told Noailles: 'All that [persecution of the Huguenots] is part of the other reign. In this one, it would be preferable to convert them with reason rather than by the means employed in 1684. Remember too, Monsieur le Cardinal, that it is with reason that attempts should be made to convert you and those of your party.'

In 1720, the archbishopric of Cambrai became vacant and Dubois asked the Regent for it. He was not ordained, so he took a short course in the priesthood, and went from minor orders to diaconate to priest to bishop in nine days, an uncontested record. There was a rumour that he had a wife in his hometown of Brive, but it was probably unfounded, since he left Brive at the age of sixteen. When he was consecrated archbishop the Regent gave him a pastoral ring worth 120,000 pounds. Having become a man of the cloth, which was to him no more than a form of livery, Dubois discovered the great merits of the Unigenitus Bull. He understood that the price of a cardinal's hat meant persuading the refractory French priests to accept that controversial papal document. He used his influence to bring the Regent closer to the Jesuits and the policies of the Roman church. With a mixture of cajolery and threats, he persuaded the dissident prelates, even the Cardinal de Noailles, to accept the Bull and its condemnation of 101 propositions in the Jansenist work of Father Quesnel. Still the biretta eluded him. It was only when Pope Clement XI died, and Dubois used his influence to elect the new pope, Innocent XIII, that the grateful father of the church made him a cardinal, on July 16, 1721. Unfortunately, the armistice between Jansenists and Ultramontanes which Dubois had engineered was only temporary, and most of Louis XV's majority was troubled by renewed quarrels over that most irritating of documents, the Unigenitus Bull. As for the Huguenots, they had to wait another fifty years, until the reign of Louis XVI, to attain legally recognized religious tolerance and civil rights.

Dubois was now a half-mad old man, feverish, insomniac, cadaverous, and prey to fits of temper during which he jumped over tables and chairs, insulting whoever was in earshot. But he still pursued honours with the same obstinacy, and was elected to the

Adadémie Française, and the academies of sciences and inscriptions Despite his failing health, he took on the jobs of Lord Privy Seal and Superintendent of Posts in 1721. A year later he badgered the Regent into naming him Prime Minister, his final Richelieu-like triumph. 'What is so surprising about making a pimp a minister?' the pamphleteers asked. 'Didn't Caligula make his horse a Roman consul?' Dubois did not live to enjoy his triumph. An abscess had rotted his bladder and he was operated on in August, 1723, at the age of sixty-seven. In those days surgeons were executioners more often than healers, and Dubois did not survive the operation. Mathieu Marais wrote in his diary of the Regency: 'And now this great cardinal, Prime Minister of France, is encased in lead like the others, although he did not even have the consolation of carrying his private parts into the next world, for the surgeons had cut everything off.' Saint-Simon estimated that Dubois had an income of a million and a half livres a year at the end of his career, which included the income from seven abbeys and archdiocese of Cambrai, his salaries as Prime Minister and Superintendent of Posts, and a pension of 960,000 livres a year from England for services rendered. It was long believed that Dubois had been bribed to uphold the English alliance, but no evidence of payoffs has ever been found in either French or English archives. Finally, Dubois goes down as a statesman who made sound decisions for questionable motives. He gave France a peaceful interim with the English alliance, and also tried to patch up France's religious quarrels.

The last and most daring of the Regency's experiments concerned the chronically chaotic state finances. One of the Sun King's bequests to his successor was a national debt in the vicinity of 3 billion livres. To finance his wars, Louis XIV had depended on loans from private bankers and anticipations on future income. At the end of his reign he was borrowing at interests as high as 400 per cent; money owed to court furnishers alone amounted to 185 million livres. The Regent was responsible for his uncle's debts but could not even meet current expenses, much less the interest on the national debt. Like a surgeon examining a gangrenous limb, he had to amputate. He appointed the four Paris brothers, financiers of humble origins who had made fortunes selling supplies to the army, to 'revise' letters of credit, that is, reduce their value. They inspected the accounts of all the businessmen who had dealt with Louis XIV. If their claims were just they were allowed to exchange their unpaid bills at a loss for promisory notes at 4 per cent interest; 650 million livres of debts were thus ex-changed for 250 million livres' worth of notes. If they were suspected of dishonesty they were turned over to a Chamber of Justice which dealt summary justice to profiteers. During the year it sat, there were 4,410 convictions and the state recovered about 400 million livres. The new rich of the Sun King's reign were moved from their confiscated Paris mansions to the Bastille; their gold and silverware, furniture, and art collections were carted to government warehouses. Two tax collectors convicted of graft were dragged through the streets with signs around their necks that said 'thieves of the people.' In-formers were promised one-quarter of the sums recovered, and one dishonest but shrewd businessman informed on himself.

Such harshness was not in harmony with the lenient liberalism of the Regency, and Philippe was disgusted by the success of his own measures—he loathed informers. There were also attempted reforms. The budget for the king's household was reduced from 15 million to 4 million livres, a saving made possible because Versailles was in mothballs. This spirit of thrift was fleeting, and in 1717 the Regent was persuaded to purchase for his greater glory a 125-carat diamond for 2 million livres. Other reforms, such as lower duties on foreign goods and a single tax based on land ownership, were either stillborn or short-lived.

Chambers of Justice and impulsive frugality were stopgap mea-sures, not fiscal policy. The finances of the Regency remained un-sound. Money was tight. Loan sharks discounted promissory notes at 30 per cent interest. It was in this climate of pessimism that the Regent resorted to the financial soothsayer of the century. As early as September, 1715, the month Louis XIV died, the duc de Noailles, who was head of the Financial Council, noted in a report: 'Monsieur Fagon exposed Monsieur Lass' project to establish a bank in Paris. . . . Monsieur Lass claims that the utility will be that everyone will be charmed to have banknotes instead of money, since it is so much easier to make payments with paper, and because of the assurance of being paid on sight. He adds that it is impossible that there be more banknotes than money, since banknotes will only be printed according to the quantity of money.'

Monsieur Lass was of course John Law (the French could not pro-nounce the *w*), the picaresque son of an Edinburgh goldsmith. He lived on the Continent because he was under sentence of death in England for having slain a gallant named Beau Wilson in a duel over a lady's favours. He migrated from country to country, earning his living at the card tables of the well-to-do. In his travels he had studied and admired the Bank of London, founded in 1694, and the Bank of Amsterdam, founded in 1609. When Louis XIV was still alive he had written a memorandum suggesting the foundation of a national bank in France, but it was ignored. As Law explained it, money was like blood, it had to circulate to make the body healthy. He proposed a beneficial transfusion of paper money, which would restore the economic health of France. Coin, he reasoned, is heavy, cumbersome, and sluggish. Paper money issued by the state and backed by gold and silver reserves would encourage trade, enrich the state, and absorb the national debt. Law's ideas were welcome alternatives to the tired expediencies of *ancien régime* finances. They gleamed with promise like newly minted gold coins. The international drifter who had tried in vain to interest the Duke of Savoy and the Emperor of Austria in his schemes had at last found a sympathetic listener, the Regent, a man with whom he had great affinities: both were bold, unscrupulous innovators. Law was the rainmaker, the mysterious stranger who comes to town and promises to end the drought and save the crops. The Regent decided against the advice of his ministers and gave the rainmaker a chance. Thus a foreign Protestant adventurer became the economic czar of Europe's richest nation. In the five years that the Law experiment lasted, France became the proving ground for a form of economic planning two hundred years ahead of its time.

Law began in a relatively modest manner. On May 2, 1716, a patent letter from Parlement gave him permission to start a private bank, which opened its doors in late May with a capital of 6 million livres. He reasoned that lack of public confidence in government finances stemmed from changes in the value of currency (an often-used fiscal device was an arbitrary drop in the gold value of the livre), and decreed a fixed value for his paper currency. Thus was the banknote born in France. Law was the first public official to accomplish the miracle of separating a Frenchman from his gold. Depositors entrusted him with their nest eggs because he promised to redeem them at the same rate, whereas official currency fluctuated wildly. He invested his depositors' money wisely and his bank thrived. Reassured by this initial success, the Regent began using the banknotes as official currency in 1717 and gave Law the monopoly of colonial trade in Louisiana, which he turned into a shareholding corporation

Three-quarters of the purchase price of shares had to be paid in Law banknotes. Since the government kept altering the gold value of the livre, more and more depositors exchanged gold for banknotes, which they converted into shares in the colonial company. In 1719, Law's bank became the Royal Bank and he was given the monopoly of all colonial trading companies, which he fused into one India Company. At the same time, Law took over the collection of indirect taxes (on salt, tobacco, and most other consumer goods) and established an economic empire. His genius was in understanding the role of credit in economic expansion. His bank, with branches in Lyon, La Rochelle, Tours, Orléans, and Amiens, each of which had two windows, one to exchange coin for paper, the other paper for coin, stimulated the economy by turning the gold hoards of the citizenry into working capital. But his mistakes were the encouragement of speculation and the fusion of his bank with his India Company, which pegged the value of his banknotes to the fortunes of colonial trade, since banknotes and shares were mutually convertible.

He launched a misleading publicity campaign to make the shares of the India Company rise. Paris was covered with posters that showed French explorers on the Mississippi admiring mountains of copper, silver, and gold. The copy said that since natives did not know the value of precious metals they exchanged them for trinkets. The search for an emerald boulder in this fairyland of riches was described. Indians were brought to France and shown like freaks. A marriage between an Indian princess and a sergeant in the guards was arranged. Law had forgotten his original promise to print no more paper money than he had gold reserves for. He now believed he could print an indefinite quantity of banknotes and keep up their value by using the very method he had intended to abolish, juggling the gold value of the livre.

Saint-Simon, an early critic of *le Mississippi*, sneered at Law's efforts to suppress the use of gold and silver, 'as if, since the time when Abraham paid cash for Sarah's burial, the world had been in error.' But the rest of the nation trundled bags of gold to the banks and waited in line for hours for the privilege of exchanging coin for paper. Law was a visionary, but he was also a gambler who approached state finances like a roulette player with a martingale, convinced that he can beat the bank. Unfortunately, he was the bank. His colossal self-confidence made him believe he could avoid panic and keep the system under control. He encouraged speculation, reasoning that the more money there was in circulation the more profits there would be for the state. He sold shares in his India Company at 50 livres, offering to buy them back in three months at 100 livres, which made their paper value rise. A first stock issue of 50,000 shares was quickly sold out. He floated a second issue, but buyers had to own four shares on the first in order to buy one share of the second (they were called daughters, and every daughter had to have her dowry). A third kind of share, the granddaughters, was sold to whoever had five daughters. These methods made the paper value of shares soar. At the height of speculation, a 500-livre share was quoted at the open-air stockmarket on the rue Quincampoix at 18,000 livres. This tiny street became the headquarters of the get-rich-quick delirium. Its iron gates were open during daylight hours to the frenzied trading of swarms of speculators. Law liked to visit the street and throw money out of a window to watch the crowds scramble for it. Fortunes were made and unmade in a day. Adventurers from all over Europe flocked to the Paris bonanza. Law was the most popular man in France. The Regent's mother wrote that 'Law is pursued to such a point that he knows no rest, night or day. A duchess kissed his hand in front of everyone. If the duchesses behave this way, what will other women kiss?' In its brief lifetime, the India Company floated 624,000 shares at 500 livres each, which were traded at an average of five times their nominal value.

The rush for riches imposed its own social patterns on the Regency. Dukes and princesses rubbed shoulders with their valets in the beckoning democracy of greed. Montesquieu, learning that chimneysweeps and waiters had become millionaires, wrote in the *Persian Letters* that 'God himself does not pull men from nothingness more quickly.' He added: 'In every heart, I saw the sudden birth of an insatiable thirst for wealth. I saw formed in a moment the detestable plot to make money by ruining the prince, the state, and the citizens rather than by honest labour and generous industry.' It was the reign of the unscrupulous, the shady dealers, the favourseekers, the stock-jobbers and stock-kiters, the shysters, and the usurers who made 'clock loans' at 2 per cent an hour. It was Babylon with banking hours. Great lords not only licked Law's boots for tips on the market, they profited from the inflation that came with sudden wealth by hoarding goods, which they sold when prices soared. The nobility was banned from retail trade under pain of derogation, which did not prevent the duc d'Antin from selling cloth, the duc d'Estrées from dealing in coffee and chocolate (then luxury products as expensive as caviar today), and the duc de La Force from owning a general goods store. Parlement tried La Force, a member of the Regency Council, as an example to other speculators of noble birth, and let him off with a warning to 'be more circumspect in the future, to behave in the irreproachable manner, suitable to his birth and his dignity of duke and peer.' Crime as well as speculation broke through social barriers. In 1720, Count Antoine-Joseph d'Horn, member of a famous Dutch family distantly related to the Regent, stabbed one of Law's brokers to death in a tavern while robbing him of 150,000 livres' worth of shares. He was seized by other patrons and turned over to the police. The Regent sentenced him to death despite pressures from his family to have him freed or declared insane.

The social consequences of the 'system' were not only the disturbance of public order and the further loosening of public morals. Law's principal lesson to courtiers was that they could become wealthy outside the closed circuit of court favouritism. The power of money to make money was substituted for the power of the monarch to grant gifts and pensions. This discovery of an alternate road to wealth, finance capitalism, also shook the foundations of the old society.

The glittering period of overnight fortunes and a boom economy lasted roughly from June, 1719, to February, 1720. In that brief but magnificent interval, Law, dizzy with success, ran France like an energetic Croesus. Never had so many measures been taken in so short a time: the free circulation of grain, a uniform tax on wine, lower meat prices, and the elimination of such useless sinecures as oil inspectors, cloth measurers, coal weighers, warehouse commissioners, and funeral criers, whose salaries amounted to an indirect tax on goods and services.

But as he accumulated responsibilities, he also accumulated enemies: Parlement, which had tried to stop him in 1718 by ruling that no foreigner could be involved in state finances; the General Farmers (sixty bankers to whom the monarchy farmed out the collection of indirect taxes), whose profitable duties Law had taken over; and the Regent's ministers, who feared the Scotsman's growing political influence. A first rush on the bank in July, 1719, failed when Law cut the gold value of the livre. Banknotes were still considered pre-

ferable; but the real crisis came after Law had fused his bank with
the India Company. He had promised dividends of 40 per cent on
his 500 livre shares, and it was a promise he kept, but for those who
had bought shares at inflated prices the spoils were meagre: 40 per
cent on a share worth 500 livres meant 2 per cent to the person who
had bought it at 10,000 livres. The speculators began to cash in their
winnings. The very lords Law had steered to enormous fortunes precipitated the system's collapse. On March 2, 1720, the prince de
Conti brought four carts into the courtyard of the bank, on the rue
Vivienne, and turned in 14 million livres' worth of shares for gold.
The next day Monsieur le Duc, even though he was superintendent
of the young king's education and a member of the government,
redeemed 25 million livres in gold. It was another example of the
nobility's irresponsibility and lack of foresight. The lords were sabo-
taging the first regime for over a century which had given them
any real power. The Regent was so furious that he had an apoplectic
fit. He told Monsieur le Duc: 'It seems, sir, that you take pleasure
in destroying in a single moment what we have taken great pains
to establish. Is this a way to uphold the interests of the state? Is it
not a means of destroying the bank to withdraw twenty-five million
as you have done, or fourteen million as Monsieur le prince de
Conti has done? What you do need so much money for?' 'It is true,'
replied Monsieur le Duc, 'that I have withdrawn twenty-five million
owed me by the bank, because I have a great love of money.' The
rush was on. The same gullible crowds which had queued up to
convert their gold to paper now stampeded the bank to convert paper
to gold.

Law had been named to the country's highest ministerial post,
Controller General of Finance, in January, 1720, after an expedient
conversion to Catholicism. Now, only two months after his triumph,
he had to use every resource at his command to save his bank. The
believer in free enterprise was forced to pass a series of restrictive
measures. He prohibited the hoarding of gold and silver and the
flight of capital. Individuals were not allowed to keep more than
500 livres in cash. The bank was closed without warning on certain
days. The value of the banknotes was cut, which further reduced
confidence. Each day there were new decrees about money and
property. The India Company shares were converted into state bonds
at 2½ per cent interest. On days when the bank was open there were
frightful mob scenes. Investors climbed trees from which they threw

themselves onto the compact mass below for a better place in line. There were fifteen killed in a single day. On May 29, Law resigned as Controller General and was placed under house arrest. In October the bank locked its doors for good. The shares and banknotes were worth exactly the cost of the paper they had been printed on. A month later, Law left France secretly with a passport provided by the Regent. He fled to the Low Countries and eventually made his way to Venice, where he died a poor man. His personal fortune of some 40 million livres was tied up in his own ventures, and when the bank failed he was one of the victims. He wrote to the Regent twice from Venice, requesting funds, but never received a reply.

At the Regency Council of January 24, 1721, the Regent, who had made possible the Scotsman's escape, said that 'Law should have been hanged.' The state returned to classical methods of financing. The Paris brothers were called from exile to liquidate 'the system.' They announced that banknotes and shares in the India Company would be redeemed at a fraction of their real value, ranging from 5 to 15 per cent. Eight hundred clerks sat in improvised offices in the Louvre and processed the shares and banknotes of an estimated 511,000 persons who rushed to beat the March 20 deadline. There were 3,200 million livres' worth of notes in circulation, and after the deadline had lapsed 728 million still had not been turned in. The holders kept them, like imperial Russian bonds after the October revolution, in the hope of better times. The collected banknotes were piled into an iron cage and burned. The policies of the Regency's first years were renewed. A 1722 tax on speculators brought in 188 million livres.

The 'system' had promised a golden age and delivered a full-scale economic crisis, with suicides, bankruptcies, and unemployment. Thousands of small investors were ruined. Barbier wrote in January: 'I had 60,000 livres in banknotes and now I don't even have enough to give my servants their Christmas tips.' A favourable long-range effect was that by accepting his own banknotes in payment of India Company shares Law managed to pay off half the national debt. An adverse long-range effect was to create a lasting suspicion of credit in the French popular mind, and a return to the sugar bowl mentality of hoarding gold. It is no accident that the Bank of France was not founded until 1800. Law was the father of buy-now-pay-later, of the advertising campaign, of free trade, and of the friendly neighbourhood banker. But he naïvely believed that money is an arbitrary sign of value, and that its circulation is enough to make real wealth increase. He is still described in French history textbooks as 'a foreign adventurer,' but if he had been both supported and restrained by an intelligent government, instead of undermined by greedy nobles and envious ministers, the 'system' might have endured. Its failure is consistent with the failure of most Regency reforms, and with the absence of civic resposibility among the privileged classes.

The Regency was coming to a close. Cardinal Dubois was dead. John Law was in exile. Louis XV had reached the age of royal adulthood, fourteen. At forty-nine, Philippe was exhausted by his excesses, an impotent libertine reduced to voyeurism at the orgies he hosted. He named himself Prime Minister at the death of Cardinal Dubois, and his health was further affected by the new work load. On December 2, after a long day's work, he asked to see his last mistress, the blonde and lovely Madame de Falaris, who sat in front of the fire near his armchair.

'Do you believe in good faith that there is a God, a hell, and a paradise after this life?' Philippe asked.

'Yes, my prince, I believe it utterly.'

'If what you say is true, you must be very unhappy about the life you are leading.'

'I hope God will forgive me.'

Philippe swallowed a few drops of a cinnamon-flavoured drink and slumped in his chair. Efforts to bleed him did not help and he died less than an hour later, of apoplexy.

Few of the Regent's innovations survived him. He made the University of Paris tuition-free and opened the Royal Library to the public. He increased the salaries of soldiers by 15 per cent. He was a liberal and imaginative man, blessed with a quick mind, but he was also weak, inconsistent, unreliable, and vacillating. For most of his life he behaved 'like an eighteen-year-old musketeer,' in the words of Saint-Simon. He favoured progress, hated hypocrisy and cant, but that is not enough to govern a nation. He drifted with events instead of shaping them, and did nothing to prepare Louis XV for the task of reigning. His two lasting achievements are that his was the first regency in French history to avoid civil war, and that it also avoided serious foreign wars and established the conditions of a European peace. Aside from that, the Regency left a style, *bergère* chairs, hooped dresses, masked balls, Watteau paintings. The word, unfairly, remains synonymous with elegant debauchery. The Littré dictionary defines 'regency manners' as 'worthy of the rakery of the Regent's court.'

IV

THE PLAGUE OF MARSEILLES

Now the countries keep guards lest infectious persons should from the city bring the disease unto them. Most of the rich are now gone, and the middle sort will not stay behind; but the poor are forced through poverty to stay and abide the storm. The very sinking fears they have had of the plague hath brought the plague and death upon many. Some by the sight of a coffin in the streets have fallen into a shivering, and immediately the disease has assaulted them; and Sergeant Death hath arrested them, and clapt to the doors of their houses upon them, from whence they have come forth no more till they have been brought to their graves.

—VINCENT, *God's Terrible Voice in the City*

IN MID-MAY, 1720, a French merchant ship, carrying silk, muslin, cotton goods, and a small number of passengers out of Syrian ports, requested permission to put in at Cagliari, the capital of Sardinia. The viceroy of Sardinia refused, flouting international conventions that all ships should be granted harbour privileges if their papers were in order. Ships which sailed to the Near East were inspected at each port of call and given bills of health as long as no traces of disease could be found on board. As the captain of the *Great Saint Anthony*, Jean-Baptiste Chataud, pointed out to the Viceroy's emissaries, he had clean bills of health from Tripoli, Sidon, Famagusta, and Leghorn. The Viceroy replied that if the *Great Saint Anthony* tried to land at Cagliari, he would blow it out of the Mediterranean with his shore artillery. His advisers thought he had gone mad.

The Viceroy's uncharitable attitude was based on a dream of the night before, in which an infested ship had landed at Cagliari and brought the plague to his island. He had seen his subjects black-tongued, suppurating, and feverish, their unburied bodies rotting in the streets; he had seen his own palace assaulted by enormous, disease-carrying rats; he had seen all of Sardinia ravaged by a pestilence so implacable that there were no survivors. He had dreamed of the plague as early civilizations saw it, as a disaster of demonic origin—Ptah, the Egyptian god of destruction, was depicted by sculptors holding a rat in his outstretched hand.

Refused admittance at Cagliari, the *Great Saint Anthony* sailed towards Marseilles. The ship could have obtained its bills of health only through negligence or bribery. In Tripoli it had taken on a few Turkish passengers, one of whom died on board. The two sailors who threw the body into the open sea used iron hooks to avoid contamination, but within days they too fell ill and died. The captain shut himself off from his crew, eating from private stores off pewter no one was allowed to touch. Five more sailors and the ship's doctor died before the ship reached Leghorn, but they did not show the characteristic swollen glands of plague victims. Italian health inspectors attributed the deaths to fever and gave the captain a letter stating that there was no suspicion of plague.

Despite long acquaintance with the plague (fourteen epidemics in the sixteenth century), Marseilles was an overcrowded city of 80,000 with open sewers, dungheaps in gateways, and a large floating population of well-travelled sailors and rats. The harbour had been called a cesspool by François I and a cesspool it remained. France's second city was particularly vulnerable to what was to become the worst epidemic of the plague since the Black Death of the fourteenth century, a circumscribed but total crisis which showed that *ancien régime* society, advancing haltingly into the eighteenth century, retained many medieval traits.

To the clergy, still the most influential body in France, the plague was a punitive measure from heaven. The buboes were pricks from a lance held by one of God's retributive angels. A Biblical scourge fell on societies disintegrating through excess of pleasure. Only faith could heal. As a Dominican preacher had told his flock during another plague, in 1630: 'Scourges are the soldiers with which God combats hardened hearts.' The plague was not a disease that could be fought with government assistance and medical care, but a divine mystery to which sinning and powerless mortals must submit. Such

THE RUE QUINCAMPOIX, OUTSIDE JOHN LAW'S BANK, 1720
Engraving by Humblot

THE PROCESSION FOR LOUIS XV'S CORONATION AT RHEIMS
OCTOBER 25, 1722
Engraving by Martin

attitudes were still prevalent in a France which had emerged from the seamless theocracy of the Middle Ages to enter what became known as the Age of Reason. Montesquieu's *Persian Letters* were published in 1721, the same year the Marseilles plague spread through forty-nine communities and took more than 90,000 lives. But the Sodom and Gomorrah syndrome dies hard, and even the nineteenth-century historian Jules Michelet unintentionally subscribed to it when he wrote with reference to the Marseilles plague that periods of low morality coincide with periods of high mortality.

The city government was run by four magistrates recruited among prominent merchants and lawyers. The chief magistrate was a wealthy merchant named Estelle, who traded with the East and was said to have 100,000 crowns' worth of merchandise aboard the *Great Saint Anthony*. It was further alleged, although no documentary evidence of the transaction was ever found, that Estelle had closed a deal to send his cloth to the famous Beaucaire fair, so that if the cargo were detained as suspect he would suffer a business loss. When Captain Chataud landed on May 25, he played down his ship's misfortunes. He said his crewmen had died of food poisoning. Normally, suspect ships were taken to the offshore island of Jarre, where the cargo was disinfected and a lengthy quarantine imposed on crew and passengers. But Captain Chataud's declaration convinced health inspectors that the *Great Saint Anthony* was a safe ship. A routine two-week quarantine delayed the passengers, while the crew and cargo were confined to the Lazaretto, a sprawling, run-down quarantine station. It was poorly guarded, with walls full of gaps. As early as May 26 quarantined sailors off the *Great Saint Anthony* were selling contraband calico prints to second-hand clothes dealers in the rue de l'Echelle. The quarantined passengers were released on June 14 in apparent good health, and left Marseilles for Paris and Amsterdam. Soon after, residents of the rue de l'Echelle neighbourhood began dying without apparent cause. One was an elderly woman, whose death on June 20 was attributed to carbuncles because she had a dark pustulent growth on her lip. No one yet dared to consider the possibility that Marseilles was menaced with an epidemic of the bubonic plague, probably caused by plagued fleas released from the bodies of dead rats, which had infested the bales of cloth that were carried ashore. It was only on July 12, when Marseilles had already recorded about fifty mysterious deaths, that the

D   97

Great Saint Anthony and the part of the cargo not already smuggled into the city were taken out to Jarre island.

Instead of preparing Marseilles to cope with an epidemic, the city fathers deliberately covered up the gravity of the crisis because of the economic loss involved. They knew that commerce, the lifeblood of the city, would come to a standstill if the plague were declared. A blockade would seal the harbour. No city would buy the goods which filled its warehouses. Marseilles would be isolated and its citizens would panic. The magistrates also knew they could not count on the central government—French provinces had long since learned the hard lesson of self-reliance. Nor could they count on the two highest provincial officials: Pierre Cardin Lebret, Royal Intendant of Provence, and the maréchal de Villars, Governor of Provence, who in twenty years of governorship visited his province three times. Both these gentlemen were conspicuous by their absence during the entire three-year plague period.

The magistrates decided that the best course for their own and the city's affairs was blind optimism. On July 15 they reported that 'health is good in the city.' When officials from neighbouring towns inquired about the alarming rumours of disease, the magistrates wrote back that they were 'fairy tales.' By this time, several persons were dying each day, and some had the inescapable symptom of the plague—a bubo under the armpit. The magistrates reported: 'We hope there is more fear than harm in all this.' Particularly optimistic bulletins were sent to cities like Aix-en-Provence, with which Marseilles did much of its trading. The bulletins were unconvincing, for on July 31 the Aix Parlement voted to interrupt all commerce with Marseilles. The magistrates complained that the decision was 'unduly harsh.'

In the dog days of August, contagion quickened its languid pace, and entire families were wiped out. The magistrates admitted that 'there died various persons of a disease believed contagious,' but still they would not employ the dreaded word. Reassuring placards were posted in the streets, advising against leaving the city. The magistrates insisted the deaths were due to bad food. They said the sick were vomiting worms and 'the best proof that it is not the plague is that only the poor have been stricken.' The dead were buried secretly at night and their graves were covered with quicklime, but soon the nights were too short. The magistrates berated as alarmists those doctors bold enough to call the plague by its name. The first to do so

was a Marseilles doctor named Sicard, on August 1. The magistrates
hired other doctors to discredit his diagnosis. Their conclusion:
'How could Sicard recognize the plague since he did not even touch
the sick and examined them from afar?'

There were two schools of thought about epidemics, the one holding that they were caused by contagion, the other by fever. As the
death toll rose in Marseilles, the most respected medical faculties of
France argued in learned papers whether the cause of the disease was
a miasma, a poison in the atmosphere, poor nutrition, earthworms
that flew like birds and swam like fish, or tiny insects that entered
the skin. When a second Marseilles doctor said it was the plague, the
city magistrates reported that 'the doctors want to make "a Mississippi" of this affair.' They refused to consult studies of previous
plagues or existing health regulations concerning epidemics.

The magistrates were supported by the Regent's personal physician, Chirac, the most prominent member of the anti-contagion
school. He agreed, although he had not seen a single victim, that
'this is only a very ordinary malignant fever caused by the poor
nutrition of the little people.' His remedy for a population famous
for hyperbole and overdramatization (although 510 had died by
August 8) was to 'hire some violinists and trombone players and
have them play in every neighbourhood to give young people the
chance to forget sadness and melancholy.' He accused the Marseilles
doctors who had recognized the obvious of 'holding the public in a
climate of terror and fear to serve their own interests.'

On the Regent's personal order, however, Chirac sent a team of
three doctors from the Montpellier faculty to Marseilles in early
August. One of the three was his son-in-law and eventual successor.
The doctors arrived August 12, stayed five days, and came to the
personal conclusion that it was indeed the plague. But they gave in
to the pleas of the distraught magistrates and made out two reports.
The first, public report stated that the disease was a malignant fever
due to poor nutrition. Duly signed by the eminent medical authorities, it was placarded all over the city to reassure the population. The
private report, sent to Paris on August 18, said Marseilles was in the
throes of 'a veritable pestilential fever which has not yet reached its
final stage of malignance.' By this time Marseillais were falling as
thick as summer hail, and the dead-carts piled with bodies wrapped
in linen sheets or rags had become a familiar sight.

The magistrates' ostrichlike behaviour did not prevent panic.

Marseillais practically tore down the city gates in their rush to flee. Troops guarded exits and heavy fines were imposed on those caught trying to escape. But the haemorrhage continued, and spread the plague through the rest of Provence, even though citizens of Marseilles arriving in other towns were as welcome as lepers.

Having disregarded the plague when it was still controllable, the magistrates were now helpless as it spread. They fixed food prices, evicted beggars, gathered the indigent into Charity Hospital, closed off streets where plague victims lived, mobilized eighty commissioners to count the dead and assist the living, and appropriated buildings to use as quarantine stations and infirmaries. The Regent ordered seventeen doctors and ninety-seven surgeons to Marseilles—three of the doctors and thirty-one of the surgeons died there. But these measures, which would have been useful two months earlier, were hopelessly inadequate in the scorching autumn of 1720, when the daily mortality toll reached 1,000. The magistrates lured doctors by offering extravagant salaries, but the doctors only added to the impression that Marseilles was living a ghastly throwback to the Dark Ages. Their remedies were poultices made of ground celery leaves, flour, and egg yolks, and mysterious potions. One was a mixture of white onions, live snails, and chopped snakes. Quacks sold preventive pills, sovereign cordials, royal antidotes, and universal remedies, some of which were fatal. One of the most popular was called 'the four thieves,' a blend of absinthe, mint, rosemary, and rue—it was moderately useful as a disinfectant. The doctors looked like members of a religious procession during the time of the Inquisition. They wore long black robes with pointed hoods, leather gloves, boots, and masks with glass eyes and long beaks filled with bergamot oil. At their waists they wore amulets of dried blood and ground-up toads. Before approaching a plague victim they doused themselves with vinegar and chewed angelica. Their elaborate precautions were futile, and four out of five persons who contracted the plague died from it.

It was not a pretty death. The first signs were red, inflamed eyes, irregular breathing, and foul breath. Doctors said the breath of a plague victim would kill a bird and leave scum on warm water. Then came seizures of hiccoughing and sneezing, terrible stomach pains, and a high fever. Still able to walk, the sick would most often leave their homes to spare the rest of their family—in some cases they were evicted at the first symptoms. Certain that no hospital would admit them, and convinced in any case that the disease was fatal, they dragged themselves to one of Marseilles' broad, tree-shaded avenues, which had become dumping grounds for plague victims. There they would sit moaning and vomiting under the trees among their own kind as the dark ulcers began to burst through their skin, begging passers-by for water to moisten their parched and blackening tongues. Doctors administered their remedies, and those who dared approach the victims lanced their ulcers. The doctors with their useless medicines gave way to priests with the last sacraments. The priests were brave, in many cases reckless. Henri de Belzunce, the Jesuit bishop of Marseilles, had complete faith in his own immunity. 'God will not afflict the flock to the point of condemning the pastor,' he said. But when priests whose evangelical zeal made them disregard health precautions perished, Belzunce established safety rules. Priests were to turn their backs on those whose confessions they heard. The consecrated communion host was to be left at a safe distance from the communicant, sandwiched between two unconsecrated hosts. Extreme unction, the sacrament most in demand, was delivered at a distance, with the priest extending a perch from which dangled pieces of cotton soaked in holy oil. Citizens who refused to leave their homes for any other reason still went to Sunday mass, however, and churches became centres of contagion. The plague was often in the next pew. In their eagerness to serve, the priests were like those crusaders who had made heaven accessible to infidels by bringing them at the same time baptism and death.

The bishop of Belzunce became, in the popular imagery, the hero, almost the saviour of the Marseilles plague. It was indeed inspiring to see him walk unescorted through streets piled high with bodies, comforting the sick and distributing his personal fortune to the needy. In other ways he was a dangerous bigot. The most urgent problem was the burial of plague victims, who littered the city like refuse and were the principal cause of contamination. Belzunce refused the city magistrates permission to use the network of catacombs under his churches for burial. He said it would be a sacrilege. He was overruled, and the churches were opened by force. Nor did he forget the church's doctrinal quarrel with Jansenists. He prevented an Order of Oratorians suspected of Jansenist leanings from giving sacraments to the dying. Even his charity had a nasty side. He wanted control over his donations, so that when the magistrates asked him to contribute to a general food and medicine fund he replied: 'I am not the city treasurer.' He was at the same time generous and restrictive, dedicated and narrow-minded, a humanitarian and an Ultramontane. Later, when the plague had lifted, he would not allow municipal authorites to disinfect the churches. No matter how grave the crisis, the possible encroachment of civil authority in church affairs was graver.

Belzunce advised the people of Marseilles to pin crucifixes to their sleeves and nail the prayers of Saint Francis of Assisi to their doors so that God might recognize His own. The instructions of the city magistrates were hardly more practical—implore the assistance of God, eat heartily, stay home, and stay at a safe distance from other people's breath.

The plague settled in, so that it became customary for Marseillais to end their letters with this salutation: 'Yours, until it pleases the Lord to put a stop to the scourge that afflicts this city.' Grass grew on the pavements of main thoroughfares, over which carriages no longer passed. The few shops that stayed open kept jars full of vinegar into which customers threw their coins. Each day, hundreds of persons ventured into the streets and met ubiquitous death, who was bride, mother, and midwife. The rich and powerful who had stayed in the city were not spared, for even if they were able to avoid contact with others, their servants were not. The plague was equalitarian.

'There is no pity in a time of plague,' the magistrates wrote to Intendant Lebret. The plague exposed both courage and cowardice, deep personal reserves of strength as well as concealed weaknesses. There were priests who gave the last sacraments until they could no longer advance through the piles of decaying bodies, and priests who boarded themselves up in their convents and walled the windows. There was a hospital director who requisitioned ewes so that infants who had lost their mothers would have milk, and a hospital director who turned away plague victims. When the rumour arose that domestic animals were plague carriers, dogs and cats became tangible objects of revenge and were savagely destroyed—but they were not buried, and their carcases became carriers.

There was such close cohabitation of the living and the dead that the two states seemed somehow to overlap—a patient admitted to a hospital was put in a bed evacuated by a corpse; the sheets were not changed, but the occupants were. Burial was the insoluble problem.

At first the cemeteries sufficed, but from August on, bodies were left in the street to decompose in the summer sun. They were chewed at by marauding dogs and swathed the city in malignant vapours. The magistrates thought of piling the bodies into a creaky merchantman, towing it out to sea, and sinking it, but they voted down the plan because the fish, an important source of revenue for the area, might become contaminated. As it was, many Marseillais had sought refuge in the harbour, which was crowded with skiffs, wherries, ketches, dinghies, scows, and other types of small craft. The plague reached them too, and soon bodies were bobbing on the surface of the scummy waters.

An army major in Toulon wrote to the magistrates: 'I thought I would inform you of the manner I saw bodies that had been festering eight or ten days buried on the battlefield . . . you must get quicklime and dig great ditches thirty to forty feet square . . . cover your gravediggers' noses with rags dipped in vinegar and drag the bodies to the pits with ropes . . . men with hooks can go into houses to remove the bodies . . . cover them with quicklime and earth and at night light fires over the graves.'

The magistrates began to recruit peasants to dig the ditches and bury the dead. But the peasants balked, and the city authorities summoned one of the few groups which, by virtue of its seclusion, had remained immune to the plague. Between August 10, 1720, and January 4, 1721, 784 convicts and galley slaves were forcibly freed from their prisons in Marseilles and Toulon to do a job no one else would touch. The gravediggers (bodysnatchers would be a more appropriate term, since they did not hesitate to carry off the dying with the dead to expedite their task) were called Crows, and devised several profitable sidelines—they looted the bodies and sold the contaminated goods, and they accepted bribes from families who wanted quick service. They were promised freedom if they survived. Did they realize that handling plague victims was a virtual death sentence? Even though they used shovels, enormous pincers, and tumbrils, and were well fortified with wine, it was usually enough to touch a body to become contaminated. Moreover, the navy was hostile to the plan and gave the city its weakest and oldest galley slaves. It is all the more surprising that 241, or nearly one-third, of the convicts, did survive.

On September 4 the Regent seemed finally to realize the extent of devastation and named a governor extraordinary for Marseilles, a bailiff named Charles-Claude de Langeron with a reputation for sternness and honesty. The nomination was an indirect admission that the two highest provincial officials were useless in the crisis. The correspondence between Royal Intendant Lebret, who had taken refuge in his country home instead of occupying his Intendant's residence in Marseilles, and the Governor of Provence, de Villars, who was a pillar of the Regent's court, speaks for itself. Lebret wrote to Villars: 'If I did not have so many children I might have gone to Marseilles . . . what is worse, no one wants to help; the sick cannot and the others think only of protecting themselves and profiting from the misfortune of their brothers.' Villars replied that he had begged the Regent's permission to go but that 'I am not sure His Royal Highness will allow me to share your perils and your woes.' On September 8 he wrote: 'I have a strong urge to leave for Marseilles so that I could perform services which I flatter myself would be decisive because of the way I could carry out what is useful and necessary.' However, Villars decided that the state of his finances did not permit him to travel. When the Marseilles magistrates asked him for money, he wrote with astonishment that he thought money was plentiful in Provence, and whined about his own financial problems—he was living on credit, he might have to sell his furniture, no one could imagine the difficulties he was going through. Villars was like the fellow on the home front who complains to his friend in the trenches about the inconvenience of soap rationing.

The situation improved with Langeron's arrival. He was ruthless with the convicts. Two who were caught looting the dead were hanged the same day. Those who violated sanitary ordinances and sold contaminated clothing were publicly whipped. Langeron established a dictatorship, and with his convict-gravediggers, saved what was left of Marseilles. More ditches were dug, and twenty tumbrils rattled through the streets day and night with the convicts hawking their only goods, corpses. Finally the streets were cleared and the magistrates could turn to the problems of financial aid and supplies for the sealed-off disaster area. The central government held back, hoping Marseilles could obtain private financing. It was common then for provincial and city governments to ask private banks for loans. But the bankers of Avignon evidently did not think much of Marseilles' credit and turned the city down. This lack of solidarity in time of crisis was repeated when Law, as Controller General of France, asked all the provinces to help the stricken Provence; the neighbouring provinces of Languedoc and Auvergne refused. Appeals were also made to France's 130 bishops, only four of whom replied. However, Pope Clement XI sent three ships laden with grain to Marseilles, along with special indulgences for those who had given the sick food and drink. Bishop (later Cardinal) Fleury, the tutor of Louis XV, who was then ten years old, gave 6 louis (about 120 livres) in the future king's name. Times were hard. Law's disgrace had come in November, 1720, and an economic crisis followed. Nonetheless, Marseilles was grateful to Law, the only member of the government (with the exception of a gift of silver coins from the Regent in November) who made a personal gift to the city—100,000 livres sent in September.

On October 23, the magistrates wrote to Lebret: 'Is it possible that at court no one has been moved by the pitiable state we are in, and that a city like Marseilles will be allowed to perish? The plague has taken a third of our inhabitants and the remaining two-thirds will succumb to their misery.' The magistrates wrote directly to influential courtiers, but the government did not respond until August, with a promise of 200,000 gold livres and 500,000 livres in banknotes of doubtful value, since the plague had struck at the time the Law bubble burst. The first regular government assistance, a gift of 60,000 livres a month, was not decided until December, 1720. After that, several loans were arranged through private financiers like Samuel Bernard, and through the government. Thus financial assistance did not begin until the worst of the plague was over. From June, 1721, to January, 1723, the government advanced a total of 3,278,571 livres to the stricken communities. The plague areas were also granted a tax exemption in November, 1723, of 4,500,000 livres, to be spread over fifteen years.

The Regent was not a callous or a miserly man. It was simply that the notion of civic responsibility as it is understood today did not exist under the *ancien régime*. Each parish, town, city, and province was expected to assume its own relief needs, and the royal government only acted after every other possibility had been exhausted. Because of poor communications and the nature of court life, a plague in Marseilles was not very different from a plague in Switzerland—one was sympathetic, one did what one could, but one did not allow events to interfere with life at court. The royal entourage at Paris and Versailles had built up an immunity to unpleasantness.

Whatever lay beyond its tapestried walls was neither good nor bad, but merely remote. You could not accuse the maréchal de Villars, who, despite his painted eyebrows and padded cheeks, was the hero of the famous battles of Malplaquet and Denain, of cowardice. He was guilty of nothing stronger than lack of interest. The Regent never once considered visiting the disaster areas. The Great Admiral of France never once showed interest in the welfare of the convicts under his jurisdiction. The memoirists of the period treated the plague as an event hardly worth mentioning. Saint-Simon, who could devote hundreds of pages to court controversies like the right of royal princesses to sit on stools in front of the queen, disposed of the plague with a few lines.

Within the limitations of his time, the Regent did what he could— he sent medical teams to Marseilles, asked Law to look into the city's finances, authorized the use of convicts over the navy's objections, and arranged loans and gifts of supplies. But government assistance came too late to have any serious effect on the mortality rate of the plague. Wheat and other staples were left at the city gates. The magistrates never lacked wheat, but the bakers had fled. An August 26 ordinance summoned them to return within five days under penalty of death. There was never a danger of famine, but food prices soared and speculation thrived. Black marketeers sold fresh meat from the Auvergne on street corners.

With these rare and tardy exceptions, Marseilles was left to its own resources. By October, 1720, the plague had abated; the daily death 'bill' had dropped to twenty-five or thirty. New cases were attributed to peasants coming into the city for the winter and to the eagerness with which families of the deceased collected their inheritance. They settled into the houses of the dead and inherited the plague. But to a city under death's dominion for three months, life slowly returned. Shops reopened. Convalescents left hospitals. Families were reunited. Civil servants went back to work. So did barbers. In December there were only forty deaths. The city magistrates wrote: 'The danger is past.'

Bishop Belzunce, in an expiatory ceremony, exorcised the plague from the top of the belfry in the church of Accoules on November 15. He built an altar on an open landing in the belfry from which he shouted liturgical imprecations on the plague, turning first north, then west, then south, then east. Disinfection began. 'Perfumers' instead of gravediggers now did the rounds. They burned clothing and contaminated objects, doused houses with disinfectant, set off gunpowder in each room, and protected themselves with vinegar baths and a special diet of garlic, onions, figs, nuts, and plenty of wine. Disinfected houses were marked with a red cross.

As the plague lifted, it was followed by an epidemic of marriages. Bailiff Langeron had to rule that no marriage could be contracted without a health certificate. There were too many cases of women who had been widowed two or three times in a single year. 'One would have sworn,' wrote Michelet, 'that death had served as a marriage broker.' Five years after the plague there had been so many births that the Marseilles population was almost back to normal.

The plague was not officially over until February, 1723, when a letter from Louis XV ordered a Te Deum sung in all the churches of his realm. There was little to rejoice about. Seeping out of Marseilles into the rest of Provence, the plague had taken 93,290 lives out of a total provincial population of 292,165. Aix, Toulon, and Arles were among the worst-hit cities after Marseilles, which had about 39,000 dead, or half its total population.

In 1722 there was a brief relapse but this time Marseilles was ready. The same authorities who had not wanted to admit the plague's existence in 1720 now saw it everywhere. Doctors who had mistaken plague symptoms for malnutrition now mistook malnutrition for plague symptoms. The blockade of Marseilles continued until January 7, 1723, and was severely enforced. Captured smugglers could choose between the noose and the firing squad.

The *Great Saint Anthony* was burned off the island of Jarre. Captain Chataud was jailed in the state prison of Château d'If on another offshore island. He remained there three years, protected from the plague and the Marseilles mob that was clamouring for his head. In 1723, he was cleared of responsibility by the Regent and released. The Regent had recruited the convict gravediggers with the promise that survivors would be freed, but that promise was not kept. Of the 241 survivors, only those who could prove they had previously exercised a trade were freed; the 108 others were sent back to the galleys. It is to the city magistrates' credit that they made repeated appeals to the Regent for the convicts' release. Their appeals were heard, and by the end of 1723 there was only one galley slave who had not been freed, because he was listed as dead. But that clerical error was eventually straightened out.

V

THE FRAGILE ESSENCE

*The court, the court, the court! In that word lies all
the evil. The court has become the nation's sole senate,
the least Versailles valet is a senator, chambermaids
take part in government, if not to command, at least
to prevent laws and rules from functioning . . . this
ascendancy of the court began with the creation of
a special capital for it . . . the court prevents every
financial reform and increases disorder . . . it prevents
the king from reigning.*
—MARQUIS D'ARGENSON, *Mémoires*

*They say it takes one hundred thousand roses to
make a single ounce of the attar used by Persian
kings; in the same way, this drawing room is a
slender flagon of gold and crystal containing the
substance of a human vegetation. To fill it, a great
aristocracy had to be transplanted to a hothouse where
it was made barren of fruit, bearing only flowers,
which were distilled in the royal alembic until their
exhausted sap was concentrated into a few aromatic
drops. The price is exorbitant, but it is the price for
very delicate perfumes.*
—HIPPOLYTE TAINE, *Origines de la France
Contemporaine*

AS FRENCH monarchs consolidated their power, the court
became their natural environment. A king is not a hermit,
and must be attended, just as a priest must have altar boys
and a general aides-de-camp. Court life did not spring into full-blown
existence with the reign of Louis XIV. In the thirteenth century
Saint Louis surrounded himself with warriors who formed a martial,
masculine court. He wore sable and embroidered garments to dis-

tinguish him from his companions. Under the influence of the dukes of Burgundy, who were the tastemakers of their time, and the small Italian courts of the early Renaissance, lavishness became the court's identifying badge. In the fourteenth century, under the first Valois kings, the court absorbed one-third of the king's revenues. The proliferation of servants began; there was a staff of seventeen for the pantler's office alone. Kings surrounded themselves with young noblemen whose only duty was to make themselves agreeable. The more powerful the French king grew, the more favours he was able to dispense, and the more sought-after life at court became. A ritual based on religious symbolism was adopted. 'Why do the pantlers and cupbearers hold superior rank to the cooks and the carvers?' asked the fifteenth-century writer Olivier de la Marche. 'Because their occupation concerns bread and wine, to which the sacrament gives a sacred character.'

The court's ceremonial was liturgical, but its pleasures were profane, and depended increasingly on the presence of women. The early kings had recognized some of their natural children but discarded their mothers. The first king publicly to recognize a mistress was Charles VII in the fifteenth century, who made Agnes Sorel the equal of princesses. This was probably the single most important development in court life, for the royal mistress became either heroine or villainess of many reigns to follow. At her best and at her worst, she was not merely the king's supine diversion, but an active strategist of his reign who eclipsed the influence of other courtiers, and ministers. The tradition of the political mistress begins with Agnes Sorel, who was credited with awakening the courage of Charles VII and persuading him to oust the British from France. Thanks to her, writes the sixteenth-century chronicler Brantôme, 'the king left his gardens and hunts and put the bit between his teeth.'

The royal mistress is one of the earliest expressions of French nationalism. In a country where women could not rule and the queen, for reasons of state, was always a foreigner, the mistress was the nation's emissary to the monarch's bed. The function of the imported Spanish and German princesses who became queens was to bear an heir to the throne, not to meddle in affairs of state. Those who did, like Marie Antoinette, were vilified by public opinion. The mistress, on the other hand, was French, and had earned the king's favour, while the queen had merely acquired it. She alone could be blunt with the king, and use her Gallic common sense to offset royal blunders. In whom else could the king confide? Who else dared point out his shortcomings? When the duchesse de Châteauroux died, Louis XV lamented: 'Ah, and who is left now to tell one the truth?' The mistresses also usurped their power. They were often grasping and extravagant, protected their own favourites, set themselves up as sole intermediaries to the king, and were sometimes responsible for political decisions to which they applied the frivolous standards of a court amusement.

Under the growing influence of women, court life became more formal. It was Catherine de Medici, in the sixteenth century, who first insisted on 'policing matters.' It was her son, Charles IX, who inaugurated the practice of arising and retiring in front of a group of privileged courtiers. It was Henri III in 1585 who wrote a breviary of court life, describing 'the order the king wishes upheld at court in the department of hours and in the manner in which he wishes to be honoured and served.' Kings began to distribute titles and lands to diligent courtiers, but parsimoniously, for under Henri II, France counted only 20 dukes, 8 marquisses and 150 counts. They were expected to leave their provinces, where they still retained considerable influence, and attend court, thereby making the transition from feudal lord to titled aristocrat. The court travelled from castle to castle (François I had 12,000 horses to carry his baggage), and the itinerant courtiers often slept under tents or in draughty, barely furnished country manors. They understood that their principal virtue was obedience. They laughed when the king laughed, and never disagreed. They were already known as 'chameleons, wind-sniffers, and tablecloth-hangers.'

Louis XIV took a court which was still flexible, still nomadic, still spontaneous, and stamped it with his gloomy discipline. Life became as aimless and methodical as life aboard an ocean liner, of which the king was both captain and purser. Like scheduled shipboard amusements, there was gambling on Sundays and Fridays, concerts on Mondays and Wednesdays, comedies on Tuesdays, tragedies on Thursdays, and Italian farces on Saturdays. Meals were as important and love affairs as transient as shipboard meals and shipboard romances. The difference was that although the liner Versailles was motionless, its passengers were convinced that they could be no better off elsewhere than on board. As Stendhal noted: 'Louis XIV's masterpiece was to invent *ennui*, in the original sense of the word;

the *ennui* of exile.' There was no pretence in the lords' eagerness to belong to the court at Versailles. They did not have to be coaxed into living in its draughty rooms and sharing its mournful splendour. They desperately wanted to be a part of it. They gladly obeyed the absurdities of Ludovican etiquette, the first purpose of which was that each man might measure the distance that separated him from the king.

What Saint-Simon called the *mécanique* of the court was so involved that it contained its own contradictions, like a street that is one-way in both directions. For instance, cardinals had to be seen to the door by whoever they were visiting, but royal princesses were never supposed to see anyone to the door. There were graceful compromises: royal princesses feigned illness when cardinals came to call and received them in bed. Courtiers believed that the marks of prestige obtained from the king were real rewards, just as marks of royal displeasure caused genuine suffering. Philippe Dangeau, who wrote a court diary under Louis XIV, wrote that 'the exact observation of etiquette is the only way of showing respect for the king and his family.'

There is more than a jest in this advice from an old courtier to a new arrival: 'You have only three things to do. Say nice things about everyone, ask for whatever sinecure is available, and sit down when you can.' The simple act of sitting down was at a premium. Women considered that a long career at court was crowned with success if they received what Madame de Sevigné called 'the divine tabouret'—a simple wooden stool on which certain women were allowed to sit in the presence of Their Majesties. Another privilege concerned the names of guests scribbled in white chalk on the doors of their rooms at Marly, a small royal castle, invitations to which were highly prized. It was considered a special distinction if the name was preceded by the preposition 'for.' The duchesse de Bracciano fainted with pleasure when she saw on her door: 'For the duchesse de Bracciano.' A duke could be immediately recognized, not by his courage or virtue, but because he was allowed to place a small cloth square under his knees at church. Everything that touched the king served to differentiate him from other mortals and therefore had to be rare, sumptuous and overelaborate. At meals, the king's napkin reposed on perfumed cushions inside a miniature gold ship guarded by two armed men.

Louis XIV perfected a style of living, which, however spurious,

was convincing. The court was a tiny minority of overdressed aristocrats which passed itself off as France. (There were an estimated
200,000 nobles in France in 1715, but only 4,000 families had been
presented at court, and only 2,000 of them lived at court.) Versailles
was the seat of government and the temple where the cult of the
Sun King was practised. But the style could not outlast the man.
It underwent subtle changes, and the two kings who followed
Louis XIV indulged the cumbersome formalities of Versailles out
of habit rather than conviction. What had been a necessity under
Louis XIV became a convention under Louis XV. The mesmerism
no longer operated, and court life became far worse than corrupt:
it became superfluous.

There was a period immediately after the death of Louis XIV
when the cage opened and the birds flew out. The Regent, Philippe
d'Orléans, brought the five-year-old Louis XV to Paris, and for
seven years the great palace was empty. The Minister of Finance,
the duc de Noailles, suggested tearing it down to save on maintenance. But the pull was too great, and in 1722 Louis XV returned
to Versailles.

Under the young and amiable Louis XV, the court lost its constraint and primness. The Versailles of Louis XV evokes nacreous,
perfumed afternoons, furtively passed love notes, and padded,
womblike interiors. The setting was the female rococo. Stucco and
gilt softened and disguised architectural lines; rooms and their
furnishings followed the undulations of the feminine form. There
was less building, but more interior decoration, with upholstered
walls, paintings over the upholstery, carved wood panelling, smaller,
more comfortable rooms, painted panels over doors, curved mirrors
over fireplaces, winter furniture and summer furniture. There was
a new decorative freedom and variety; cabinetmakers found ways
of making chairs without crosspieces; there were twenty styles of
bed, and as many new kinds of specialized pieces of furniture
designed to heighten the feeling of intimacy—the *canapé,* where
languorously recumbent ladies could receive callers, the *bonheur du
jour,* a small desk ideal for writing and storing love letters, and other
additions to drawing rooms with feminine names like *marquises,
bergères,* and *veilleuses.* The boudoir was a room specifically designed for seduction. The architect de Mézières called it 'the sojourn
of voluptuousness.' The spirit of the court emerged in rustling satin
and skirts under skirts; in the use of masks, which excused the

boldest of advances; and in the basic harmlessness of rococo, with its shells, garlands, palm fronds, and cupids whose arrows always remain in their quivers.

It was, instead of Louis XIV's obsession with the grandiose, the refinement of minutiae. Madame de Pompadour commissioned a theatre in the king's small apartments which could seat only forty spectators. The tickets of admission designed by the court engraver Cochin showed the *commedia dell'arte* characters Columbine and Leander in various stages of courtship, with the buffoon Pierrot's head peering through a stage curtain.

The spirit of the court was preserved by its painters. Watteau, although he died in 1721, belongs spiritually to the court of Louis XV. His misty feasts captured the elusive moment when courtiers are forming couples, when glances are lowered, conversation stops, and arms are interplaced; they also caught the secret melancholy of enforced pleasure. Boucher's simpering mythology showed wigged and powdered shepherds and shepherdesses exchanging silken caresses under a turquoise sky. Fragonard fixed instants of pleasure, a young man surprising his mistress at her sewing and stealing a kiss, a pretty girl on a swing throwing off her satin slipper to a reclining courtier whose gaze explores the ruffles of her pink skirt. Frivolity's setting required rich textures, pastels, crowns of flowers, the play of mirrors, and fans with tiny monocles concealed in their folds so that women could see without being seen.

It was the last magnificent banquet of the courtier before joining Neanderthal man in the graveyard of extinct species. Rococo was a hopelessly fragile style; its grace became mannered, its wit became precious, its softness became mushy, like an overripe pear, its line grew slack, and its decorative effects became grotesque, like the stucco figures winking through their tears to show that their suffering is a game, or the pink cherubs trying on bishop's mitres, or the bat's wings in the Hôtel de Soubise. Reality was smothered in the court's love of fable, *double entendre,* allegories, allusions, and periphrases. Every inch of wall space had to be occupied. There was a proliferation of knickknacks and curios, Chinese porcelains, tobacco boxes, candy boxes, snuffboxes, and miniatures, all of which, like the bronze mirrors and ivory combs uncovered at Pompeii, bear their own patina of doom. The cartouche, originally a family's representation of its coat of arms, lost its emblematic function and was appropriated by rococo engravers for their free-style experiments.

The nobility suffered an identical loss of purpose, having itself become little more than a decorative element.

Artists not only portrayed the quest for pleasure, they catered to it. Madame de Pompadour commissioned from Boucher a series of pornographic paintings for the boudoir of Louis XV. The amorous inclinations of kings were always a popular topic of the *ancien régime,* since their principal function was to procreate, to give the nation not only an heir, but a male heir. Whenever a king married, the fishwives of Les Halles offered the traditional gift of truffles as 'an excellent remedy for generation.' Queens gave birth in public so that there could be no question about a dauphin's origins. At the pleasure-oriented court of Louis XV, the king's love life, both conjugal and illicit, was the main event. The duc de Bourbon, who arranged Louis XV's marriage with the Polish Princess Marie Leczinska, reported that on his wedding night the king 'proved his tenderness seven times.' The minister d'Argenson noted in his diary that 'the king and queen slept together two nights running, which caused great joy.' The manner in which Louis XV occupied his nights was as familiar to the courtiers as his schedule during the day. Memoirs of his reign are spiced with stories no one would have dared tell about his predecessor. On one occasion, the king's valet and procurer, Lebel, brought the wife of a wealthy General Farmer to his private apartment for the night. Louis XV told her to get undressed and into bed while he went through the paces of retiring in public. A while later he returned and said: 'Madam, you must excuse me, I am no longer young; I am sure that your person deserves every tribute, but a king is no more of a man than anyone else, despite the greatest good will and desire. . . .' Louis XV left the lady to dress unassisted and find her way out alone through the gloomy corridors of the palace. But two days later Lebel apologized in his name, saying: 'His Majesty regrets that a momentary indisposition prevented him from giving you a longer audience. He hopes you will accept this casket, which contains 4,000 crowns [12,000 livres].' Courtiers and, although less informed, the rest of France, followed the failures and triumphs of the king's love life with the diligence of diplomats at treaty negotiations.

Louis XV was equally curious about the sex lives of his subjects. Weekly police reports were written exclusively for the king about the private activities of courtiers and visiting notables, describing who was being cuckolded, who had been caught 'a galantry,' and who was keeping whom. The reports, based mainly on the information of courtesans, were written with Rabelaisian verve. A woman of easy virtue was described as 'a baptismal font in which every passerby has the right to clean the tips of his fingers.' The feats and foibles of well-known figures were graphically described. The duc de Chartres (the king's cousin) 'makes the jumpers fly' and 'bores through the cabbage.' The governor of the Bastille 'always carries a dozen English riding-coats on his person; he would forget his rosary sooner than his condoms.' A visiting aristocrat, the Russian Prince Rasomowsky, 'whose corpulence announced a proud virility, spent the evening of the 16th with Mademoiselle Grécourt, who was looking forward to a feast, since she thought she was getting a vigorous athlete; but she was most disappointed, for not only does she need a microscope to see his frivolity, but after the first run does not get another sigh out of him . . . an impressive capital with little yield, in other words.' A cousin of the king, the prince de Conti, 'passes for a heroic lover . . . but I know from a *bona roba* that he has only the appearance. It is agreed that he is still capable of a slight erection, but to keep up his reputation, at the moment of climax he withdraws, pretending reasons of health, does his business in a white handkerchief he always carries, and then starts again. Our *bona roba* let him have at her twice with an air of trust, but having adroitly seized the handkerchief and seen that it was dry, she let him know that all his grand airs were at best to the credit of an apprentice locksmith, that is, one who knows only how to file down.'

On the surface, the king's activities had not changed since Louis XIV. Louis XV continued arising, eating, and retiring in front of his court, continued to hunt (he ran down 3,000 stags from 1732 to 1749), attend mass daily, gamble, and take walks in the gardens of Versailles. But behind the formal façade, Louis XV led a private life. In 1783 he abandoned 'the visible centre of the monarchy,' the Sun King's bedroom, in favour of small apartments he had built in the right wing of the palace, overlooking the marble courtyard, where Louis XIV had kept his art collection. He continued to retire in public in Louis XIV's bed, but when the last courtier was gone he climbed a private staircase to reach a second, less ceremonious bedroom. Louis XIV had been as punctual as the sun, arising and going to mass at the same time each day. Louis XV often went to bed late and liked to sleep late. The timing of ceremonies became flexible, which led to negligence. In the evening the pages in the

ceremonial bedroom, who never knew when and whether Louis
XV would arrive, sometimes stretched out on the bed, and the chap-
lains sprawled on chairs. Louis XIV had always eaten in public,
usually alone, but Louis XV had a dining room in his small apartments where he entertained his favourite courtiers, and occasionally
made and served coffee himself.

Louis XIV had banned pleasure; Louis XV enforced it. But there
was an undercurrent of despair in the relentless amusements of a
once-great order. Woman, once the 'warrior's recreation,' became
his only remaining form of conquest. As Voltaire noted, 'constant
pleasure is not pleasure'—it was, rather, another sign of the nobility's
decline. Interest in the game was kept up thanks to the elaborate
stylization of courtship, in which the man pretends physical impatience in the guise of eternal love, and the woman pretends to be deeply
moved by the admission that his destiny depends on her favours.
Libertinage became an end in itself, with its inventory of conventions and disguises: outrageous compliments, secret meetings, stolen
moments, and the special language of seduction. The eighteenth-
century courtly tale *Angola*, by the chevalier de la Morlière, perfectly
expresses the overrefined wantonness of Louis XV's court. The book
is in the form of advice to a fledgling courtier. He has 'an arranged
affair with a lady,' who must 'retain a spark of virtue,' for 'one must
not revolt by being too obvious.' The courtier must 'in the interest of
pleasure . . . adroitly manipulate all the mechanisms of the heart.'
Having been admitted to the lady's boudoir, he moves to a chaise
longue 'which seemed tacitly to designate the use for which it was
destined.' The lady offered 'a light resistance, with which a woman
who knows the way of the world must never dispense.' She 'im-
plored the heavens for assistance which she would perhaps later have
been grateful not to receive.' The courtier 'asked to be forgiven for
his indiscretions while preparing to commit greater ones,' and by
this time 'everything was permitted him in the hope that he would
take unfair advantage of the permission.' Thus, 'one reaches by
degrees the most intense of pleasures,' and one must give 'reiterated
proof of one's passion.' Behind the vows of perfect love is the mutual
awareness that 'we took each other out of convenience, we kept each
other without formality, and I imagine that we will leave each other
without sorrow.' The author, while writing a court manual like
Castiglione or Lord Chesterfield, shows in his final description of a
ball scene the vision of a moralist saddened by Versailles' fraudu-

lence: 'The ball was almost over, the candles had shortened, the
musicians, drunk or asleep, no longer made use of their instruments.
The crowd had dispersed, everyone was unmasked, rouge and
powder flowed down the painted faces and exposed livid, flaccid,
blotched patches of skin, which offered the eye the disgusting spectacle of dilapidated stylishness.'

Like the courtiers' ruined complexions exposed by the running
cosmetics, the cracks in the veneer of persiflage revealed complete
cynicism. While accepting the conventions of courtship, men of
fashion agreed with Chamfort that love was 'the contact between
two epiderms,' and with Talleyrand that 'every woman is worth a
compliment, very few are worth a regret.' The corollary of multiple
feigned passions was to make conjugal love unfashionable. The
bond of marriage had to be a loose one for libertinage to operate, and
jealousy was ridiculous because it betrayed feeling. In 1750, a play
called *The Fashionable Prejudice* was performed at Versailles. Its
plot concerned a husband afraid to show his love for his wife for fear
of appearing doltish. Correct behaviour was expressed by the
husband who said: 'I allow you everything except princes and
valets.' The duc de Lauzun, asked what he would do if he learned
that his long-estranged wife was pregnant, replied: 'I would write
to her: "How delighted I am that heaven has finally blessed our
union; take care of your health. I will come tonight to pay you my
court."'

Cynicism was the foundation not only for the relations between
the sexes, but for the stylish form of court wit which set off the 'man
of good company,' eighteenth-century successor to the seventeenth-
century *honnête homme*, or gentleman. The man of good company
always kept his aplomb, like the marquis who was interrupted
during a game of biribi with the news that his house was on fire and
replied, as he continued playing: 'I never interfere with household matters.' The woman of good company subjugated feelings to
fashion, like the young lady whose eyes stayed dry during a tragedy
and who explained to a surprised friend: 'I would have wept willingly, but I am dining in town.' The man of good company inclined
towards gallows humour, like the courtier who told a young widow:
'How fortunate you are to bear the name of a man who can no
longer make a fool of himself.' And like the cosmopolitan prince de
Ligne, who had teased Catherine the Great about the unimpressive
size of an artificial river. When a workman drowned in the river,

the czarina asked Ligne: 'What have you to say to that?' 'The man is a flatterer,' he replied. The man of good company took nothing seriously except pleasure: at the age of fourteen, the duc de Richelieu was 'expert in all the details of gallantry.' When he died at the age of ninety-two, it was said that four unopened notes from ladies were found on his person, each pleading for a single hour of his nights. In the intervals of a busy court career, Richelieu found the time to be received by the Académie Française. His speech was highly praised, and he said he would thank the scribbler who had written it, Monsieur Roy, as soon as he learned court manners. The man of good company was as servile with the king as he was disdainful of outsiders. Louis XV, who loved coarse practical jokes, summoned the comte de Sourches, and when he arrived, slapped him full in the face. Dufort de Cheverny, court Master of Ceremonies, remarked in his diary: 'How pleasant and gay.'

Finally, the man of good company had a repartee for every occasion. Someone told the queen, Marie Leczinska, that the hussars were holding their annual war games. 'What if I run into a troop of hussars and am poorly defended by my guards?' asked the queen. 'Well, Madam,' said Monsieur de Tressan, 'they would "hussar" Your Majesty.'

'And what would you do, Monsieur de Tressan?'

'Madam, I would imitate the dog in the fable, who after having defended his master's dinner, began to partake of it like the others.'

Women were as powerful at court as in an Amazonian tribe. The queen, although she did not meddle in affairs of state, controlled enough patronage to attract her share of sycophants. And while there was only one queen there was a succession of mistresses, each of whom protected a group of favourites and ministers, and based her position of power on the simple fact of accessibility to the king. Courtiers bribed or flattered valets and chambermaids to gain access to women of influence. The laws of survival at Versailles were matriarchal. The duc de Croÿ noted in his diaries that 'not having courted Madame de Pompadour enough, at the end of the winter I lost the advantage of dining [with the king] in the small apartments.' The minister Maurepas joked that 'my wife governs me, and I govern France.' Maurepas eventually lost his job because he had incurred the wrath of Madame de Pompadour.

The influence of women meant the tyranny of fashion, and both sexes spent as much time preening for public occasions as actors in their dressing rooms. Women's clothes became increasingly un-reasonable during the eighteenth century, with the introduction of whalebone hoops, multiple skirts, and high, powdered headdresses. The most influential women were the slaves of their hairdressers, who thought of themselves as great inventors and devised forty kinds of curls. So much powder was used that hairdressers were called mackerels because they looked like fish coated with flour and ready for the frying pan. Flour was actually used, and it was said that the amount of flour on Versailles headdresses could have fed the poor of Paris. Cosmetics were also time-consuming, and it took dozens of lotions and creams to achieve the properly wan 'convent complexion' so highly prized. Few women dared face the sun with-out a velvet mask, or retire without a 'handkerchief of Venus,' a wax-coated band to keep the brow wrinkle-free. Another popular item was a cream to mask the ravages of smallpox.

Women ruled over the entertainments which helped to fill the court's day. The conscientious courtier had to keep up with dance fads and learn dozens of quadrilles, among them the 'feasts of Paphos,' the 'pretty boys,' the 'all too brief,' and the 'Marseillaise' (before becoming the national anthem of the republic, the 'Marseil-laise' was danced to a different tune at the court of Louis XV). Balls often required months of preparation, and courtiers were asked to come disguised as their favourite proverbs, as Chinese mandarins, or in some other fanciful garb. Louis XV met Madame de Pompadour at a ball where he was disguised as a potted yew tree and she was the huntress Diana.

Finally, women were tastemakers in art and literature. The role that Madame de Pompadour played in the development of rococo has been exaggerated, for by the time she had become official mistress the style had already blossomed. But thanks to royal patron-age, she and other mistresses were responsible for keeping artists and architects busy. Madame de Pompadour had her brother, the mar-quis de Marigny, appointed Intendant des Batîments, which made him the employer of hundreds of artists and master craftsmen. Her passion for the accumulation of beautiful objects and the decoration of her many houses were enough to make her a patroness of the arts. In addition, she had a china factory installed in the village of Sèvres, near her property of Bellevue. She gave her name to a shade of Sèvres pink. Madame de Pompadour also encouraged the writers of the Enlightenment and helped make them popular at court, so that

Voltaire lamented her death with the cry: 'After all, she was one of us.'

Women governed the Paris salons which flourished under Louis XV: Madame du Deffand, whose 'invincible obstination' displeased Rousseau; Madame de Tencin, who gave Monday dinners for artists and Wednesday dinners for writers, and to whom the abbé de Saint-Pierre replied, when she praised his brilliant conversation: 'I am but an instrument which you have brilliantly played;' Mademoiselle de Lespinasse, who had been Madame du Deffand's assistant and raided her clientele to form her own salon, and who proclaimed that 'my only passion is reason.'

With all its exotic natural life, its water lilies, flamingoes, and orchids, the court remained a swamp that reeked of boredom. The courtiers thrived on a daily diet of inconsequence. A platitude in the king's mouth became a conversation piece. Inane remarks were recited with self-importance within the framework of ritual. At dinner one night, the queen was sitting alone at a table large enough to seat twelve, while a dozen courtiers in attendance watched her gobble her food with her nose in her plate. 'Monsieur Lowendal,' she called. A handsome man of military bearing stepped from the group, bowed, and said: 'Madam?'

'I believe this stew is a fricassee of chicken.'

' Madam, I am of the same opinion.'

Casanova, who described the scene, added: 'I was delighted to have seen the famous warrior who subjected Berg-Op-Zoom, but it hurt me to see such a great man obliged to discuss a chicken fricassee with the same tone of voice as if he was pronouncing a death sentence.'

The most trivial incident could cause endless controversy. In his memoirs for 1738, the marquis d'Argenson, a minister under Louis XV, wrote ominously that 'Republicanism is piercing at court, there is no more respect for royalty.' What he meant was that when the queen wanted to play a hand of lansquenet, no one offered to cut the cards.

'They say I do not want to start playing early,' complained the queen. 'It would be more accurate to say that they do not want it; I was mulling the matter over a moment ago, during the sermon.'

'Perhaps that is what brought about the misfortune,' suggested Madame de Boufflers, a lady-in-waiting.

'Perhaps the sermon was on gambling,' offered d'Argenson.

'No, it was on slander,' said the queen.

'Well, Madam,' he replied, 'a sermon against slander must exhort its listeners to gamble, for when one is gambling one cannot slander.'

'Should then sermons against gambling exhort to slander?' inquired the queen.

Every member of the royal family was afflicted by the enforced triviality of his life. The dauphin, Louis de France—who died nine years before his father, Louis XV—was gambling with Madame de Ventadour. After the game he asked Monsieur de Châtillon:

'Did you remark that I was bored at cavagnole?'

'No, Sire.'

'Nonetheless, I was very bored.'

Infantile behaviour was another symptom of boredom. On one occasion, Louis XV addressed his mistress, Madame de Mailly, who was too busy working on a tapestry to reply. The king, in a kind of tantrum, cut her tapestry into four pieces with a knife. The boredom of courtiers also came out in their readiness to fight duels over puerile arguments, such as whether a certain person sat a horse well, or small annoyances, such as one carriage brushing against another. At the Opera, Monsieur Duperron, chamberlain of the King of Sweden, ran into the comte de la Marck.

'Is it true, Monsieur le comte,' he asked, 'that you have accused me of cowardice and that you claim I refused to join my regiment during the last war?'

'That is perfectly true, sir. I said it and I repeat it; it is completely my opinion.'

'In that case, Monsieur le comte, will you do me the honour of meeting me tomorrow?'

'With pleasure, sir, I am at your service, if only to make sure that sometimes you do show yourself.'

The duel took place as scheduled and the chamberlain was killed.

The court was changing; its standards were wavering. No one, apart from an old guard of true believers, had much faith any more in the daily miracle which Louis XIV had performed. And yet the machinery still turned, largely thanks to etiquette and money. Despite Louis XV's retreat into privacy, and his separate bedroom, public ceremonial was still taken seriously. Concern for etiquette is the main topic of the duc de Luynes' memoirs, seventeen volumes about daily problems of rank and manners that might have been written with embalming fluid. For Luynes, there were still great battles of rank. The duchesse de Châtillon, he writes, sat down before Mademoiselle (a royal princess), who observed: 'Madam, you are in a great hurry.' Madame de Mazarin replied that the queen had given the *tabouret* to the duchesse. ' Madam, the queen may do as she judges best,' said Mademoiselle, 'but it is the king who decides rank in France, and he did not give the *tabouret* to Madame de Châtillon; the queen cannot confer rank, even were she Regent.' Luynes discussed the arguments that raged for days on whether the salutation of a letter from the dauphin to the king should be 'your very faithful son and subject,' or 'your very humble and very obedient servant, son and subject.' Nothing affected him more adversely than changes in the etiquette established by Louis XIV. He feared a dangerous innovation when Louis XV had newly named peers kneel in a semicircle instead of stand in line according to seniority. He was shocked because Monsieur de Rochefort, who was in uniform, was invited by the king to join him in his carriage —'under the late king, this was not done.'

The queen, who, after bearing Louis XV ten children, had little else to do, was also careful to enforce etiquette. On one occasion, she was visiting the dauphin and asked for a cream puff. The duchesse de Châtillon brought it to her on a napkin. The queen was in a huff, observing that her lady-in-waiting, the duchesse de Luynes, should have given it to her host, the dauphin, to give to her.

As in the days of Louis XIV, the same total attention was paid to the monarch's person. La Peyronie, Louis XV's doctor, proudly noted that 'he was accustomed to go to the water closet twice a day, and abundantly.' But Louis XV did not inherit the Sun King's capacity to inspire awe. The sons of courtiers who had made flattery an art openly criticized him. The duc de Richelieu said in front of fourteen persons that the Treaty of Aix-la-Chapelle, which ended the War of the Austrian Succession in 1748, was 'a masterpiece of stupidity, if not of corruption.'

Most courtiers could not afford to criticize, for the race for pensions and privileges was still on. The luxury of the court remained unchanged. The civil household of Louis XV had twenty-two branches, such as the Trivial Pleasures Department, the Chapel Music Department, and the Department of the Mouth, which fed the king and his guests such dishes as pigs' tongues stuffed with stag's-horn jelly, pheasant with carp and iris-root sauce, and trees

with caramel trunks, marzipan branches and candied flowers. There
were sixty doctors and pharmacists to bleed and purge the king
when he overate. There were offices whose origins were lost in the
dust of past reigns, like the ten men in charge of crows and the six
men in charge of blackbirds. The king's military household, which
had mainly ceremonial functions, numbered 10,000 men, including a
fife and drum corps which accompanied him to mass, and 150 horse
grenadiers who were reputedly the best-looking men in France. The
total expense of both households could reach 30 million livres a year,
and there were many lucrative sinecures nestled among the household expenses: the Master of the Queen's Wardrobe, who supervised
the packing of her chests when she went on trips, was paid 24,000
livres a year. The maids who held the candle concession were said to
earn at least 50,000 livres a year from the resale of candles which
were only used once.

Courtiers still spent fortunes to keep up with the royal family. A
comfortable income was 500,000 livres a year. A woman's dress
could cost 1,000 livres, and men's clothes were no less sumptuous—
the marquis de Stainville wore a suit of silver cloth embroidered in
gold and lined with sable which had cost 25,000 livres. Whereas the
taxable Third Estate often had to hide its wealth, the tax-exempt
nobility had to display a wealth it often did not have. The forms of
display were the number of servants one had (the household of a
man of quality required a staff of seventy-five), the number of estab-
lishments one kept up, the clothes and jewellery one wore, one's
prodigality at the gaming tables of Versailles, and the luxuriousness
of one's carriages (lords had runners with Great Danes on leashes to
open the streets of Paris for their carriages—Jean-Jacques Rousseau
was knocked down by one in 1776 and split his upper lip). The
eagerness to display external signs of wealth was such that when a
tax on doors and windows was enforced the marquis de Castellane
had new windows pierced at his castle of Villandry. Another memorable extravagance was the marble mausoleum which prince Louis
de Bourbon-Condé erected for his pet monkey, McCarthy. Favouritism and the king's bedchamber were still the principal roads to
affluence. No lady ever left the king's bed empty-handed, and the
official mistresses made fortunes for themselves and their families.
Madame de Pompadour is estimated to have received 36 million
livres during the eighteen years she was *maîtresse en titre*. Madame
du Barry's house at Louveciennes had lapis lazuli fireplaces,

gold-plated bronzes, painted walls and ceilings, pilasters of white marble with bronze capitals, and floors made from precious, fragrant woods. The court nobility is neatly summed up in this exchange from *The Marriage of Figaro*:

Figaro: I was born to be a courtier.
Suzanne: They say it is a difficult profession.
Figaro: Receive, take, and ask, that is the secret in three words.

Beaumarchais' mockery was part of a general spirit of irreverence which the court itself adopted rather than resisted, particularly in religious matters. Louis XIV, who considered himself God's terrestrial agent, did not tolerate lack of respect for the church. Louis XV was more superstitious than pious, and while he carried out his own religious obligations (at mass he moved his lips so that courtiers could see he was following the service), he could not impose them on the court. His mistress, Madame de Mailly, tried to convince him that hell was an old wives' tale. The chevalier de Lorenzi, whose mistress wanted to take him to mass, asked: 'Is it still being said?' The duc de Croÿ, a member of the old guard, was made fun of because he refused to eat meat on Friday, and the marquis d'Argenson noted in his diary: 'No one dares take the clergy's part in conversations, for fear of being considered an advocate of the Inquisition . . . during the Paris carnival, no one had ever seen so many people disguised as bishops and monks.'

Events, as well as the spirit of irreverence and criticism, shook the court's stability. The death of Madame de Pompadour in 1764 was one such event, for Madame du Barry, who succeeded her, lacked her authority, and the court, more than ever, divided into quarrelling factions. It was after Pompadour's death that court pillars like the duc de Nivernais began to abandon Versailles. Another result of her death was that the duc de Choiseul, who had snubbed Madame du Barry, was exiled in 1770. Choiseul's elegance and prodigality had set the tone at Versailles under Madame de Pompadour. When he retired to his Loire castle of Chanteloup, elegance retired from court. He auctioned his magnificent collection of paintings in order to maintain his standards of extravagance. He built a seven-story pagoda where the names of the 210 courtiers who had deserted Versailles to visit him in exile were engraved. He created an alternate court. Versailles under Madame du Barry, wrote the prince de Montbarey, was made up of 'all those who insisted on calling themselves relatives of her so-called husband, of all the male and female hangers-on of the maréchal de Richelieu, of the duc d'Aiguillon and the other leaders of the cabal, of the rabble of favour-seekers, great and small, and of all those who had arrived by coach from Bordeaux and the other meridional provinces of the kingdom drawn by the lure of profit . . . and with nothing to lose or risk.'

With the advent of Louis XVI in 1774 the court underwent other changes. The new monarch was awkward, coarse, and humourless. He was the first Bourbon who kept no mistresses, and his own marriage was not consummated for seven years. Louis XVI had the erotic Bouchers removed from his grandfather's boudoir. He said he wanted to be remembered as 'Louis the Severe.' Marie Antoinette had the private parts of the male statues at Marly covered with stucco shells. Boudoirs in the small apartments were turned into laboratories, where the king made locks and watches and studied geography and physics. The interest in Greek and Roman antiquities, born under Louis XV with the exploration of Herculaneum and Pompeii, gradually led to a neoclassic style which replaced the rococo and was labelled Louis XVI. It was sober and stiff, a return to symmetry, tables and chairs with straight legs, allegorical statues, a pronouncement that the era of graceful pleasure was over.

At the same time, it fulfilled the court's need for a new fashion that could be followed as fervently as the rococo. Almost overnight, everything became *à la grècque*: architecture, jewellery, decoration, furniture, hair styles. Horace Walpole wrote in 1764 that the French 'are as formal as we were in Queen Anne's day and believe they make discoveries when they adopt what we have had these twenty years. For instance, they begin to see beauties in the antique—everything must be *à la grècque*—accordingly the lace on their waistcoats is copied from a frieze. M. de Guerchy [French ambassador to the English court] seeing a Doric fret on a fender at Woburn, which was common before I went abroad, said to the Duchess of Bedford: "Why, Madam, you have there some *à la grècque* without knowing it." ' Paris architects favoured heavy neoclassic structures with Doric columns, like the School of Medicine and the Mint. Buildings of every purpose, from theatres to churches, had to look like Greek temples.

True feeling and the cult of Rousseau replaced persiflage. Romantic melancholy became fashionable, and found its proper setting in the English garden, with its moss-covered bridges, artificial ponds lined with rushes, and fake ruins in a variety of styles—Dutch wind-mills faced Gothic towers; minarets coexisted with druidic temples, Chinese pagodas with Russian isbas. The passion for the exotic and the absence of a truly national style under Louis XVI provided an eclectic setting for a society whose own values were being ques-tioned. The island of Ermenonville, designed by Hubert Robert, boasted a temple of philosophy which was left unfinished, like human knowledge.

Alongside the Greco-Roman inspiration, artists began to find sub-jects outside the court, and to paint the lives of humble people. The anecdotal paintings of Greuze were admired by the Philosophes, for they showed the virtuous behaviour of the common man. Other writers were shocked by the absence of grandiose themes. Bachau-mont, commenting on a 1762 art exhibit in his secret memoirs, wrote: 'The portrait is very fashionable; this style, worthy of little praise, is only worthwhile when persons who deserve the applause of the nation are depicted. One sees a great many untitled men and women, unworthy of interest.'

The last stronghold of absurd extravagance was clothing. Gentle-men wore brocaded waistcoats depicting hunts and battles, and buttons that were miniature portraits of French kings, or the twelve Caesars, or their own mistresses. A courtier called decorated waist-coats 'the historical monuments of our age.' Women's fashions reached a degree of ridiculousness unmatched in French history. Fashionable colours were Carmelite's Stomach (an off-white), King's Eye (a royal blue), Paris Mud, and Goose Dung. A strand of Marie Antoinette's hair was sent to the Gobelins tapestry-works in Lyon so that its colour could be faithfully reproduced. A dress worn by a fashionable actress in 1780 was described as 'in the Suppressed Sighs style, decorated with Superfluous Regrets: in the centre a point of Perfect Candour, garnished with Indiscreet Complaints, and ribbons in the Insistent Tribute manner: Queen's Hair shoes embroidered with diamonds in Perfidious Blows and Come and See It emeralds . . . a muff of Sentimental Agitation.' Hair styles were sometimes two and three feet high, and considerable acrobacy was required for the simplest movements. The Baroness Oberkirch in 1782 adorned her powdered hair with flowers in tiny flasks half-filled with water, which she called 'spring in the middle of the snow.' Other hair-pieces were decorated with miniature windmills and a three-masted sloop in honour of a naval victory. Hairdressers were so inflated with self-importance that they petitioned for severance from the wigmakers' guild and assimilation into one of the scientific guilds. Beauty marks were mandatory, and were called 'wenches' on the nose, 'Coquettes' on the upper lip, and 'Receivers of Stolen Goods' when they were masqueraded over a real mole.

Marie Antoinette at first followed fashion and was ridiculed in Paris street songs because of the number of dresses she bought each year. Her dressmaker, Rose Bertin, was called 'the minister of fashion.' But when she began to wear simple clothes, and was painted in 1783 by Madame Vigée-Lebrun in a white percale dress, people said she dressed like a chambermaid. Since there were no mistresses at court, Marie Antoinette was the first unrivalled queen of Versailles. Her influence was great, but she used it to further simplify etiquette rather than uphold it. She soon grew to detest the monotony of daily representation and sought escape from the court's exacting conventions. She nicknamed the bluestocking comtesse de Noailles 'Madame Etiquette.' She complained about the 'odious' system of passing her clothes from one lady-in-waiting to the other as she waited, shivering. She turned the court into a coterie of intimate friends with whom she spent most of her time, and found refuge from the formality of Versailles in the miniature farm at the Petit Trianon. There, in a landscape of rustic simplicity Rousseau would have admired, one felt '100 leagues from the court,' according to the writer Grimm. To make her privacy complete, there were sliding mirrors that covered the windows and a secret passage in the artificial grotto. Once the queen had turned her back on Versailles general attendance slackened, and many courtiers began coming only once a week, so that 'six days a week the court seemed a private society or a family united by affection.'

Thus, as the Revolution approached, the court underwent a transformation of its own against the system of Louis XIV. The following conversation between Marie Antoinette and one of her young pages, the comte de Tilly, with its tone of bantering familiarity, marks a half-way point between the cold formality of the Sun King and the brazenness of the Paris mobs who came to Versailles in 1789 to fetch 'the baker and the baker's wife.'

The queen received Tilly in her private apartments and said:

'Good day—where did you dine?'
'With Madame de Beauvillier, Madam.'

'Does she serve supper?'

'Yes, Madam, at least to me, whom she knew as a child and does not have to be formal with.'

'If Monsieur de Champcenetz [a notorious rake] had been at Versailles you could have dined with him.'

'Madam, he has some wit and much gaiety.'

'Oh, that is charming, that will take him far. Well, sir, what is it you wish?'

'Madam, there has arrived a gentleman, a sort of magistrate to whom my parents and I wish well; he seeks a vacant office in Alençon . . . it depends on Monsieur de Miromesnil. My man is an excellent subject and I would be most happy to see him get the office. A word from the queen to the Lord Privy Seal and it is clear . . .'

'Well, it is clear . . .'

'Yes, Madam, that he could not refuse.'

'Return tomorrow and the letter will be written. Goodbye.'

'I do not know how to express all my gratitude to the queen.'

'By behaving!'

Even card games could serve to reveal the changes at court. Card suits are the symbolic representations of social orders—the word 'spade' comes from the Italian *spada* (sword) and represents the ruling feudal class; hearts (shown in Spanish cards of the period as chalices) are the clergy, diamonds are the pavement blocks trodden by the urban bourgeoisie, and clubs are the emblem of the lowest or peasant class. The favourite card game at Versailles had long been quadrille, in which the ace of spades, or *spadille*, is always the highest card, whatever the trump suit. The *spadille* is an absolute ruler and cannot be deposed by another card. But under Louis XVI, quadrille lost ground to English whist, in which the ace of spades is no longer invulnerable. Trump is the master. Any order may rule. The ace of spades may be deposed by a lowly club.

Although only a handful of ancient courtiers seemed any longer to take it seriously, the system perfected by Louis XIV continued to work on its original momentum until 1790, a year after the start of the Revolution. In its twilight, the court was like a faded beauty who continues to wear the gowns and jewellery that enhanced her youth and still expects compliments from gentlemen. Courtiers still scratched on doors with their combs instead of knocking, still glided

THE STOLEN KISS
By Fragonard

THE CHEVALIER D'ÉON IN FEMALE CLOTHES
Engraving by Condé

rather than walked, still addressed the king in the third person: Did His Majesty sleep well; is His Majesty over his cold? The king was still protected by Swiss guards wearing ruffs and plumed hats, and by his personal guard of nobles in blue jerkins and red, silver-trimmed trousers. When he mounted a horse a page in a blue twill coat and leather leggings held his stirrup. When he ate, it still took ten servants to serve him a dish of meat. The splendour of Louis XVI's surroundings was not very different from the Sun King's. His chapel had a staff of 75, his library of 15,000 volumes kept 43 persons employed, his medical staff numbered 48, his stables of 1,857 horses required a staff of 1,500 and the Department of the Mouth still numbered nearly 500 valets, waiters, stewards, cup-bearers, overseers of the roasts, masters of the pantry, carvers, master cooks, dish handlers, herbmen, saucemen, kitchen supervisors and scullions. There were still more than 100 servants of the King's Wardrobe, including tailors, yeomen of the laundry, starchers, ushers and secretaries. The total military and civilian royal house-hold staff on the eve of the Revolution was in the vicinity of 15,000 persons, and despite repeated attempts at economy, absorbed about 13 per cent of the budget (including pensions). The single item of wine in 1789 amounted to 60,899 livres. Versailles still had its zoo, stocked with lions, tigers, pelicans, ostriches, and calves for the king's table, who were fed only egg yolks, orange juice, and milk.

After the violent days of 1789 and the rush of citizens on Versailles in October, the royal family moved to the Tuileries in Paris, and there, in the shadow of a new age, the court continued to go through its motions, unaltered by events and the first defections of emigrating nobles (including the king's brother, the comte d'Artois). Presentation at court continued until June, 1790. Louis XVI still arose and retired amid his faithful courtiers and attended mass publicly in a drawing room converted into a chapel. He gave formal dinners on Thursdays, and those courtiers who had not emigrated were comforted by the fact that there was less competition over invitations. But the Revolution could not absorb the court. In the confrontation between republican and courtier the latter seemed obsolete, the former crude. When Jean-Marie Roland was named Minister of the Interior in 1792, the Minister of Foreign Affairs, General Dumouriez, took him to court to be presented to the king. It was Roland's first visit. He wore a simple round hat, and his shoes were tied with ribbons. The Master of Ceremonies said in a shocked whisper to Dumouriez: 'But sir, he has no buckles on his shoes.' 'Good heavens,' replied Dumouriez with mock consternation, 'all is lost.' Ten months later, Louis XVI was guillotined.

VI

THE WELL-BELOVED

The reign of Louis XV is the most deplorable period of our history: when one searches out its characters one is reduced to rummaging in the ante-chambers of the duc de Choiseul, the wardrobes of Pompadour and du Barry, and one cannot see how these names can be elevated to the dignity of history. All of society was in decomposition: statesmen became men of letters and men of letters became statesmen; great lords were bankers and bankers were great lords. Fashions were in ridiculous bad taste; shepherdesses in hoops were painted in salons and colonels did embroidery. Everything was decayed in mind and manner and forecast the revolution to come. Magistrates were ashamed of their robes and ridiculed the gravity of their fathers; priests in their pulpits avoided naming Jesus Christ and talked instead of the legislator of Christians. Ministers fell one after the other and power slipped from all hands; it was supremely fashionable to be English at court and Prussian at war, anything, in fact, except French. All that was said, all that was done, was a series of inconsistencies.

—FRANÇOIS-RENÉ DE CHATEAUBRIAND

The reign of Louis XV was the great era of French administration. . . . Louis XV did not reign over a France plagued by misery, but over a France at the peak of prosperity. . . . It was a time of farmers, businessmen, ironmasters, shipbuilders and civil servants. Certainly, there was some depravity, but without hypocrisy . . . there were no more sermons, and, as yet, no romantic tears. People knew the art of living and lived.

—PIERRE GAXOTTE, *Le Siècle de Louis XV*

LOUIS XV is one of the most baffling of French kings. His reign of fifty-one years is the monarchy's second-longest. He showed sufficient authority to keep the system from collapsing in his lifetime, although he accurately predicted that 'things as they are will last as long as I do myself.' But in the half-century he spent at Versailles, even those who were close to him admitted that they did not understand him. To the marquis d'Argenson, who served as his minister, he was 'undecipherable.' To the duc de Luynes, his loyal courtier, he was 'undefinable.' To his mistress, Madame de Pompadour, he was equally perplexing, a man who needed constantly to be diverted, a task at which she could never be sure she had succeeded. The story of his many mistresses has been magnified out of all proportion, so that he is most commonly remembered as a kind of male nymphomaniac, or in the words of Carlyle, 'a fabulous Griffin, devouring the works of men, daily dragging virgins to thy cave.'

It is not in mythology, however, that an understanding of Louis XV can be found. He was, more than anything, a Shakespearean king, beset by too many human failings, unequal to his task, racked by self-doubt, subject to fits of apathy and pessimism. He was self-indulgent and lacking in conviction. His obsessions would by modern clinical standards probably make him a pathological case, for in addition to his tireless sensualism he was morbidly preoccupied with death and showed symptoms of sadism, a word which was yet to be coined. Finally, he was an absolute monarch reluctant to believe that any decision of his could change or improve matters.

Setting aside his private failings, this judgment of the public figure by Frederick II in a letter to Voltaire is one of the shrewdest: 'He was an honest man whose only fault was being king.' He lacked Louis XIV's unwavering faith in the power and mystical authority of the monarchy. Louis XIV was consistent, even in his worst mistakes. There is about the reign of Louis XV the feeling of a man watching helplessly as the world around him alters. When he acted, it was often at cross-purpose. He spent years eroding his authority in a sterile struggle with Parlement to protect the Jesuits, only to banish the Jesuits for reasons which have never been fully understood; for years he conducted secret diplomacy to defend French interests in Poland only to stand by helplessly when Poland was divided by Austria, Prussia, and Russia; he gained small pieces of territory like Corsica and Lorraine but lost a vast colonial empire;

he tried to impose tax reforms but instead gave in to pressures and exiled the minister who had suggested the reforms; his only successful measure, the suppression of the Parlements in 1771, was undone by his successor, Louis XVI, who called them back.

Louis XV was a beautiful child, with liquid, lustrous black eyes, long curly eyelashes, a small crimson mouth, and a well-proportioned specimen of the Bourbon nose. He worked hard at his lessons, and several hundred translations from the Latin in his schoolboy's hand have been preserved. But quite early his character was the cause of alarm, and in 1721 Cardinal Dubois wrote to the Doge in Venice: 'Be assured that all the malicious talk you have heard on the weakness of the king's temperament and on his melancholy is completely false. His health is perfect. He is stronger every day. . . .' Despite the cardinal's denials, melancholy proved to be one of Louis XV's principal characteristics. Another was cruelty. One of his pages, the marquis de Calvière, noted in his diary that when the king was twelve he tortured three kittens to death. 'The king's cat, named Charlotte,' wrote Calvière, 'had four very pretty kittens and the king caressed them a great deal, but tormented them to the point that three out of four died within twenty-four hours.'

He liked also to torment his courtiers. One of them, Jean-Potentin Darboulin, was complaining about his attacks of gout when Louis XV suddenly stamped on his foot with his heel and said: 'Is this where you have the gout?' 'It took all the strength I could muster not to shove him,' Darboulin told Madame de Pompadour, 'for he can have no idea of the pain I felt . . . let him keep his caresses for others.' Coupled with his cruelty was an abnormal fascination with death, partly explained by the fact that when he was two, his father, mother, and brother died within the period of a week. As the duc de Luynes noted, 'All too frequently, his [the king's] conversations dwelled on the details of illnesses, operations, questions of anatomy, and the places where one expected to be buried.' He liked to tease his courtiers about their illnesses. 'That cough of yours has the scent of pinewood,' he would say. 'How much will I profit when you die?' he once asked the maréchal de Villars (meaning profit in vacant offices that could be resold, and pensions). 'Sire, I do not know what Your Majesty's profit will be, but to the late king my death would have been a loss.' He liked to warn his courtiers of their impending deaths and was pleased when his predictions were accurate. Anything to do with death engrossed him, and once when he was driving by a cemetery in his carriage he sent an equerry to see whether there were any freshly dug graves. There were almost daily examples of the king's morbidity, and the marquis d'Argenson noted that 'His Majesty speaks joyously of the death or the sickness of his subjects. Not long ago I heard the queen ask him for news of one of his surgeons who had fractured his skull while hunting; the king laughingly said he had nearly died.' Although he laughed about the deaths and suffering of others, he was himself a physical coward. In 1757 a would-be assassin stabbed him in the side with a penknife, inflicting a superficial wound. 'What was most singular about the king's fear was that he had only been scratched,' wrote the duc de Choiseul, 'which would not have prevented anyone with a little more courage from sleeping at Trianon, as he was intending to do before he was wounded.' When he was dying in 1774, the duc de Liancourt, Grand Master of Ceremonies, said that 'the king's fear and pusillanimity were inconceivable.'

He was not a lazy man, for he spent long hours closeted with ministers and confidants, kept his own files, sought out exact information, and wrote his letters and reports in a brisk and direct style. He also expended considerable energy on hunting (he was estimated to have run down a total of 6,300 stags) and the pursuit of women. But he was prone to periods of deep apathy. Days would go by when he would refuse to sign an official paper, and attended council meetings with a vacant, indifferent air. There were also occasions when two different ministers would bring him conflicting reports and he would approve them both. He was so profoundly convinced of the futility of human endeavour that he once said of a newly appointed minister: 'He displayed his merchandise like the others and promised the most marvellous things in the world, none of which will take place. He does not know this country; he will learn.' He told his minister Choiseul that he knew his servants were robbing him but that there was nothing he could do about it.

Perhaps it was only in his amorous intrigues that Louis XV could overcome the fundamental apathy of his nature. It did not bother him that Madame du Barry was widely believed to have started her career as a Paris prostitute, because, as he said, she was the only woman in France who could make him forget that he was sixty. His first experience with the opposite sex, however, made him cry. In 1721, when he was eleven, he was informed by the Regent that a marriage had been arranged for him with the Infanta of Spain, a round-cheeked blond baby of three. Courtiers who saw him after he had learned the news noted that his eyes were inflamed and moist. The Infanta arrived in France in 1722, clutching a doll, and Louis XV waited for her outside Paris, in Montrouge, and welcomed her courteously but without enthusiasm. It was now a matter of waiting for the Infanta's puberty and guarding the twelve-year-old king against corruption. When half a dozen of his teenage playmates were caught in the Versailles woods performing homosexual experiments, they were discreetly removed from court, and the ringleader, the Marquis de Rambures, was jailed in the Bastille. Louis XV asked where his playmates were and was told they had been punished for knocking down picket fences; 'picket-fence-puller' (*arracheur de palissade*) thereafter became a euphemism for pederast. The duchesse de Retz was also exiled because she had secluded herself with the king and tried to 'touch him in secret places.'

In the same year that the 'picket-fence-pullers' were banned, the Regent forced the resignation of the king's superintendent, the maréchal de Villeroi, a fatuous relic of the court of Louis XIV who saw plots to kill the king in every bowl of soup. He was replaced by the great-grandson of the grand Condé, Monsieur le Duc, who was both ambitious and unintelligent, and whose appearance was forbidding—he was tall, thin as a splinter, one-eyed, with a short torso and spindly, storklike legs, sunken cheeks, an overlong chin, thick lips, and tiny, darting, rabbitlike eye. When the Regent was dying, in 1723, Monsieur le Duc, without waiting for the moment of death, rushed to the king's apartments to solicit the job of Prime Minister. He held the post for two-and-a-half years, and is remembered for a law branding beggars on the arm with the letter M (for *mendiant*) and for the repudiation of the Spanish Infanta, to hasten the king's wedding day.

Prodded by his mistress, Madame de Prie, whom Viscount Bolingbroke called 'the most corrupt and ambitious jade alive,' Monsieur le Duc in 1725 asked a Secretary of State to draw up a list of eligible European princesses. He secretly hoped to pass off one of his cousins on the young king, and it was felt that in any case that the king's health was too fragile to delay the making of an heir. The initial list of a hundred princesses was reduced to seventeen after subtracting 'forty-four who are too old to marry a young prince, twenty-nine who are too young, and ten with whom a match would be inconvenient.' The English princesses were set aside because of their religion, while the daughter of the Czar, Princess Ann of Muscovy, 'was born of a mother of low extraction and brought up in the midst of a still barbarous people,' and the Infanta of Portugal 'does not have a fertile nature and the communication of her blood is believed perilous.'

The weeding-out process left only one possibility: Marie Leczinska, a homely, superstitious Polish princess who was seven years older than Louis XV. Her father Stanislas had been king of Poland for five years. After being ousted by the Russians, he took the fragments of his court to Lorraine, where he lived in genteel poverty under French protection. He was a vain and self-important man who continued to sign his letters 'Stanislas king,' but was reduced to begging French ministers for a pension which never arrived on time. On the day the good news came he sought out Marie and said:

'Ah, my daughter, let us fall to our knees and thank God.'

'Why, Father, are you called to the throne?'

'Even better; you are queen of France.'

The Spanish Infanta had to be returned to her parents, like a trinket bought on approval. It was a terrible insult to Spain. Diplomatic relations were broken off and Philip V signed an alliance with France's enemy, Austria. Spanish peasants crossed the Pyrenees and cut the tendons of cattle grazing in French valleys. The marquis de Santa Cruz, who had brought the Infanta back to Madrid, showed the Spanish court pieces of coarse black bread which he claimed was part of the Versailles diet.

Not long after Louis XV's wedding plans had been announced there were rumours that Marie Leczinska had two fingers stuck together and was an epileptic. Monsieur le Duc proved that the rumours were false, but he could not quiet the discontented murmurs of 'misalliance' at the French court. Louis XV 'will be, I think, the first of our kings to marry a commoner,' wrote the duchesse de Lorraine to a friend. Mathieu Marais, the Regency diarist, reflected popular opinion when he wrote: 'We will have to take the Polish one and have a queen whose name ends in ski. It is a terrible name for a queen of France.'

On his wedding night, September 5, 1725, the fifteen-year-old Louis XV was 'fully satisfied,' Monsieur le Duc wrote to the father of the bride. Marie Leczinska was not beautiful or amusing. She ate too much and tended to dourness. She was so frightened of ghosts that a lady-in-waiting had to hold her hand when she went to bed at night. She did, however, perform her essential function, and gave the king ten children between 1727 and 1736 (including twin daughters), of whom five girls and two boys survived, 'a great assurance for the tranquillity of the kingdom.' After that, exhausted by childbearing, she gave herself up to court pursuits, strummed the guitar and coloured canvases on which a court artist had already painted in the backgrounds and sketched the figures.

Her one intrusion into affairs of state may have turned the king against her. Grateful because he had arranged her marriage, she supported Monsieur le Duc in his struggle with André Hercule de Fleury, bishop of Fréjus, who had been the king's tutor from the time he reached the age of seven. Each morning Louis XV had a working session with Monsieur le Duc, which was also attended by Fleury. Monsieur le Duc wanted to see the king alone to discredit Fleury, and prevailed on the queen to arrange it. Monsieur le Duc was waiting in the queen's apartment with his briefcase, and handed Louis XV a letter from the cardinal de Polignac which was full of fantastic charges against Fleury. The king read the letter, frowned, and handed it back to Monsieur le Duc, who asked: 'Have I had the misfortune to displease Your Majesty?' Louis XV replied that he had. In the meantime, Fleury, finding the king's apartment locked and guarded by order of Monsieur le Duc, wrote to the king an affectionate letter of farewell. He asked for permission to spend the rest of his days in religious retreat and left for the Sulpician monastery of Issy without waiting for an answer. Louis XV had him brought back to Versailles the next day and said, 'I hope you will never leave me again.' Three months later, in June, 1726, Monsieur le Duc and his mistress, Madame de Prie, were banished from court. Louis XV punished his wife's meddling by giving Fleury a letter for her which said: 'I beg you, madam, and if need be I order you, to do all that the bishop of Fréjus tells you as though it came from me.'

From 1726 until his death in 1743, Fleury governed France with the powers but without the title of Prime Minister. He was never obsessed by the external signs of greatness, although he accepted the cardinal's hat in November, 1726, and his administration was successful because he used power with restraint and had earned the confidence of the king. Fleury, the son of a Languedoc tax collector, had been plucked from an obscure bishopric to give Latin lessons to Louis XV. He was already in his seventies when his duties changed from teaching to governing, and he was subtle enough to make old age, modesty, and feigned weakness instruments of power. He was France's last great cardinal-minister, encumbered neither by the greed of a Dubois nor the intrigues of a Mazarin. He insisted that he did not want 'an historic ministry,' and under his discreet but masterful tutelage, the *ancien régime* knew an interim period of peace and financial stability. He was guided by a simple aim, the good of the state, and asked of the restive and intriguing courtiers: 'When will we be given common sense in exchange for fine wit?' Fleury's rule was the rule of common sense. With the reform of 1726, France had a stable currency for the first time in her history. In 1738 the budget was balanced for the first time since 1672. In foreign affairs, Fleury preserved Dubois' English alliance, convinced that France and England had played for too long a perilous cat-and-mouse game in which each side thought it was the cat. He was fortunate, from 1726 to 1742, in that he dealt with Robert Walpole, a mercantilist minister who considered war an unfortunate interruption in trade. Even when he was forced to take part in the War of the Polish Succession in 1733 he sent a small force so that England would not be alarmed. Fleury tried to quiet those eternal dissenters, the Jansenists, but instead revived the resistance of the Parlements, and the exhausting round of appeals, memoirs, decrees, deputations, remonstrances, beds of justice, exiles, and sealed letters. In 1732, Louis XV put on a show of strength, summoned Parlement to Versailles, and said: 'This is my will. Do not force me to show you I am the master.' It was simply another episode in the struggle, about which Fleury was able to do little.

In his late eighties, half-blind and totally deaf, Fleury continued to work twelve hours a day. One of his pleasures was denying rumours of his death. He said old age was a defect which he hoped he would not have to cure for a long time. In 1740, the Austrian Emperor Charles VI died, leaving the crown to his daughter, Maria Theresa. The temptation to challenge Maria Theresa's claims to the throne and win a piece of the Austrian empire in the bargain was strong in Europe, and the first to succumb to it was Frederick II, who invaded Silesia in December, 1740. The initial reaction of Louis XV was pacific. 'The only thing to do is to stay on Mont Pagnotte,' he said (Mont Pagnotte was a hill in Chantilly forest from which the king often watched the fleshing of the hounds). Fleury agreed, but he was ninety, and no match for the courtiers who insisted on war with Austria. His efforts to keep peace were fruitless, and in 1743,

the year of his death, France entered the War of the Austrian Succession. Fleury left an unfillable vacuum, for Louis XV told his
other ministers that he would henceforth govern himself, without
intermediaries. Louis XV had changed. He was now a handsome
thirty-three, with a hint of softness in the face and a slight pout to
the cupid-bow mouth. While Fleury had handled affairs of state
so well and so effortlessly, Louis XV had devoted himself increasingly to his private affairs. The court noticed his growing disaffection with the queen. When she was pregnant he seldom spent his
nights at her side. He refused to alter his hunting schedule to visit
her during an illness. Conversely, her annual births gave the queen
an excuse for long periods of continence. The king surrounded himself with courtiers of his own age, gave the first of his *petits soupers,*
and spent more and more time away from Versailles and the queen.
In 1732, at a gay champagne dinner at the château de Madrid, in a
suburb of Paris, the king set tongues wagging by toasting 'an unknown woman.' It soon became apparent that this mysterious figure
was the large and boisterous Madame de Mailly, reputedly one of
the ugliest women at court. She was one of the five Mailly-Nesle
sisters, and it is a tribute to the thoroughness with which the king
conducted his extramarital life that he is believed to have had affairs
with all five.

It was winter when courtiers arranged the first private meeting
between the king and Madame de Mailly, and she said her feet were
cold and moved closer to the fire. The king touched her foot and
moved his hand up her leg to her garter. 'Sire,' said Madame de
Mailly, 'if I had known that Your Majesty had summoned me for
this I would not have come.' Nonetheless she remained, and became
the king's first official mistress. She boasted that sixteen painters had
done her portrait. Her mistake was inviting her sister, Madame de
Vintimille, to suppers and parties with the king. In 1740 Louis XV
told Madame de Mailly, 'you bore me' and replaced her with
Madame de Vintimille, who was even larger and more homely. Her
husband said she had the soul of a devil in the body of a billygoat.
She was also bad-tempered and one day when she refused to answer
a query from the king about her health he told her: 'I know very
well, Madame la comtesse, the remedy you need. It is to have your
head cut off, which would suit you because your neck is too long.'
Louis XV was nonetheless genuinely fond of Madame de Vintimille,
and when she died in 1741 while giving birth to his child he asked

for a wax mould of her face. She had died in convulsions with her mouth open and it took 'two strong men to hold her jaws closed.'

Next in line for the succession was Madame de la Tournelle, who was better-looking and more demanding than her sisters. She negotiated her conditions of capitulation: the title of duchess, a large apartment at Versailles, an unlimited allowance, public pregnancies, legitimatized bastards, and the exile of her sister, Madame de Mailly (who became known as the Widow). Thus did Madame de la Tournelle become the duchesse de Châteauroux. She was an ardent patriot who urged the king to take part in the campaigns of the War of Austrian Succession. In 1744, she accompanied him to Metz, where he fell deathly ill. The duchesse left his side so that he could be given the last sacraments and absolution, while at the sacristy of Notre Dame 6,000 masses were requested for his recovery. It was during this bout with an undiagnosed fever that he earned the name of Well-Beloved. Louis XV recovered, but the duchesse de Châteauroux did not. She was ill in Paris when the king sent for her again, and as she dressed to leave for Versailles, she collapsed and died of peritonitis, at the age of twenty-seven.

The marquis d'Argenson had written in 1743 that 'after two years of Châteauroux, His Majesty is what one might call surfeited.' He sought variety in a fourth Mailly-Nesle sister, Madame de Flavacourt, but gave her up when faced with an ultimatum from the bossy Madame de Châteauroux. Her death saddened the king, but the court knew he was over his grief when he failed to carry out his Christmas obligations that year. The fifth and last Mailly-Nesle sister, the duchesse de Lauraguais, briefly served as the king's mistress, and received as a reward the income from the chain of shops in Nantes, which amounted to 18,000 livres a year. The loves of Louis XV had become the favourite topic of Paris gossip, and the saga of the Mailly-Nesle sisters was immortalized in verse form:

> The first is forgotten, the second is turned to dust,
> The third has her foot in the stirrup,
> The fourth is waiting for her chance
> To give way to the fifth.
> Is it faithlessness or constancy
> To choose an entire family?

It was only after thirteen years of faithless constancy with the Mailly-Nesle sisters that Louis XV began finding mistresses outside the court, which was an implied insult to the women who surrounded him at Versailles, and a mockery of class distinctions. France could forgive a costly war or an unrewarding peace much more easily than a royal mistress lifted from 'the dregs of the people.' Madame de Maintenon had been of poor but noble birth. Madame de Pompadour came from the world of finance and was a commoner. Her maiden name was Poisson, and it inspired more anonymous pamphlets (called *Poissonades*) than any other subject of discontent during the reign of Louis XV.

Madame de Pompadour was the last of the great authoritarian mistresses who appear at regular intervals in the monarchy, sometimes to guide it with firm and manicured hands, sometimes to precipitate its falls. The prevailing view, echoed to this day in encyclopedias, is that 'she became the mistress of Louis XV in 1745 and until her death was the virtual ruler of France.' This is an oversimplification of both the reign of Louis XV and feminine psychology. Madame de Pompadour was an ambitious, single-minded woman whose rise to power is another example of the flexibility of eighteenth-century French society. She controlled considerable patronage, was responsible for the disgrace of certain ministers and the rise of others, served as go-between in treaty negotiations with Austria, and was a vigorous patroness of the arts. But in no way did she rule France. The king did not trust her completely and never made her a privy to his secret diplomacy. She was herself ruled by anyone who flattered her with diligence, and one of her protégés, the abbé de Bernis, wrote that 'she judged affairs of state like a child.' The two major policy changes that took place while she was at court, the banning of the Jesuits and the Austrian alliance, were far more the result of events outside her control than of any conscious manipulation on her part. She had, like every royal mistress before her, permanent access to the king, and knew how to use it. The duc de Croÿ wrote that 'it was most agreeable to deal with such a pretty prime minister, whose laughter was enchanting and who was such a good listener . . . there was perhaps not a single office or favour that had not come from her.' At the most, this meant that she was the principal intermediary between the king and the court. But her influence was limited, for there were entire areas of policy about which she knew nothing.

Madame de Pompadour represents the eighteenth-century alliance of moneyed capitalism with the aristocracy, which contributed greatly to social mobility. Her father was an agent for those Regency financiers the Paris brothers, one of whom was her godfather. Monsieur Poisson was involved in a wheat fraud in 1725 and fled to Germany to avoid arrest. Madame Poisson accepted the protection of Le Normant de Tournehem, a former ambassador to Sweden who had made a fortune as a General Farmer. When she was nineteen, the pretty, fresh-faced Jeanne-Antoinette married the nephew of her mother's protector, Le Normant d'Etioles, and had a daughter by him named Alexandrine. She had the money and the taste to entertain well, and began her social climbing at the family château of Etioles, in the forest of Sénart. Montesquieu and Fontenelle were among her guests there. She was a sort of French geisha, who could sing, dance, and play the clavichord at parties. She had her portrait painted by fashionable artists like Nattier and Boucher. She called on the titled dowagers of neighbouring châteaux, in the hope that her calls would be repaid. Louis XV liked to hunt in the forest of Sénart and Madame d'Etioles learned to drive a phaeton so that she could follow the hunts. In February, 1745, she was invited to a ball at Versailles in honour of the dauphin's marriage to the Spanish Infanta Maria-Theresa-Raphaele. The court noticed the unmasked king in a corner with the unmasked Madame d'Etioles. Soon she began appearing at court functions. In April, she attended the Italian theatre in a loge facing the king's. In May, Louis XV left for a four-month trip to the front. He sent the abbé de Bernis and the marquis de Gontaut to Etoiles to teach the alluring bourgeoise court manners. After the victory of Fontenoy, the king wrote to her that he was reviving the extinct marquisate of Pompadour as her court title. Her coat of arms would be three castles on a field azure. Upon the king's return, the newly minted marquise was presented at Versailles, where she remained until her death in 1764.

The mark of a great royal mistress is the ability to negotiate the delicate transition from passion to comradeship, keeping her position even though she is no longer the object of the king's physical desire. Madame de Pompadour succeeded admirably. Sex was always a trial for her, but she rose to the task by taking an aphrodisiac diet of hot chocolate with triple vanilla, truffles, and celery soup. The king complained that she had the temperament of a coot, a cold-blooded aquatic duck. Nonetheless he slept with her for about seven years. A courtier, seeing her with the maréchal de Saxe, said: 'There goes the king's sword with the king's scabbard.' In 1749, the marquis d'Argenson, who is seldom kind to the marquise, wrote: 'Madame de Pompadour changes every day and is becoming skeletal. The lower part of her face is yellow and dried up, as for her bust, it is kinder not to mention it. However, the monarch still used her carnally, more than ever; several courtiers saw him the other day, cynically caressing her behind a screen.' There was, as Louis XV himself remarked, little natural warmth in Madame de Pompadour's nature, but she was skilful in keeping the monarch's affection after aphrodisiacs were no longer necessary. She successfully parried intrigues to have her replaced with various court debutantes. She invariably sacrificed her own interests to the king's. When her mother died in 1745 and Louis XV offered to postpone a trip to Marly as a sign of mourning she said that 'the death of my mother is not important enough to disturb the court and the ladies who have made expenses for Marly and would regret not going.' She knew how to listen. There were, however, many secrets he did not tell her which she tried in vain to pry from the prince de Conti, who spent long hours closeted with the king discussing the secret diplomacy. Finally, she did not discourage Louis XV's growing fondness for teenage girls, or the establishment of the Deer Park. The most celebrated *Poissonade* is the mock epitaph which says: 'Here lies a woman who was fifteen years a virgin, ten years a whore, and twenty years a pimp.' In fact, she did no recruiting for the Deer Park. There were valets who specialized in tracking down young ladies whose beauty had impressed the king. But she considered the ageing monarch's indiscriminate lechery a preventive measure against her own replacement. As long as the king had the Deer Park he would not seek another official mistress at court.

A great deal of lurid nonsense has been written about the Deer Park. One imagines Louis XV with a pointed beard and cloven hooves chasing dozens of frightened young things in loose tunics through fern and forest. Stripped of legend, the Deer Park is sadly anti-climatical, more of a tired businessman's retreat than a royal orgy-house, and a very modest contribution to the annals of debauchery. The Deer Park was a small house with an enclosed garden in a residential neighbourhood of Versailles where Louis XIII had once raised stags for his hunts, hence its name. Louis XV bought it in 1755 under the name of Louis de Bourbon and staffed it with a housekeeper named Madame Bertrand, commonly known as 'the abbess,' a guard, a nurse, a maid, and two elderly valets. The girls who boarded there were called Madame Bertrand's nieces. There was generally only one at a time and never more than two. They were recruited from various levels of Paris society by the king's valet-pimp, Lebel, and brought to a secret two-room apartment at Versailles called 'the bird-trap.' If they passed muster, they were sent to the Deer Park house, which Louis XV visited under the guise of a Polish lord. One of the girls recognized him because of his resemblance to the profile on the silver crown. It appears that the king used the Deer Park because he liked variety, admired youth, and feared disease. According to Barbier's diary, he had as a young man contracted gonorrhoea from a butcher's daughter. Two years before the purchase of the Deer Park house, d'Argenson wrote: 'Being weary of the marquise, he wanted a very new young lady, fearing syphilis with good reason. He had this one's virginity; she had never even menstruated when he had her.' D'Argenson is referring to the ravishing Mademoiselle Morphise, whose backside Boucher immortalized, and affirms that she was fourteen when the king had her in 1753. Her birth certificate has been found in Rouen, however, and shows that she was sixteen that year. Available information indicates that the youngest inmate of the Deer Park was the fifteen-year-old Mademoiselle de Tiercelin, and that the total number was far smaller than the 'hundreds' which critics of Louis XV have conjured up. Those who became pregnant were handsomely provided for, and it was a popular jest to say that just as every man is descended from Adam, every Frenchman is descended from Louis XV. The king sold the Deer Park house in 1771, for by that time Madame Pompadour was dead and had been replaced by Madame du Barry.

One reason for Madame de Pompadour's influence at court was that, between the death of Fleury in 1743 and the appointment of the duc de Choiseul in 1758, there were no statesmen with enough authority to assume the responsibilities of Prime Minister. Madame de Pompadour helped to fill the power vacuum. She was a stubborn and sometimes tyrannical woman. She wanted to be accepted in the queen's entourage and rebuffs did not discourage her. She asked to be one of the fifteen ladies who helped the queen wash the feet of the poor on Holy Thursday and was politely turned down. She asked to help take up the collection at Versailles chapel on Easter Sunday and again the reply was a discreet but final no. The following spring she asked for permission to travel in the queen's carriage. Weary of refusing, the queen capitulated.

Everything she touched was organized with a matriarchal thoroughness. Her theatrical troupe had regulations in ten articles: 'no member can refuse a role under the pretext that it does not suit him or that it is too tiring,' said article six; 'the actresses only will have the right to pick the plays performed by the troupe,' said article seven; 'each actor must be at rehearsal on time or pay a fine to be decided on by the actresses,' said article nine.

She was proud of her ability to do favours and quick to take credit for them. 'Not only do I have all the nobility at my feet,' she boasted to the abbé de Bernis, 'even my little dog is beset by homages.' In 1760, the new Controller General, Etienne de Silhouette, was received by the king. 'Are the beams in your office varnished?' asked Louis XV. Silhouette was struck dumb by such an unexpected query, and the king, annoyed by his silence, turned his back on him. Silhouette described the incident to Pompadour, who said: 'But sir, one must always reply to the king.' 'But . . .' mumbled Silhouette. 'Yes, sir, one replies, one says yes, one says no.' 'But I haven't noticed whether the beams are varnished or not.' 'Imbecile, do you think he is going to check up on you? Now he is in a bad mood—it will take me eight days to put you back into his good graces, and it took only one word to have you named Controller General.' Silhouette was sacked eight months later, in spite of the marquise's patronage.

D'Argenson wrote that Madame de Pompadour 'considers the king's ministers her own. She tells departing ambassadors: "Continue, I am very pleased with you; you know that I have long been your friend." ' It was of course in the interest of ministers and ambassadors to flatter the king's mistress. But the times when an appointment or a disgrace can be decisively attributed to her are few over a period of eighteen years. She persuaded Louis XV to disgrace Jean-Fréderic Phélypeaux de Maurepas in 1749. Maurepas, a minister since 1718, was widely believed to have written a scurrilous rhyme about the marquise which described her secret infirmity, a chronic discharge.

Another minister Madame de Pompadour did not like was comte Marc-Pierre d'Argenson, who served as Police Lieutenant and Secretary of War. In January, 1757, when an assassination attempt was made against Louis XV, she was separated from the king during his convalescence. She asked d'Argenson to remove hostile pamphlets from the post he showed the king, who was in a state of depression.

D'Argenson said it was not his custom to censor the king's post. The more Pompadour insisted, the more he stiffened. The marquise finally lost her temper and said: 'Sir, you have exhausted my patience and it would be useless to prolong this conversation. Your hope is that I will leave this court and the insulting advantages you would derive from my departure are clear. I have not seen the king for five days and perhaps will never see him again. But if I do, you may be sure that one of us will be banished.' After the king had recovered, the marquise again tried to sway d'Argenson. 'Sir, it is essential to keep these abominations [the pamphlets] from the king,' she said. 'He loses sleep over them; he is tormented by them. Continue to watch over his safety, but do not mention them.' 'Madame,' replied d'Argenson, 'I could not agree with you more. But tell the king, in one of those moments of kindness when he refuses you nothing, not to ask me for them. I would be only too glad to hold my tongue, but I cannot when he questions me.' 'So you would rather be a good valet and see him unhappy' snorted the marquise.

On February 1, d'Argenson was taking an aromatic bath for the treatment of his gout when a sealed letter informed him of his disgrace. He blamed it on 'that unfortunate woman.' Madame de Pompadour was also blamed for the disgrace that same month of the Secretary of the Navy, Jean-Baptiste Machault d'Arnouville. However, whereas the king's sealed letter to d'Argenson was sullen, Machault's notification of exile was cordial and regretful. Louis XV wrote Madame Infante that he had jettisoned Machault, not to please Madame de Pompadour, but to placate Parlement. 'They [Parlement] have gone so far,' he wrote, 'that they have forced me to sack Marchault, a man according to my own heart—I will never get over it.'

The two men whose careers the marquise most advanced both paid her the supreme favour of ridding her of younger, more attractive rivals. The comte de Stainville (better known as duc de Choiseul, which he became in 1758) was a pudgy, red-haired courtier with the face of a heavy-lidded mischievous child. He was famous for his wit and elegance, and was able to afford the latter because he had 'manured his lands' (married a rich woman). Destiny for him took the form of betrayal. In 1752, one of his cousins, Madame de Choiseul-Romanet, aspired to replace the marquise and was encouraged by affectionate letters from the king. Choiseul read the king's letters when he tried to persuade his cousin to leave the court and avoid a family scandal. He passed the information and some of the letters on to Madame de Pompadour, who made a scene. Louis XV hated scenes almost as much as indiscretions about his private life. He blamed Madame de Choiseul-Romanet for both and exiled her. She was pregnant by the king, and died in childbirth. Choiseul became Madame de Pompadour's protégé. He was appointed ambassador to Rome, and stayed in her good graces with gifts and witty letters. After he sent her a large opal in 1756 she had him named to the Order of the Holy Spirit and wrote to him: 'Finish your work so well begun. That is the reward I want for the blue ribbon. Dare to say after this that I am not involved in court affairs. . . .' After Rome, Choiseul was sent to Vienna with a bonus of 50,000 livres. In 1758 he was named Minister of Foreign Affairs and operated as unofficial Prime Minister until 1770, when he was banished by order of another mistress, Madame du Barry.

As Foreign Minister, Choiseul replaced another Pompadour protégé, the abbé de Bernis. It was Bernis who had been sent to Etioles in 1745 to teach the marquise the rudiments of behaviour *en ce pays-là,* as the court was known to its members. He was thus one of her earliest flatterers and became her confidant. Despite her patronage, it was a long time before she could obtain a post for the abbot, who had a reputation as an inconsequential jester. Finally, he was made ambassador to Venice, where he did surprisingly well, and in 1755 he became Minister of Foreign Affairs. Bernis rescued Madame de Pompadour when the king began showing too much interest in the marquise de Coislin, who could not keep from boasting that she had received his most ardent attentions. Bernis offered the king his resignation if there was to be another official mistress, and Louis XV decided to give her up.

Before becoming minister, Bernis had been involved in the negotiations which reversed France's traditional foreign policy and made her the ally of Austria. A Franco-Austrian alliance was the long-range goal of Prince Wenzel Anton von Kaunitz, who had served four years as Austrian ambassador to Versailles and thereafter directed his nation's destiny as chancellor, becoming known as 'the coachman of Europe.' Under the guise of extravagant foppery, Kaunitz was probably the shrewdest diplomat of his time. At Versailles he was talked about because of his intricate coiffure, called 'love's laces'—he had four valets with bellows blow the powder off his wig so that only the finest particles remained. Depending on the weather, he wore from one to nine black silk coats. At meals he picked his teeth in front of everyone with elaborate instruments of his own invention. Madame de Pompadour, who admired and understood him, said that his eccentricities were like 'Alcibiades cutting off his dog's tail, to give Athenians something to talk about and put them off what he wanted to conceal.' Kaunitz had broached the subject of an alliance in 1748 with the French Minister of Foreign Affairs, Puysieulx, but said that it was like 'trying to make a canary digest an ox.' The principal accomplishment of Kaunitz' mission was securing the friendship of Madame de Pompadour with the help of friendly letters from Empress Maria Theresa. In 1755 Kaunitz renewed his bid for a Franco-Austrian alliance and chose Madame de Pompadour as go-between. The new Austrian ambassador, Stahrenberg, brought the marquise secret proposals from the empress. Madame de Pompadour was partial to the proposals because of her friendship with Kaunitz and her dislike for Frederick II of Prussia, against whom the alliance would be directed, and whom she called 'the Attila of the north.' She brought the proposals to the attention of Louis XV. There was a great deal of resistance from his ministers, who saw no reason for an alliance with France's traditional enemy. The decisive factor was not the influence of the marquise, but the news that Frederick II had secretly concluded the Treaty of Westminster with England. France would be isolated if she turned down the Austrian alliance. Louis XV, who considered Frederick a dangerous hothead, liked the prospect of an alliance with another Catholic nation against two Protestant powers. He did not realize that Austria was bent on war with Prussia to recover Silesia. On May 1, 1756, the Treaty of Versailles was signed. It was an unpopular treaty because public opinion could not fathom why the former enemy was now the ally. After 'working for the king of Prussia' in the War of the Austrian Succession, France was now working for the Austrian empress. The treaty also precipitated France into the Seven Years' War, which destroyed her empire.

Madame de Pompadour's good offices did not make her responsible for the treaty, although she received expensive gifts from the empress as a reward. However, during the Seven Years' War she took it upon herself to tell generals in the field how to conduct their campaigns. The comte de Clermont, who had received some of her advice in the midst of a difficult retreating action on the Rhine in

1758, replied with annoyance: 'Be assured, madam, that an army does not move like a finger on a map.'

The abbé de Bernis, Madame de Pompadour's appointee, was unequal to the strain of high office. He was a whining, pessimistic hypochondriac who constantly complained of headaches and liver attacks. Like other ministers of Louis XV, he saw the irresistible decline of the *ancien régime*. 'We live like children,' he wrote. 'We shake our heads when the weather is bad and we laugh at the first ray of sunshine. Our government is directed by the will of children. We expect money as though it were due from the sky, without taking the measures to obtain it . . . it would be better to row in a galley than be responsible for affairs of state at a time when everyone is allowed to do what he wishes. Our anxieties do not make the king anxious, nor does our embarrassment embarrass him.'

In 1758 Choiseul replaced him and eventually took over the war and navy ministries, subletting foreign affairs to his cousin, the duc de Praslin. He was, like the marquise, totally committed to the Austrian alliance. He shared Louis XV's aversion for Frederick II, whom he called 'a drunken Don Quijote.' In the public mind, however, it was still Madame de Pompadour who ruled. When the Jesuits were banished it was said that she had finally obtained revenge against a Jesuit confessor who had refused to give her holy communion. Explaining history by the marquise's whims, however, only serves to obscure the forces that were challenging the monarchy.

The Jesuits represented blind submission to Rome and were thus the natural enemies of the Jansenists and the Gallican Parlement. They were a favourite target of the Philosophes. D'Alembert called them 'grenadiers of fanaticism and intolerance.' In France they were solidly entrenched. They ran the country's best schools, more than a hundred of them, and they supplied confessors to the king, which gave them a strong position at court. The order was a vigorous, conservative institution which supported all the tenets of divine-right monarchy; it was one of the last strongholds of orthodoxy in an age that questioned every traditional value and belief. Throughout Europe, however, the Jesuits were tarnishing their reputation by mixing in political affairs. They were expelled from Portugal in 1759 after becoming implicated in a plot to kill the king.

The order was wealthy, and active in business enterprises. A French Jesuit, Father de la Valette, had started a colonial trading

company in Martinique with borrowed money. But an epidemic, a
cyclone, and British privateers ruined him. One of his creditors sued
the order to recover the sum of 1,500,000 livres. Inexplicably, the
Jesuits took the case on appeal to their worst enemy, the Paris Parlement. In May, 1761, Parlement ordered them to pay their debts.
The Jesuits argued that the constitution of their order did not allow
them to. This gave Parlement the chance to examine their constitution and attack the order on more serious grounds. Parlement soon
found the Jesuit constitution seditious. The order was accused of
teaching 'probabilism, simony, perjury, prevarication, homicide,
and regicide.' The Jesuits were not allowed to speak in their own
defence. Louis XV, influenced by Choiseul, did nothing to save
them. As Choiseul wrote, 'Either Parlement had to be destroyed or
the Jesuits had to be banned . . . the king took the easiest way out,
which was the banishment of the Jesuits.' They had to relinquish
their schools and were exiled from France. This was one of the worst
inconsistencies of Louis XV's reign. After quarrelling with Parlement and the Jansenists for thirty years, with the Jesuits as his allies,
Louis XV turned against the order and closed down the schools
where respect for the monarchy and obedience to its institutions
were most convincingly taught. It was another example of the
monarchy acting against its best interests. A courtier like the prince
de Ligne was so struck by the banishment that he exaggeratedly
attributed the Revolution to it. He wrote to Catherine the Great in
1790: 'Although I am neither a prophet in my own country or a
sorcerer abroad, I said long ago that if the Jesuits had not been
expelled we would not be witnessing this damned spirit of independence, of chicanery, of definition and aridity which spreads like
a torrent and overthrows or threatens all the thrones of Europe.'

The job of official mistress was no sinecure, and its demands were
telling on Madame de Pompadour's health. She had as many daily
appointments as a cabinet minister and wrote up to sixty letters a
day. She was generally accepted as mediatrix of the king's graces.
When the president de Meinières, who had written many of Parlement's remonstrances against the king, wanted a cavalry commission
for his son, it was Madame de Pompadour he went to see, as the
only person who might mollify the king. She complained that her
life was 'like that of the early Christians, a perpetual struggle.' She
suffered from insomnia and headaches, and her digestion was poor.
She was so short of breath that she could not climb stairs, and moved

to a ground-floor apartment. Her doctor advised her to run around her room, lifting weights. In 1764 she had a bad inflammation of the lungs and knew that the time had come to put her affairs in order. She sent her pets to the naturalist Buffon and her jewellery to friends, she wrote to her husband to ask his forgiveness, and in April she died. The English ambassador, Lord Hertford, wrote that she had died poor, refuting the 'imputations of rapacity that popular clamour had thrown upon her.' Popular clamour cannot be so easily dismissed when her total expenses at Versailles are tallied—they amounted to 36,924,140 livres, or more than 2,000,000 livres a year for the eighteen years that she was royal mistress. She was, like her era, profligate and stylish. She applied the sinuous tactics of court intrigue to affairs of state, and was too easily swayed by flattery. But she had the disciplined ambition to attain a position that was not hers by birth and to defend it successfully against all contenders.

Whereas Madame de Pompadour had wanted to command, her successor wanted only to please. Madame du Barry was a docile, good-natured, easy-going beauty, quite unprepared for the campaign of slander which heralded her arrival at Versailles. Louis XV had to sack his principal minister and put pressure on members of his family to impose her on the inimical court. She was the last royal mistress, but she was not in the lineage of the Maintenons and the Pompadours. She took little or no interest in public affairs or appointments, apart from the mock appointment of her Bengalese page, Zamore, as governor of her country house in Louveciennes. She was the graceful ornament of the king's last years, who made him forget that he was sixty.

Louis XV had recruited Jeanne-Antoinette Poisson from the rich bourgeoisie. He reached much lower to find Jeanne Bécu and make her the comtesse du Barry. Jeanne's father was unknown. He may have been a monk named Brother Angel. Her mother took her to Paris when she was five and found work as a cook for a wealthy contractor. The contractor was impressed by the child's beauty and paid for her schooling in a convent until she was sixteen. Jeanne worked as a hairdresser, as companion to the widow of a tax collector, and as a salesgirl in a millinery shop. Her looks were dazzling, and they were noticed by Jean-Baptiste du Barry, a gambler who wrote off his losses as purveyor of pretty women to fashionable gentlemen. Du Barry offered to complete Jeanne's education, and gave her the more euphonious name of Jeanne de Vaubernier. She stayed with him four years. She was not a prostitute, for she had no police record and her name is not listed as an inmate of the brothel operated by Madame Gourdan, where she was widely believed to have worked. But she was the eighteenth-century equivalent of a call girl, and police reports list her as 'du Barry's current milk cow.'

It was this semiprofessional training which pleased the king, who said that he found with her 'a sensual enjoyment of an entirely new sort.' The duc de Noailles suggested that this was because Louis XV had never been to brothels. Her origins were no secret at court, where more than one lord had known her in the Biblical sense. Louis XV heard about her many admirers, and remarked: 'They say I am the successor of Saint Foix [one of her recent lovers].' 'Yes, sire,' came the reply, 'just as you are the successor of Pharamond [a Frankish chieftain of the fifth century].' Louis XV had met Jeanne in July, 1768, when she was twenty-five, and wanted her to attend court, but she needed a marriage and a title. Jean du Barry married her off to his brother Guillaume, who arrived from Toulouse for the wedding, and went home the next day without having consummated the union, but richer by the sum of 5,000 livres a year.

The duc de Choiseul encouraged a mud-slinging campaign against the comtesse du Barry to prevent her reception at court. Pamphlets describing in vivid detail her life as a Paris whore were circulated at court and in Paris. One by Pidansat de Mairobet affirmed that she had repeatedly sold her virginity with the help of astringent lotions 'which removed all vestiges of virile penetration.' Louis XV insisted on her presentation, and the comtesse de Béarn agreed to sponsor her after the king promised to pay her gambling debts. On April 22, 1769, before the court and the king, who had his arm in a sling as the result of a hunting accident, the comtesse du Barry, her hair powdered white and her delicate neck circled with diamonds, kicked back her train and made her three backward curtsies without a misstep. She sat down, as did the other ladies being presented. But after the presentations were over there was a vacant chair on either side of her.

Louis XV wrote Choiseul a carefully worded, tactful letter asking him to end his resistance to the new mistress. 'You handle my affairs well,' he said. 'I am pleased with you: but beware of intrigues and givers of advice, which is what I have always hated and what I hate more than ever. You know Madame du Barry . . . I had thought of making her acquaintance before her marriage. She is pretty, she satisfies me, and each day I advise her to beware of intrigues and givers of advice, for you can see there is no shortage of them. She has no hatred towards you, she admires your intelligence and wishes you well. The attacks against her have been horrible and for the most part unfounded. Everyone would be at her feet if . . . that is the way of the world. . . . She is very pretty, she pleases me, that should be enough. Should I take a lady of condition? If the archduchess were to my liking I would marry her with great pleasure [attempts had been made to marry the king to a sister of the Austrian empress]; but I would like to see and know her first. Her brother sought me out and did not succeed. I think my vision is clearer than his, for there must be an end to this, and otherwise I would be constantly troubled by the weaker sex. For most assuredly you will never see me take a Madame de Maintenon. I think that will be enough for this time.' It was not enough for Choiseul, who continued to snub Madame du Barry and was exiled to his castle of Chanteloup in 1770. Marie Antoinette, who had arrived in France that year to marry the future Louis XVI, joined the anti-du Barry faction and refused to speak to the king's mistress. Louis XV had to mention her behaviour to the Austrian ambassador. On New Year's Day, 1772, when Madame du Barry was paying her respects to the royal family, Marie Antoinette broke her two-year silence with the memorable words: 'There are a great many people at Versailles today.'

After the death of Louis XV Madame du Barry was briefly sent to a convent for retired actresses but was eventually allowed to return to her sumptuous home at Louveciennes, where she lived the tranquil life of a widowed mistress until the Revolution forced her to flee to England. She foolishly returned to France in 1793 and was accused of being a royalist agent and squandering the funds of the state (her total expenses in five years at court had been 12,429,559 livres). Zamore, her Bengalese page, testified against her. Fouquier-Tinville, her public prosecutor, compared her to every famous wanton of antiquity, and she was sentenced to death. As she reached the scaffold she told the executioner: 'Please don't hurt me'—words more poignant than the famous and declamatory last phrases so often put in the mouths of famous victims of the Revolution. They are somehow appropriate words for a harmless and lovely courtesan, an errant butterfly offered as a sacrifice in the name of all the ladies who had over the centuries attended the pleasures of kings.

Louis XV had banished the Jesuits to soothe Parlement, even

though he admitted that he preferred the clergy to the lawyers. He also believed that he could control Parlement through bribes. He had told Madame de Pompadour: 'Fortunately there are a few in the Parlement on whom I can count and who pretend they are very bad although they know how to soften. It costs me an abbey here, a secret pension there . . . the Regent made a big mistake in giving them back their right to remonstrate. They will finish by dooming the state.' 'Ah, sire,' said Monsieur de Gontaut, who was present, 'the state is too strong to be shaken by these little lawyers.'

But each year, the resistance of Parlement became better organized and more clamorous. In 1771, with the support of an energetic chancellor, René Nicholas de Maupéou, Louis XV suppressed the Parlements in a *coup d'état*. 'Do we have a single sovereign or is France subjected to a dozen aristocracies?' asked Maupéou. When the Paris Parlement disobeyed the king's order to sit, on January 18, 1771, Maupéou sent musketeers to the home of each member with a summation to answer by a simple yes or no whether they were prepared to carry out their duties. Nearly all refused and the following night they received sealed letters of exile. In February, the Paris Parlement was dissolved and replaced by six new councils. A common legislation for the entire nation was announced. A single court for registering laws and for appeals was established. Provincial Parlements were also scheduled for replacement. The venality of offices was abolished.

Maupéou's decree was resolutely worded. He promised what France had never had, fair and equal justice. 'The venality of offices,' he said in part, 'often prevents those most deserving by their merit and their talent from acceding to the magistrature. We owe our subjects prompt, free, and unbiased justice. Any confusion of interests can only offend the delicacy of magistrates whose duty it is to maintain the sacred rights of honour and property . . . the excessive jurisdiction of the Paris Parlement is infinitely prejudicial to those who seek justice.'

Public opinion scoffed at the 'Maupéou Parlements,' and there were recruitment problems, but they were nonetheless installed. The members of the old Parlements predicted that they would soon be back in office. They were right, for Louis XV's most vigorous and sensible decision was repudiated by Louis XVI.

The reign of Louis XV was a time for taking one's distance from absolute monarchy. The clergy refused its financial assistance, the

nobility flirted with the Philosophes or became the allies of Parlement in a conservative reaction against reform, while the Parlements
tried to become legislative bodies which could control the state's
expenditures. All these groups fought the king, although their privileges depended on a strong and stable monarchy. In addition,
popular faith in the monarchy was shaken by the rising tide of
written and oral criticism and by the scandals of Louis XV's private
life. Louis XV was still popular when he visited Le Havre in 1749.
His subjects volunteered for roadwork to catch sight of him. When
the carriages went downhill, twenty-five or thirty persons threw
themselves against the wheels to brake them. The eighteen leagues
from Rouen to Le Havre were lined with two solid hedges of people.
Only a year later, however, the duc de Luynes wrote that the king
avoided crossing Paris for 'it is probable that in present circumstances there would be few acclamations, none perhaps, at his passage.' At the end of his life, Louis XV admitted that he was no
longer the well-beloved, and had become the 'well-hated.'

To lay all the errors of the reign at his feet is palpably unfair. He
realized that the monarchy was besieged by new forces and fought
back with a few vigorous measures like the suppression of Parlements. During his reign Corsica and Lorraine were won, meagre
compensation for the loss of a colonial empire but (in the case of
Lorraine) another step in the monarchy's quest for the French
hexagonal. Louis XV had found the treasury in a terrible state and
left it not much improved, thanks to wars and court expenses. He
wavered curiously between indecisiveness and abrupt moves like the
banishment of the Jesuits and the reversal of his alliances. When he
was ably seconded by Fleury, times were good. Afterwards, the
country seemed to slip from his grasp. There was a lack of clear
planning, a failure to recognize France's real interests. He was,
finally, a rather ordinary king, but his were not ordinary times.

Louis XV died of smallpox, which in the eighteenth century killed
more people than wars. On April 27, 1774, he was at Trianon with
Madame du Barry and a few courtiers when he was stricken with
trembling and chills. He was taken to Versailles where his six
doctors, five surgeons, and three pharmacists could not agree on a
diagnosis, and therefore bled him. His pulse was taken every ten
minutes. The doctors believed the king had already had smallpox in
1728. A few days later little pink papules appeared on his face and
hands. Louis XV stared at his outstretched hands and said: 'If I had

not already had smallpox, I would think I had it now.' Only immune courtiers continued in attendance. The doctors bled the king regularly. His body was covered with pussy, suppurating boils, and the doors and windows had to be kept open because of the stench. On May 10, he died, and there was a stampede to leave Versailles. Louis XVI, his brothers, Marie Antoinette, and the royal princesses, forgot decorum and fled to Choisy. The First Gentleman of the Bedchamber, the duc de Villequier, told the First Surgeon, Monsieur d'Andouillé, to open and embalm the body. The order was a death sentence. 'I am ready,' said the surgeon, 'but while I operate you must hold the head as your own duties command.' The body was neither opened nor embalmed. No autopsy was performed. Louis XV was the first Bourbon whose heart was not cut out as tradition demanded and placed in a special coffer. He was buried almost surreptitiously. Alcohol was poured into his coffin and his remains were soaked in quicklime. On the night of the 12th to the 13th, the body was taken to Saint-Denis cemetery with an escort of three carriages, 100 guards, and pages with torches. The only courtier who accompanied the procession was the prince de Soubise. The nocturnal funeral procession passed wineshops from which drunkards shouted 'tally-ho, tally-ho,' imitating the king's high-pitched halloo when he followed the hounds.

VII

DAMIENS

FREDERICK-MELCHIOR GRIMM, a German man of letters living in Paris, is visiting his friend Denis Diderot, whom he considers a modern Socrates. He wonders why there is such a gap between philosophy, which recognizes the need for wise and benevolent rulers, and history, which allows ignorant despots to reign. The modern Socrates perorates on the contagion of virtue, the power of reason, and the invincible philosophic spirit. A valet bursts in and shouts: 'The king is dead.'

Madame Campan, who will one day become Marie Antoinette's first chambermaid, is in the middle of supper with her family and a few friends. A haggard late-arriving guest says: 'I have awful news. The king is murdered.' Two of the ladies present faint, and a soldier playing solitaire throws down his cards and says: 'I'm not surprised. It must be those rascals the Jesuits.'

It is six in the evening on January 5, 1757. Courtiers with their hands in fur muffs are shivering in the snow-covered marble court-yard of Versailles. A valet is holding open the door of a carriage and two guards rein the horses. The courtyard is lit by torch-bearing Swiss guards. The court is at Trianon, but Louis XV has spent the day at Versailles visiting his daughter, Mademoiselle Victoire. He is descending the stairway to the courtyard, leaning on the arm of his equerry, Henri de Beringhen. A shadow darts between two guards and crosses behind the king. The duc d'Ayen, captain of the 1st Guards company, orders: 'Arrest that drunkard.' 'Duc d'Ayen, someone has punched me,' says Louis XV. The shadow has dis-appeared behind the row of guards. The king touches his right side and stares at his bloody hand. 'I am wounded,' he says. 'Arrest that man but do not kill him.' The man is Robert Damiens, a forty-two-year-old unemployed servant.

The duc de Croÿ, chronicler of the minutiae of court life, when informed of the assassination attempt reflects that 'that's what happens when you talk in front of the servants.' Damiens is undressed and a horn-handled, two-bladed penknife is found in his trousers, along with thirty-five gold and silver louis. One of the knife blades is bloody. Jean-Baptiste Machault d'Arnouville, the Secretary of the Navy, orders the soles of Damiens' feet burned to make him talk. He is given an emetic in case he has taken poison.

Louis XV is also given an emetic, in case there was poison on the blade. The king is warmly dressed. The blade went through a fur-lined coat, a black velvet jerkin, a white satin shirt and a flannel undershirt before touching skin. The wound between the fourth and fifth ribs is superficial, but the king believes he is mortally struck, and says: 'I am hit and I will not recover.' Everyone is at Trianon, there are no doctors, no priests, not even sheets for his bed. Louis XV has two obsessive fears, hell and syphilis, and at this moment he dreads the approach of the former and calls for a confessor. His confession takes over an hour, and by that time his first doctor, Sénac, has arrived, pushes the confessor aside, and dresses the wound. The queen and the dauphin have also arrived. Louis XV tells the queen: 'Madam, I am assassinated.' Still convinced that he is dying, he gives the dauphin a bit of deathbed advice: 'You were born more fortunate than I. Administer this kingdom with the wisdom that God gave you. Make your people happy.'

An old soldier named Landsmath, who serves as the king's chief huntsman, hands him a chamber pot and says: 'Piss.' There is no trace of blood in the king's urine. 'Spit in my hand,' says Landsmath. There is no blood in the spittle. 'This wound is nothing,' says Landsmath. 'It missed you. Neither your lungs nor your bladder have been touched. In a week we will run down a stag together.' Landsmath opens his jerkin and displays a scarred chest. 'Look,' he says, 'these wounds were drinking troughs for flies, and I am still here.' The king keeps to his bed for nine days, with the curtains of the canopy drawn, refusing to see Madame de Pompadour because he has promised his confessor virtue in exchange for absolution. When he finally sees his mistress he says he is convinced that Parlement is involved in the assassination attempt. 'If it were not for these counsellors and presidents I would not have been struck by that gentleman,' he tells Madame de Pompadour. 'Read the indictment; it is the conversations of these men that muddled his brain.'

Damiens, a tall man with a pushed-in nose and deep-set eyes, is locked in Montgomery Tower, previously occupied by Ravaillac, the assassin of Henri IV. He is questioned eight times but his replies are incoherent. He has a history of erratic behaviour, never holding a job, stealing from his employers. Sometimes he says he acted alone, sometimes he mentions accomplices. Questioned about his motive, he replies: 'If they had chopped the heads off five or six bishops this would not have happened.' The duc de Croÿ, in charge of the inquiry, concludes that Damiens is 'an illiterate madman who has long been obsessed with attacking the king.' On March 26 he is brought before the High Chamber of the Parlement of Paris—5 princes, 22 peers, 12 first presidents, and 32 counsellors. He is charged with 'divine and human lese majesty' and sentenced to be quartered in the Place des Grèves. Every trace of his passage on earth is to be erased. His parents will be exiled from France, the house where he was born will be razed, and no other will be built on its site. Damiens tells Parlement's surgeon that he hopes he has a good seat for the execution.

On March 28, the day of the execution, he is taken to the Bonbec tower for the Question. Guards tie down his arms and legs with iron rings. One guard is filling his pipe and Damiens compliments him on his fine gold tobacco pouch. He is questioned for two hours and a half. When he is put to the torture of the boot, he screams and faints and is revived by water spiked with wine. The execution procession leaves for the Place des Grèves—two priests reciting prayers, lawyers, and guards. In front of Notre Dame, Damiens repents and declares that he has committed 'a very detestable parricide.' The execution area on the Place des Grèves, with its rows of seats, has been fenced off, and the roofs are covered with spectators. Windows overlooking the square have been rented for as much as 100 livres. An *aficionado* named George Selwyn has come from London to attend. An executioner finds him a front-row seat, saying: 'Make room for this gentleman—he is an Englishman and a connoisseur.' From a mezzanine window rented for three louis, a Venetian visitor named Giovanni Casanova watches the sixteen executioners in black uniforms and hoods prepare the scaffold, light the fire and melt sulphur in pans. Casanova wants to impress a lady, Mademoiselle de la Meure, and has invited her with her aunt and Count Tiretta de Trevise to watch the spectacle. The ladies are leaning on the windowsill, with the men standing behind them. Count Tiretta has raised the aunt's skirts to avoid stepping on them.

Damiens arrives and the crowd applauds. He lies down on the scaffold, with a mound of straw for a pillow, and his right hand, clutching his penknife, is chained to an iron bar. Heavy iron rings are placed on his shoulders and thighs. An executioner pours hot sulphur on Damiens' right hand. Another skilfully plucks bits of flesh from his arms, legs and chest with pincers. A third heats a mixture of resin, sulphur, wax, lead, and oil, which he pours into the open wounds.

Damiens screams, and Casanova turns his eyes away and puts his hands over his ears. But the ladies do not betray the slightest emotion. A young horse is hitched to each of Damiens' limbs. The horses are whipped and started but Damiens' strong body resists. The executioners, cursing, whip the horses for more than an hour. Women in the crowd call out: 'Oh, the poor horses.' Charles-Henri Sanson, the chief executioner, expertly cuts Damiens' muscles and tendons like a butcher carving a side of beef. The horses gallop off with Damiens' limbs trailing, as the crowd cheers.

Casanova again looks away and sees Tiretta's hand moving under the skirt of Mademoiselle de la Meure's plump aunt. 'For two hours,' he writes, 'I heard the rustling of cloth . . . I admired Tiretta's appetite even more than his boldness, and even more I admired the beautiful resignation of the pious aunt.' Damiens is still alive, his chest is heaving. Executioners pick up this living trunk of a man and throw him in the fire. It takes four hours to consume him and the ashes are thrown to the wind.

The king did not attend the execution, but for days he could talk of nothing else to courtiers and visiting ambassadors. Thereafter, he always kept a guard hidden near his bedroom. In 1762 a guard impatient for promotion simulated an attack on the king. He ripped his clothes, inflicted several wounds upon himself, broke his sword, and called for help. He said he had repulsed two men who had tried to force their way past him. The overzealous guard was found out and hanged after being led through the streets of Paris with a sign around his neck that said 'imposture against the safety of the king and the loyalty of the nation.'

VIII

THE KING'S SECRET

At my court I enjoy less power than an advocate at the Châtelet, over my armies less power than a Colonel. It is thanks to the Secret that I regain what I have lost. —LOUIS XV

During all of Louis XV's long reign, France was manœuvred by England, Prussia, and Austria. —ROGER GLACHANT, *Histoire de l'Inde des Français*

THE SEVENTEENTH CENTURY had its Richelieus and Mazarins, the eighteenth century its Walpoles and Pitts. The penury of gifted French statesmen is one reason for what became known as the century of English preponderance. Absolute monarchy, which lifted a king's mistakes and vacillations to the level of policy, is another. A myopic vision that blurred whatever lay beyond the limits of continental Europe is a third. Times changed, but France's diplomatic goals did not. The monarchy remained stubbornly unaware that the underlying cause of much eighteenth-century conflict, as well as the richest prize of victory, was colonial supremacy.

France in its almost definite shape, much as we know her today, is the product of three treaties signed during the minority and reign of Louis XIV. The first two, the Treaty of Westphalia and the Peace of the Pyrenees, are models of diplomatic success. French diplomats, after all, knew how to manipulate their own language, in which most negotiations were conducted. It was an advantage simply to have mastered the subjunctive tense, described in Webser's International Dictionary as 'that mood of a verb which represents an attitude toward, or concern with, the denoted action or state not as a fact but as something simply entertained in thought, contingent, possible. . . .' Finesse of language helped put a French Bourbon on the Spanish throne. Cardinal Mazarin had won for France a natural southwestern border in the Peace of the Pyrenees in 1659, along with the Rousillion and important territorial gains in Flanders. The treaty stipulated the marriage of Louis XIV and the Spanish Infanta. Once married, the Infanta would give up her rights to the Spanish throne, *moyennant* (in consideration of) a dowry of 500,000 gold crowns, which Mazarian knew the Spanish king, Philip IV, was unable to pay. The convenient word *moyennant* later helped Louis XIV press the claim of his grandson, the duc d'Anjou, to the Spanish throne, after d'Anjou had been chosen by the dying Spanish king, Charles II. The nonpayment of the debt gave France another argument for its rights to the Spanish throne. Eleven years before the Peace of the Pyrenees, the masterfully drafted Treaty of Westphalia had given France Alsace and three important fortress-cities, and reduced the Holy Roman Empire and the House of Hapsburg to a disconnected federation of small states.

The third treaty that shaped France was the Peace of Utrecht in 1713, which ended the War of the Spanish Succession. Utrecht was the start of a period of decline in the conduct of French foreign affairs that lasted almost a century, until Napoleon became emperor in 1804. Utrecht was as much a failure as Westphalia and the Pyrenees had been successes. Louis XIV recognized the claim of the House of Hanover to the British throne. The French fortifications at Dunkirk were destroyed. The dismantling of France's colonial empire began with the loss of Newfoundland and the Hudson's Bay territory to England. France failed in her attempts to annex Savoy and Nice and gained them permanently only in 1860. France restored the right bank of the Rhine to the Austrian empire and never regained it. The dominance of England in eighteenth-century foreign affairs begins at Utrecht.

The eighteenth century has been called the third Hundred Years' War. The first pitted Capetians against Plantagenets from 1154 to 1259; the second started in 1334 and was never ended by treaty, so that even Queen Victoria claimed the title of Queen of France. The third begins in 1688, with the formation of the League of Augsburg against Louis XIV, and continues until 1815, with the defeat of Napoleon at Waterloo. During that 127-year period, France and England were at war for a total of sixty years: the War of the League of Augsburg lasted nine years; the Spanish Succession, eleven years;

the Austrian Succession, seven years, followed by the Seven Years'
War; the American War of Independence, five years; the coalition
against French revolutionary governments, nine years; the coalition
against Napoleon, twelve years. True, there was a twenty-three-
year peace between the hereditary enemies, from 1717 to 1740,
thanks to the policies of two cardinals, Dubois and Fleury. But
treaties were then the most fragile of truces, to give the belligerents
time to recruit new armies and build new navies.

After 1740 France became involved in a long, fruitless period of
dynastic squabbles and profitless wars which eroded her prestige,
crippled her economy, and amputated her empire. France's foreign
policy in 1740 was based on equal parts of misconception and
European expansionism. The principal misconception was that the
Austrian Empire was still dangerous and that France, for its own
security, had to keep pursuing the goal of 'weakening Austria.' The
expansionism was based on the traditional goal of making France's
borders coincide with those of ancient Gaul. England's genius lay
in conducting successful colonial expansionism while finding continental allies to fight her European wars.

Each time there was an open succession it was questioned by other
sovereigns who showed rash contempt for the very dynastic laws
which were keeping them in power. The Spanish questioned the
French Regency after the death of Louis XIV; the French and the
Prussians questioned the accession of Maria Theresa to the Austrian
throne in 1740; the elective Polish succession was always the subject
of contention; the English succession was threatened by the Jacobites. Succession was such a problem that Gustavus III of Sweden
had to invent a sham revolt and stage a *coup d'état* to keep himself
in power in 1772. It was a time when parcels of territory were
handed out from monarch to monarch like party favours, on the
occasion of a peace treaty, a marriage, a victory, or a defeat. Thus
could Charles VI of Austria exchange Sardinia for Sicily with
Victor Amadeus of Savoy, just as they might have exchanged pieces
of furniture. Thus did obscure territories like the Banat of Tem-
esvar change hands, ceded by Turkey to Austria in 1718 at the Peace
of Passarowitz. Thus did the Austrian empire, as a result of these
many accretions, include such disparate lands as Sicily and the
southern half of the Lowlands (present-day Belgium) and stretch
from Bavaria on the west to Turkey on the east.

In the midst of this round robin of conquest, Louis XV's gift for self-delusion made him imagine that his diplomatic failures were successes. In a curious set of instructions drafted in 1757 for his ambassadors, he argued that French participation in the War of the Austrian Succession had been rewarding. He claimed that he had used Frederick II of Prussia to deprive Austria of Silesia. It was just the other way around, as Louis XV was to learn when Prussia turned against France in the Seven Years' War. The War of the Austrian Succession was started by that foremost exponent of preventive warfare, Frederick II, and served to make Prussia a major European power. There was no legitimate reason for France to enter the war. She had accepted the Pragmatic Sanction, according to which the Austrian throne could be inherited by a female successor, under whom all Hapsburg lands were to remain intact. But when Charles VI died in 1740 and was succeeded by his daughter Maria Theresa, France joined Prussia in an anti-Austrian coalition. The Treaty of Aix-la-Chapelle, which ended the war, gave rise to the Parisian expression 'as stupid as peace.' France was the victor on the battlefield but gave up all her advantages during negotiations. A popular print of the period shows a masochistic Louis XV being whipped by the Empress Maria Theresa as England recommends to 'hit him hard' and Holland says 'he will throw up everything.' The maréchal de Saxe, commander-in-chief of the successful Lowlands campaign, wrote that 'France, by giving up her conquests, was warring against herself. Her enemies remained as powerful, only she was weakened, with a million subjects less and almost no finances.' The French still use the expression 'working for the king of Prussia' to describe profitless labour.

The Seven Years' War was further illustration of the damaging inconsistencies of French policy. After devoting his reign to diminishing Austria, Louis XV in 1756 made his famous 'reversal of alliances' and became Austria's ally. Several French historians date the divorce between the king and the French people from the Austrian alliance. Louis XV was personally partial to an alliance with another Catholic monarchy. He disliked Frederick II because he was a Protestant and because he was 'a madman ready to risk everything to win .. although he has no morals, no religion, and no principles. He wants to create a stir and he will. After all, Julian the Apostate did.' France, which had a few years earlier emerged weakened from a war against Austria, was now drawn into another long war fought mainly for the interest of the Hapsburgs. It was clear that Austria

welcomed the Seven Years' War, to try to recover Silesia and reduce Prussia to a third-rate German principality. It was less clear
what France stood to gain when it agreed to mobilize a huge army
and pay annual subsidies to Austria and Russia. France had first of
all to give up her traditional foreign policy props—alliances with
Turkey, Poland, and Sweden, countries which in the past had provided second fronts against her Germanic enemies. Far more crucial,
the continental war led to an eruption of the long-smouldering
colonial conflict between France and England, and here again
French policy was woefully shortsighted.

It is a corollary of France's absorption in the quarrels of the European powers during the reign of Louis XV that not a single French
statesman grasped the importance of her colonies. France's American conquests in Canada and Louisiana were a considerable source
of wealth, but they were appallingly underpopulated. There were
only 90,000 settlers in Canada and 10,000 in Louisiana when the
Seven Years' War broke out, while there were about one million
settlers in the English colonies, who had been waiting for the chance
to push the French west of the Alleghenies and control the profitable
Canadian fishing and fur trades.

It was natural for England to understand the meaning of colonies.
Islands are inexpansible, and England had no hope of territorial
gains in Europe. France gave priority to border security and trouble-
some neighbours, problems which England did not have. England
gave priority to opening new trade routes, realizing that the fulcrum
of the balance of power was no longer somewhere east of Paris. At
a time when France was still stretching towards its natural boundaries, England was realizing its destiny as a world power. 'Rule
Britannia, Rule the Waves,' is, after all, an early-eighteenth-century
song. In England, William Pitt, Earl of Chatham, had the magnificent vision of empire, while France's Minister, the marquis
d'Argenson, said he would willingly trade France's colonies for the
head of a pin. Montesquieu wrote in his *Persian Letters* that colonies
weakened the mother country. Voltaire could not understand why
French troops in Canada were fighting over 'a few acres of snow.'
The duc de Choiseul, Minister of Foreign Affairs at the time of the
Seven Years' War, said that 'one square league in Holland is worth
more than a colony.' Canada was an icepack. Louisiana was a
swamp inhabited by cannibals. 'France can be happy without Quebec,'
was a favourite Parisian expression.

The irony is that thanks to their successful Indian policy and the quality of their leaders, the French settlers had a secure hold on their sparsely populated American empire. With help from France, they could probably have hung on to part of the vast territory. Powerful tribes like the Algonquins had settled on the banks of the Saint Lawrence and became the devoted allies of such French leaders as the marquis de Montcalm and Cavelier de la Salle. But the French settlers were hopelessly outmatched in military and naval power. There were 70,000 British regulars to back the army raised by the settlers, and 140 English ships to 60 French. Louis XV had committed his army to the campaign against Frederick II, and could not send reinforcements to the colonies. When the French navigator Louis de Bougainville was sent to Versailles by Montcalm to describe the desperate situation of the Canadian defenders, he was received by the Secretary of the Navy, Berryer, who mumbled: 'Ah, sir, when the house in on fire, one doesn't try to save the stables.' 'Not unless one happens to be a horse,' replied Bougainville.

Nothing could shake the indifference at Versailles. The duc de Choseul treated the heroic defence and capitulation of Montreal in 1760 as a joke. 'If you were counting on me for furs this winter,' he wrote to Voltaire, 'I hereby notify you that you had best address yourself to England.' To Louis XV and his ministers, the war in North America and India was an annoying marginal episode in the classic European war being fought on familiar battlefields by the usual protagonists. The bluff *coureurs de bois* and their Indian scouts who were dying for New France were as alien to the king as men from another planet. There were men who raised the storm signals, but they were ignored. The marquis de la Galissonière, governor of Canada, wrote that it should be retained at all costs, 'inasmuch as that is the only way to wrest America from the ambition of the English, and as the progress of the empire in that quarter of the globe is what is most capable of contributing to their superiority in Europe.'

Louis XV would have been astonished at the verdict of history, for the Seven Years' War has become known as the Great War for the Empire and the most important event of his reign. The results of the war were so far-reaching that historians like Lawrence Henry Gipson argue that the American Revolution is the necessary aftermath of the Seven Years' War. The meaning of the Anglo-French confrontation in North America was not the conquest of land or the emergence of England as the most powerful European power. Basically, although neither side realized it at the time, it was a struggle to decide what type of civilization was going to dominate the North American continent—a French Catholic civilization which assimilated the Indian populations, settled the country slowly, and received only sporadic support from the home country; or an English Protestant civilization, militant in transforming the land and pushing back the Indians, conscious of empire, and with strong ties to the home country, until it revolted, won its independence, and gave an example of revolution to the French.

The Treaty of Paris which ended the Seven Years' War in 1763 was one of the most humiliating episodes of the French monarchy. France abandoned India (except for five commercial counters), Canada, and the left bank of the Mississippi. Most of the French navy was at the bottom of the sea. Fortifications at Dunkirk had to be dismantled, under the supervision of an English commissioner. France still held New Orleans and lands to the west of the Mississippi, but it was clear that the Treaty of Paris was the first stage of total abandonment of the New World. Choiseul, consistent in his shortsightedness, called the Treaty of Paris 'a good joke we have played on the English.' French opinion was gulled into believing that France had lost the milk but kept the cream of her colonies. The sugar islands of the Caribbean were still French, and France still held commercial counters in India and fishing rights in America. Choiseul, reasoning like a grocer, said France had the commercial advantages without the political entanglements. French prestige sank to a low point for the century. The absolute monarchy of Louis XV suffered from comparison with the regimes of successful nations, such as England's parliamentary monarchy or Prussia's enlightened despotism. The French monarchy had through its foreign policy failures exhibited its archaism.

While Frederick II routed superior French forces at Rossbach, while General James Wolfe carried his troops over the Saint Lawrence River by night to defeat Montcalm at Quebec, while the comte de Lally, son of an Irish Jacobite and French general, surrendered to the English at Pondicherry, Louis XV was busy unravelling the threads of his secret diplomacy, which was totally unconnected with these events. Unravelling the threads in the sense of a Penelope, who at night undoes the work of the day. For one of the most mysterious matters managed by this most mysterious of monarchs was a 'Black

Cabinet' which for thirty years pursued its own policies, without the knowledge of and sometimes in direct contradiction to the programmes of his ministers.

Every eighteenth-century power employed spies and conducted secret negotiations. The times were profitable for double agents who infiltrated friendly courts and served up a weekly or monthly hash of gossip and political analysis. These sometimes amateurish secret services worked with the other departments of the government. But the Black Cabinet of Louis XV was something very different.

Louis XV had cabinet ministers following one policy with his consent, which his secret agents would then endeavour to cancel, again with his consent. There were two distinct decision-making channels, both directed by the king, but acting independently, sometimes pursuing the same, sometimes different, objectives. The king's schizophrenic conduct of foreign affairs illustrates what a complicated figure he was, not to be written off simply as a man dominated by his vices and too lazy to do an hour's work. The minister d'Argenson wrote that 'the king . . . abhors work and consequently his ministers cannot even get one hour of work out of him. He is suspicious of all of them and confides in no one.' D'Argenson did not then know about the secret diplomacy.

No mistress, no secretary, ever had access to the voluminous secret correspondence. It was kept in a desk the key to which was always on the king's person. At this desk Louis XV spent many long and patient hours bent over a cipher pad, working out in his long, slack hand the code messages that were sent to his agents in major European capitals. The secret correspondence, in which he amended and sometimes cancelled decisions he had reached the same day with his cabinet ministers, was closed with three different seals and sent by special courier. The estimated cost of the king's secret diplomacy was 10,000 livres a month. The king's upbringing and character help to explain his penchant for double diplomacy. During his minority, his guardian, the maréchal de Villeroy, had a maniacal attitude about his safety, tasting his food, inspecting his linen and even his handkerchiefs, and frightening him with stories about imaginary plots to poison him. After the death of the Regent in 1723, Louis XV remained the pupil of Cardinal Fleury for twenty years. By the time Fleury died, the king was thirty-three, at once inordinately suspicious and lacking in self-confidence. 'His views were better than those of others, but he always imagined he was wrong,' wrote the duc de Croÿ in his memoirs. He loved secrecy, first, because he was pained by the gossip about his private life, second, because it was impossible for him to trust anyone completely, and third, because he had many characteristics of the voyeur. He had, for instance, resumed Louis XIV's practice of reading his subjects' mail. The postmaster, an obsequious fellow named Robert Jarrelle, kept six clerks working full-time in a bureau with a secret entrance. With a mercury mould they made copies of the red wax seals which closed letters, melted the seals over a double boiler, copied the letters, and resealed them with the new seals struck from the mercury imprints. The clerks looked for evidence of plots against the state, criticism of the king and his entourage, and titillating stories, particularly those involving priests and seminarians. Every Sunday, Jarrelle arrived at Versailles with a briefcase bulging with private samplings of public opinion. The practice was openly criticized by François Quesnay, a leading physiocrat and Madame de Pompadour's personal physician, who said: 'I would no more dine with the Intendant of Posts than I would with the executioner.'

The secret diplomacy began in 1744, after the death of Fleury, and lasted until the death of Louis XV in 1774. It was concerned with two futile obsessions of the king—placing a Frenchman or a friend of France on the Polish throne and landing an invasion force in England. Both these plans were total failures. The remarkable thing is that, while the map of the world was changing to the detriment of France, Louis XV stubbornly continued to indulge his preoccupation with Poland. It is a little like the captain of a sinking ship worrying whether his tie is on straight. The muddled background of this minor issue is that the Elector of Saxony, Frederick Augustus, became King Augustus III of Poland thanks to Russian support, and ousted King Stanislas Leczinsky in the process. When Louis XV married the daughter of ex-king Stanislas, he tried to help his father-in-law recover his throne. Louis XV failed to grasp the eighteenth-century emergence of Russia as a European power. His attempts to bring Poland within the French orbit broke on the shield of Russian influence east of the Hapsburg empire.

In 1744, for the first time in many years, Louis XV sent an ambassador to Warsaw, the Comte de Saint-Séverin d'Aragon. The ambassador reported that there was a faction of the Polish nobility which opposed King Augustus III and would support a French-backed candidate to the elective throne. France was in the midst of the War of Austrian Succession, and the Foreign Minister, the marquis d'Argenson, paid scant attention to the dispatches of his Polish ambassador. The ambassador complained to his friend Louis-François, prince de Conti, that his dispatches were ignored. Conti persuaded Louis XV to initiate a parallel line of communication, originally intended only for Polish affairs. Conti was a visionary whose father had been elected to the Polish throne in 1697 but had never been able to occupy it. He was disdainful of the French foreign ministry officials, whom he called 'pocket viziers.' He gradually saw possibilities to regain the throne for himself and also informed Louis XV of his grand design for Europe. He wanted to contain Russia's influence, isolate Austria and build a network of French alliances with secondary powers—Turkey, Poland, Sweden, and Prussia. He still believed what Frenchmen a hundred years earlier had believed, that Austria was the gravest threat to France.

The pro-French faction in Poland obtained financial assistance from Louis XV, while the official French position was one of non-intervention. For a time there were two French ambassadors in Warsaw, an official one, who reported to the marquis d'Argenson, and a covert one, who reported directly to Conti and the king. In 1747 d'Argenson was disgraced, partly because of his opposition to the policies pursued by the Black Cabinet. In 1752, the thirty-two-year-old Comte Charles-François de Broglie was sent to Warsaw as ambassador with two sets of instructions and secret funds to advance the prince de Conti's cause. He was given an autograph note from Louis XV which said: 'The comte de Broglie will believe whatever he hears from M. le prince de Conti and will not repeat it to a living soul.' Broglie had to send double sets of dispatches, informing the king of the progress he was making with the pro-French nobles, and reassuring his minister that the country was steeped in anarchy and unimportant to France.

The treaty concluded in 1756 between Prussia and England shattered Conti's dream of a 'Northern League' allied with France and led instead to the 'reversal of alliances,' a Franco-Austrian pact. Conti was unable to digest the Austrian alliance and in 1756 the king dismissed him for 'sulking.' Two years later the comte de Broglie was recalled from Warsaw and became the new head of the Black Cabinet. The network was expanding, and at its height Louis XV had secret agents in Turkey, Holland, Sweden, Russia, England, Switzerland, Austria, Poland, and the Kingdom of Naples.

Their main purpose seemed to be to make life impossible for the accredited French ambassador. Thus, in Russia, during the Seven Years' War, the French ambassador had instructions to obtain Russia's participation in peace negotiations, while the king's secret agent had been ordered to prevent Russian participation, for fear that she would play too important a role. This was one of the reasons that made an early settlement of the war impossible.

Louis XV took conspiratorial precautions with his agents. When he sent the chevalier Douglas (a Scotch Catholic émigré) on a secret mission to Russia in 1755, he told him to pose as a fur merchant and word his reports like letters of exchange concerning the sale of pelts. If the anti-Austrian faction dominated the court at Saint Petersburg, Douglas wrote that 'ermine is fashionable this year.' If the pro-Austrian faction made gains he wrote that 'the price of lynx is going up.' He was told to use tiny handwriting and conceal his reports in the false bottom of a tortoiseshell tobacco case. The chevalier d'Eon, an agent who was to cause untold embarrassment to the king, was recruited by Conti the same year as Douglas.

'Sir, would you like to go to Russia?' Conti asked d'Eon. The Czarina Elizabeth was about to form an alliance with Prussia and England against France. D'Eon arrived in Russia disguised as a woman, with secret instructions sewn into the morocco binding of a copy of Montesquieu's *Spirit of Laws*. Later, for missions in London, d'Eon used a code in which the king was 'the lawyer,' the French ambassador, the duc de Nivernais, was 'honey,' the Minister of Foreign Affairs, the duc de Choiseul, was 'porcelain,' the Secretary of the Navy, the duc de Praslin, was 'bitter,' and he himself was 'dragon's head.' Once, the curious Madame de Pompadour picked the king's pocket and found coded correspondence from d'Eon. Confronted with the messages, Louis XV said they were 'from a woman of letters of no importance in England who has my permission to give me special news.'

The king's security measures were futile, and he was forever complaining that his codes had been broken and his messages intercepted. A good part of his autograph correspondence with agents concerned security. 'For some time I have known that England has discovered our code,' he wrote. 'Is the leak in some office? In some secret correspondence? It cannot be from my cabinet because everything is under lock and key and the key never leaves my person. I do believe it may come from Sweden; perhaps from Prussia . . .

however, let us in the future be more careful about the expedition of secret packets.' The comte de Broglie was so inept an agent that his coded messages were stolen by the Prussians while he was on a brief mission to Dresden. In Vienna, Austrian intelligence services magnanimously turned over decoded copies of secret French messages to the French ambassador, the prince de Rohan, who sent them back to the king. Thus, in most of the important courts of Europe, the French king's intelligence network was a farce. Only the French ministers and diplomats were kept in the dark, although there were exceptions. The duc de Choiseul, Minister of Foreign Affairs from 1758 to 1770, knew about the secret but considered it the innocent diversion of an ageing monarch, like a general in his dotage playing with tin soldiers.

One of the key sharers of the secret was Jean-Pierre Tercier, the first clerk of the foreign affairs ministry and 'a man who had the map of Europe in his head.' Choiseul, when he became minister, promptly kicked Tercier upstairs to direct the ministry's archives. Tercier nonetheless continued his secret role, naming parallel agents when Choiseul appointed ambassadors and receiving much of the secret correspondence at his home. When Tercier died in 1767 the king ordered his papers impounded. On the same day Choiseul approached the king and said very casually: 'I have heard that Tercier might have some letters belonging to Your Majesty.' 'I don't think so,' replied the king, 'but since he has been chief clerk someone will be sent over to see what is there.' When Choiseul was told the search of Tercier's papers had proved fruitless, he said: 'Someone was up earlier than we were.'

The king refused to believe that Choiseul knew. The tone of letters between the monarch and the comte de Broglie concerning mutual indiscretions is that of two petulant children. Broglie evidently felt that the king was incapable of keeping a secret. He complained that someone had informed Choiseul, and the king replied in August, 1768: 'Monsieur le duc de Choiseul may have notions which he is trying to confirm, but he has never mentioned your correspondence with me, so that you may be sure you have been rudely lied to. Or else you are sounding me out. In any case I answer only for myself.'

In 1770, Madame du Barry questioned the comte de Broglie about letters she had seen on the king's desk, and again the hotheaded Broglie charged his sovereign with indiscretion and the king had to excuse himself. 'Madame du Barry saw your letter about the Arras government,' the king replied. (Broglie had been offered the governorship and was holding out for something more important.) 'That was not a secret. About the large packet, she found it on my table and wanted to know what it was. I did not want to show it to her. The following day she insisted. I told her it was about the affairs of Poland, and that since you had been ambassador there, you still had contacts who reported to you. That is all I said and did. . . .'

Thus secrecy was not the forte of the king's Black Cabinet. Nor was competence. In 1763, Augustus III of Poland died and the elective throne was available once again. France's official position was that the election should be open and free. The secret policy was to support one of the Polish lords. As soon as France and Austria had announced their intention of guaranteeing free Polish elections, Russia moved in troops.

Louis XV was not prepared to fight Russia over Poland. After twenty years of efforts to put a French protégé on the Polish throne his clandestine policy had come to a disappointing end. His intrigues had proved illusory before Russian might. A Russian-backed prince, Stanislas Poniatowsky, became Polish king, and was recognized by France. In 1772 the partition of Poland by Russia, Prussia, and Austria consecrated the failure of the secret diplomacy. France watched helplessly as 'the Very Holy Trinity . . . because of the fear of the total decomposition of the Polish state' (to quote the preamble of the partition treaty) committed an act of international banditry. The holy trinity 'carved up the cake,' to use Frederick II's felicitous phrase, and in 1795, after the third partition, Poland disappeared from the map of Europe.

The king's secret, however, continued to thrive. Louis XV kept his agents in foreign courts. When Catherine the Great took power in Russia in 1762, Louis XV directed the French ambassador, the baron de Breteuil, to send him private reports: 'If there are secrets which, for special reasons, you do not wish to entrust to my minister, you must realize that there can be no secrets where I am concerned, and you must instruct me by secret means, while observing all necessary precautions to keep your letters from being intercepted.' Louis XV kept writing long, detailed letters to his agents, analysing European policy, the character of monarchs, the various court factions. But his new pet project was the invasion of England. The king's red seal was hardly dry on the humiliating Treaty of Paris that ended the Seven Years' War in February, 1763, when he began studying detailed invasion plans drawn up by the Comte de Broglie, and sending spies to study the English coastline for landing possibilities. Briefly, the plan involved a diversionary landing in Scotland while the bulk of the French fleet landed in channel ports and disembarked troops to march on London. The Spanish, if their help could be obtained, would land in Ireland.

In June, 1763, Louis XV wrote to his London agent, the chevalier d'Eon, to 'receive my orders through the Comte de Broglie or M. Tercier, on the subject of reconnaissance in England, of the coastline and the interior, and conform to all prescriptions as though they came directly from me. My intention is that [you] keep the utmost secrecy about this affair and in no case inform a living soul about it, not even ministers.'

The following month the marquis de la Rozière, an army engineer, left for England to inspect beachheads. After studying the problems of a French landing in England, logistics, transportation, bivouacs, occupation of London, de la Rozière returned to France and spent months studying the French Atlantic coastline, from Dunkirk to Saint Jean de Luz. In January, 1765, however, the plan to invade England was compromised by a complication which also proved highly embarrassing to the king. A courier for the comte de Broglie named Hugonnet, on his way to London with unciphered messages, was arrested at Calais on suspicion of espionage. Hugonnet was thrown into the Bastille, along with a secretary of the comte de Broglie named Drouet, who had signed the messages. The king's secret was threatened with exposure. The imprisoned man, if questioned, would admit that they had been acting not for a foreign power but for the French sovereign. To prevent this ludicrous denouement, Louis XV had to resort to involved stratagems. He summoned the chief of police, Gabriel de Sartine, and sheepishly confided that the two men in the Bastille were his agents. Sartine agreed to remove incriminating material from the impounded papers found on Hugonnet. Then the governor of the Bastille, Jumilhac, had to be let in on the secret, so that the two prisoners could be coached before questioning. They were told to say they had acted alone. The inquest was conducted by the duc de Praslin, who said afterwards: 'Someone is making a fool out of me.' Drouet was released, but Hugonnet languished in the Bastille for thirty months. The king made no effort to help him.

In June, 1765, the comte de Broglie gave the king his invasion plan. He observed that France had been twice defeated by England in primarily naval wars. He proposed an unprovoked war on England, pointing out the advantages of a surprise attack. The resources of the kingdom had been underestimated, he said, despite the drain of the Seven Years' War. He proposed that the Spanish navy join in the initial attack, which would consist in seizing and destroying the largest possible number of British ships, and looting the English trading posts in India. A blow to English naval might and English commerce would be a favourable start for the war. In the next phase, Spain would draw away British forces with diversionary tactics—the siege of Gibraltar, an attack on Jamaica, a raid on Ireland, and a troop concentration on the border of England's ally Portugal. Next, an invasion army of 60,000, protected by a Franco-Spanish fleet, would make cross-Channel landings at Rye, Winchelsea, Hastings, and Pevensey, and converge on London.

Louis XV already saw himself as a second William the Conqueror, marching into London at the head of his troops and avenging France for humiliations dating back to the Hundred Years' War. But Broglie's grandiose plans strained the limited means of the secret diplomacy. To invade England, negotiations must be begun with Spain and alliances signed with Austria and the Northern powers. Louis XV's first impulse was always enthusiasm, but then projects often slipped into a kind of limbo. Broglie knew the invasion would be stillborn unless it were sponsored by the Ministry of Foreign Affairs. Louis XV was reluctant to mix secret and official affairs, but finally allowed Broglie to present his plan to the duc de Choiseul, without mentioning that it already had royal approval. Choiseul examined Broglie's project, promised to mention it to the king, and suggested an inspection of French coasts. All the work that had been done secretly now had to be repeated officially. In March, 1768, an Irish officer at the service of France named Brawn went home on a secret mission and reported that Ireland was ripe for a French landing. The project was still under examination in 1770, when Choiseul was disgraced. His successors showed little interest. The king, in his last years of life, became resolutely peace-minded. The bellicose de Broglie fell out of favour and was exiled to his castle in Normandy. The English invasion plan, like the king's Polish ambitions, was shelved. The king's secret diplomacy was not destined to have tangible results, but to remain a network of private information, a source of ideas, a royal plaything like the Deer Park and the château of Compiègne.

The king's London agent, the chevalier d'Eon, embodied all the flaws of the secret diplomacy: he went to great lengths to perpetrate an absurd masquerade, he was rash, obsessed with trivia, flamboyantly indiscreet, and incapable of grasping important issues. One reason Louis XV dropped the English invasion plan was exasperation with d'Eon. It would have been hard to find a more inappropriate secret agent. Charles Geneviève d'Eon de Beaumont had first used a transvestite disguise in Russia, where he claimed to have become, as the lady of breeding Lia de Beaumont, the confidant of Czarina Elizabeth. He seems rather to have earned a reputation for tactlessness. When a Russian officer observed that with his pink face and powdered hair he looked like the Christ child, he replied: 'You are right, for I am in a very filthy manger.'

Louis XV was grateful for his services, however, and gave him a diamond-encrusted tobacco case and a captain's commission in a dragoons regiment. He served as aide-de-camp to the maréchal de Broglie, and was wounded in the head and thigh and cited for gallantry in the Seven Years' War. In 1762 he was sent to England as the king's agent, again dressing as a woman, and encouraging the gossip that he belonged to the fair sex. He developed a persecution mania, imagining that the official French ambassador, Monsieur de Guerchy, wanted to have him killed. He adopted a tone of deliberate insolence in his official dispatches, at one point writing to Guerchy that he was a stupid and evil thief. D'Eon's erratic behaviour came to the attention of Broglie and Tercier, who realized that the king's secret was in thoroughly unreliable hands. Tercier wrote d'Eon a letter that was a miracle of tact, in which he said: 'I beg you to abstain from jests, which although excellent in their place, can only offend and have a worse effect than was intended . . . you cannot betray the king who has confided in you . . . we have too high an opinion of your zeal to believe that you would prefer movements of temper to duty.' D'Eon ranted in reply that he was being subjected to 'diabolical injustices, infamies, vexations on the part of the inexorable sacrificers of public affairs, who form a triumvirate of illustrious crooks. I think they have sworn to usher me into a better world . . . we are ruled by knaves who want to invade and engulf everything . . . but I, with one blow, will destroy the column and the mountain of their lies.' D'Eon's behaviour finally led to his recall, but he refused to leave England. He did not hesitate to blackmail the king to finance his continued stay there. He had an autograph note from Louis XV confirming his mission and mentioning 'the subject of the reconnaissance of England.' What would the English say if they learned that the king of France, a few months after signing a peace treaty, had sent spies to England to plan an invasion?

When process-servers came to d'Eon's London apartment to recover the papers in December, 1763, he shouted that he would die first, grabbed a loaded rifle, and pointed it at them, saying: 'The king's papers are at the end of the barrel, come and get them.' D'Eon's next outburst was the publication of his private correspondence with French ambassadors and with the Minister of Foreign Affairs. The frontispiece inscription was a quatrain by Voltaire with the line: 'Pardon the soldier who is a bad courtier.' He omitted papers dealing with the king's secret, but the published correspondence nonetheless caused a scandal in London.

To retrieve his compromising note, Louis XV had to negotiate for three years with d'Eon as with an equal. In 1766 d'Eon returned the autograph note, which was concealed in a false brick in his cellar, against an annual pension of 12,000 livres. However, he still had his secret correspondence with the comte de Broglie, including the detailed invasion plans. He turned this correspondence over for safe-keeping to two members of the English Parliament, Mr. Cotes and Lord Ferrers. Louis XV had to humour him, keeping him on as a secret agent while specifying in the margin of a letter: 'Do not employ d'Eon for anything.' D'Eon continued sending political reports and was used for certain menial tasks, like buying off the authors of anti-French pamphlets.

The secret agent had become a London celebrity. Bets were made in coffeehouses and taverns on whether he was endowed with what the French call 'Father Barnabas' crutch.' He was offered £1,000 to divulge the secret of his sex. Voltaire called him 'amphibious,' and verses were written about him: 'Hail, thou production most uncommon, Woman half man and man half woman.' Horace Walpole, who met d'Eon at dinner, was not impressed. 'I found her loud, and vulgar,' he wrote. 'In truth I believe she had dined a little on dragon. The night was hot, she had no muff or gloves, and her hands and arms seem not to have participated in the change of sexes, but are fitter to carry a chair than a fan.' Even Louis XV's curiosity was aroused, and in July, 1772, the comte de

Broglie was able to report: 'The suspicions we had about the sex of this extraordinary individual are founded. Drouet [Broglie's secretary], whom I had asked to verify the matter, assured me upon his return that he had been able to do so and could certify, after a careful examination, that the said sire Eon was a girl and nothing but a girl, with all the attributes and the periodic distresses. What is curious is that she had never had the least attraction for pleasure, although in her conversation she indulges in all the liberty which her dress authorizes.' The king replied: 'D'Eon's sex is a mighty strange thing. Make sure she does not trick us with her changes.' Louis XV died in 1774 believing d'Eon was a woman, and bequeathed to his successor, Louis XVI, the unexpected burden of his secret diplomacy. Since there was no more Poland and since the England invasion plan had been momentarily forgotten, the only unresolved matter was what to do about d'Eon. Louis XVI decided that the secret diplomacy was a dangerous extravagance and wrote to the comte de Broglie: 'This correspondence is useless.' He ordered the agents recalled and the correspondence burned. He sent an envoy to London to retrieve the remaining papers in d'Eon's possession. D'Eon, who had already successfully blackmailed one king, replied with a preposterous expense account which included items like 'reimbursement for a 6,000-livres diamond I should have but did not receive from Prince Poniatowski during my mission in Saint Petersburg.' 'I have never seen such impertinent and ridiculous demands,' wrote Louis XVI to Broglie. 'If he did not hold important papers I would send him packing.'

Louis XVI entrusted the delicate negotiations with d'Eon to the picaresque author of *The Marriage of Figaro,* Pierre-Augustin Caron de Beaumarchais. Travelling under a false passport made out to the 'chevalier de Ronac,' Beaumarchais had already carried out several secret missions under Louis XV. Arriving in London, Beaumarchais was startled to find a delicately featured, fine-boned woman who appeared younger than her forty-three years and who, modestly lowering her eyes, admitted that she had all the attributes of her sex. Beaumarchais was touched and wrote to Louis XVI: 'When one considers that this persecuted creature belongs to a sex to whom everything is forgiven the heart is moved to sweet compassion.' D'Eon convinced Beaumarchais that he was the victim of a thousand injustices. He played on the playwright's vanity by feigning an ardent infatuation. Beaumarchais wrote to his Foreign Minister, the comte de Vergennes: 'Everyone says the girl is mad about me; but who the devil would have imagined that to serve the king well in this matter I would have to become the gallant of a captain in the dragoons?' His vivid imagination led him to compare d'Eon to Joan of Arc.

Assisted by these tender feelings, the negotiations came to a successful end in October, 1775. D'Eon agreed to turn over the secret correspondence in return for an increase in his pension and a safe-conduct to France. The only condition was that he would be 'prohibited from appearing in the kingdom with any other clothing than that suitable for women.' D'Eon agreed to 'publicly declare my sex, to end all equivocation as to my condition, and to wear women's clothes until my death.' He was authorized to wear his royal decoration, the cross of Saint Louis, in his corsage. He promised to leave his male attire in England and was given 2,000 crowns for a trousseau. On October 21, 1777 ('Saint Ursula's day,' as d'Eon said), the chevalier appeared at Versailles with a fashionable three-decker coiffure and a blue taffeta dress with a puce border. The contrast between his fashionable costume and his blue chin and dragoon's stride kept the court laughing for days. He was then exiled to his home in Tonnerre, where he settled down to the peaceful existence of a lady of independent means, answering the letters of the curious. In 1781 he was invited to a banquet given by his old regiment and replied: 'Sir, the sensitivity of a young girl's heart added to that of an old dragoon captain was touched by your invitation.'

Eventually, however, he returned to England, where he had made many friends and would not be so closely watched. He died in 1810 at the age of eighty-three, the last survivor of the king's secret diplomacy. He did not take his own secret to the grave. On May 25, 1810, there appeared in the London *Times* an autopsy notice signed by T. Copeland, Surgeon, Golden Square, which read: 'I hereby certify that I have inspected and dissected the body of the chevalier d'Eon, in the presence of Mr. Adair, Mr. Wilson, and the père Elisée, and have found the male organs in every respect perfectly formed.' Confirming the findings of the autopsy is an autograph letter in the British Museum's Slade collection, signed by a notary public named George Silk who had viewed the corpse: 'I . . . can assure you that the late chevalier, called when living Mlle. d'Eon, had the visible organs of generation of a male, and was a very man.'

IX

FONTENOY

The battle of Fontenoy gave the monarchy a forty-year reprieve.

—NAPOLEON

THE GREAT war machine that had echoed with the names of warriors who made Europe tremble, like Condé and Turenne, was creaky and corroded. The armed might that had policed Europe for more than a century was wasted in a series of useless wars. The reigns of Louis XIII and Louis XIV had kept the engravers of victory medals busy. The reign of Louis XV was, with one great exception, notable for defeats. At the Saxon village of Rossbach in 1757, Frederick II routed a French army twice the size of his own, which was led by a protégé of Madame de Pompadour, Charles de Rohan, prince de Soubise. 'I am writing to Your Majesty in boundless despair,' reported Soubise with considerable candour after the battle. 'The rout of your army was total. I cannot tell you how many of your officers were killed or captured.' For centuries the coalition armies of Europe had feared what the Italians called *la furia francese*. Under Louis XV, French generals fled from the field. Prince Louis de Bourbon Condé, a descendant of the Grand Condé, reached friendly lines during a rout and asked: 'Where are the others?' 'You are the first, Monseigneur,' he was told. Examples of cowardice became common. After the defeat of Dettingen in 1743, the comte de Choiseul accused the duc d'Ayen of hiding behind his horse during the fighting. The comte de Saint-Germain, later Minister of War under Louis XVI, covered the Rossbach retreat, and wrote to a friend in Paris: 'I am commanding a band of thieves and assassins, who run without firing a shot and are always ready to mutiny . . . never has an army fought so poorly.

The king has the worst and most undisciplined army on earth . . .
our nation has no more military spirit; honour has been abolished. One can only tremble when leading troops, and expect the
worst.'

The decline of the army was linked to the decline of the aristocracy. Nowhere in Europe (except Prussia after the Sergeant-King)
was the aristocracy's function so exclusively military as in France.
In other kingdoms the nobles still held political power. In France,
the Gothic prejudice that the nobility's principal duty was to pay
the blood tax on the battlefield still held sway. The origin of the
nobility's privileges lay in its readiness to die by the sword when
summoned. There was an almost mystical belief in the nobility's
heroism and willingness to spill its own blood. The belief no longer
corresponded to reality. The aristocrat-warrior had become the
aristocrat-courtier. His function had decayed from fighting in
defence of the king to paying attendance on him. Feudalism was
extinct. The external characteristics of a martial caste atrophied
like the second horn on a rhinoceros. Tapestries replaced armour
on the walls of feudal castles, the moats were stocked with fish, and
the towers became dovecotes. The sword the nobleman wore at his
side for protection became a foil, a mere mark of distinction. The
king's elite guard, the Maison du Roi, included a high percentage
of young noblemen. In the seventeenth century, Marlborough had
said in tribute to its courage: 'You cannot defeat it, you can only
destroy it.' Under Louis XV, it became a band of highly born, effete
youths who escaped discipline because they answered directly to
the king. And under Louis XVI it was reduced to a symbolic unit
because it was considered expensive and useless.

The nobility still clung to army commissions, less from a willingness to fight than as a source of privileges. Since the army was one
of the few careers open to them, they wanted to keep it exclusively
theirs, even though they were 'more often seen in salons doing petit
point than on battlefields.' At the same time, the army was subjected
to the venality of offices. Commissions were sold like meat at a
butcher's, and wealthy commoners could raise their social standing
by buying a regiment. The price varied from 25,000 to 75,000 livres
in the infantry and could reach 120,000 livres in the cavalry. Thus,
the army was the simultaneous victim of the nobility's efforts to
monopolize commissions and the central government's promptness
to sell them. Unnecessary commissions were created to raise money

and made the army top-heavy. The Minister of War in 1787, the comte de Guibert, found that there were 1,261 generals for an army of 200,000 men, a greater number than the combined total of generals in all the other European armies. A commission could be bought at any age, and there were teenage colonels called 'bib colonels.' The prince de Montbarey was wounded in battle at the age of twelve, with his tutor by his side. Buying a regiment was also an investment, and a few unscrupulous regimental commanders created non-existent companies so they could sell captaincies and lieutenancies. The nobility grumbled that too many commoners were becoming officers, and was able to have restrictive measures enacted. In 1750 Louis XV founded a Military Academy financed by a tax on playing cards and restricted to the provincial nobility, often too poor to afford commissions. The Academy did not necessarily produce the best officers, and Taine wrote that at examinations for artillery commissions, the noble cadets lacked ability and the able cadets lacked nobility.

In 1775, the comte de Saint-Germain, a provincial nobleman and an officer who had been promoted in the field, became Minister of War and decided to put a stop to the abuses of bartered commissions by ruling that all officers must henceforth prove four degrees of nobility. Thanks to this measure, which he inspired, but which was not enacted until 1781 under a new minister, the comte de Ségur, commoners were excluded from the officer corps in the final years of the *ancien régime*. In 1789, out of a total of eleven Marshals of France, there were five dukes and one prince; there were 109 infantry regiments, and only 6 untitled regimental commanders; there were, out of 10,946 officers, 8,001 nobles, 1,100 soldiers of fortune (promoted in the field), and 1,845 commoners. Saint-Germain's intentions were full of merit—he wanted to make the army a fighting force at the service of the king rather than a piece of property belonging to a group of rich officers. But in doing so he served the feudal reaction and angered the bourgeoisie. In 1787, the comte de Guibert enacted even more drastic reforms to ease the financial burden of the army. He reduced the size of a number of famous but undisciplined regiments. He replaced the Military Academy of Paris with twelve provincial military colleges. There were eighteen Marshals, whose pensions totalled 2 million livres a year, and Guibert said that 'with this sum the Emperor of Austria and the King of Prussia pay nearly all their generals'; he reduced the number of

Marshals to twelve. He reduced the number of superior officers and increased the pay of the simple soldier.

Reform-minded war ministers could do little about the ingrained court habits which officers took with them on military campaigns. Frederick II, who repeatedly defeated larger French forces during the Seven Years' War, said that he had found fifty cases of lavender water among the loot at Rossbach. Officers went to battle with their carriages, their valets and their mistresses. The chevalier de Quincy even took his bass viola to the front, because he found it was useful in his amorous pursuits. Officers carried tons of luggage and insisted on eating elaborate meals off silverware during sieges. An army on the march looked like a gypsy caravan, with horse-drawn cannon, slogging foot soldiers, the emblazoned barouches of officers, sutlers' wagons, and carts full of camp followers. The latter were such a problem that in 1760 the duc de Broglie had their faces blackened with a product said to be indelible for six months so they could be kept out of his camp. Entire shopping centres followed the armies, despite the soldiers' reputation for not paying. Thanks to the stately pace of eighteenth-century warfare, campaigns dragged on for years, with armies hibernating during the winter months and laying sieges that lasted through spring and summer.

The deterioration of the army was an accepted fact. When the duc des Cars bought the Cambrai regiment of dragoons in 1774, his friend the marquis de Castries told him: 'Your regiment has always attracted attention because of its ignorance and lack of discipline—you will find it full of gamblers and drunks; as for the cavalry officers, half of them do not know how to ride and the other half do not own horses.' Soldiers were no better than their officers. The esteem in which they were generally held is illustrated by the signs which prohibited the use of public gardens to 'dogs, whores, lackeys, and soldiers.' Little could be expected from soldiers shanghaied by recruitment officers who worked on commission and offered any able-bodied man over the age of sixteen willing to eat the king's bread for six years a 30-pound enlistment bonus plus one louis for every inch over five feet.

Desertions were so common that the Minister of War d'Argenson supplied this astonishing statistic: 30,000 deserters were put to death between 1728 and 1732. The only way to keep the army from dissolving altogether was to pursue deserters relentlessly. Pyrenees border posts built to keep invaders out now served to keep deserters in. The execution designed to impress would-be deserters involved slicing off the nose and ears, branding a fleur-de-lys on the cheeks, and hanging. For minor infractions, soldiers ran a gauntlet of their comrades-in-arms armed with switches as drummers beat a special charge. When the comte de Saint-Germain tried to replace this primitive punishment with Prussian-style beatings with the flat of a sword, there was such a hue and cry about the blow to French pride that the gauntlet was restored.

There were still incidents of gallantry and unsung heroes in the French army. At the siege of Prague in 1742, when French troops were scaling the ramparts with ladders, there was this classic exchange between Colonel François de Chevert and an unnamed sergeant:

> 'You will climb the ladder.'
> 'Yes, sir.'
> 'The sentry will fire at you.'
> 'Yes, sir.'
> 'He will miss you.'
> 'Yes, sir.'
> 'You will kill him.'
> 'Yes, sir.'

But out of the crowd of pink-cheeked, dimpled, powdered 'little generals,' there emerged no leaders. The scarcity of military talent was so acute that in 1744 the bastard son of a Saxon Protestant prince became commander in chief of the French army. Maurice de Saxe was a perfect example of the eighteenth-century condottiere who could say, like Sir John Suckling: 'I can fight, whether I am i' the wrong or right, devoutly.' His father had become King Frederick Augustus II of Poland due to one of those accidents of succession common to the period. His mother was the Swedish Countess Maria Aurora of Koenigsmarck, the king's long-time mistress.

Born in 1696, Maurice de Saxe went to war when he was twelve and fought in the Hungarian and Russian armies against the French until he was twenty. He served in the coalition army under Marlborough and Prince Eugene of Savoy which defeated the French at Malplaquet. In 1720 he joined the French army and eventually served against his own half brother in the War of the Polish Succession. For when Saxe's father died in 1733 there were two pretenders to the Polish throne: Stanislas Leczinsky, the father-in-law of Louis XV, who had already been forced out of Poland once, and Saxe's brother, Augustus III, who was supported by the Russians and Austrians.

Son of a king and brother of a king, Maurice de Saxe was haunted by the idea of sovereignty. He was briefly Duke of Courland, a tiny Baltic duchy between Prussia and Latvia. But his election was revoked thanks to Russian pressures and he left to seek his fortunes elsewhere. Later, when he was overwhelmed with honours by Louis XV, he asked for sovereignty over the island of Madagascar, which he wanted to settle with impoverished German families. When that was refused he seriously considered founding a Jewish state in America. He wanted to be king of the Jews. Disappointed in his regal ambitions, his natural habitat became the battlefield. Peace was to him the name of the interval between wars. He said once that 'generals are like raincoats. No one thinks of us except when it pours.' He might have added that he lived in an age when it rained constantly, and could have said with Othello that 'the tyrant custom . . . hath made the flinty and steel couch of war my thrice-driven bed of down.' He was in fact accused of prolonging wars by refusing to pursue a defeated enemy. His aide-de-camp, the marquis de Valfons, wrote that he was 'too important in time of war to wish for peace and obtain it thanks to decisive action.' Saxe's reply to critics was: 'I know that worthy Paris bourgeois who live between their butcher and their baker are shocked because I do not make my army advance ten leagues a day.'

His feats of bravery in the War of the Austrian Succession led to his nomination as commander in chief of French forces and Marshal of France. He was the first Protestant to be thus honoured. He had the right to be addressed as 'dear cousin' by a king whose great-grandfather had revoked the Edict of Nantes. He thereby earned the envy of other French generals, who spent their time second-guessing him and derisively said that 'he fought like a Tartar.' However, he knew how to wage successful campaigns and amuse the king. When he captured Ghent, a city famous for its veal, he announced the victory by sending Louis XV a side of veal in a basket. When he was nominated for the Académie Française, he replied that he could not even spell, let alone write.

His military strategy was based on suspicion of firepower. This was a curious attitude at a time when improved weapons were changing the classic pattern of attack. With the introduction of light field artillery like the Swedish 600-pound cannon that could fire ten rounds a minute, battles could no longer be won, as they had been in the seventeenth century, with massive charges in open fields. Generals were slow to adapt their tactics to improved weapons (it seems to be a rule of warfare that strategy lags behind weaponry). Troops still advanced in great glutinous masses, as though obeying an enemy injunction to form the ideal artillery target. Engravings of eighteenth-century campaigns show the long rows of soldiers lined up as though for a parade. Against the evidence of the battle-field, French generals (with the exception of Saxe) continued to insist on the use of the massive advance as better suited to the pugnacious French temperament. It was also supposed to give the soldier a sense of security to advance in a herd, elbow to elbow. The musket-armed infantry was lined up three or four deep, with the first row kneeling when it stopped.

All the rows fired together, and there followed a long moment of total helplessness as all the rows reloaded. The English system of three alternately firing rows was more successful. Battles were fought with a kind of stately lethargy, for it took the troops hours to deploy in their cumbersome units. The problems facing the eighteenth-century infantryman are described in this extract from a French military manual on the correct method of firing: 'Tear off the cartridge case with your teeth and pour powder into the pan; close the pan, holding it with two fingers; bring the gun upright and ram the cartridge down the barrel with a single stroke of the rod; aim along the top of the barrel.' With this easy-to-do-it system, a deft soldier could fire one round a minute with an effective range of 300 yards. The French had finally adopted the iron ramrod introduced by Frederick II and the fixed bayonet introduced by the Swedish King Gustav III. But the 1717 model musket still in use remained an unwieldy affair, so heavy that foot soldiers wore little bags of bran on one shoulder to cushion the stock, so long that when firing from a prone position the barrel had to be held up with a kind of fork.

The effectiveness of light field artillery required from generals a more intelligent use of the terrain, flanking movements, separate missions for separate corps, and light infantry to be used for harassment. Maurice de Saxe understood all this, and preferred a defensive position where he could dig in and make full use of the terrain for large-scale, massive attacks. Ultimately, he believed, battles were won by the army which held the best position, and by cold steel at close quarters. 'I have seen entire salvos that did not kill four men,' he wrote, 'and I have never seen any, nor, I think, has anyone else, which did enough damage to stop an advance and the vengeance of great bayonet thrusts through the kidneys and point-blank gunfire; that is where the damage is done. . . .' As two battalions moved towards each other, he believed, the advantage went to the one that held its fire. Firing early, he wrote, 'is more noisy than harmful and always leads to defeat.' Although he had too much confidence in the devastating effect of bayonet attacks and did not fully grasp the advantages of field artillery (Frederick II was the first to use mounted artillery teams which could move a cannon over the battlefield with relative speed), Maurice de Saxe's campaigns are the link between the battles of Condé, which were won by the cavalry, and the battles of Napoleon, where artillery had become decisive.

The fragile equilibrium of eighteenth-century Europe seemed to require constant wars in which allies changed like partners in a quadrille. The only constant factor was that after 1740 France and England were always on different sides. It was during the War of the Austrian Succession, from 1740 to 1748, when France fought an Austro-English coalition, that Maurice de Saxe earned his page in French history books. In 1745 he chose Fontenoy, a Flemish hamlet in a valley between the Escaut River and thick, ravined woods, as the ideal site to wait for advancing English and Hanoverian armies. The low fields of Flanders were the French kings' favourite battlefields. They were not French soil, they were the only common border between France and its frequent enemy, the Austrian empire, and they offered an excellent view of the action whenever the king and his court chose to visit the front. The armies could be deployed as though for a *Kriegspiel*, with the king watching the magnificent spectacle from a safe but neighbouring hilltop. The population was accustomed to being fought over and went placidly about its occupations, indifferent to wars, the causes of which they usually ignored. The political map of the Low Countries was as patchy as a Harlequin's coat, but its geography was particularly suited to eighteenth-century warfare.

The campaign of 1745 began sluggishly. The contending armies faced each other for months without combat. Maurice de Saxe, once so strong that he could bend a nail into the shape of a corkscrew with one hand, was so weakened by dropsy that he had to travel in a small wicker carriage he called his cradle. He was content to fight the slow, classic war of sieges. In April he broke the trench before the fortress of Tournai, part of the so-called 'Barrier,' a line of defensive positions built by the Dutch at the end of the seventeenth century. But upon learning that a large allied force was moving towards him, he moved the bulk of his troops to the Fontenoy position, leaving behind 30,000 men to continue the Tournai siege.

Saxe had been studying battle positions for months. He knew the coalition army was spread over a 250-mile front, from Ostend to Luxembourg. He knew the allies had been paralysed by disunity, finally placing at their command the twenty-two-year-old Duke of Cumberland, second son of King George II. The allied army advancing towards him, Saxe knew, could not be superior to his own in size and was commanded by a brave but inexperienced youth seconded by an ancient veteran, the seventy-five-year-old Austrian Marshal Koenigsegg. He had enough time to prepare a strong defensive position through which the allies would have to pass to reach Tournai. His army of 56,000 men had its back to the sea, it was cut off from Paris and supply lines, and its precarious escape route was three bridges over the Escaut River. Retreating troops would probably panic at the river, and he would have to abandon his artillery. Above all, he was risking the capture of the king, who had decided to attend the battle. But Saxe was confident that he could mousetrap the allies at Fontenoy.

As it happened, he was right, and gave the French monarchy its last great victory. Voltaire wrote that French kings had done nothing so glorious for 300 years. The presence of Louis XV and the dauphin turned the battle into an historic event. It was considered part of the 'royal profession' to attend battles. The king at the head of his troops was an image that stirred the hearts of his subjects. From a safe vantage point, he could watch his men fight and die, convinced that his presence was inspiring them to heroism. Louis XV had already made the traditional wartime pilgrimage to the Low Countries twice. In 1744 he had fallen gravely ill while joining his troops at Metz. Now, in the spring of 1745, the prospect of a full-scale exercise in eighteenth-century armed choreography brought him back to the front.

In addition, here was an opportunity to settle a 400-year-old score with France's hereditary enemy. French and English royalty would be meeting on the battlefield for the first time since the stinging defeats of the Hundred Years' War. At Crécy in 1346 the English longbowmen under King Edward III had annihilated the ponderous French cavalry led by King Philippe VI. At Poitiers ten years later King Edward's son, the Black Prince, had taken prisoner the French King Jean le Bon and his son, Philippe le Hardi. Louis XV, who was concerned about his drop in popularity, saw in Fontenoy a glorious opportunity for redemption. Leaving Versailles on May 6 with the sixteen-year-old dauphin, he reminded the courtiers in his entourage that no French king had won a personal victory from the English since Saint Louis in the thirteenth century. Fontenoy was the high point of his reign. Forgetting his natural timorousness, he would willingly have died at the head of his troops. At one point of the battle he donned his breastplate so that he could join a cavalry charge and had to be forcibly restrained. He moved within range of the British artillery and one of the horses in his personal guard was killed. When a cannonball fell near him, he said with regal disdain: 'I want nothing from these people. Pray return it to them.' Saxe gallantly said that the presence of the king was 'worth 5,000 men, as much for the morale of our troops as for the impression it will make on the enemy, which does not think we are here in force.' Privately, he considered the king's presence a mixed blessing. He was not only responsible for winning the battle, but for the king's safety. He had to divert troops to protect the royal entourage. He had to reserve a bridge over the Escaut for an eventual royal retreat and man it with three battalions of guards.

Moving across the green fields of Flanders with his 51,000 men, Cumberland was confident of victory. He planned to destroy Saxe's army at Tournai while the duc d'Arenberg defeated a second French army led by the prince de Conti on the Rhine, after which the two victorious armies would meet in Paris. Cumberland boasted that if he did not reach Paris he would eat his boots. To which Saxe later replied that he would be glad to cook them. Cumberland's optimism was shared by the allies. The Minister of Sardinia at the Hague looked forward to new French trophies for his museum. At a dinner given by Lord Chesterfield in London, the envoy of the Elector of Cologne wondered aloud which member of the coalition would be responsible for French prisoners.

Saxe was criticized by his officers for immobilizing part of his troops at the Tournai siege. Moreover, he was himself a casualty before the battle had begun. 'Doctors gave him at most a few months to live,' wrote the duc de Luynes. His doctor, Sénac, had accompanied him to the front and treated his dropsy with punctures, extracting pints of liquid each time. He could not ride a horse, and kept to his wicker carriage, drawn by two horses. And yet he was so suspicious of the French officers under his command that he insisted on making every decision himself and on being everywhere at once. The only officer he trusted was Count Ulrich von Lowendal, like him an adventurer and a professional soldier, who had previously fought against the French for the Elector of Saxony, and like him a royal bastard, for he was the natural son of the king of Denmark.

Tournai was girdled with forests, and Saxe reasoned that Cumberland's army could reach the fortress only by crossing an oval field half a mile wide and about a mile long. The field, four miles from Tournai, was bounded by woods and the twisting Escaut River. Saxe preferred to leave the initiative of attack to the enemy so long as he could choose the field of battle. The steep, narrow ravines between the patches of wood were considered unpassable by an armed column. The villages of Fontenoy, in the centre of the oval field, and Antoing, on the bank of the Escaut, could be turned into bastions.

Saxe placed his army in a triangular position, with the base of the triangle parallel to the river in a north-south axis. The forward point of the triangle was the village of Fontenoy, and its base points were the village of Antoing and the Bari wood. Saxe had built half a dozen redoubts between Fontenoy and the two other points so that wherever the allied army attacked along the V-shaped front it would be caught in cross fire. Each redoubt was at least a battalion strong and armed with artillery. The Bari wood had been invested by the Grassins, a light infantry corps made up of volunteers (often Paris vagabonds) armed with crossbows. The Grassins were skilled fighters in difficult terrain, a kind of eighteenth-century guerrilla unit used for harassment. Behind this front line of redoubts and infantry battalions Saxe had massed his cavalry. Further to the rear, at a point where the field abruptly sloped, he had grouped his reserves, out of sight and shot of the enemy. Saxe had committed 55 infantry battalions and 101 cavalry squadrons to the battle, a total of roughly 50,000 men. The Anglo-Hanoverian-Dutch force numbered perhaps 1,000 men more.

Louis XV, the dauphin, and their suite, arrived on May 8 and took up temporary residence in the village of Calonne, on the safe side of the Escaut. They slept in barns, and the king was in high spirits despite the Spartan accommodations. On May 9 he reviewed the troops, and one major lined his battalion up in a formation that spelled *vive le roi*. The king was in gold lace, with the diamond of the Order of Saint Espirit around his neck, and each officer saluted as he passed by extending his musket vertically at arm's length, bayonet pointed towards the ground. In the evening, Louis XV told off-colour stories and sang the endless couplets of barracks songs. The comte d'Argenson, Minister of War, wrote to Voltaire that 'there was never a ball night so gay, never so many bon mots,' as on this eve of battle. By May 10, Cumberland's troops had advanced to two cannonball lengths of the French forward positions. Cumberland secured advance positions of his own after some inconsequential skirmishing, and it was clear that he planned to attack on the 11th, at the customary time: one hour before dawn.

On the morning of the battle, May 11, Louis XV awoke at four and sent d'Argenson to get the final order of battle from Saxe. The king and his court took up positions on a hill behind the village of Antoing. Some of the courtiers climbed trees to get a better view. Nearby was the Calonne bridge, the king's escape route. Saxe had piled bundles of wood beneath it and planned to set it on fire once the king had crossed. Cumberland's plan was a simultaneous attack on the three French strong points. The Dutch would storm Antoing, he would attack Fontenoy, and Lord Ingoldsby would occupy the Bari woods. A thick milky fog had settled on the Fontenoy plain, masking the advance of Cumberland's army. When it lifted, the men in the French advance positions could see the blurred outline of combat regiments moving slowly towards them like gigantic centipedes.

The dawn attack was repulsed on all three fronts. The Dutch were routed at Antoing by an artillery cross fire from the village and from concealed French batteries on the other bank of the Escaut. The Dutch regiments retreated behind a small rise and spent the rest of the day there. Marshal Koenigsegg, who later had to explain the defeat to the Austrian Empress Maria Theresa, blamed it on the Dutch, who 'threw themselves into the first ditch they could find, so that there was no way to make them support the English.'

Lord Ingoldsby fared no better at the Bari wood. His regiment of Scots was cut down by a hail of arrows from the Grassins concealed in the foliage. Ingoldsby misjudged their strength and retreated under the pretext of asking for artillery support. Cumberland galloped up to the Bari wood to repeat his orders personally to Ingoldsby, but the retreat had become a rout and the unfortunate general was later court-martialled for his part in the battle.

At Fontenoy, Cumberland and Saxe faced each other. The Saxon, sucking on a lead pellet to keep his feverish throat moist, could see the successive charges of the red-coated English infantry break under the fire of the French artillery. General Campbell, commander of the British cavalry, was ordered to provide cover for the infantry and had his head blown off by a cannonball. On the French side, the duc de Gramont, commander of the elite guards regiments, died from a thigh wound when his horse was blown from under him.

The first phase of the battle was over. The French line had held. The cross fire from the improvised redoubts barred the advance of Cumberland's infantry. An overconfident officer congratulated Saxe on his triumph. 'It's not over, sir,' he replied. 'Let us find the British; they will not be so easy to digest.'

Cumberland decided to mass all his infantry in an attack on the French centre. He rallied the four battalions which had been repulsed at the Bari woods and advanced at the head of his troops, into a ravine littered with fallen trees, between Fontenoy and the Bari woods, where he hoped to escape the lethal French artillery cross fire. As the allied cavalry attacked in a diversionary action, Cumberland saw that there was a break in the French line of defence at the point he had chosen. The British dragged their cannon along the bottom of the ravine and kept their tight ranks in the difficult terrain. They advanced with the same grave imperturbability they might have shown at field manœuvres. The officers straightened the barrels of their men's muskets with their canes just as they did at target practice to improve their aim. By 10.30 A.M. Cumberland's phalanx had advanced 800 yards and reached the end of the ravine. As they clambered up its slope to the plain they found themselves face to face with four battalions of French guards and two battalions of Swiss guards. There was no more than sixty feet between the two armies—the French guards with their black, silver-fringed cock hats, and their blue coats with furled skirts, and the English infantrymen in red coats and yellow mitres. Each was led by the flower of its nobility, and the scene had the unreal quality of courtiers meeting in a drawing room—the duc de Biron, the comte de Chabannes, the Count of Albermarle, Robert Churchill (the Duke of

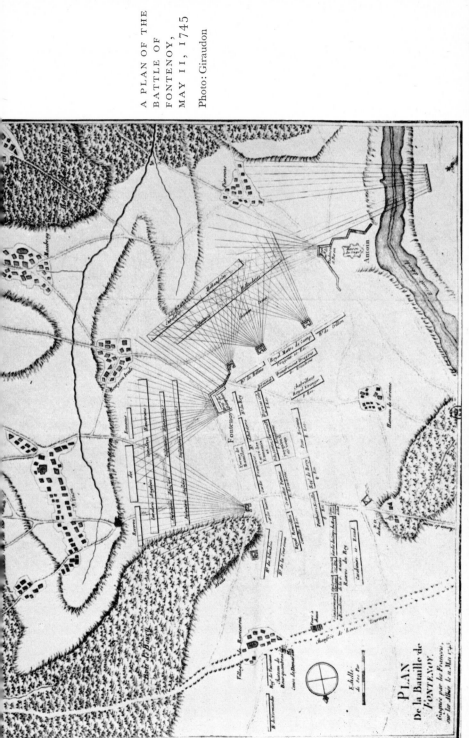

A PLAN OF THE
BATTLE OF
FONTENOY,
MAY 11, 1745

Photo: Giraudon

LE DÉJEUNER DE FERNEY, 1775: VOLTAIRE IN HIS NIGHTSHIRT
Painting by Huber

Marlborough's bastard son), and Lord Charles Hays. At this point took place the incident every French schoolboy knows by heart. It was described by Saxe's aide-de-camp, the marquis de Valfons, in his *Souvenirs*:

'The engagement was at such close quarters that the English officers, at the moment when they halted their troops, doffed their hats in a salute to us; our officers having replied to this courtesy, a captain in the English guards named Lord Hays emerged from the rank and advanced. Count Joseph d'Anterroches, a grenadier lieutenant, went out to meet him. "Sir," the captain said, "have your men fire." "No, sir," replied d'Anterroches, "we are never the first to fire." And having saluted again, each returned to his lines.'

This apparently absurd display of battlefield etiquette is often used to illustrate the foolishness of eighteenth-century 'lace warfare.' In fact, the gesture was not so much a matter of courtesy as of sound military tactics. One of Saxe's theories was that 'a troop must never be eager to fire first, for if it fires in the presence of the enemy it will become disorganized, so long as the enemy holds its fire.' Reloading eighteenth-century muskets was so complicated an operation that whoever fired first was at the mercy of his foe. Both sides knew this, and at close quarters the military advantage went to the line that fired last.

Even as d'Anterroches made his celebrated reply, the undisciplined French guards began to fire. The English received the scattered French volley at thirty feet without budging. They moved stolidly closer to the French line, and when they finally fired, their volley was lethal. The first row of French guards stumbled and fell; d'Anterroches himself was killed. The other rows of French guards vacillated when they saw their comrades and one of their officers fall, and the tight battle formation broke. They panicked and ran. Monsieur de Puységur, who tried to stop them, was thrown from his horse and stampeded. The guards bayoneted the horses of other officers who tried to regroup them. The official French account of the battle says euphemistically: 'The guards brigades having promptly fallen back, our affairs began to go very badly.' The guards had left 98 dead and 313 wounded. The rout had not lasted more than fifteen minutes. French cavalry squadrons which had been backing up the guards suddenly found themselves facing the staunch British line and turned tail.

As d'Argenson wrote in his account to Voltaire, the panic was spreading. 'No one knew what was happening or where the king was, but you could hear a great deal of noise and see smoke on the horizon. I arrived at the pontoon bridge on the Escaut at the worst moment of the affair. Deserters forced the bridge's guard and almost drowned me in the process. Fortunately I am a good rider and that was the only risk I ran. I did not know where the king was, for he had just executed a manœuvre [he had moved back 200 paces to be out of the range of English cannons]; I noticed great disorder while looking for him. . . .'

Cumberland now had a compact force of 15,000 men on the plain and had outflanked Fontenoy, which he could take from behind. Many on both sides thought the rout of the guards meant English victory. Men watching the battle from the besieged ramparts of Tournai were already shouting their hurrahs. The duc de Noailles told Louis XV the battle was lost and urged him to flee, which gave rise to the epigram that during the battle the duc de Biron changed horses three times, the maréchal de Saxe changed shirts three times, and the duc de Noailles changed his trousers three times. Louis XV, who was watching his troops deploy through a spyglass, summoned Saxe and asked him if he thought he was defeated. Saxe lost his temper and shouted, 'Who is the poltroon who told you that, Sire?' Saxe saw the situation very differently. He still had his redoubts, which could catch the British force in cross fire. The British army held the centre of the Fontenoy plain in a formation like three sides of a square but it was cut off from its own rear and was dangerously exposed. The British were, according to the military historian Colin, in the position of 'a child who has grabbed a lobster claw with one finger.'

Cumberland seemed astonished at his own success and stopped his advance. 'I looked at the column,' wrote an eyewitness, 'and it was motionless in the middle of the plain. It seemed as though it was led by no one.' Saxe, although grey with exhaustion, mounted a horse and ordered cavalry attacks on the flanks of the British columns. He told his cavalry officers that he wanted to see the breaststraps of their horses touch the uniforms of the British infantry. The cavalry attacks were designed to slow the British advance and give him time to regroup his troops. He knew there were intact battalions at various points of his original line. The cavalry was butchered while performing its mission with great gallantry. Sabre in hand, the horse squadrons charged the British column like cossacks and were beaten

back. Some squadrons made eight consecutive charges. Only the
squadron of the marquis de Wignacourt was able to make a dent in
the line, 'which was like a wall, but a wall that repaired its own
breaches.' He broke through the wall, but his entire squadron was
annihilated, except for ten men taken prisoner. He died of two
bayonet wounds in the stomach.

Saxe was now ready for his decisive attack, and threw every able-
bodied man he could find into it—the king's personal guard, cooks
and valets, the bridge guards, and ten intact battalions that had been
brought from less threatened points. The duc de Richelieu discovered four forgotten Swedish cannon at the Calonne bridge, which
had been set aside to cover the king's retreat. He moved the cannon
up and chipped at the corners of the British square, at the same time
drawing the bulk of enemy fire away from the attack which was
coming from another direction. Saxe led the charge himself. Too
weak to don a breastplate, he wore instead several taffeta doublets.
'One final push, my dear Lowendal,' he told the Danish-born general, and galloped towards the British. It was the monarchy's last
demonstration of *furia francese*. Cavalry and infantry attacked in
waves, the foot soldiers following the horsemen and cutting in front
of them when they were blocked to clear their way. The French
were so rabid they nearly charged the Irish Bulkeley regiment,
which was fighting on their side (it was Sergeant Wheelock of the
Bulkeley regiment who captured the only British flag). As d'Argenson wrote: 'Nothing resists French vivacity. With this secret weapon,
the battle was won in ten minutes.' The duc de Croÿ, who was
watching developments with the king, said he saw the English infantry 'running for their lives.'

Saxe was on the point of collapse and did not pursue the retreating
army past his own defensive line. It was 2 P.M. and the battle had
lasted nine hours. There were 2,500 dead and 5,000 wounded on
each side, and the English had left forty cannon on the battlefield.
English historians later accused French troops of loading their guns
with bits of glass and uniform buttons but otherwise a spirit of
perfect courtesy prevailed. The wounded of both sides were picked
up in carts, taken to hospitals as far as Lille, and given identical
treatment. The Dutch prisoners were released after promising they
would not take up arms against the French again. The dead
were buried where they lay. General Campbell received full military
honours. The behaviour of the French won the admiration of Cum-

berland, who wrote to Louis XV: 'I am touched by the orders which your Very Christian Majesty has seen fit to give with respect to General Campbell, as well as for the relief of our wounded soldiers. People in their circumstances are indeed worthy of such generous attention. I can assure His Majesty that, for my part, I will neglect nothing to soften the misfortune of your wounded, who will be given every possible care, delighted as I am for the opportunity of demonstrating my regards for His Majesty. I am, sir, your affectionate friend.' The ability to wage war without a trace of rancour and with genuine respect for one's enemy was a natural consequence of *ancien régime* society. It may seem surprising that Cumberland could sign himself the affectionate friend of the man who had just crushed him in battle. However, officers of enemy armies were members of the same class and might in peacetime be each other's guests. Their relations were governed by mutual esteem. During the Seven Years' War, the son of the Duke of Brunswick, Prince Henry, was shot in the chest, and the prince de Soubise sent his two best surgeons to save him—in vain. And in 1742, at the siege of Prague, French officers made bets with their Austrian counterparts as to whether the relief army would arrive in time to save the garrison. There was a strong cosmopolitan spirit among the upper classes. Cumberland and Louis XV were royal 'cousins' first and enemy commanders second.

Louis XV reviewed the troops, embraced Saxe, and made a number of field promotions. The king then asked for paper and pen and, surounded by his troops and the bodies of the fallen, wrote a letter to his wife on a drumhead: 'The enemy attacked us this morning at five o'clock. They were badly beaten. I am well and so is my son. I haven't the time to say any more since I must reassure Versailles and Paris. As soon as I can I will send you details.' Louis XV had been so impressed by the battle that he took his son on a tour of the Flemish field where hundreds of English and French bodies lay in their crimson and blue uniforms. Perhaps he noticed that the dauphin was overjoyed at enemy losses. 'Do you see what victory costs?' he asked. 'The blood of our enemies is still human blood. Real glory consists in sparing it.'

The English reaction was expressed by Horace Walpole, who wrote to his friend Sir Horace Mann on the day of the battle: 'We don't allow it to be a victory on the French side; but that is, just as a woman is not called Mrs. till she is married, though she may have had half a dozen natural children. In short we remained upon the field of battle three hours; I fear too many of us remain there still! Without palliating, it is certainly a heavy stroke. We never lost near so many officers . . . the whole hors de combat is above 7,300. The French own the loss of 3,000; I don't believe many more, for it was a most rash and desperate perseverance on our side.'

Saxe wrote to the Princes of Holstein with justified pride that 'the English got a sound drubbing; the affair lasted nine hours. Although I was dead on my feet I stood up to the day with vigour.' The victory brought him new honours. He was given the right to enter the Louvre in his carriage, an annual pension of 40,000 livres, the governorship of Alsace and the château de Chambord. After Fontenoy, he swept through the Low Countries and captured the channel ports of Ostend and Nieuport. His army seemed invincible, and it was thought that he would invade England. The war, however, returned to the slow pace of sieges and in 1748 the Peace of Aix-la-Chapelle was signed. Disgusted by Louis XV's inability to profit from his victories, Saxe retired to the life of a well-to-do country squire at Chambord, where he installed, for a little Saxon warmth, an enormous stove of pink porcelain which stands there still. He died in 1750 at the age of fifty-four. The rumour at court was that death had found him in bed with a lady, and in Paris, streetsingers made popular the following couplet: 'Whores will weep and Englishmen will laugh, The time has come for Maurice's epitaph.'

The French army could also weep, for with his passing it fell into a period of decline from which it was to be revived only fifty years later by another Frenchman by accident named Buonaparte.

X

THE PEN AND THE CROWN

*The several structures of political thought that
arose in France, and clashed in the process of revolution, were not directly responsible for the outbreak.*
—LORD ACTON, *Lectures on the
French Revolution*

*The French Revolution was caused 'by a group of
writers who believed themselves to be thinkers.'*
—LOUIS MADELIN

LOUIS XIV ordered style and content from his artists just as
he ordered the colour and cut of his servants' livery. The great
writers of the seventeenth century were in his keep, and, with
the exception of Fénelon, who was exiled, would no more have
thought of criticizing the regime than they would have appeared at
court in their underclothing. Muted voices were already announcing
the major themes of the eighteenth century, but official thought
prevailed and was controlled by royal patronage. The great change
that took place in the eighteenth century was not so much the
acceptance of new ideas as the monarchy's alienation from them.

The monarchy could not condone the writing of the Encyclopedists, with their emphatic attacks on the church, and thus became
opposed to and divorced from the new intellectual movement. Nor
could it suppress works which found their most ardent supporters at
court, or provide the alternative of a new orthodoxy. A literary
establishment independent of the monarchy, with powerful allies at
court, was formed. Royal prohibition served some of the same functions as royal patronage; a burned book was sure to become a successful book and fill the pockets of its author. In the seventeenth

century, a writer could not succeed unless he praised the king. In the eighteenth century, the most successful writers were the most irreverent, and the few writers who continued to proclaim their loyalty to king and church were hounded like renegades.

The change in the writer's condition, the monarchy's inability to sponsor intellectual change, and the development of a social climate in which the ideas of the Enlightenment could thrive, can be illustrated by comparing two extraordinary literary careers: that of Jean Racine, the supreme practitioner (with the possible exception of Corneille) of seventeenth-century classicism, and that of François-Marie Arouet, who governed the eighteenth-century republic of letters under the name of Voltaire. Each was the most successful writer of his age. Each had an early vocation and a precocious talent. Each was devoured by ambition and knew how to pull the strings of favours and friendships. Each received court pensions and was named to the coveted sinecure of Royal Historiographer. Each won the consecration of the Académie Française, as well as popular success. Each was of humble origins but proved as buoyant as cork in rising to the top of his compartmentalized society. Each had powerful patrons at court. But Racine was a domesticated spirit while Voltaire represented the triumph of free enterprise. Racine was a courtier who wrote; both his life and his work were an uninterrupted hymn of adoration to the monarch. Voltaire was an independent man of letters who broke with the court and scorned all forms of adulation (except perhaps those directed at him). What Racine achieved through determined sycophancy Voltaire obtained through irreverence and independence of mind. One is the bard and valet of absolutism and a proof that the system in his lifetime was still meaningful; the other is a triumphant sceptic who cast adrift from a court which had abdicated control of arts and letters as it was eventually to abdicate political control.

Jean Racine was born in 1639, one year after Louis XIV, in La Ferté-Milon, forty miles from Paris. His father was a minor civil servant. He was orphaned at the age of three and raised by his godmother, a nun who lived in that stronghold of Jansenism, the abbey of Port-Royal. Had his parents lived, he would probably have inherited from his father the obscure existence of a minor functionary in a seventeenth-century provincial town. Orphanage freed him from family tradition and provided an education to which his social background did not entitle him. He decided very early that he wanted to write (there were not many solutions for a youth who was both educated and poor) and was encouraged by a relative who managed the affairs of the powerful duc de Luynes. He said goodbye without regret to the puritanism of Port-Royal. In 1660, the marriage of Louis XIV to the Spanish Infanta Maria Theresa seemed an apt literary subject, and Racine wrote a congratulatory ode which was singled out by Nicolas Chapelain, the king's unofficial poet laureate. Racine began to cultivate influential courtiers and practise his natural gift for flattery. When the king caught the measles in 1663, Racine wrote an ode on his convalescence which earned him a 600-livres annuity. Chapelain drafted a charter which stated that all art must be at the service of the king's glory and enlisted Racine as one of his 'courtiers of Parnassus.'

Through his court contacts, Racine was admitted to the king's *lever* (awakening), which was a major victory for a writer of low birth, for it meant not only that his work was appreciated but that he could pass for a gentleman. Now that he had a pension, Racine sought a protector, and found one in the comte de Saint-Agnan, a member of the Académie Française who later became First Lord of the Bedchamber. Racine dedicated his first tragedy, *La Thébaïde*, to the comte. Dedications were the most obvious and rewarding form of flattery for a writer. Not only was the recipient pleased, it was also customary to give the author a financial reward. A minor scribbler named Boursault had dedicated a tragedy entitled *Mary Stuart* to the same comte de Saint-Agnan. 'He told me that my book would be the favourite one in his library,' wrote Boursault, 'and asked if I would not be offended by a feeble attempt to make up for his obligation by giving me 100 louis. I replied that his kindness in receiving my book was thanks enough. He said he could see that my reticence came from disbelief that he could afford the gift, so that he would give me twenty louis now and the rest on a monthly basis.' Racine used dedications as stepping-stones in his social ascent. His first great success, *Andromaque*, performed at Versailles in 1667, was dedicated to the king's sister-in-law, Henrietta of England, with the words: 'The court looks upon you as the arbiter of whatever is agreeable.'

The patronage of Henrietta of England guaranteed the play's success, for courtiers applauded it in the hope of pleasing the patroness. Similarly, when he wrote his first comedy, *Les Plaideurs*, Louis XIV was kind enough to laugh. Racine's dual ambitions were interwoven

—his position at court propelled his literary career and his success as a writer advanced his social ambitions. He had a gift for self-publicity, reading excerpts of his plays to select audiences before they were performed, and managing to have two plays running concurrently in Paris. He was lampooned, an unmistakable sign of success. A satire called *The Mad Quarrel* recounted for three acts the arguments of a gallant, who praised *Andromaque*, with his mistress, who didn't like it. He was honoured with a pirated edition of his works printed in Cologne. At the age of twenty-eight, he was France's most famous playwright and at the age of thirty-three he was elected to the Académie Française. For thirteen years, from 1664 to 1677, he continued producing, at the rate of about one every two years, pompous, majestic, grandiose tragedies which rolled on for five acts in thumping alexandrines. *Britannicus* was dedicated to the duc de Chevreuse, and *Bérénice* to Louis XIV's de facto prime minister, Colbert. After *Bérénice*, judging that he had arrived, and that there was, finally, something vulgar about flowery dedications, Racine stopped them altogether. He ignored the intrigues and scandals of the Paris theatre and began writing exclusively for Versailles. The premiere of *Iphigénie* in 1674 was part of an all-day feast celebrating the king's victorious return from a military campaign. During the day Louis XIV accepted 107 flags captured from the enemy, and that night he attended Racine's new play, which the Parisians were to see only eight months later. It took a great deal of money to attend court, and Racine assiduously increased his income. Seventeenth-century writers did not live from their pens but from royal favour and fringe benefits. The theatre was unprofitable, for royalties, which the author shared with the actors, were paid only on the first run, normally limited to twenty or thirty performances (the theatre had a restricted public even in Paris, partly due to the high price of seats— from 15 sous for standing room to 6 livres for seats on the stage). Racine, once he was established, received preferential treatment and sold the rights to his plays for fixed periods, reselling them when the period had lapsed. He probably earned about 1,500 livres a year from his writing, including the published versions of his plays. His most lucrative talent lay in accumulating pensions. He was awarded the income from a priory, about 300 livres a year. Colbert gave him a treasurer's office, worth 2,400 livres a year, which included the right to be called Chevalier, and to be buried wearing gold spurs. His author's pension was increased to 2,000 livres in 1679 'in consideration of the beautiful plays he has given the public.' His income was comfortable enough for him to invest capital which returned 1,000 livres a year. He lived in the Hôtel des Ursins, which overlooks the Seine, surrounded by rich tapestries, precious furniture, and 53 kilos of the finest silver.

But money derived from the pen was still considered tainted at court. An indignant memoir of the period notes that 'the art of composing has become, so to speak, a profession to earn one's living.' Saint-Simon wrote glumly in 1695 that the death of the poet La Fontaine had created more of a stir than the death of the duchesse d'Uzès. Racine's prominence at court helped dispel the prejudice that it was gauche and inelegant for a gentleman to apply himself to the written word, and helped to substitute the notion that artists are valuable men. At one end of the spectrum we have the Duke of Gloucester telling Edward Gibbon: 'What, another one of those damn, fat, thick books, Mr. Gibbon? Always scribbling, eh, always scribbling.' At the other end we have the Emperor Frederick II of Prussia rising from the dinner table to kiss Voltaire's hand. Somewhere in between, there is Racine, who persuaded the court to tolerate talented men.

Cabals were mounted against Racine, but he was too solidly entrenched at court, and more gifted than his envious rivals. It was not they who put an end to his playwright's career, but His Majesty's service. Racine had no sacred concept of the writer's mission, no message for the world, no demons tormenting him to create. Writing was a profession which had given him prosperity and an enviable court position. Now, after writing *Phèdre*, which some critics still consider the outstanding masterpiece of French literature, he showed that the theatre was no more than a parenthesis in his court career. When Louis XIV offered him the job of official historiographer in 1677, he accepted it without regrets for what it was—a court promotion. He was ordered to give up other writing and devote himself exclusively to chronicling the king's glory. He received an additional pension of 6,000 livres a year. The sublime tragedian who had made the marquise de Sévigné spill 'more than six tears' at *Andromaque* and 'more than twenty' at *Bajazet* became a mealy-mouthed manufacturer of elaborate compliments, a sort of court toiler available for the most menial writing tasks so long as the request came from within the magic circle of the king's entourage. It was as though Shakespeare had been hired to write

Queen Elizabeth's court Calendar. There was considerable speculation about Racine's decision. People said he was dispirited by the
cabals against him; or that with the court turning to piousness under
the influence of Madame de Maintenon, he was giving up the theatre
as too frivolous. It was also in 1677 that Racine married a daughter
of the gown nobility, Catherine de Romanet (who had an income
of 5,000 livres a year), and it was said that his wife had made him
promise to give up verse. But there is no evidence that he had any
motive other than his court career.

As official historiographer, a position he shared with the poet
Nicolas Boileau-Despréaux, Racine vowed to be a faithful recorder
of events, not an incense-bearer. In practice, he was more like an
evangelist following Christ. In a speech to the Académie Française
in 1685 he said: 'In the history of the king, everything lives, everything marches, everything is action. One has but to follow him, if
one can, and study him and him alone. It is a continuous delight of
marvellous deeds, which he both begins and ends, as clear and intel-
ligible when they are finished as they are impenetrable beforehand.
In a word, miracle follows miracle.' If Racine's historical writing
was in the same vein, it is fortunate for his memory that most of it
was destroyed in a 1726 fire at his family's country home in Valin-
court. For twenty years, he was the chief proponent of the Louis
XIV personality cult, forming with Boileau a two-man ministry of
propaganda. He studied previous historians to choose a method.
He questioned multiple witnesses of the same event to cross-check
his sources. Illness made Boileau sedentary, and it was Racine who
followed the king on the field of battle, interviewing officers and
survivors and inspecting battle plans like a seasoned war corres-
pondent. Vauban, the king's chief engineer, delegated one of his
assistants to explain to Racine the fortifications of cities and the plans
of attack. Courtiers muttered that he could barely sit a horse and
blanched at the sight of trenches, and that as a bourgeois he had no
notion of military valour. Louis XIV, however, seemed to appreciate
his travelling historiographer and even made memorable remarks
for him to leave to posterity. In 1678, the king showed Racine seven
captured cities in front of Valenciennes and said: 'Now you will see
Tournai, which is well worth my risking something to conserve it.'

Racine had other chores besides writing history. He was leader of
the chorus of praise at the Académie Française, which was in the
process of revising its dictionary to purify the language. The diction-

ary too, said Racine, was an instrument to serve the greater glory of
the king. Language itself must be taught to genuflect. He was also a
member of the 'little academy,' or 'Academy of Inscriptions and
Medals,' which composed captions for medals struck to commemorate the king's deeds. Racine's speciality was Latin inscriptions on
medals and statues. When a medal was struck for the duchesse de
Bourgogne, whose education the king was supervising, Racine suggested the sun's ray shining on a rosebud with the inscription:
Firmat et Ornat. He also wrote the librettos of allegorical operas
with music by Jean-Baptise Lully in which Louis XIV was pictured
as a god who banished discord to Hades.

Pleasing the king was not enough. Racine had also to please his
mistresses. When Madame de Montespan was in favour he wrote an
introduction to a volume of stories by her seven-year-old royal bastard, the duc du Maine. He rewrote a play which Madame de
Thianges, Montespan's sister, offered the king in 1683, and corrected
a translation of Plato's *The Banquet* for another Montespan sister,
the Abbess of Fontevrault. Finally, he wrote the preface for an illustrated book of the king's victories in Holland which Madame de
Montespan offered the king. It must have been with considerable
relief that Racine saw Madame de Maintenon, with her reputation
for censorious piety, replace such an eager patroness of the arts as
Madame de Montespan. But Madame de Maintenon did not allow
Racine's talent to lie fallow. He was put to work rewriting the
constitution for the finishing school she had founded at Saint-Cyr.
Then Madame de Maintenon had the untypical urge to have her
young ladies perform plays during the carnival season that preceded
Lent. Racine was asked to work up something edifying that could
be played by innocent young girls. In 1688 he wrote *Esther* and personally rehearsed the novice actresses. Louis XIV liked *Esther* so
much that he attended at least a dozen performances and commissioned another sacred tradegy. But *Athalie,* the sequel to *Esther,*
was never officially performed because Madame de Maintenon gave
in to extreme elements in the church who criticized her for teaching
young ladies to act. Racine's return to the theatre as an author for a
girls' boarding school had lasted a brief two years, and he never
wrote another play. He remained in Madame de Maintenon's good
graces by composing the inscription on a cross offered her by a
charitable organization: 'She is our faithful guide, All our felicity
comes from her.'

Since Racine was not at Versailles by birthright, but because of his talent, he had to make it available. At the same time he was a naturally gifted courtier. Tortuous politeness and elaborate periphrases came easily to him, and he was always ready to jettison his personal convictions to follow court fashion. Although his inclinations carried him towards Jansenism, he publicly claimed 'a childish submissiveness to all the church believes and commands, even in the tiniest matters.' He was careful to banish criticism from his writing, and never had an unfavourable word for the king, even during the merciless persecutions of the Huguenots. He repudiated his past as a playwright. When the king stopped attending the theatre, so did Racine, who also forbade his son to attend. He criticized a former mistress, the actress Champmeslé, for refusing to renounce the stage in an age when actors were still refused absolution by the church.

Racine's resolute hypocrisy won him new riches and honours. He now had an income of 20,000 to 25,000 livres a year, enough to live like a lord. Each time he accompanied the king to battle he earned hardship and risk bonuses amounting to several thousand livres. He was careful about his fortune. He dabbled in real estate, speculated on grain, and loaned money to friends at 5 per cent interest. He cultivated the bourgeois virtues of prudence and economy. He made his son Jean-Baptiste break off marriage negotiations with a young lady who was assured a dowry of 84,000 livres because that was not enough. As he grew richer, he became more miserly. Postage was expensive in the *ancien régime* and it was paid by the recipient of a letter, not its sender. Racine asked his son not to write to one of his friends because the friend might reply. 'Remember,' he said, 'that you are not the son of a merchant.' In 1690, he was made one of the twelve Gentlemen of the King's Household, which conferred nobility, and three years later the king made his nobility hereditary. Racine acquired ancestors and a respectable genealogy. Friends testified that he belonged to an ancient family which had distinguished itself under Henri III and Henri IV. He was listed in the court 'Who's Who.' He was given an apartment at Versailles which had belonged to the marquis de Gesvres and which was claimed by a royal princess after his death. When the king was ill, Racine read Plutarch at his bedside, even though there were official readers. When Racine had laryngitis, the king inquired when he would recover the use of his voice. He belonged to the inner circle. Courtiers were dumbfounded when in 1694 he walked into the king's bed-chamber without being announced by an usher.

Racine died in 1699, at the age of fifty-nine, after a brief profane and a prolonged sacred period. There are signs that in his final years he realized that he could not come to terms with the divided existence of an artist trying to portray some form of truth and a courtier sweating hypocrisy. He had given up his work and accepted the duties of the courtier willingly, but his life remained a contradiction. He returned to Port-Royal often, which did not alarm the king because he was the nephew of a nun there. He secretly wrote the history of Port-Royal, a work which should have been incompatible with his official history of the king, who was persecuting the abbey. But he managed to compartmentalize his loyalties, and there is nothing detrimental to the king in his history of Port-Royal. When he was accused of Jansenist sympathies in 1698, he reminded Madame de Maintenon in an apologetic letter that he had written under her instructions 'nearly three thousand verses on the subject of piety.' But in the last eighteen months of his life he became disenchanted with the court and seldom attended. He asked in his will to be buried in Port-Royal. A courtier made the cruel but probably accurate jibe: 'He would never have asked when he was alive.'

And yet Racine did contribute to social change. Not through his work, which does not contain a single breath of reproach, but by making literature a career acceptable at court. He was in a sense the pathfinder for the eighteenth-century writers who were lionized by the aristocracy. Perhaps his one courageous statement was that the works of the other great seventeenth-century tragedian, Corneille, would contribute to the Sun King's glory in the same way as feats of arms. By placing writers on the same level as generals, he broke military valour's monopoly on greatness. Voltaire, who was taken up by the court like a pet until it was realized that he was not house-broken, is indebted to him.

Voltaire was by turn on the best and the worst of terms with the monarchy, but they were usually his own terms. He was twice imprisoned in the Bastille, but he also won many of the same honours which Racine had stooped so low to conquer. Where Racine had been an ornament of the French court, Voltaire became an international celebrity who achieved personal independence to the extent of holding his own court at his property of Ferney. At the end of his life it was not the king, but the city of Paris, which made him into a national hero. The monarchy sulked while 'King Voltaire' was crowned.

Born in Paris in 1694, François-Marie Arouet was the son of a notary who traced the origin of his family to a fifteenth-century tanner. He showed his contempt for genealogy by inventing his own name, Voltaire (a limping anagram of Arouet), which made him the first of his line. He was educated by the Jesuits and wrote his first verse at the age of twelve as a punishment for playing with his snuff-box in class (snuff was recommended for colds). He began his career, like Racine, with official poems for Louis XIV. In 1712, when he was eighteen, he wrote an ode to the Virgin for a contest sponsored by the king. His entry was noticed, but he did not win the prize. After the death of Louis XIV there was no more court to send odes to. Instead of the royal charioteer who kept artists in harness, there was the licence and experimentation of the Regency. Perhaps Voltaire decided that the quickest way to literary success in a period which encouraged scandal was to criticize the regime. He wrote a poem in which he listed the evils of his time, ending each stanza with the line: 'I have seen these evils who am not yet twenty.' There was no official reaction. But when he wrote a poem charging that the Regent had committed incest with his daughter, the duchesse de Berry, he was locked in the Bastille for eleven months. In 1718, Voltaire's first play, *Oedipe*, was performed. One scene had been lifted almost word for word from Sophocles, and some lines were anticlerical, such as: 'The science of our priests is based on our gullibility.' Times had changed. The Regency approved of anti-clericalism, and the Regent was not a vindictive man. Voltaire was given a 1,500-livres annuity. The style of Voltaire's plays is a timid imitation of the 'noble style' of seventeenth-century writers. Like Racine, he believed that only lofty language could transmit lofty ideas, and was shocked by the 'barbarism' of Shakespeare. He could not forgive Shakespeare for writing a phrase like 'not a mouse stirring,' when ladies would be in the audience. It was not Voltaire's plays that were new, but his wit, irreverence, and gift for ridicule. He remarked about an academic poet's 'Ode to Posterity': 'I do not think this ode will ever reach its destination.' After the performance of one of his tragedies he said of the audience: 'They cried just as noses bleed.' The court had broken up, and its members had re-turned to their provincial estates and needed to be amused. Voltaire was received in a dozen castles, and often had to turn down invitations on the grounds of grave illness, an expediency that was to become familiar. The nobility had adopted him. So had the salons of Paris. Madame du Deffand wrote to him: 'Keep in mind my amusement. Do not forget that you have promised me insolences.' When the Regency ended and Louis XV resurrected Versailles, Voltaire made another attempt to fit in at court. He offered verse to the new queen. But Louis XV kept him at a distanec, sensing that he was not a tractable courtier and that under the proffered gloved hand there were sharp claws.

In 1725, Voltaire discovered that there was still a residual contempt among some lords for upstart writers of humble birth. The chevalier de Rohan-Chabot insulted him, and later hired ruffians to give him a drubbing. But even the chevalier gave him a backhanded compliment as he watched the beating from his carriage and ordered: 'Don't strike his head, something worthwhile may come out of it.' Voltaire wanted to defend his name and his honour in a duel, but the powerful Rohan family had him sent to the Bastille for a second visit. In 1726, on the advice of the minister Maurepas, he left for England, which was like sending a pen to be dipped in ink. Voltaire, unlike Racine, was cosmopolitan. He took advantage of a Europe awakening to itself, and alive to new ideas. He spent three years in England, learned the language, and admired what he saw. He returned to Paris in 1729 to find that Louis XV had suppressed his pension. The contradiction in Voltaire's situation was that while he burned for literary honours, like membership in the Académie Française, he kept writing books that offended the authorities and kept honours out of reach. He had to use extravagant subterfuges to publish his books, and his allies were the lords. His history of Charles XII was clandestinely published in Rouen, and the 25,000-volume first edition was carried by barge to a suburb of Paris, where it was distributed in small lots with the help of the duc de Guise. His *English Letters,* praising England's form of government and religious tolerance, appeared in 1734. All the copies that could be rounded up were publicly burned in the courtyard of the Palace of Justice on June 10. Voltaire fled to Lorraine, still an independent province, where he accepted the hospitality of his mistress, the marquise du Châtelet. Thanks to money inherited from his father and earned from his books, which he had judiciously invested, Voltaire had a comfortable income. At the marquise du Châtelet's castle of Cirey, he lived in a luxurious wing decorated at his own expense. His bedroom was blue and yellow, and even his pet dog's basket was faithful to the colour scheme. He had an amber writing desk, curtains of embroidered muslin, a bedspread of blue watered silk, and a marble and porcelain bathroom.

Since his rude verses on Joan of Arc had appeared (*La Pucelle*), everything Voltaire wrote was automatically banned. The French court was closed to him. He turned to greener pastures, and began his long, bizarre literary flirtation with Frederick II of Prussia. Frederick was so fond of the French language that he called his own subjects 'Iroquois' because they could not speak it. When he was not extending the borders of his small kingdom through conquest, Frederick played the flute, composed music, wrote doggerel (in French), and admired Voltaire. He sent Voltaire a cane which had a gold bust of Socrates for a knob, while addressing him as 'the Virgil of the century.' Voltaire took to calling Frederick 'the Solomon of the North.' They exchanged fatuous alexandrines and pedantic quatrains. 'I dream of my prince as one dreams of one's mistress,' Voltaire wrote. When Frederick was crowned in 1740 Voltaire addressed him as Your Humanity instead of Your Majesty. He was summoned to meet the monarch at the castle of Moylard near Cleves in September of the same year (he prudently asked for travel expenses), and admitted that he was drunk with the glory of having a king with an army of 100,000 men sitting on the edge of his bed and chatting with him like a boarding-school room-mate.

When it served his purpose, Voltaire could be as base a flatterer as Racine, although he was more far-ranging and less consistent. Prussia was France's ally in the War of the Austrian Succession, but in 1742 Frederick double-crossed France and signed a separate peace with Austria. Voltaire sent him a letter of congratulation. To separate Voltaire from France and draw him to his own court, Frederick had his agents distribute copies of the letter all over Paris. Madame de Mailly, one of the more patriotic of Louis XV's mistresses, flew into a rage and asked that the traitor be punished. Louis XV's aversion for Voltaire probably dates from this incident.

Frederick offered a house in Berlin, lands in Prussia, a generous pension, and a title. Voltaire still hoped for glory at home. To soften the resistance of the forty immortals, who could not forgive his militant impiety, he wrote a maudlin tradegy called *Mérope,* which dealt with maternal love. In pursuit of a worthy cause Voltaire could even feign piety, and he wrote to the abbé de Bernis, Minister of Foreign Affairs, about the 'pages of his works which are sanctified by religion.' The Académie was not swayed, so Voltaire proposed himself for the academy of sciences on the basis of such works as a *Memoir on the Nature of Fire*. In the same inconsistent vein, at the very moment he was writing against war, he speculated in military supplies. Using one of his cousins as a front, he was awarded in 1743 the lucrative concession for supplying fodder and uniforms to the French army.

Voltaire used his friendship with Frederick to get back into the good graces of his own government. He voluteerd for a secret mission to Berlin, to try to detach Frederick from his English alliance and bring him back within the French orbit. He told Frederick about Dutch arms smuggling in Prussia to try and involve him in a war with Holland. He gave Frederick a list of written questions on his political aims, with blank spaces where the king was supposed to write in answers. Frederick answered every question . . . with nonsense rhymes, which sums up the value of Voltaire's mission.

Nonetheless, the mission helped to reconcile him with the crown, as did a poem on the events of 1744 addressed to the king. Louis XV had fallen gravely ill during a military campaign in Metz and Voltaire wanted him to know that 'I was burning three candles in the window.' In 1745, he was on good enough terms with the monarchy to move to Versailles, where he confessed that he felt 'like an atheist in church.' He played the courtier, even though it bored him to be 'a fifty-year-old jester.' His play *La Princesse de Navarre* was performed at Versailles for the marriage of the dauphin. On the basis of that success he asked for Racine's old job, official historiographer, and got it, with a pension of 2,000 livres. He was fortunate in his first important assignment, which was to describe the victory of Fontenoy. He wrote a poem on the battle, which he dedicated to 'our adorable monarch.' It sold more than 100,000 copies. His historical description had to include the names of as many officers as possible, so that it reads something like a guest list. But it too was a great success. Voltaire took his new job seriously, and spent many hours poring over the archives of the war ministry to write a fuller account of the victory.

He had influential friends like the duc de Richelieu and the marquis d'Argenson, who obtained entrees for him, so that, like Racine, he attended the king's rising and became a Gentleman of the King's

Bedchamber. Just as Racine had invented a genealogy, Voltaire invented a coat of arms, three flames gules on a field azure.

He renewed his manœuvres for membership in the Académie, this time going as far as Rome to pay his court. He dedicated his play *Mahomet*, a denunciation of the Moslem faith which discriminating readers might interpret as a veiled attack on Catholicism, to Pope Benedict XIV. He humbly requested, through several influential channels, a portrait of the new pope and some holy medals. By enlisting the pope's support and pulling a great many other strings, Voltaire was admitted to the Académie Française in 1746, over the objection of Montesquieu, who said it would be 'shameful' to make him a member.

Having obtained the honours after which he had lusted so long, Voltaire made an honest attempt to settle down to the life of a courtier, but restraint was not in his nature. In October, 1747, Madame du Châtelet was gambling at the queen's table and lost 103,000 livres in the course of the evening. This was more than the thrifty Voltaire could bear. 'Can't you see that you are gambling with scoundrels?' he blurted out in English so that other courtiers would not understand. But someone did understand. The indirect insult to the queen could not be forgiven. Voltaire and Madame du Châtelet left Versailles that night. Voltaire was famous and rich and could go where he pleased. He now had an income of roughly 100,000 livres a year, only a small part of which came from his writing. He had invested in colonial companies, which gave a return of 25 per cent, he had his contract with the army and his historian's pension, and he loaned money at high interest rates. Like Racine, he prospered, although he was more daring and less scrupulous in his financial affairs. With Madame du Châtelet he briefly visited the court of Louis XV's father-in-law, ex-King Stanislas, at Lunéville, in the northern province of Lorraine. It was one of those miniature courts which imitated the elegance but not the formality of Versailles. In Stanislas' entourage there was a Jesuit, a mistress, and a dwarf named Bébé, who sometimes arrived at dinner inside a pastry shell which was sliced open at the table.

In 1749, Madame du Châtelet died as a result of an illness that followed childbirth. Voltaire was not the father, and mourned his companion of seventeen years but briefly. He soon replaced her with his niece, Louise Denis, the widowed, middle-aged daughter of his sister. Most of Voltaire's contemporaries believed that this heavy, coarse woman was no more than his servant and housekeeper. But his correspondence leaves no doubt as to the nature of their relationship. In one of several letters which sound as if they had been written by a moonstruck and lascivious adolescent, he applied 'a thousand kisses to your round breasts, your thrilling buttocks, and your whole person, which has given me so many erections and has made me dive into a river of delights.'

Voltaire had again found protection at court under the aegis of Madame de Pompadour, who had his tragedy *Alzire* performed in her small private theatre, but he was restless, and accepted in 1750 the Prussian king's invitation to add lustre to his Potsdam court. For three years, he stayed at Sans-Souci, a palace inspired by Versailles, where the first rule of etiquette was to speak French. He had the title of Chamberlain and a pension of 20,000 livres. His contract listed every expense, down to the number of candles he was entitled to burn daily. Here, far more than at Versailles, he was a jester who brought laughter to the mournful northern court. At meals he amused the company. Between meals he played chess with the king's brothers and edited Frederick's verse. He called himself the king's grammarian. Voltaire's capacity for mischief saved him from being buried alive at Potsdam. After invading Saxony, Frederick had forced the defeated government to redeem at full value some almost worthless Saxon bonds held by Prussia, which resulted in brisk but illegal speculation on the bonds. Voltaire, incorrigible in money matters, sent a Berlin Jew named Hirsch to Saxony to buy shares at their low value, so that he could cash them in at the price set by Frederick. He revealed his own dishonesty when he accused Hirsch of swindling him. Frederick, in the midst of a campaign against speculators, could not protect his jester. He scolded Voltaire in a letter which warned that if he could not live like a philosopher, free from childish excesses, he should leave Potsdam. Voltaire left in 1753, taking with him a thin volume of Frederick's poems which had been privately printed in a 500-copy edition. Frederick was so angry that he had Voltaire held in Frankfurt until the volume was returned. For the philosopher-speculator, this was another example of despotic aggression against a defenceless individual, as bad as the beating he had been given in his youth by the chevalier de Rohan. Voltaire's opinions were often the result of his personal experiences. Imprisonment, beatings, and illegal seizure made him the champion of individual liberties, just as land ownership was later to make him hostile to the education of peasants. The Potsdam fiasco was his last attempt to play the courtier. In 1755, he bought Les Délices in Geneva for 87,000 livres, and three years later he bought Ferney, across the border in France. For the last twenty years of his life he was the lord of two manors, with one foot in Switzerland and the other in France. Ferney became a shrine where a long procession of famous pilgrims came to worship a shrivelled, bent, toothless country squire who walked with a cane, wore a ridiculous floppy turban, threw things at his servants, and fell suddenly ill as soon as someone bored him. The duc de Villars came with a suite of forty. Boswell came, and asked Voltaire if he still spoke English. 'To speak English,' he replied, 'you have to put your tongue between your teeth and I have no more teeth.' The prince de Ligne stayed eight days and wrote a delightful portrait of his host. When Voltaire said Rousseau was a monster, Ligne jokingly pretended that he had just seen him running through the garden pursued by his enemies. 'Where is the poor fellow?' exclaimed Voltaire. 'Bring him here! My arms are open . . . go and get him! Have him brought to me, everything I own is his!' If there had been a guest book it would have read like a European *Who's Who*. The Austrian Emperor Joseph II was expected, but rode through Ferney without stopping. It was the only time Voltaire was snubbed.

Those who could not visit Ferney kept up with Voltaire through his prodigious output. Towards the end of his life, his anticlericalism seemed to become obsessive. He said he always had a Bible handy because you had to know what the enemy was up to. He signed his letters with the cipher ECRLIN F, or *écrasez l'infâme* (crush the infamy, i.e., the church). He wrote that Saint Francis of Assisi was a madman and that there was no beauty in the Bible. One of his pamphlets was called 'The Snails of the Reverend Father Cockchafer,' who amused himself by cutting the heads off snails and claiming that new heads grew. But he was less virulent in his private deeds and opinions. Travelling through Colmar on Easter Sunday, 1754, he went to communion because he was afraid of the public reaction to impiety. 'If I had 100,000 men I know what I would do,' he wrote to a friend, 'but since I do not have them I will make my Easter communion and you can call me a hypocrite as much as you like.' At Ferney he built a church with the inscription: 'Voltaire built this for God.' The pope sent him relics from Rome and the Christ painted on the wall bore a marked resemblance to the landlord. His attitude towards religion was practical. His watchmaker God was not a principle of creation but a skilled craftsman, a maintenance man of the universe. He wrote that if a single woman had been prevented from cuckolding her husband from fear of God, then God had proved his usefulness. The key to his deism was utility. Once at Ferney when Condercet and d'Alembert were arguing at the dinner table about the existence of God, he made the servants leave the room. It was better that they should believe.

He even had a soft spot for the Jesuits, and wrote to his friend the marquis d'Argens after the order was banned in 1762: 'I don't know whether it is a good thing; those who replace them will feel obliged to affect greater austerity and pedantry. Nothing was more acrimonious and ferocious than the Huguenots, because they wanted to combat loosened morals.' In 1764 he took in Father Adam, a fleeing Jesuit from Dijon. Father Adam stayed thirteen years. He said mass and played chess—he was a better player than Voltaire, but also knew the art of losing.

The patriarch of Ferney's belief in progress was equally practical and limited. Progress meant that a full stomach is better than an empty one, that health is an improvement over sickness, that justice is preferable to injustice. It went no further than that. Thanks to his wits, Voltaire had become a landowner and a millionaire (his annual income at the end of his life was estimated at 200,000 livres). It was natural for him to believe in the class distinctions of the mind, the aristocracy of the intelligence. He called the farmers on his property 'the rabble.' He fed and clothed them but provided no school for them. He wrote to Monsieur de la Chalotais, who had written an essay on education: 'Thank you for proscribing education for labourers. As one who works the earth, I want farmers, not tonsured clerks. Send me ignoramuses to drive and harness my ploughs.' Voltaire was purposely overstating his case to make a point. He did not believe in keeping the people ignorant but rather in suiting the form of education to the social level, which of course did not mean teaching illiterate peasants philosophy. He remained in favour of the monarchy, not because he liked the king, but because of a deep suspicion of his fellow man. 'I prefer to obey a single tyrant than three hundred rats of my own species,' he wrote. Progress to him did not mean equality or democracy. Before making philosophers of tenant farmers famines should be eradicated. There was a hierarchy of social distress. He declined to write controversial articles for the

Encyclopédie, limiting himself to topics like 'fire,' and his final opinion of it was that 'it will never be anything but a jumble.'

Voltaire's greatest merit was not as a thinker but as a man of deeds. His philosophy might be shallow, but he was willing to practise it. In 1761 the eldest son of a family of Huguenots named Calas, who lived in Toulouse, was found hanged on a crossbeam of the ceiling in their textile shop. The parents lied about the cause of death to save family honour. French Protestants were still a perse-cuted minority, easy to victimize. The rumour arose that the parents had murdered their son to prevent him from converting to Catholi-cism. Three members of the family, a servant, and a guest who happened to be there when the suicide was discovered, were arrested and tortured. They were tried by the Toulouse Parlement. No evidence of wrongdoing was found, but the fact that they were Huguenots was enough. The sixty-two-year-old father was put to death.

Voltaire turned the Calas trial into the Calas Affair. He investi-gated for months to get at the truth. He questioned the younger Calas son and mobilized his court contacts to pierce Parlement's curtain of silence. Like so many major French *affaires* (Dreyfus, Ben Barka), this was essentially a matter of a branch of government, in this case Parlement, covering up the truth to avert criticism. Voltaire wrote a best-selling pamphlet about the case and won the support of the powerful minister Choiseul. In 1764 the verdict of the Toulouse Parlement was overruled. Madame Calas was received at Versailles, although the king hardly saw her, because his attention was dis-tracted by someone falling as he passed her. It was, wrote Voltaire, 'a play according to the rules, the most beautiful act five in the world.' It was much more than that. It was the triumph of public opinion over constituted bodies of the state. Voltaire's crusade spurred a royal commission to reverse the verdict of the Toulouse Parlement. It is in the Calas Affair that the change in the writer's condition, from a timorous valet of the crown to a crusader able to change the course of public affairs, can best be appreciated.

Voltaire was acclaimed in France, but he was also persona non grata. With typical cunning, he supported the candidacy of a gov-ernment censor named Marin to the Académie in the hope of obtain-ing a passport from him. No passport was forthcoming, so Voltaire came to Paris with his reputation for credentials. He arrived in February 1778, two months before his death, a spry, lucid old man of eighty-four. Louis XV was four years in the grave, but Louis XVI, a genuinely devout young man of twenty-four, refused to receive a miscreant at court. Paris, however, received Voltaire as Rome had received Pompey. The Académie held a special session for him. He arrived at a meeting held in his honour by the Masonic lodge of Nine Sisters on the arm of Benjamin Franklin. The fact that the monarchy was sulking did not mar Voltaire's reception. The seventeenth-century situation was reversed. The crown could do nothing for Voltaire, whose triumph did not depend on court patronage. But Voltaire could have stimulated the popularity of Louis XVI, if the monarch had only recognized a matchless opportunity in public relations and participated in his welcome.

On his deathbed Voltaire asked for a priest and signed a retraction of what he had written against the church. He refused communion because, he said, he did not want the blood he was spitting to be mixed with God's. He died in May and was buried outside Paris in the village of Seillières, but his remains were transferred to the Panthéon in 1791. Madame du Deffand wrote to Horace Walpole that he had died 'from an overdose of glory which overagitated his wild machinery.'

The monarchy was never able to adopt a consistent policy towards eighteenth-century thought. It was like a man in a boat who is bailing water with one hand and pulling out the plug with the other. There were, of course, repeated efforts to silence the voices of discord, such as the ordinance of April, 1757, which said: 'Anyone convicted of composing, ordering, or printing writings tending to attack religion, heat spirits, threaten our authority or disturb order and tranquillity will be put to death.' But censorship and punishment served only to turn often innocuous works into forbidden fruit. We who live in an age where the last defences of censorship and modesty have been breached may find it almost enviable that books were once dangerous enough to send their authors to jail, require denunciations from throne and pulpit, and be seized and destroyed like contraband arms. The writers of the eighteenth century knew that book-burning is preferable to apathy. Jean-Jacques Rousseau realized he was a success when he heard from a Swiss friend in 1765: 'Will you not smile, my very distinguished compatriot, when you learn that I saw burn in Madrid, in the main Dominican church, at the end of the high mass, before a large number of ex cathedra imbeciles, your *Emile*, in the form of an in-quarto volume? Which resulted in several Spanish lords and ambassadors from foreign countries wanting to obtain it at any price. . . .'

In practice, the monarchy found it awkward to deal harshly with writers and books which had become popular at Versailles. At the end of Louis XV's reign, court fashion was evolving from Italian conceits, mythological romances, pastoral paintings, and the witty and affected frivolity of Marivaux, to philosophy and politics, from preciousness to erudition, from the kingdom of pleasure to the republic of letters. Every woman at court had a geometer, wrote the abbé de Bernis, just as every woman had once had a page. Horace Walpole overstated the case when he wrote in 1765: 'Do you know who the philosophes are? . . . in the first place it comprehends about everybody; and in the next, means men, who avowing war against popery, aim, many of them, at a subversion of all religion and, still many more, at the destruction of regal power.' But it was true that these writers found wide credit at court. The new vocabulary on the lips of lords who, involved in nothing, could discuss everything, was reason, nature, humanitarianism, imprescriptible rights, sensibility, public good, freedom, citizen, patriotism. The monarchy absorbed the vocabulary, without realizing it, and Louis XVI when he was crowned said he intended to 'reign according to the spirit of reason,' an idea which would never have occurred to any of his predecessors. The writer was now courted instead of courtier. The *Almanac of Authors* of 1755 noted that 'to be a writer today is a condition, like being a soldier, a magistrate, a clergyman or a financier.' This did not mean that writers prospered from their pens. Editions were pirated, royalties were irregular, publishers were greedy, copyright agreements were nonexistent, and the reading public was small. Literacy, measured by the percentage of couples able to sign marriage certificates in parish registers, rose at the end of the old order to 47·5 for men and 26·8 for women. Rousseau copied music to earn a living. Montesquieu was a member of the landed gentry. Voltaire was a shrewd businessman. Diderot had a small income from his father's estate and a pension from Catherine the Great. A writer's natural audience was the minute portion of the population which could both read and afford books, that is, the aristocracy and bourgeoisie. Writers still depended on court patronage, but patronage no longer meant control over content. In 1776 the duc d'Orléans gave a young writer 1,200 livres, and the writer asked what his duties would be. 'Your only duties are to work more and more towards your own glory,' was the reply.

The tension between the risks of reprisal and support at court turned publishing into a drama. Read today, the *Encyclopédie*, the first volume of which appeared in 1751, is tiresome, repetitive, badly edited and full of mistakes. But its publication, involving as it did a conspiracy to prevent its suppression, was a matter of great excitement. As volume erratically followed volume over a period of nearly thirty years, it became clear that the *Encyclopédie* offered nothing less than an alternative to the church's explanation of the universe. The reader was given a simple description of what was then known about the visible world. The *Encyclopédie* questioned the value of slave trade, penal harshness, torture, taxes, and wars. It stated, with transparent irony, that 'the true Christian must rejoice at the death of his child which assures the newly born eternal felicity.'

Diderot, its chief editor, was jailed, and publication was suspended. The church denounced it and treacherous printers made deletions in it. But in their camp the Encyclopedists had Madame de Pompadour, who was painted with a volume of the work within her reach, which showed that she read it. There was even a rumour that she had written the article on rouge. They were protected by Lamoignon de Malesherbes, an outspoken admirer of the Encyclopedists, who had become Director General of the Library (chief censor) in 1750. Diderot wrote Malesherbes a thank-you note in the pages of the *Encyclopédie*: 'Under the new auspices of Monsieur de Malesherbes, the library changed its complexion and took on a new form and a new vigour.' Malesherbes also made possible the publication of Rousseau's *La Nouvelle Héloïse* in France, asking him only to delete the phrase: 'a charcoal burner's wife is worthier than a king's mistress.' There was something for everyone in the *Encyclopédie*, so that even a member of the old guard like the duc de Luynes praised the work for the amount of knowledge it dispensed while warning against its dangerous ideas and its 'principles tending towards deism and even materialism.'

The king was badly served. The best minds were in the anti-church, rationalist camp. The Encyclopedists dominated the century's thought to such an extent that it became more perilous to defend church and crown than to attack them. A writer like Elie Fréron (1718–1776), by conviction a conservative monarchist, had continued censorship trouble. 'As for me,' he wrote, 'I belong to no cabal of fine spirits, to no party, unless it is that of religion, morals, and honesty.' Fréron was ordered by Malesherbes to suspend publication of his magazine *L'Année littéraire* because of an article attacking the Encyclopedist d'Alembert. Fréron published another periodical, *Le Journal Etranger*. The Philosophes wrote pamphlets against him, tried to get his writing banned, even forged letters to incriminate him. When he published travel notes by a doctor who had visited Spain in 1756, his enemies persuaded the Spanish ambassador to make a formal complaint against him which resulted in a month's imprisonment in the Bastille. When Diderot was invited to join the Berlin academy of Frederick II, he accepted on condition that Fréron be blackballed. Fréron wrote a pamphlet proving that Diderot's *The Natural Son* had been lifted from Goldoni's *Il Vero Amico*. The pamphlet was banned by Malesherbes. On the other hand, a pamphlet in which Voltaire falsely accused Fréron of stealing money from his sister was allowed to appear. Fréron was the king's knight, waging single combat against the regiments of Encyclopedists, and he lost every battle. Voltaire, a maker of barbs who did not like to receive them, wanted to 'reduce the rascal to mendacity.' Fréron wrote that only twelve members had shown up for a meeting of the Académie Française. 'Will you allow this scoundrel to insult the Académie with impunity?' Voltaire wrote to the secretary. 'There was a time when he would have been punished.'

The Philosophes formed a clan which drew the courtiers away from Versailles and into the Parisian salons. Marie-Thérèse Geoffrin could not be received at court because she was the bourgeois wife of a glassworks director. But she was a living denial of the duc de la Rochefoucauld's quip that 'the court does not make me happier but prevents me from being happy elsewhere.' For forty years her salon in the rue Saint-Honoré was an alternate court ruled by a commoner who received royalty. King Gustav III of Sweden and Emperor Joseph II of Austria were her guests and watched her navigate the conversation of brilliant men like a harbourmaster, into the favourable winds of wit and away from the eddies of controversy and the shoals of boredom. Salons such as hers proved the existence of a mobile, polycentric society. There was no longer Versailles and the void, but a number of smaller planets where the courtier could meet the man of letters and frivolity rubbed shoulders with enlightenment.

Not only did courtiers protect the Encyclopedists, but the king himself was powerless to prohibit what he considered seditious. In 1783, Louis XVI and Marie Antoinette, alone in one of the king's cabinets, summoned the lady-in-waiting Madame Campan. On a small table across from them lay a thick manuscript. 'It's Beaumarchais' comedy [*The Marriage of Figaro*],' the king said. 'You must read it to us. Some passages are hard to read because of erasures and insertions; I have already scanned it but I want the queen to hear it. You will tell no one that you have read this.' As Madame Campan read the manuscript aloud, Louis interrupted, saying: 'This is in very poor taste. This man is continually bringing back to the stage the habits of the Italian *concetti*.' After Figaro's celebrated monologue, in which bureaucracy and state prisons are attacked, the king leapt from his chair and said: 'This is detestable! It must never be staged! If the performance of this play were not to be a dangerous inconsistency, the Bastille would have to be torn down. This man ridicules everything that should be respected in a government. . . .' 'Then it will not go on?' asked the queen. 'Certainly not,' replied Louis XVI, 'you may be sure of that.' He sent the manuscript to Armand-Thomas de Miromesnil, the Lord Privy Seal, with the handwritten annotation: 'The censor must permit neither its performance nor its publication.'

It is easier to understand the king's anger if one knows that this first version of the play was set in France and mentioned the Bastille and other monuments of Paris by name. In his second version, Beaumarchais shifted the setting to Spain, deleted attacks on the clergy, and muffled much of his criticism. The Comédie Française began rehearsing the play, but a new prohibition came on the opening night, June 13, 1783. This time the play's forthcoming performance had been publicized and Beaumarchais presented himself as a martyr of tyranny and oppression. Louis XVI was swamped by pressures from so many different sides that three months later he agreed that the *Marriage* could be performed once in the private theatre of the comte de Vaudreuil. Madame Vigée-Lebrun, the court painter, wrote of the performance in September, 1783, that 'dialogues, couplets, everything was directed against the court, a large part of which was there, without mentioning the presence of our excellent prince [the king's brother, the comte d'Artois, who had supported the play] . . . Beaumarchais . . . ran here and there like a man beside himself, and when there were complaints that it was too warm, he did not wait for the windows to be opened but broke the panes with his cane, so that it was said that he had broken the windows in more ways than one.' It took seven months and arbitration by a panel of men of letters before the play could be put on in Paris. By that time the *Marriage* was already a *succès de scandale*, and it ran for seventy-eight consecutive performances, a record for the French eighteenth-century theatre. The Baroness Oberkirch was one spectator who sensed that she was applauding the end of an age. She wrote that she was 'furious at having been amused . . . the great lords were tactless and immoderate in applauding it. They slapped their own cheeks; they laughed at their own expense, and what is worse, they made others laugh. They will repent someday. . . . Beaumarchais showed them their own caricature and they replied: that is it, the resemblance is excellent. What a strange lack of vision. . . .'

The importance of *The Marriage of Figaro* was not, as Danton was later to say, that 'Figaro killed the nobility.' Beaumarchais was not a political thinker. He was himself a member of the nobility, for he had taken the trouble to purchase a title. He wanted to amuse, not incite to revolt. He was writing in the traditional *commedia dell'arte* form of the valet who tricks his master. Molière had used the same device a century earlier in *Les Fourberies de Scapin*. The satire against the regime was far milder than in many other contemporary works which created less furore. Against military service, Beaumarchais wrote: 'Are we soldiers who kill and are killed for interests we ignore? As for me, I want to know why I am angry!' Against the nobility, he wrote: 'Because you are a great lord you think you are a great genius—nobility, fortune, rank, offices; all that makes one so proud! What have you done to deserve it? You took the trouble to be born, that is all.' Finally, Beaumarchais, along with Voltaire and practically every other eighteenth-century French writer, railed against censorship. 'Printed foolishness is important only in those places where efforts are made to suppress it,' he wrote; 'where there is no freedom to blame, there is no true praise; and only petty men fear petty writings.' Which is an excellent summary of Beaumarchais' own case. The efforts of Louis XVI to suppress the *Marriage* publicized it, while his final failure to suppress it exposed his own weakness. The most seditious line in the play was unwritten: it was that the king had abdicated all authority.

To what? In many cases to that ubiquitous and amorphous eighteenth-century creature, public opinion. It is hard to imagine Louis XIV appointing a minister to please public opinion, and yet this is precisely what his successors did. Louis XV said with resignation: 'I name ministers and the nation sacks them.' Louis XVI dismissed his Minister of Finance, Jacques Necker, and then brought him back because 'the nation clamoured for him.' The public will was not formed by the Revolution, it was already a force to be reckoned with in the final seventy years of the monarchy. The Regent's repudiation of Louis XIV's policies stamped the century with irreverence. Kings and members of the royal family were lampooned with unprecedented viciousness. The pamphleteers of Paris broke down the time-honoured respect for the king. The government of France, it was said, became 'a monarchy tempered by epigrams.' Public curiosity and public concern were matched by interest in public welfare on the part of reform-minded ministers, who were influenced by the ideas of the Enlightenment. The real innovation of ministers like Turgot was not this or that reform but the recognition of a public will, so that decrees were called, instead of the king's will, 'a benefit which appears to be the general wish of his subjects.' Necker believed in 'King We . . . a king without visible throne, without pomp, without display; and yet everyone trembles and obeys at the sound of his voice. A singular king who is master in things both great and small.' Public opinion could have a direct bearing on royal decisions. During the Bohemian campaign of 1742, General Mallebois was ordered to the rescue of the French army surrounded at Egra. There was such a public outcry when he failed that he was recalled and replaced. And when Madame de Pompadour decided to plant an enclosed vegetable garden on the Champs Elysées, six-foot-high walls were already up when the citizenry began to complain about the encroachment on the promenade area, and she gave up the project. This public ferment was not in itself revolutionary, just as the political thought of the eighteenth-century writers was not revolutionary. None of the writers of the Enlightenment wanted to overthrow the monarchy.

It is curious that the direst forecasts of revolution came not from the Philosophes but from ministers who were in a privileged position to observe the shortcomings of the regime they were serving. To quote only two, Jean-Baptiste Machault d'Arnouville, Controller General under Louis XV, wrote: 'I am an old man but I will see the monarchy in its grave before I am in mine.' He was right, for he died in 1794, in prison during the Terror. The marquis d'Argenson, who was Secretary of State for Foreign Affairs under Louis XV, was by nature a pessimist, but hardly exaggerated when he wrote in 1749: 'All the orders are discontent; everything is combustible, an uprising can become a revolt, and the revolt a revolution where veritable tribunes of people could be elected and where the king and his ministers would be deprived of their excessive power to harm.'

It is futile to speculate on the influence of the Philosophes in forming public opinion. Diderot believed that he was the product, not the cause, of the eighteenth-century intellectual climate. 'In another age,' he wrote, 'I would never have conceived the ideas that I am capable of nourishing today.' The rash of coffeehouse criticism that followed the death of Louis XIV coincided with the first great works of the Enlightenment. There was no lag between Voltaire, Montesquieu, and the man in the street. Police reports of the period show an increasing preoccupation with seditious discussions. In the words of a 1729 report: 'There are in Paris a number of so-called *beaux esprits* who discuss religion as a chimera in cafés and other places . . . if this is not dealt with, the number of atheists and deists will increase and many will devise their own religion, as they have in England.' Nor was the monarchy spared in these curbstone forums, and a 1725 police report tells us that 'there were a great many assembled, some seated and some standing. . . . The one who seemed to be directing the conversation said the policy of kings was to ruin the people, and that this was the surest way of subjecting them; another, who is a maker of edge-tools, replied that kings were tyrants and could be done without, and that republics could govern themselves and be the happier for it. The first said he should think such things without expressing them because walls had ears. The second . . . replied that all the nobles in France had neither faith nor law, that religion was not made for them, that it was a mask for the prince and a brake for the people, and that those who made the laws did not observe them.'

Supplementing these oral protests were clandestine tracts. They were handwrittten, usually anonymous, and passed from reader to reader. One historian has traced 102 such tracts from 1697, when Pierre Bayle's *Historical and Critical Dictionary* was published, to 1748, when Montesquieu's *Spirit of Laws* appeared. The brunt of criticism in these tracts fell on the church and religion, but in a divine-right monarchy, any attack on the church was bound to strike the regime by ricochet.

Here again the aims of the Philosophes and the popular protest were identical; both focused on the church, but for different reasons. To the disgruntled subject seeking a target for his discontent, the church was a privileged order which paid no taxes and grew rich on the tithes of the faithful. The upper clergy were ostentatious lords whom they saw drive by in handsome carriages, but seldom in church. To the writers of the Enlightenment, the church was a roadblock in the way of reason, progress, and happiness. The church taught that man was flawed from birth because of original sin. It was not reason which could perfect him, but faith. Social progress was meaningless because suffering was retributive and this life was only a way station for heaven or hell. Natural laws were part of a divine order. There was no supremacy of reason, only a divine intelligence. To the church, still in the grip of the medieval concept that it must govern men's lives to prepare their deliverance, happiness was suspect, progress was futile, and reason without faith was a ruse of the devil. This fundamentalist view had prevailed long past its medieval historical context thanks to the great orators like Bossuet and Massillon and the piousness of Louis XIV. But in the eighteenth century there were no great Catholic orators. The talent was in the enemy camp, which believed that religious despotism was incompatible with human nature and social growth. Piercing the tongue of a blasphemer with a hot iron was not only cruel, it was anachronistic. The church represented worn-out, untenable notions. The Philosophes, who differed on many other topics, were united in their assault on revealed religion. It had to be exposed as superstition before the century could be delivered of the Age of Reason. Voltaire tried to invalidate the Bible by pointing out its inconsistencies, i.e., that the devil could not have seen the whole world from a mountaintop. Montesquieu explained that miracles had natural causes. In Naples he saw the blood of Saint Januarius bubble and said it was because the reliquary had been taken from a cool place and warmed by candles and the priest's hands. Religious tolerance was another way to attack the state religion, and Voltaire wrote in his *English Letters* that 'an Englishman is a free man who goes to heaven along the path he likes.' The monarchy was committed to the defence of the church. Diderot was twice jailed for his attacks on

THE CHAPEL AT FERNEY, 'DEO EREXIT VOLTAIRE', 1761

BENJAMIN FRANKLIN RECEIVING A LAUREL CROWN FROM
MARIE ANTOINETTE AT VERSAILLES
By Jolly

Photo: United States Information Service

religion, in 1747 and 1749, and had to sign a statement that he would write nothing more against religion and morals.

On the level of popular, anonymous pamphlets, the attacks against the church became increasingly violent. A pamphlet on the life of Christ in 1770 described Him as 'a clumsy juggler who tried to seduce the people of his class . . . the error must finish sooner or later. But what is the substitute? Reason.' The number of anti-clerical pamphlets and the tenor of café discussions show that resentment against the church was widespread, from the Philosophes to the common people (although it remained essentially an urban phenomenon). The state of the eighteenth-century clergy helps to explain why it was unable to keep the respect of the faithful. It was, first, riddled by internal disputes—Jesuit against Jansenist, and Gallican against Ultramontane. These quarrelling factions absorbed much of the energy of the eighteenth-century Catholic church in France and broke down ecclesiastical discipline. Moreover, there was a second, even graver split between upper and lower clergy. The upper clergy was recruited from the nobility. In 1789, all of France's 136 bishops were aristocrats. Certain families had hereditary strangleholds on lucrative bishoprics. Strasbourg, with annual revenues of between 300,000 and 400,000 livres, had been in the Rohan family for over a century. With few exceptions, the princes of the church were greedy, luxury-loving, unenlightened men who bore out Voltaire's thesis that religion is a method of exploitation. A successful bishop was one who could spend more time at court than in his diocese. Cardinal de Polignac died in 1741 without having once seen the city of Auch, whose archbishop he had been for fifteen years. Monsieur de Simiane, the bishop of Langres, paid a surprise visit to his diocese to practise billiards so that he could beat Monsieur de Vendôme when he returned to Versailles. Bishops held the lower clergy in the same contempt that courtiers reserved for the Third Estate. Christophe de Beaumont, archbishop of Paris, refrained from making pastoral visits during which he would have to mix with lowly parish priests. Court practices were obeyed to the detriment of religious obligations. The bishop of Mans, Monsieur de Grimaldi, could be seen on Sundays wearing a red suit, white stockings, and carrying a game-bag. Once, when leading a hunt, he rode through a religious procession which was singing litanies to the Virgin. He had the ringing of churchbells stopped in his diocese because it kept one of his lady friends from sleeping. It should not seem surprising that episcopal letters posted on church walls were often splattered with mud in eighteenth-century France.

By contrast, the lower clergy, which numbered 40,000 pastors and 5,000 curates in 1789, was often poor, familiar with the problems of the Third Estate, and accessible to the ideas of the Enlightenment. The lower clergy was later to provide a number of revolutionary leaders, such as the Abbé Sieyès. But much earlier some of its members were in open revolt against the church. They joined Masonic lodges and gave 'Greek-style' sermons during which they delivered philosophical discourses instead of reading the gospel. The abbé de Prades in 1752 advanced in a Sorbonne thesis that there was nothing singular about the miracles of Christ. The thesis was condemned and he had to write a retraction to his bishop. Father Berruyer, a Jesuit, wrote that the New Testament was obscure and ambiguous. Father Jean Meslier, who died in 1729, left an angry diary in which he expressed the hope that 'all the lords and nobles on earth will be hanged and strangled with the guts of priests.' The revolt of the lower clergy may have been fanned by the works of the Enlightenment and the general climate of irreverence. It was more certainly the result of direct observation. An eighteenth-century parish priest was chaplain to the disinherited. He kept municipal registers, ran the schools, drafted wills, and read from the pulpit official news about battles, treaties, royal births and deaths, and declarations of war. He was involved in civic improvements and sought to protect his parishioners from unfair taxes and feudal obligations. His influence and popularity were great, as they still are in French villages where the traditional triumvirate of power is the priest, the schoolteacher, and the mayor. He was in a better position than most to observe the inequities of the regime. The schism between upper and lower clergy came out at the Estates General of 1789, when the clergy's unity as an order was broken and the lower clergy went to sit with the Third Estate.

The writers of the Enlightenment had proceeded like a demolition team, specialized in the clearing and removal of church influence. They were able at the same time to impose themselves as the literary establishment. The Académie Française, that club of conservative thinking and pure language, was integrated. From 1760 to 1770, out of fourteen new members, there were nine Philosophes. The essay subject for 1757 was 'What is the philosophical spirit?' Editions of new works were costly, and usually ranged from 500 to 4,000 copies.

But Voltaire's *Candide* went through forty-three editions in thirty years and Rousseau's *La Nouvelle Héloise* topped that with eighty editions in forty years. The expensive *Encyclopédie* was called 'the cornerstone of all libraries,' and in 1753 there were 4,000 subscribers. Recent studies on the contents of 500 private libraries under Louis XV show the most widely represented work to be Pierre Bayle's *Dictionary* (288), followed by Buffon's *Natural History* (220), Voltaire's *Henriade* (181), and the *Encyclopédie* (82). Authors became public figures. At the Saint-Germain fair in 1784, the traditional wax statuettes of the king and queen were on sale next to those of newcomers Voltaire, Rousseau, and Benjamin Franklin. The monarchy was still popular, but so were the Encyclopedists. There was in fact no reason why they could not coexist. Having emancipated man from the pulpit, the Enlightenment presented him as a rational, sensible creature, who seeks pleasure, avoids pain, and aspires to that state in which there is more pleasure than pain, called happiness. Faith in happiness on earth was substituted for faith in the afterlife. New virtues were needed for the new morality—tolerance, social progress, justice. There was a chorus of praise for England's constitutional monarchy, because it allowed the individual greater freedom. Even Rousseau, who did not share the Encyclopedists' views of social and material progress, wrote that England was 'the only remaining nation of men among the various herds that cover the earth.'

It was also from England that the Freemasons came, not, as some historians still maintain, to plot the overthrow of the monarchy, but to add yet another discussion forum where social classes could mix; from 1776 to 1789 the number of lodges grew from 198 to 629, with roughly 30,000 members. Were they more than eating clubs with principles of tolerant companionship (in some lodges Protestants were allowed) who laughed at the ritual of court life while creating an even more ridiculous ritual of their own? No serious evidence bolsters the intriguing thesis of a Masonic conspiracy. Was there, any more than a revolutionary plot among the Masons, a revolutionary thinker among the writers of the Enlightenment? Voltaire believed in limited progress stimulated by enlightened kings. His distaste for the 'rabble' made him the spokesman of the liberal bourgeoisie. Men could believe in a government in which they had a vested interest—'a good field, whose owner, comfortably lodged in a well-run house, could say: "this field I till, this house I built, are mine." ' Montesquieu, who wanted a 'gothic' government controlled by the aristocracy which could check a tyrant's ambitions, and who advocated the separation of powers, had dual and opposite influences: his *Spirit of Laws* became the Bible of the feudal reaction under Louis XVI as well as an important source book for the drafters of the American Constitution. Finally, these men of reason were also men of faith who believed that the monarchy did not have to be overthrown because it could be overhauled. They were the temperate vanguard of a prerevolutionary generation still too involved with monarchic society to consider a final solution, or any solution other than gradual change. They were, one might say, only the first stage of the rocket.

Rousseau, whose link with the Revolution is more direct because of his theory of the social contract, went through three periods of thought, each one less kindly disposed toward democracy. At first he affirmed that democracy could work in small countries like his native Switzerland; then he said democracy was impossible for men, it was only for gods; finally he came to fear it, writing that 'no one ignores how dangerous for a great state is the moment of anarchy and crisis that precedes the establishment of a new regime . . . what man endowed with common sense would dare abolish the old customs, change the old maxims, and give another form to the state than that which has lasted for 1,300 years.' The monarchy was, after all, a social contract in which the king was meant to be in perfect communion with his people. Breach of contract is the story of the monarchy's decline. Rousseau in fact believed with complete seriousness that he had prevented a revolution from breaking out in France in 1754. 'Those were the days of the great quarrel between clergy and Parlement,' he wrote. 'Ferment was extreme; everything pointed to a forthcoming uprising. My brochure (a *Letter on French Music*) appeared and all other quarrels were instantly forgotten. All thoughts turned to the perils of French music and all uprisings were directed against me . . . those who read that this brochure may have prevented a national revolution will wonder whether they are dreaming. And yet it is a very real truth.'

Not only were the Philosophes non-revolutionary, they were for the most part non-equalitarian and non-nationalistic. Voltaire and Montesquieu believed devoutly in class distinctions. Rousseau, despite his celebrated cry that 'man is born free but is everywhere in chains,' nursed no hope that the primitive state of innocent equality could be recaptured. The levelling forces of the eighteenth century, the battering rams of class barriers, were not ideas—they were first of all money, the equality of speculation under law, the marriages of aristocrats with wealthy commoners, the growing number of business ventures in which the nobility was associated with the bourgeoisie; then there was the equality of Masonic lodges, of the salons, and of the Académie, where foundlings like d'Alembert sat next to dukes. Finally, there was the equality of sex, illustrated by Louis XV, who chose each successive official mistress from a lower social 'milieu.'

Nationalism was no more than a misty notion that people who lived within the same boundaries shared common interests. It was not developed by eighteenth-century writers, who were more concerned with forming a united Europe of the intellect. Voltaire, who said that he belonged to Europe, travelled to England and Prussia. Montesquieu visited Italy and Diderot went to Russia. There was a European society eager to exchange ideas, with a uniformity of manners and language. Men of letters travelled with their reputations for passports, spoke French in Saint Petersburg or Potsdam, and everywhere met a literate and cosmopolitan elite. Voltaire was read at the English court, and in turn introduced Newton and Shakespeare to the French. He was a member of the Royal Societies of London and Edinburgh, of the Academies of Berlin and Saint Petersburg, and of six Italian academies. The Enlightenment was the first secular movement of ideas which was truly international.

Freemasonry, although it was condemned by Pope Clement XII, flourished and contributed to the feeling of international fellowship. In 1731, François de Lorraine, husband of the Austrian Empress Maria Theresa, was received into a Masonic lodge by the British ambassador to Vienna, Lord Chesterfield. Montesquieu, Voltaire, Choderlos de Laclos, Lessing, Goethe and Mozart were all Masons (the *Zauberflöte* is the allegorical representation of a Masonic initiation). France and England were at war for thirty years between 1700 and 1789, but as soon as there was a lull in the fighting, the 'milord whatthens' and the 'goddems' (two French nicknames then current for the English) invaded France, which was the starting point of that cultural marathon invented in the eighteenth century, the Grand Tour. Gibbon estimated that 40,000 Englishmen visited Italy in 1745.

France was still the cultural sun of Europe, although politically she had been eclipsed by the rise of England, and had lost her colonial empire while pursuing a series of continental wars. In 1777, the Neapolitan ambassador to Paris, Caraccioli, wrote a book called *French Europe* in which he said: 'A dominant nation can always be recognized by the efforts to imitate it.' In a roundabout way, he was right, for England was then the dominant nation of Europe and France was in the midst of 'Anglo-mania,' a passion for things English, the 'redingote' (a deformation of riding coat), afternoon tea, horse races, water closets (*lieux à l'anglaise*), and English gardens. In the rest of Europe, however, France's cultural reign continued unchallenged. It was in the eighteenth century that French became the language of diplomacy. A treaty between the Russians and the Turks was drafted in French in 1774. No non-English man of letters used the English language, but many non-French writers used French— Casanova wrote his memoirs directly in French, and Gibbon wrote an *Essai sur l'Etude de la Littérature*. When the duc de Nivernais translated Horace Walpole's essay on gardens, Walpole said: 'You have allowed me to speak the universal language.' Frederick II wrote poetry in French to Voltaire, Maria Theresa of Austria corresponded in French with her daughter, Marie Antoinette, and Catherine the Great wrote to Diderot in French. The Russian minister to Versailles, Prince Galitzine, could speak French better than his own language. Voltaire, exulting at his success in the 'language of Europe,' boasted that he had four kings in his hand. The French court continued to dazzle foreign visitors. The monarch never went abroad, and indeed, rarely departed from the fixed environment of Versailles and other royal residences. But foreign monarchs, wide-eyed and open-mouthed, came to see the splendours—Peter the Great, Joseph II of Austria, Christian VII of Denmark, and Gustav III of Sweden.

Far from making French men of letters chauvinistic (Chauvin was, after all, a soldier under Napoleon), their country's intellectual dominance favoured their membership in European society. They became cosmopolitan, sometimes to the point of treason. Voltaire in the twentieth century would probably have been tried as a traitor for praising the victory of Frederick II over the French at Rossbach. In 1759, he wrote to Frederick:

> Northern hero, I well knew
> That you had seen the backsides

Of the Very Christian King's warriors
When you put them to rout.

To which Frederick replied that the French were:

A foolish and fickle people,
As valiant at looting
As it is cowardly in combat.

Voltaire's pen was for hire. He praised the French king too when
it was to his advantage. But patriotism escaped him. He turned
France's most sacred legend (Joan of Arc) into a smutty story (*La
Pucelle*). However, he did not, like the blind Madame du Deffand,
famous for her salon, go as far as to give military information to the
enemy. Blinded also by her senile adoration for Horace Walpole,
she wrote him in 1779, when France and England were at war: 'You
may be sure that although French by birth, I do not adopt the sentiments of my nation,' and 'I am sending you a list of our officers
and troops. . . . I heard yesterday that 8,000 men are being sent into
the Roussillon.' Serving one's country was another nebulous notion.
The eighteenth-century cosmopolitan gravitated toward whoever
appreciated his services. The greatest general of the eighteenth-
century French monarchy was Maurice de Saxe, a German. The
two men who had the greatest influence on the monarchy's finances
were John Law, a Scotsman, and Jacques Necker, a Swiss. Warriors
and artists were often mercenaries. Marshal Schulembourg, another
German, ended his career as a Venetian general after serving Denmark, Poland, and Holland. Irishmen and Jacobites like Count
Bulkeley and Lally-Tollendal fought for France. The Scotch Earl
George Keith represented Frederick II in Paris and Madrid. The
comte de Saint-Germain, French Minister of War under Louis XVI,
had been a minister at the Danish court. French artists glorified
French defeats in foreign courts. Dominique Serres, the official
painter of the British navy, recorded Lord Howe's victory over the
French fleet at Gibraltar. Diderot acted as middleman for Catherine
the Great, who depleted France's art heritage by purchasing the
famous Croizat collection of paintings.

The prototype of the eighteenth-century cosmopolitan was the
prince de Ligne. Born at a time when Belgium was part of the
Austrian empire, he had allowed his genealogist to convince him
that he was a descendant of Charlemagne. His country was not a

territory but a rank, whether he occupied it in Flanders, France, Russia, or Austria. He had grace, ease, poise, and a natural elegance which made him feel at home in any court. 'I like to be a foreigner everywhere,' he wrote, 'French in Austria, Austrian in France, one or the other in Russia, that is the way to be happy everywhere and depend on no one.' Another man for the age was Prince Eugene, Italian-born, French-bred, serving the Austrian empire as a general. A true cosmopolite, he signed his name Eugenio von Savoie.

It was not until the popular armies of the Revolution began to proselytize Europe that nationalism became Messianic and countries began to believe they were the custodians of sacred truths. It had never occurred to the maréchal de Belle-Isle when he occupied Prague in 1742 that the national aspirations of the people might be used against the Austrians. The eighteenth century was much closer to our own attempts to create a united Europe, much closer to Montaigne's generous and fruitful attitude: 'I respect all men as my compatriots and will embrace a Pole as I will a Frenchman, placing the national link behind the common and universal one.'

How could writers who did not even have a clear idea of France as a nation preach the gospel of revolution? It is difficult to accept Taine's description of France as a healthy individual who fell on the ground foaming at the mouth after drinking poison (the writings of the Enlightenment). France had no subversive elements plotting a new order. Rousseau's *Social Contract* appeared in 1762 and was burned in Geneva because it was believed to apply specifically to that republic. Who can prove that Rousseau's influence was greater in fostering revolutionary sentiment than in making English gardens popular with the phrase 'nature never plants in straight lines'?

French eighteenth-century writing seems to be less a cause of the Revolution than part of a multifaceted phenomenon of breakup which led finally to the Revolution. While none of the major literary figures called for a revolution, they contributed to the social decomposition which made it necessary. Like the vibrations of an explosion which shatter windows far from the target, their attacks against religion weakened the monarchy because it could not dissociate itself from the church. Also, they wrote at a historical moment in which the liberated word had the force of a blow. Their programmes were less dangerous to the state than their tone of voice, which marked the end of timorousness, the beginning of provocation. Finally, they had a receptive audience. Ideas have no built-in capacity for distribution and growth. They must 'take' as a vaccine takes. The opinion quoted by the marquise de Crécy is oversimplified but still apt: 'They are wrong to impute the fall of the *ancien régime* to the Encyclopedists: the old house collapsed by itself, and they furnished the materials to build a new one. They are no more responsible for its fall than the rocks that go toward building a new house are responsible for the fire that destroys the old.' Had they lived, they would probably have been victims of the Revolution. Condorcet, the only Encyclopedist who lived through it, poisoned himself during the Terror. Robespierre pronounced their epitaphs as counter-revolutionaries in a speech on the 18 Floréal (May 8) of the year II (1793): 'The most important and most illustrious [sect] was that known under the name of Encyclopedists, which included a few estimable men and a great number of ambitious charlatans; several of its leaders had become important citizens in the State. . . . In politics, this sect always asked for far less than the rights of the people; in morals, it went much further than religious prejudices. Its leaders sometimes inveighed against despotism, although they received pensions from the despots; sometimes they wrote books against the court, and sometimes dedications for kings or speeches and madrigals for the courtiers; they were proud of their work and crawled in anterooms. This sect zealously propagated the opinion of materialism. . . . We owe it in large part the practical philosophy which, making a system out of selfishness, looks upon human society as a war of wits, success as the measure of justice and injustice, honesty as a matter of taste or convention, and the world as the heritage of clever egotists.'

XI

THE PARADOX OF PROSPERITY

> *The revolution was not to break out in an exhausted country but, on the contrary, in a flourishing land on a rising tide of progress. Poverty may sometimes lead to riots, but it cannot bring about great social upheavals. These always arise from a disturbance of the balance between the classes.*
> —ALBERT MATHIEZ, *La Révolution Française*

> *The evil consists in this, that the nation, from the highest to the lowest, is organized so as to go on producing less and less, and paying more and more. She will go on declining, wasting away, giving, after her blood, her marrow; and there will be no end to it, till having reached the last gasp, and just expiring, the convulsion of the death-struggle arouses her once more and raises that feeble body on its legs—Feeble? —grown strong perhaps by fury!*
> —JULES MICHELET, *Histoire de la Révolution Française*

JOHN LAW believed that money was the blood which irrigated the national anatomy and kept it healthy. A regime with a prosperous economy, sound fiscal policies, and a fair tax basis, unblemished by pockets of misery, like refuse on the steps of a palace, was immune to that most communicable disease—discontent. But the blood of the eighteenth-century monarchy was thin and anaemic. A graph showing the unequal rise of prices and wages, and the inverse ratio of taxes to income, appears, with hindsight, as the sawtooth forecast of a revolution. The statistics were hardly seditious, however, since they show that France was Europe's richest country and the eighteenth century was a period of inflationary prosperity. Despite these favourable conditions, the monarchy was incapable of enacting economic and financial reforms. The result is the paradox of prosperity: increasing national wealth matched by increasing personal poverty, rural misery in Europe's granary, the danger of overproduction alternating with the threat of famine. The situation bore an uncomfortable resemblance to the description of France by an Italian diplomat at Versailles as a country where 90 per cent of the population was dying of hunger and 10 per cent of indigestion.

The essential preoccupation of the vast majority of eighteenth-century Frenchmen was the procurement of their daily bread. This meant, in cities, having the money to buy it, and in the countryside, having a sufficient harvest. Famine is not an invention of pro-revolutionary historians to blacken the regime. Much of the population lived on the razor's edge of sustenance, so that a harsh winter was enough to cause insurmountable difficulties. 'The people,' wrote Taine, 'may be said to resemble a man attempting to wade through a pool with the water up to his chin, and who, losing his footing at the slightest depression, sinks and drowns.' The price of a four-pound loaf of bread varied from 8 to 20 sous between 1700 and 1789, while on the eve of the Revolution an unskilled worker earned 25 sous a day, a carpenter 50, and a goldsmith 100. The margin of survival could depend on a 3-sou rise in the price of a four-pound loaf. The eighteenth-century worker was expected to spend half his net income on bread for himself and his family, which made the food riot the classic form of protest. The chorus of the hungry lifted their voices with alarming regularity. In the famous winter of 1709, when the coast of the Mediterranean froze, and crops, fruit trees, and domestic birds were killed, the famine was aggravated by short-sighted officials who continued to allow the export of grain reserves in spite of the disastrous harvest. The situation was so desperate that Louis XIV sold some gold plate. In 1725, there was a riot in Paris' working-class faubourg Saint-Antoine when a baker abruptly increased the price of his bread by 4 sous. Police fired on the rioters, arrested eight, and hanged three. In 1740, the price of the four-pound loaf rose to 20 sous. There were fifty dead in a prison riot protesting the reduction of the bread ration. The marquis d'Argenson said more Frenchmen had died of misery between 1738 and 1740 than in all the wars of Louis XIV (although the population of France increased steadily during the eighteenth century). The threat of famine in eighteenth-century France led to restrictions on the sale of grain, hoarding, and speculation. Experiments to establish the free circulation of grain failed. But it is clear that the single most important economic fact of the *ancien régime* was the price of bread, and that at the same time the writers of the Enlightenment had discovered progress there were large numbers of people still haunted by the fear of famine.

And yet nothing could be more inaccurate than to say that France was poor. Rural France, and in the eighteenth century nine out of ten persons still worked the land, was a quilt of rich and poor provinces, good and bad years. This is a matter of geography and climate. There is nothing surprising about it. What is surprising is that a bad year should have such disastrous effects and that a poor province should find no relief from its blight. Foreigners were struck by the sharp differences from one region to the next. Arthur Young, an English traveller with a keener eye than many of the French king's officials, crossed western France in two journeys and visited the area between Paris and Strasbourg during a third trip in 1789. In his descriptions, prosperous areas are more rarely found than poor ones. In Amiens he saw 'poverty and poor crops . . . women are now ploughing with a pair of horses to sow barley.' In Sologne, 'the fields are scenes of pitiable management, as the houses are of misery.' In the Berri, 'chestnuts are spread over all the fields and yield the food of the poor.' Near Limoges there is 'not a vestige of any human residence . . . an American scene, wild enough for the tomahawk of the savage.' In Peyrac, 'I meet many beggars. All the country, girls and women, are without shoes or stockings, and the ploughmen at their work have neither sabots nor stockings to their feet. This is poverty that strikes at the root of national prosperity . . . it reminded me of the misery of Ireland.' In Combourg he saw that 'husbandry [was] not much further advanced than among the Hurons . . . the people almost as wild as their country . . . Combourg . . . a hideous heap of wretchedness.' In Montauban, 'the children terribly ragged, if possible worse clad than with no clothes at all . . . one-third of what I have seen in this province seems uncultivated and nearly all of it in misery.' Crossing back into France after a side trip to Spain, however, Young had a more favourable impression. 'From the natural and miserable roads of Catalonia,' he wrote, 'you tread at once on a noble causeway . . . instead of beds of torrents you have well-built bridges; and from a country wild, desert and poor we found ourselves in the midst of cultivation and improvement.' Around Pau, the land 'was all in the hands of little proprietors, without the farms being so small as to occasion a vicious and miserable population.' In the Béarn, home of Henri IV, he saw that 'each peasant has the fowl in the pot.'

Having observed a mixture of poverty and prosperity, Young drew two extremely judicious conclusions. He saw that often misery was due not to the peasant's inability to own land but to the fragmentation of land among peasant proprietors. 'The small properties of the peasants are to be found everywhere,' he wrote, 'to a degree we have no idea of in England . . . I have more than once seen division carried to such an excess that a single fruit tree, standing in about ten perch of ground, has constituted a farm.' Contemporary studies bear Young out. P. Loutchisky, who studied the land deeds of four provinces, Artois, Burgundy, the Orléanais and the Dauphiné, discovered that out of 10,374,000 acres of farmland, the peasants owned roughly 5,754,000 acres, and that only 17 per cent of the peasants owned no land at all. Thus, the privileged classes owned less than half the land in these areas. And this was a time when serfdom was still common in continental Europe, and rural labourers were employed in England's large estates. The second point Young made was that 'the misery which we see among the lowest classes in France seems quite inconsistent with a great rise in the price of commodities, occasioned by an increase of industry and wealth.' This is the key to the paradox of prosperity: a large part of the population was not involved in the cycle of economic growth and thus became relatively poorer.

Other travellers also brought back mixed impressions. Laurence Sterne in the 1760's found a peasant house on the road to Lyon with 'a potagerie of an acre and a half, full of everything which could make plenty in a French peasant's house; and on the other side was a little wood which furnished wherewithal to dress it.' But Dr. Tobias Smollett in 1763 found 'their farmhouses mean, their furniture wretched, their apparel beggarly, themselves and their beasts the image of famine . . . I cannot help thinking they groan under oppression, either from their landlords or their government; probably from both.' Lady Wortley Montagu wrote from Dijon in 1739 of 'fresh coloured lusty peasants in good cloth and clean linen,' while Philip Thicknesse in 1766 found that 'one-third [of Brittany] . . . seems uncultivated and nearly all of it is in misery. . . .' with the houses 'miserable heaps of dirt' and the staple 'black corn.' François de la Rochefoucauld, who kept a diary of his travels in the provinces from 1781 to 1783, described by turn scenes of misery and wealth. In the Limousin people were eating chestnuts because they could not afford bread while in Bordeaux the municipality was building a theatre costing 2,500,000 livres. Nantes, which specialized in the slave trade, sent 10,000 Negroes a year to Santo Domingo in exchange for coffee and sugar, while in Brittany peasants ate a kind of soup made from buckwheat. In rich provinces like Normandy and Anjou it was not uncommon to find peasants who owned fifteen or twenty horses and as many cows. A parish priest in Anjou said his parishioners always ate two main courses followed by cheese, butter, and fruit, and a parish priest in Maine said in 1783 that servants were better dressed than the mistress of the house had been twenty years ago. 'France,' in the words of Shakespeare, was 'the world's best garden,' but it was a garden that needed weeding.

A description of day-to-day life in a rural pocket of prosperity has been left thanks to a diary written between 1744 and 1759 by a peasant who lived in the tiny village of Aubais, near Nîmes. There were roughly 900 persons grouped around the castle of the marquis d'Aubais. The village seems a cheerful, well-regulated place, a corporate society in which everyone knew his appointed role and individual problems were worked out on a communal level, as though in a family. It was a tranquil, lazy life that turned with the seasons and was governed by the three familiar village wise men—the priest, the magistrate, and the lord. Food was plentiful and the rigours of winter were fought with 'that sovereign antidote, white wine.' The sale of bread and meat were village monopolies, which means that prices were controlled. The village tax or *taille* hovered around 3,000 livres a year, or about 18 livres for each of the 170 families, which was considered moderate and was attributed to the fact that the marquis had influence at court. Aubais was exclusively rural, but the neighbouring village of Gallargues made a dye from sunflowers that was exported to Holland to colour Edam cheese. The villagers were much concerned with news and gossip, which spread from mouth to ear; the diary is full of events both trivial and important, local and national, which resurrect the flavour of the time: a marquis died of epilepsy, a new military governor was appointed, a priest died while delivering a sermon, an archer fell into a well, the Margrave of Brandenburg visited Avignon, a local woman left for

Paris for a gallstone operation, two ships loaded with wheat were sunk in the port of Sète, the Garonne flooded Toulouse, in Spain there was an earthquake. Louis XV raised soldiers' pay one sou, and the Académie proposed for its 1749 eloquence prize the subject: Are riches more perilous to virtue than poverty? Feeling for the monarchy was still strong, and the diary is full of phrases like 'our invincible monarch, for whose health and military prosperity his people pray.' There is no trace of sedition or criticism. If every village had resembled Aubais the monarchy would have been eternal.

Cities were generally more prosperous than the countryside, for they were able to work out special tax deals and were also the principal beneficiaries of increased foreign trade. Santo Domingo, to which France had clung at the expense of the rest of her colonial empire, provided half the world's sugar, which arrived in French ports. Between 1763 and 1778, 245 ships were built in Bordeaux. The millionaire shipowner Bonaffé alone owned 300 ships. Every port had its monopoly; Nantes handled the slave trade, Saint-Malo shipped Breton textiles to Spain, Le Havre launched a passenger service with New York in 1783. Inland cities also thrived; the silk industry in Lyon employed 65,000, and most cities had artisans and small industries which specialized in one or two products; Blois was famous for its gloves, Rouen for its cotton goods, Le Creusot for its foundry, Langres for its knives.

The result of the boom in the cities was feverish public construction and urban development. Lyon converted the swamps of Errache into a residential district. In Aix-en-Provence the magnificent castle of the comtes de Provence was razed for a housing development. Architects in Strasbourg adopted a gridiron street plan for new neighbourhoods built in 1765. Amiens tore down its feudal ramparts and girdled the city with wide boulevards. In Marseilles, 10,000 new houses were built from 1721 to 1789. The budget of the city of Reims rose from 60,000 livres in 1710 to 190,000 livres in 1785.

The general signs of prosperity were population, which increased from roughly 17 million in 1700 to 26 million on the eve of the Revolution; the growth of trade, which quadrupled between 1716 and 1788; and taxes, which rose steadily (Necker estimated that in the last decade of the old order the income from indirect taxes was increasing at the rate of 2 million livres a year). The depression that followed Law's fiasco lasted until 1730, with a low point reached in 1725, a year of famine. The 'Mississippi,' however, was not a total mirage, and Caribbean sugar sweetened many French pocketbooks. More important, the failure of Law's bank was followed by attempts to stabilize the French pound. In 1726, a landmark in the *ancien régime's* economic history, the value of the gold louis was fixed at 24 livres and did not substantially change until the Revolution. The decision ended one of the *ancien régime's* most pernicious fiscal policies, which consisted in trying to control inflation by arbitrarily changing the value of the livre (there was no numerical designation engraved on either the gold louis or the silver crown, because their value was changed so often. Thus, one could not know by looking at it how much a gold louis was worth, although there was the consolation of knowing from which of France's seventeen mints it came, since each one had a trademark which it stamped on the coins (for Paris, it was the letter A, for Pau it was a cow).

Economic recovery followed stabilization of the livre, and led to an inflationary phase that lasted from roughly 1730 to 1778. The population, which had remained almost stationary from the fourteenth to the eighteenth century—with gains in the birthrate offset by natural disasters, famines, and wars—began to rise. The mortality rate was reduced by a third, and the average life span rose from twenty-one to twenty-seven years. Despite famine years in 1740, 1750, and 1770, the economy was in a period of expansion. Prices rose steadily. It took 165 livres to buy in 1789 what could be bought in 1740 for 100 livres. There was a sharp increase in the sale of colonial products and other luxuries. The growing population provided new consumers, business volume rose steadily, there was a good return on finance capital.

But a contraction set in shortly after the reign of Louis XVI began. Agricultural prices fell off from 1778 to 1787. Industry languished, exports declined, production slowed down, there was heavy unemployment in the silk mills of Lyon and other urban production centres. On the heels of this ten-year recession came the disastrous grain harvest of 1788, which resulted in France's worst economic crisis of the century. Hailstones as big as fists left magnificent wheat crops looking as though they had been trampled by an army. Fruit trees were permanently damaged. Food was scarce. Urban workers were laid off.

The crisis sharpened discontent, and the great mass of unemployed was to provide willing recruits for the events of 1789. Between 1726 and 1789 the price of wheat rose 66 per cent, rye 71 per cent, timber

91 per cent, and wine 14 per cent, a phenomenal overall rise despite the decline of the ten final years. But during the same period wages rose by only 22 per cent, so that the staple, bread, consumed an ever greater part of the wage earner's income. Instead of profiting from the boom, he became its victim. Nor did it profit the small land-owner, who had a small yield because of archaic farming methods, had to save one-fifth of his harvest for seed, and pay taxes, tithes, and feudal dues. He had no surplus to sell (with the exception of wine from his vineyards) and thus did not share in the profit spiral. Land ownership did not make the peasant economically independent; indeed, in an inflationary period it made him less well off than tenant farmers, whose rents rose much more slowly than agricultural prices. But once he owned land, the instrument of production, the peasant was more acutely aware of the inequities and mismanage-ment that prevented him from enjoying the fruit of his production. As long as the peasant was, in Richelieu's terms, 'a mule which, accustomed to its load, is spoiled more by repose than by work' (as was still the case in Germany and Russia), he submitted dazedly to his condition, but the small landowner in France was increasingly conscious of the disparity between his own poverty and the country's wealth.

The stagnation of 1788 shows that the whole economy could founder as the result of an early chill or a drought. It was a climate-controlled economy, far too dependent on grain production. The government was aware of the preponderant place of grain in the economy, but was unable to devise remedies for poor harvests. In principle, France produced enough grain to meet its needs. In good years, she supplied the rest of Europe and in one four-year period under Louis XV exported more than 32 million bushels. The policy since Colbert had been to impose severe regulations on the sale and distribution of grain to stop speculation and prevent famine. Farmers had to declare their yields, and could not store grain for more than two years. Grain merchants could not store more than a certain amount, and conditions of sale were spelled out in forbidding detail. Grain could not travel from one province to another without government permission. Nonetheless, speculators continued to hoard so that they could sell it when the price went up in a bad harvest year. Grain was in fact the most common form of speculation, since the economy was based on it.

Since government intervention was unable to avert periodic crises and abrupt price increases, a popular belief arose that there was collusion between the government and the speculators. A disappointing wheat harvest was sure to yield a bumper crop in rumours. In 1724, the first year of Louis XV's reign, there were rumours that government officials had bought the entire grain harvest and stocked it on the Isle of Guernsey. In 1752 Louis XV ordered grain reserves stored as a preventive measure, but the public believed he was making a million pounds a day from speculation which cost the lives of thousands of his subjects. An entry in d'Argenson's memoirs dated October 3 of that year says: 'The rumour in Paris is that the king speculates on grain.' In 1765, persistent rumours of this odious speculation were immortalized by pamphleteers under the name of 'famine compact.' The rumour was based on a contract between l'Averdy, the Controller General, and a miller named Malisset, who was asked to constitute a reserve stock of 320,000 pints of wheat, for which he was paid 24,000 livres and which he was allowed to sell at a fixed price. This was viewed by the popular mind as yet another crooked deal, although no evidence points to any wrongdoing. In 1768, when the price of the four-pound loaf reached 16 sous, the following placard appeared in Paris: 'Under Henri IV, bread was sometimes expensive because of wars and France had a king; under Louis XIV it sometimes went up because of war and sometimes because of famine and France had a king; now there is no war and no famine and the cost of bread still goes up and France has no king because the king is a grain merchant.' For four years, under another Controller General of Finances, abbot Joseph-Marie Terray, a policy of sensible economic planning was enforced. A national grain administration was responsible for stocking grain in case of famine, and importing it when necessary. But the widespread belief in the famine compact persisted, although the only thing that could be held against Terray was that he rented the grain administration storehouses on his country estate.

Against the policy of government control, there were advocates of free circulation of grain who argued that regulations did not prevent famines but caused them. For one thing, they said, regulations discouraged farmers from increasing their grain acreage, for they would have to go through a lot of red tape to sell their surplus if the harvest was good. For another, regulations made it cumbersome and slow for provinces with extra grain to send it to needy provinces. Freedom of circulation was based on the common sense argument

that by encouraging commerce instead of restricting it, and by allowing the laws of supply and demand to operate, everyone would
have enough grain. Even though the price would go up in poor
harvest years, it would still be lower than the prices imposed by
speculators.

One of the most forceful advocates of free circulation of grain was
Anne-Robert-Jacques Turgot, who became Controller General under
Louis XVI in 1774 and lost no time in putting his theories to practice. On September 13, he decreed the end of 'the imprisonment of
grain,' which could hereafter be bought and sold freely. Turgot's
timing could not have been worse, for the harvest of 1774 was paltry.
Turgot knew it, and knew that the price of grain would rise and
threaten his liberal reform, but he was impatient to act. He believed
that another reform, the creation of state-run workshops, would
allow the poor to earn enough money to buy bread and offset a price
rise. The result was unfortunate. There were never worse food riots
than under his enlightened administration, bearing out de Tocqueville's phrase that 'the most perilous moment for a bad government
is the one when it seeks to mend its ways.'

Turgot had gone too fast. Provincial authorities were confused
about the implementations of his reforms. There were transportation
problems. Rivers were frozen and grain could not be carried by
barge. In April and May, food riots broke out in France with the
swift succession of a chain of firecrackers. They have gone down in
history under the name of the 'flour war' and French history textbooks still teach that they were organized by grain speculators
whose dealings were threatened by Turgot's decree. Louis XVI himself believed that the riots were 'an odious machination.'

The price of a four-pound loaf of bread had gone up from 11 to 14
sous in a few months. The rioters did not constitute a revolutionary
crowd clamouring for liberty or equality. They were just a lot of
hungry men and women who wanted bread at 2 sous a pound. In
April, rioters attacked a miller in Dijon, and a magistrate suspected
of stocking grain had to hide in a dungheap. The military commander, Lieutenant General La Tour du Pin, caned some of the
rioters and told them: 'My friends, the grass is just beginning to
grow, why don't you go and graze?' Similar riots took place almost
daily in dozens of towns and villages. Rioters threw grain merchants
into ponds, looted mills, seized sacks of grain being carried down-
river on barges, broke into bakeries, and even marched on Versailles,

obtaining from Louis XVI the promise of bread at 8 sous for a four-pound loaf.

Government repression was severe. About 400 rioters were arrested and two were hanged for breaking into bakeries. A third man sentenced to be hanged was pardoned because he was in the service of the king's brother, the comte d'Artois. Louis XVI did not favour capital punishment, and wrote Turgot: 'If you can spare those who were swept along you will do well.' Despite popular belief that the flour war was a conspiracy, no serious evidence of concerted action has ever been found. No leaders were unmasked, no threads of any plot were unravelled. What the evidence does show is that these were independent riots caused by the scarcity of grain and the high cost of bread. The dates of the successive riots show that the example of one town led to a riot in a neighbouring town. There was no political content in the rioting. The price rise that resulted from Turgot's poor timing was close to the threshold of survival for many, and the state workshops did not have the expected result. When the price of a four-pound loaf was 14 sous, the unskilled labourer who made 20 sous a day and needed three pounds of daily bread for himself and his family was spending more than half his income on bread alone.

Thus the flour war appears as a series of spontaneous riots with limited economic objectives. In a sense, however, they announced the revolutionary riots of 1789 which overthrew the regime. People no longer blamed the seasons for high prices, they blamed the government. They were, although leaderless, testing the effectiveness of mass protests. Moreover, the number of riots showed that the oppressed were capable of common action in pursuit of that most legitimate of goals, a full stomach. Finally, the riots took place in a climate of aborted reform, whereas earlier, under Terray's economic programme, bread had reached an even higher price (16 sous for a four-pound loaf) and there had been no riots. The same consciousness that led the king to experiment with Turgot's liberal policies led his subjects to rise up against a situation they had heretofore accepted. The moral is not that good intentions are dangerous but that if they are not immediately successful they aggravate crises.

There were many other areas of the economy where the government either should have acted or did act in vain. The currency reform of 1726 stands in almost solitary splendour. The Controller General of Finance, who manipulated the nation's pursestrings, was the regime's key figure. As one of them, Pontchartrain, explained to the English ambassador Lord Portland: 'You have already seen the grandeur and magnificence with which the king is surrounded, the eagerness of his subjects to pay him their court and be gratified by his slightest gaze: well, sir! This great and majestic prince is paying constant court to his Controller General.' It was also a highly volatile post—there were twenty-six Controllers General between 1715 and 1789, an average of about one every three years, ten of them in the fifteen years of Louis XVI's effective reign. One at least, Turgot, was a great man. Some, like Law, were adventurers, some, like Calonne, were apt to confuse their own pockets with the state's, and some, like Necker, were a mixture of opportunism and idealism. One is remembered because he left his name to those shadowy, one-dimensional profiles called silhouettes (he had proposed taxes on bachelors and external signs of wealth, and remained in office eight months). Almost all of them made honest attempts to cut the gordian knot of the monarchy's finances, but were defeated by the combination of the privileged orders' resistance and the country's administrative chaos.

The main thrust was to overcome tax inequalities. The tallage (*taille*) was originally a tax against dispensation from military service, named after the incision made on a piece of wood which was the taxpayer's proof of payment, a picturesque receipt used until the Revolution in certain parts of France. There were two forms of *taille*. The first, or *taille personnelle,* was an income tax which was paid neither by the nobility which fought in the wars nor by the non-combatant clergy. The second, or *taille réelle,* was a property tax which was levied only in certain parts of France (mainly the southwest), and which nobles who owned a certain amount of property were meant to pay, although in fact they had various systems of avoiding payment, such as misrepresenting the amount of land they owned or obtaining court favours. The *taille,* as many finance ministers of the *ancien régime* pointed out, was the burden of the Third Estate, and its amount was decided each year according to information on crops and commerce. It was up to the parish and community to collect the *taille* from its residents and turn it over to the king. Tax collectors were citizens appointed by municipal assemblies, and changed each year. Collecting the *taille* from the villagers was a very unpleasant civic duty, and the *ancien régime* brings to mind an embarrassed village tax collector, impressed into service, waiting outside church on Sunday to snare laggard tax-payers. If the village or parish fell behind, its four most important citizens were jailed. There were, however, a host of special favours, exceptions, tricks and exemptions which made the *taille* fall heaviest on those who did not have a resourceful parish priest or a friendly lord to intercede for them.

It was the constant preoccupation of the Controller General to broaden the tax base. Under Louis XIV, in 1695, a *capitation,* or head tax, was devised, from which no one, in theory, could escape except the indigent. It divided the nation into twenty-two classes, much as the Chinese Ming dynasty had done, and taxed each according to its ability to pay. The highest category, including royal princes, ministers, and General Farmers, paid 2,000 livres a year, the next-to-lowest (soldiers and tenant farmers) paid one livre a year and the lowest paid nothing. But the head tax was hard to collect. Courtiers with access to the king could always find excuses (gambling debts, a new suit), and there were examples in the Berri of noblemen who tried to pass themselves off as commoners to put themselves in a lower bracket. Eventually, the categories were forgotten and the *capitation* became merely an accessory to the *taille*.

In times of war or financial crisis, which was most of the time, emergency taxes had to be levied. In 1710, during the War of the Spanish Succession, Louis XIV imposed a tax called the 'tenth,' which attempted to collect 10 per cent of his subjects' income. The 'tenth' was presented as a temporary war tax, but it reappeared again under Louis XV, in 1733 (War of the Polish Succession) and 1741 (War of the Austrian Succession). In 1749, Controller General Jean-Baptiste Machault announced a new tax called the 'twentieth,' for which there would be no exceptions. Cities would not be allowed to avoid it by paying a yearly subscription. Even the clergy would have to contribute some of Peter's pence. The 'twentieth' taxed real property, loans, mortgages, and business profits, and exempted wage earners and tenant farmers. It was the *ancien régime*'s most gallant effort to impose an equitable tax, and it drew immediate attacks from all the vested interests whose privileges were threatened. Those provinces which still kept as a feudal legacy their own tax-collecting administration—Brittany, Provence, Burgundy, Artois, and Languedoc—refused to endorse the new government budget. The Parlements incited to civil disobedience. The clergy, convened in general assembly in 1750, said: 'We will never consent to give as a tribute of

obeisance what we have always given as proof of love and respect.'
The peculiar position of the clergy was that while it was the wealthiest
of the nation's three orders it contributed the least. Its annual income
was estimated at between 150 and 200 million livres, but it insisted
that it was exempt from property taxes by divine right. Instead, it
made voluntary gifts to the king which were much lower than the taxes
it should have paid. From 1700 to 1789 the clergy volunteered contributions of 268 million livres, an average of 3,608,000 livres a year,
or about 2 per cent of its income.

Faced with the prospect of paying taxes, the clergy brandished the
hobgoblin of religious persecution and threatened to boycott the spiritual needs of the nation and retire to its seminaries. Finally, in 1751,
Louis XV gave in, and Machault's tax became, like all the others, a
victim of exceptions and special considerations. Allowing the clergy
to maintain its 'offering of love' instead of paying a realistic tax
based on its enormous wealth was one of Louis XV's most unfortunate decisions. All those whose tax burden was increased by the
clergy's immunity found new reasons for anticlericalism. It was,
moreover, another example that civil disobedience was rewarded
instead of punished. Louis XV had begun by supporting Machault's
fiscal intransigence and finally given in to the lobbies of the privileged groups. When Machault tried in 1756 to levy a second 'twentieth,' resistance was greater than ever.

Thus, the fundamental opposition to tax reforms came from the
wealthy privileged groups unwilling to share the fiscal burden with
the overtaxed Third Estate. When in 1789 the three orders sent their
written complaints to the meeting of the Estates General in Paris, the
Third Estate of Nemours remarked: 'One day people will find it
hard to believe that wealth was enough to purchase nobility, and
that nobility was enough not to pay taxes; so that there was only one
way to escape taxation and that was to make a fortune.'

If the one way to dodge taxes was to make a fortune, an excellent
way to make a fortune was to collect indirect taxes for the king.
In 1701, under Louis XIV, the Company of General Farmers was
created. It was a cartel of financiers which contracted with the king to
collect the nation's indirect taxes. The king was freed from the administrative burden of collecting the taxes himself. But more important, the financiers provided the cash advances which the monarchy
so desperately needed. If the king had collected the taxes, he could
not have reaped immediate profits. Thus, the General Farm was the

product of an already unhealthy fiscal situation in which the monarchy, its credit exhausted, developed techniques to spend its income before it was earned. Apart from an interruption during Law's brief financial directorate, the General Farm continued to operate until the Revolution, and built up a private administration of 30,000 employees which dwarfed the state's.

Every six years the General Farm signed a contract with the king, which promised the monarchy a minimum income and a share in profits. One sign of France's basic wealth in the eighteenth century is that each contract was larger than the last—80 million livres in 1726, 89 million in 1731, 94 million in 1737, and 110 million in 1765. The General Farmers were sixty capitalists, each of whom invested roughly 1·5 million livres to cover operating costs. They had 1,400 offices throughout France, a private army, and regiments of clerks and tax collectors. They formed a fourth estate of wealthy and powerful men who married their daughters to the great names of France and were able to keep their highly lucrative jobs in their families, thanks to a cat's cradle of court complicities. Each received an annual salary of 24,000 livres plus expenses, 10 per cent on the first million in profits and 6 per cent on profits above the first million. Their goal was simple: to squeeze from the nation the highest possible profit. Voltaire called the system 'organized robbery.' Once at a dinner where the guests were competing to tell the shortest tall tale, Voltaire won with: 'Once upon a time there was an honest General Farmer.'

The General Farmer had developed to a fine art the technique of bilking the government. The idea was to set a low minimum estimate, with bonus clauses for amounts over the estimate. The profits of the so-called David contract were 60 million livres, of which the king received 14,400,000, while the sixty General Farmers shared the rest. An indication of the General Farmers' prosperity is that the indirect taxes they collected were a more important source of national revenue than direct taxation. In 1725, out of a total national income of 204 million livres, direct taxes accounted for 87·5 million and indirect taxes for 99 million (the balance being made up by income on royal domains and miscellaneous items). In 1788, direct taxes made up 29·24 per cent and indirect taxes 32·47 per cent of a national income of 459,919,500 livres.

Not surprisingly, the General Farmers were known as 'the bloodsuckers of the nation,' a reputation to which some of them contributed by extravagant displays of luxury. Grimod de la Reynière, who built the Elysée palace, had solid silver feeding troughs for his horses, and Bouret, when he gave dinners, prepared two bouquets for each of his lady guests, one of flowers, the other of precious stones. It was not only ostentation, but the absurd nature of some of the taxes collected, which made the General Farm one of the most hated institutions of the old order. Twenty-five to 30 per cent of its total revenue came from the salt tax, according to which each family had to purchase a certain amount of salt a year at state-controlled prices. The General Farm had its own police to catch salt smugglers, who were often summarily 'branched' (hanged from branches).

It is hard to find any product under the *ancien régime* which was not taxed by the General Farm. There were taxes on playing cards, soap, snuff, liquor, wine, paper, leather, starch, and spices. There was a tax on tobacco, which was sold in a long twist called a 'carrot,' interlaced with a string, which the buyer had to shred. There were customs duties at the national, provincial and local level. There were taxes on transportation. Every commodity entering Paris paid a 'right of entry,' and the General Farmers ringed the capital with a high wall and sixty-six arches to stop smuggling; it was still uncompleted at the time of the Revolution. Attempts by Turgot and Necker to end the monopoly of the General Farm were inconclusive. The system had become married to the monarchy, a demanding wife unable to live within her budget. Not only did it provide short-term cash advances, it had become a long-term investor in the public debt. And the General Farmers' bribes kept them popular at court.

The disadvantages of the system were first that the monarchy did not receive the full benefit of its indirect taxes. If it had, it might conceivably have alleviated the most oppressive taxes as total revenues rose. At the same time, the General Farm made tax dodging seem almost heroic. Those who did not pay their taxes were not robbing the king, but the crooked businessmen who were themselves robbing the king. There was a conspiracy from one end of France to the other to avoid indirect taxes. Smuggling was considered a noble profession. The duty to contribute to the upkeep of the state was clouded by the General Farm's role as a private, profit-earning middleman. An eighteenth-century Frenchman could loathe the General Farm and still love the king. The people had their vengeance on May 8, 1894, when the twenty-eight General Farmers who could be rounded up, including the famous chemist Lavoisier, were indiscriminately guillotined.

The multiplication of indirect taxes and customs duties also served to fragment the French economy. In our own time General de Gaulle has commented ironically about the difficulties of governing a people who make more than 200 kinds of cheese. What then must have been the difficulties of the monarchy when there were 110 ways of measuring grain, where the unit of weight changed from province to province, where there were seven different regional rates for the salt tax and where in 1789 there were still 1,600 river tolls, 40 on the Loire River alone. The combination of lack of unity in weights and measures and local regulations was a great obstacle to commerce.

Inspectors publicly burned cloth because it did not match dyeing specifications, as though the cloth had committed heresy. Weavers rioted in Rouen in 1752 when inspectors ripped the cloth off their looms. And added to the government regulations there were the guild regulations, pitting roaster against fowler and wigmaker against barber in endless jurisdictional squabbles.

It is hardly surprising that in an economy of such kaleidoscopic decentralization, the notion of a budget did not exist. The ministers themselves admitted to having only the vaguest knowledge of the state of the nation's finances. In 1789, the Controller General was still working on accounts for 1780. At the end of each year the monarchy attempted to add up what it had spent and what it had taken in, and generally found a large deficit. In 1724, income amounted to 187 million livres and expenses to 204 million; in 1759, during the Seven Years' War, income was 285 million and expenses were 418 million. In 1756 income was 253 million livres and expenses 269 million—98 million for defence, 25 for the navy and the colonies, 30 million for the king's household and royal pensions, 62 million for annuities, 12 million for salaries and offices, and 42 million for other expenses. Until Turgot, the public had never been informed about financial affairs. The tradition was that the treasury was the king's cashbox. When he needed money he scribbled the amount on a piece of paper with the notation 'I know the employment of this sum.' That was the only accounting.

Controllers General were always scrambling to meet payments and make up deficits. Under Louis XV finances were at one point so low that stable boys could not be paid their salaries of 20 francs a day. Taxes and anticipations were not enough; ministers had to resort to selling and reselling offices, annuities, loans, and lotteries in which the losing tickets could be redeemed at the end of seven or nine years or kept at 4 per cent interest. When Abbot Terray became Controller General in 1769 there was a current deficit of 60 million livres and a national debt of more than 100 million. Revenue for 1770 had already been spent. By 1774 he had reduced the deficit to 27 million. One of his methods was voiding provincial offices and then reselling them. 'But, sir,' complained the syndic of Languedoc, 'you are picking my pocket.' 'What else would you have me pick?' asked Terray. There was little public confidence in the state, even after the currency reform of 1726, so that only high interest rates could attract lenders. In 1782, Controller General Joly de Fleury floated a high-interest life annuity. Swiss financiers thought up a scheme called 'the young ladies of Geneva.' Noting that there was a low mortality rate among wellborn ladies brought up in a healthy mountain climate, they bought Joly de Fleury's annuities and named thirty seven-year-old girls the beneficiaries.

Terray was also one of the many ministers who tried to reduce the court's expenses. He wrote Louis XV in 1770: 'If Your Majesty gave the order to save a few millions on his household or his pensions, what happiness for the state!' But preaching austerity at court was as useless as singing to deaf-mutes. Luxury was the stuff of court life. Money had a different meaning to courtiers. Sustenance level meant affording a carriage and a dozen lackeys. A courtier could be poor with an income of 50,000 livres a year, and it was up to the king to keep the machine turning with pensions and gifts. The king's household, which filled 137 pages in the Versailles almanac, consisted of roughly 6,000 civilian and 8,000 military attendants. Its estimated cost was roughly 30 million livres a year, about the same as the budget for the navy. There were thousands of pensions to pay, not only to court favourites but also to army veterans, retired civil servants, doctors, writers and inventors. There was a prodigious amount of waste. There was a street in Versailles where valets went to sell left-over food. Louis XV was not a dupe and told Choiseul: 'The theft in my household is enormous, but it is impossible to put an end to it . . . too many powerful people are involved . . . believe me, don't get excited about it and let this incurable vice subsist.'

Considering the number of pensions the king paid (more than 20,000 were listed in the Red Book drawn up by the National Assembly), the expense of his household was not that terrible a drain on the economy. It was not the cost of luxury that was dangerous, but its example in contrast to public misery. Feeble attempts were made to reduce court expenditures. In 1774, when Louis XVI came to the throne, a programme of austerity was announced—the king for dinner would eat only four hors d'oeuvres, four entrées, two roasts, and six desserts.

But this spirit of sacrifice was short-lived, and it was during the reign of Louis XVI, in the years of Versailles' decline, that the royal household was most ruinous. Turgot, the first minister since Colbert who had a complete programme of economic reform, remained in power less than two years, falling under the attacks of a court cabal. He was zealous but tactless. He had the necessary crusading spirit without the equally necessary subtlety to handle the court. Mirabeau wrote that he was like the 'cashier of a large firm.' His ambition was to reduce the expense of the king's household to 14 million livres a year. The ambition of Marie Antoinette and her greedy favourites was to increase it until it reached 62 million livres in 1789. The king's coronation at Reims was the first test. It offended both Turgot's passion for economy and his hatred of superstition. He wanted it held in Paris instead of Reims, to save money, and, wrote Condorcet, 'to destroy the prejudice which destines the ceremony to be held in Reims and uses an oil regarded as miraculous, according to a fable rejected by all critics.' The coronation was held in Reims, over his objections. He stubbornly insisted on suppressing a postal superintendence for which the queen had a candidate, thereby making a dangerous enemy. His disgrace showed that there was no remedy for the extravagance of the royal budget, which could be changed only by abolishing the court itself.

Subsequent Controllers General made token efforts. Jacques Necker, the Protestant Geneva banker converted into a minister of the Catholic French court, cut a few loose fronds from the jungle of special interests; he dismissed, among others, eight equerries who brought the king bouillon in the morning and four couriers who carried snacks in shoulder bags when he went hunting. But Necker was a courtier, and understood the importance of being generous where the queen was concerned.

It was actually Loménie de Brienne, whom historians have called a 'criminal' and an 'adventurer,' who accomplished the most impressive reforms during the sixteen months he was in office. By dismissing half the king's household, including the falconry, the wolf-hunting train, and the boar-hunting pack, he saved 4,954,000 livres a year. The merger of the large and small stable alone saved 2,460,000 livres. It was decided to sell or destroy several royal castles to save on their upkeep. Pensions were reduced and granted only once a year, to regulate the continuous flow of favour-seekers. Great savings were expected, but, in the second half of 1788, it was already too late.

After the short-lived promise of Turgot's brisk measures, the reign of Louis XVI sank into a recession which created favourable conditions for the Revolution. There was an overwhelming conjuncture of misfortunes: an economic depression brought about by a drop in agricultural prices, a financial crisis caused by French aid in the War of American Independence, an aristocratic reaction which led to the strict interpretation of feudal rights and privileges, and, finally, a severe winter in 1788 which blighted the land and spread misery.

The depression roughly coincided with the start of the reign. A heavy grape harvest led to a slump in the price of wine which ruined thousands of small growers. The price of wine dropped 50 per cent. Exceptional harvests in 1776 made the price of grain go down, which was particularly hard on tenant farmers in the north and the east, who had just renewed nine-year leases at higher rents because of the good years under Louis XV. Owners of large farms, to cut their losses, reduced their help, and unemployment rose. Unemployed rural labourers could find no work in cities, where industry and commerce stagnated because of the drop in the purchasing power of the nation's rural majority. The American war cut off the supply of cotton. An epidemic of murrain in 1785, which killed almost half the livestock in France, made the price of wool soar, apart from ruining farmers who could not plough their fields or sell their cattle. Textile production in Lyon dropped by half and thousands of workers were laid off. Industry was also affected by the 1786 commercial treaty with England, which provided for the exchange of French wheat and wine against English iron and cloth. The depression was aggravated by the blight of 1788, a severe drought resulting in a poor harvest, and a fierce winter which froze rivers and blocked transportation. Bread reached the highest prices of the century. Construction was at a standstill; hospitals were full; there was a dangerous proliferation of beggars and bandits; and peasants, months before the incident of the Bastille, began looting farms, attacking grain shipments, and refusing to pay feudal rights. Thus there was, as modern historians like Georges Lefebvre have confirmed, a 'misery factor' in the French Revolution.

At the same time, France was committed to an onerous policy of military and financial assistance in the American war. Necker estimated it cost France a total of 330 million livres, or roughly the entire national income of one year. Taxes did not bring in sufficient funds from the depressed economy, and the last three important Controllers General, Necker, Calonne, and Loménie de Brienne, resorted to the same tired expediencies which had already failed under the reign of Louis XIV—borrowing at high interest rates, which increased the public debt and prolonged the financial crisis. There was an anomalous combination of special taxes and heavy borrowing, in which the majority was overtaxed but the treasury was still empty. The ludicrous climax to this situation came in August, 1788, when the Controller General, Loménie de Brienne, learned that the state was on the edge of bankruptcy—there was in the public treasury the absurd sum of 400,000 livres, enough to keep the state functioning for about six hours. He avoided bankruptcy by floating bonds at 5 per cent interest with which the government paid its bills, but had to resign his office. That celebrated Swiss prestidigitator, Jacques Necker, returned to power and resumed his policy of borrowing from banker friends.

It was just at this time, when the rural classes were feeling the pinch of the depression, that the aristocrat landowners began to make inordinate demands on them. Influenced by the theories of the physiocrats on improving agriculture with large farms, scientific methods, and fertilized instead of fallow fields, the landowners began trying to consolidate and enclose their scattered holdings. They tried to restrict certain rights of the peasants which were as sacred as their own feudal privileges—the peasant could graze his cattle on land already harvested, collect stubble (and thus opposed the use of the sickle, which cut lower), glean in harvested fields, and chop wood under certain conditions. The livelihood of poor peasants depended heavily on these rights, which the landed nobility curtailed in its effort to transform French agriculture and pattern it on the English large estate. There was a succession of decrees which gave the landowners the right to enclose part of the communal lands and which were bitterly protested by the rural proletariat.

As part of the feudal reaction to increase their power and oppose change, the nobles were increasingly harsh in the interpretation of their feudal privileges. Their rights were listed in oft-forgotten, musty registers. Under the reign of Louis XVI there was a general move to revise these registers. In the redrafting, privileges fallen into disuse were revived and new privileges were invented. The peasant or tenant farmer or small landowner, already beset by a serious agricultural slump and increased taxes, found himself subjected to heavier feudal obligations. For fifty years the Philosophes had been announcing the arrival of social progress, but instead the peasant had to bear new feudal abuses. Often, the lord farmed out the collection of his rights, just as the king farmed out the collection of indirect taxes, and the profit-seeking collectors implemented the new rights with heartless efficiency. It was as a clerk rewriting land registers and collecting feudal rights that the revolutionary leader Gracchus Babeuf learned to hate the privileged orders. The consequences of the feudal reaction can be gauged by the fact that regions of France where the land registers were not reinterpreted and the lords did not increase their demands on the peasants, like the Vendée, remained practically immune to the revolutionary fever.

But all of France was, to varying degrees, buffeted by multiple economic disasters. Like those unfortunate persons who eat a great deal but nonetheless suffer from malnutrition, France was a rich country with an economy that could not assimilate and distribute its riches. Curiously enough, the nation suffered its worst distress from the lapses of a backward agricultural economy at the same time that pastoral conceits became fashionable at court: just as dairymaids dream that they are queens, Marie Antoinette played at being dairymaid, in her miniature farm decorated with thatch cottages, peasants washing their linen in the artificial lake, cows, sheep, donkeys, and pigeons with identifying rings to distinguish them from the unprivileged orders of pigeonhood. The image of the queen milking cows, churning butter, and proudly offering her farm-fresh eggs to favourite courtiers for their breakfasts seems a far more hallucinating metaphor of decline than the impiety of the Regent or the sense of futility of Louis XV.

XII

LOUIS THE BEHEADED

> *Let us suppose that it was not good king Louis
> who reigned at that moment but Henri IV or Louis
> XIV. Let us suppose that instead of Turgot, a re-
> markable economist and philosopher but a man
> totally lacking in common sense, Richelieu had pre-
> sided over the destinies of France. . . .*
> —A. CHOULGHINE, *History and Life*

> *During the fifteen years of Louis XVI's reign,
> almost all political, religious, and judiciary questions
> were examined and often solved. No nation ever
> obtained from its government such numerous and
> important reforms in such a short time. Louis XVI
> did not desire royalty, he accepted it as a duty.*
> —ERNEST SEMICHON, *Les Réformes sous
> Louis XVI*

THE REIGN of Louis XVI, said Alexis de Tocqueville, shows that a weak regime invites revolution when it seeks to reform itself. After the majestic disdain of Louis XIV and the gloomy apathy of Louis XV came a king who seemed to have been invented by the writers of the Enlightenment—he abolished torture and forced labour for public works (the infamous corvée), freed the serfs, gave the Protestants freedom of worship, and suppressed discriminatory taxes against the Jews. He was genuinely concerned with public welfare. He visited the overcrowded Hôtel Dieu hospital incognito and the sight of four patients in the same bed shocked him into a building programme. He wanted also to build provincial foundling homes, and schools for the deaf and dumb. He founded pawnshops, which loaned money at 3 per cent interest. He wanted to reform the prisons, close the Vincennes dungeon and raze the Bastille.

The traditional concept of divine-right monarchy, which considers the nation as personal property and subjects as the king's children, was no longer an article of faith. Louis XVI accepted the principle that his subjects had rights. He was the first Bourbon who refused to tolerate a Black Cabinet. He said the correspondence of citizens was sacred, and called the violation of private letters 'an odious method.' New language crept into official pronouncements. Citizen replaced subject and the good of the people replaced the will of the king. Louis XVI was virtuous. There were no mistresses to inspire Paris pamphleteers, no secret orgies behind locked doors to be put to verse. Inheriting the Bourbon mania for the hunt, he killed 189,251 pieces of game and ran down 1,274 stags between 1775 and 1789. But he reduced the size of his hunt to economize on court expenses. He was closer to Rousseau's natural man than he was to Louis XIV, and learned a manual trade. 'Unfortunately,' writes Madame Campan, one of Marie Antoinette's maids, 'the king showed too strong a taste for the mechanical arts. Masonry and metalwork pleased him to the point that his suite included a locksmith with whom he forged keys and locks; his hands, blackened by his labours, were more than once the subject of protests and keen reproaches from the queen, who wished he could find other pastimes.' It was against this well-meaning, progressive, modest, humanitarian, and somehow plebeian figure, this constitutional monarch without a constitution, that the nation revolted.

The two crucial deficiencies of Louis XVI were that he lacked the vocation of kingship and that he was not strong enough to make a clear choice between the reactionary privileged orders and the rest of the nation. When his grandfather died in 1774, Louis XVI bemoaned that the responsibilities of the monarchy were falling on his inexperienced shoulders and that he was not yet twenty. He was forgetting that his reign had an important advantage over the two previous ones: there would be no transitional and dangerous Regency. When at Reims he donned the gold and crimson coronation robes, was anointed with the sacred phial of Clovis, received Charlemagne's six-foot-high, gold-plated sceptre and hand of justice (an ivory hand mounted on a short rod) and bent his head to accept the gold crown, he characteristically said that it was uncomfortable.

When one of his ministers resigned in 1776, Louis XVI said: ' How fortunate you are—how I wish I too could resign.'

Like a priest who doubts his ability to achieve transubstantiation during the mass, Louis XVI had no faith in his divine majesty. He also lacked natural majesty. The Neapolitan ambassador Caraccioli wrote that 'he seemed to have been raised in the woods.' He had a weak face, its features lost in fat, and kindly blue eyes. He was pot-bellied at the age of twenty, which a gracious courtier said gave him an air of precocious majesty. His voice was thin and reedy. Beneath the fat he had the build of a manual labourer and was proud of his strength. He liked to pick a young page up on the blade of a shovel and carry him around the room. He chopped wood and went hunting for exercise, and became increasingly gluttonous. At one sitting, he downed a whole chicken, four chops, six eggs, a slice of ham, and a bottle and a half of champagne. There was some justification for the droll pamphlets which charged him with public drunkenness. (When Parisians wanted change in a café, they would throw down a silver crown decorated with Louis XVI's profile and say: 'Change this drunkard for me.') The comte de Mercy d'Argenteau, Austrian ambassador and confidant of Marie Antoinette, wrote on August 14, 1787: 'His body is thickening and the returns from the hunt are followed by such immoderate meals that they lead to an absence of reason and a kind of brusque jauntiness which is most trying for those who have to bear it. The queen is almost the only person who does not suffer from this inconvenience; she is feared and respected by her spouse.'

Louis XVI was not a stupid man. He spoke German, read Latin, and translated Horace Walpole's *Richard III*. He had a thorough knowledge of history and geography and was blessed with a trait rare in French kings—intellectual curiosity. He was interested in how things work, and the tinkerer aspect of many of his occupations was the object of court ridicule. He would stare into a telescope for hours, watching carriages arrive at and leave Versailles. Each day he consulted a barometer, writing out his own weather reports. He had a collection of atlases from which he liked to copy maps on tracing paper. The smithy in his library included two forges and over a hundred tools. He made clocks and handsome gold-plated locks.

With an accountant's lack of imagination and love of insignificant detail, Louis XVI consigned to his handwritten diary the landmarks of his life. The diary is 266 pages long and its entries are dated from

1774 to 1792. The blank pages are optimistically predated up to the
year 1806. There is almost no interpretation of events which could
help explain the king's character. A reading of this arid diary, with
its lists of daily expenses and hunting results, leaves the impression
of a man with a passion for order, categories, and keeping accurate
accounts. On the days he did not hunt, he wrote the word 'nothing,'
as though hunting were his only serious occupation. He mentions
the ups and downs of his health; he had the mumps, haemorrhoids,
indigestion, fell from his horse, was bled, drank Vichy water, and
took forty-three baths in eighteen years, as a medicinal measure. He
lists the nights he spent away from Versailles, the births and deaths
in the royal family, the number of times he went to communion or
reviewed the troops (twenty-five). Sometimes he ventures a general
remark: 'I saw a man making horseshoes on the terrace,' or 'laid the
cornerstone for the Paris school of surgery.' He listed his gambling
gains and losses, which amounted to a net loss of 104,762 livres, and
his most minute expenses: 3 francs for a bouquet for the queen, 12
sous for a pencil, 10 sous for a new glass for his watch; the almost
daily disbursements for black pudding and sweets are the mark of a
compulsive appetite. Events did not perturb the equanimity of his
diary. The most familiar entry is 'nothing,' as in: 'nothing—rain,'
'nothing—ball,' 'nothing—presentation of American deputies.' In
1789 he mentions the convocation of the Estates General in the same
breath with a stag hunt at Orsai. For July 14, the entry is again
'nothing.' And yet the conclusion that might be drawn of the king's
total insensitivity to the events of his time is not borne out by the
decisions of his reign. In fact, the diary was purposely limited to
such trivia as the number of swallows he had shot during the day or
the price of a bag of sugar-coated almonds.

A better key to his character than his diary is his marriage. He
was a henpecked husband. Marie Antoinette ruled him far more
severely than Madame de Pompadour or Madame de Maintenon
ever governed their respective consorts. The sense of inadequacy
which afflicted Louis XVI in his dealings with the queen arose from
the mishaps of their marriage. The match was arranged under
Louis XV within the framework of the Austrian alliance. The
details were decided by correspondence and the Austrian court requested that a French priest be sent to round out the Archduchess
Marie Antoinette's education. The Empress Maria Theresa was
anxious that her daughter should make a good impression. After all,

the French had been known before to send applicant queens home to their parents. The abbé de Vermond left for Vienna and reported that teaching Marie Antoinette was like 'writing on a blank sheet of paper; she could apply herself only to what amused her.' In 1770, the fifteen-year-old Marie Antoinette crossed the Rhine, and on an island representing neutral territory she was divested of her Austrian clothes and turned over to French ladies-in-waiting. The island cabin in which she dressed for Versailles was decorated with Gobelin tapestries depicting the sanguinary married life of Jason and Medea, which was later recalled as an ill omen indeed. The wedding with the sixteen-year-old dauphin was blessed by Louis XV with these words: 'Marriages are never happy but they are sometimes pleasant; let us hope this one will be.' The usual curiosity about the conjugal life of royal princes animated the court. It was noticed that Louis XVI made no public demonstrations of affection.

Marie Antoinette was not a great beauty. She had a long face with a high brow and a pendulous lower lip which was called 'the Austrian lip.' Her right shoulder was lower than her left. But she had a complexion so fine it seemed translucent, and the court painter Madame Vigée-LeBrun said that no shadow could set on it. And she had such an air of natural majesty and grace that, according to her page, the comte de Tilly, 'One would have offered her a throne as naturally as one would have offered any other woman a chair.' The fickle Paris populace approved of her at first. There were large and enthusiastic crowds on hand when she visited the city, and the maréchal de Brissac, governor of Paris, said: 'Madam, if I may be so bold in front of Monsieur le dauphin, you have 200,000 lovers at your feet.'

Louis XVI was not included in the number, for the marriage was not consummated for seven years. At first, his lack of ardour was written off to the awkwardness of youth. But the correspondence of Empress Maria Theresa expresses growing concern about the *mariage blanc*. 'The coldness of the dauphin is inconceivable,' she wrote on January 3, 1774. 'My suspicions are increasing as to the corporal constitution of the prince.' On June 2, 1775, she wrote her daughter that 'all the letters from Paris say that you and the king are in separate beds.'

The truth was that Louis XVI had a physical impediment which kept him from accomplishing the sex act. He was so secretive and anguished that the first specific mention of it in the extremely frank correspondence between Marie Antoinette and her mother was in 1776, when the virgin queen wrote: 'There is considerable change in the king, and his body seems to be becoming more consistent . . . he promised that if nothing took place in the next few days he would agree to the operation.' The king suffered from phimosis, which Webster's International Dictionary describes as 'a tightness or constriction of the orifice of the prepuce which makes it impossible to bare the glans.' Like Luther's flatulence, Jean-Jacques Rousseau's retention of urine, and the stone in Cromwell's bladder, the foreskin of Louis XVI has its place in history. His condition could not be kept secret. He was failing in the performance of the king's essential duty, to provide a male heir. His reign was cursed by impotence. Ambassadors kept their courts informed regularly about his condition. The Spanish ambassador, comte d'Aranda, graphically reported: 'Some say the foreskin is so compressed that it does not pull back at the moment of introduction and causes a sharp pain which obliges His Majesty to moderate the necessary impulsion for the accomplishment of the act. Others suppose that the foreskin is so adherent that it prevents the point from emerging, which in turn prevents the erection from attaining the proper degree of elasticity.' Paris songwriters finally had a topic worthy of their talents, and Louis XVI became forever branded as a clumsy and incompetent husband.

After seven years of nonconsummation the situation was so critical that the Austrian Emperor Joseph II came personally to Paris to see what could be done. Arriving incognito in the late spring of 1777 under the pseudonym of comte de Falkenstein, he wrote to his brother, the Duke of Tuscany, in words that put part of the blame on his sister: 'Marie Antoinette does not carry out her duties as queen and wife in a satisfactory manner . . . Louis has erections in excellent condition; he introduces his member and remains there for two minutes, perhaps without moving, withdraws without discharging and bids her good night, saying only that he was doing it out of a sense of duty and had no inclination for it.' Joseph's advice seems to have been the determining factor in convincing Louis XVI to submit to a minor surgical intervention. It was performed successfully by his doctor, Joseph-Marie Lassone, and on August 30, 1777, Marie Antoinette wrote her mother: 'I live in the most essential happiness. For more than eight days, my marriage has been most perfectly consummated; the test was repeated yesterday more completely than the first time.' Louis XVI, as Sainte-Beuve gracefully put it, stammered, but he was not speechless.

The relieved couple gave most of the credit to Joseph II, who wrote to his brother that October: 'As you know, the king of France has finally performed the great deed and the queen may become pregnant. They both wrote and thanked me, attributing events to my advice—it is true that I discussed the matter fully in a conversation with him and that I realized perfectly that the only obstacles were laziness, clumsiness, and apathy.' Less than a year later, Marie Antoinette was pregnant, and in 1781 a dauphin was born. However, the king's sexual demands remained something less than imperious, and the absence of mistresses in his life seems due less to control over his desires than indifference. As Maria Theresa wrote on March 31, 1778: 'What my daughter tells me about her conjugal state makes me doubt that we will see another child for another eight years.'

There were several political consequences of the king's condition. Doubts were often expressed as to whether he had really sired Marie Antoinette's children. The king's infirmity also helps explain his daily capitulations to his wife. It was as though by indulging her whims he was atoning for his inadequacies. Marie Antoinette was openly contemptuous of her good-natured spouse. As her mother wrote: 'She thinks the king is too apathetic and shy to ever give in to the disorders of extramarital affairs. She is so convinced of it that she told several members of her entourage that she would feel neither sorrow nor anger if the king had some momentary or passing fancy, since it might give him more vigour and energy. I strongly represented to the queen that it was no laughing matter, and that it was infinitely dangerous to speak so lightly, for if the king found out he would be terribly shocked . . . however, she persists in her opinion of the weakness of the king's character, and makes him out to be worse than he really is. The queen's conclusions are that, having so much influence over her husband, she will always have the means to control him.'

It was as though nationalities were reversed, with the king a coarse, obese, clumsy, overhearty Saxon margrave and the queen a vivacious, pleasure-loving, elegant native of Versailles. The king liked to go to bed early, and one of the standing jokes was to set the clocks ahead to get rid of his cumbersome presence even earlier. The queen liked masked balls in Paris, where she often stayed from midnight until six in the morning. The lighting between Versailles and Paris was improved at her request, at a cost of 18,000 livres a year. She liked to gamble, and often needed advances on her generous allowance to afford her favourite card game, faro. She was disdainful of the king's activities, and wrote to her friend Count Rosenberg in April, 1775: 'My tastes are not those of the king's, whose only fondness is hunting and mechanics . . . you must admit that I would look out of place working at a smithy; I could never be Vulcan, while the role of Venus would annoy him far more than my amusements, of which he does not disapprove.' The king's attitude was one of exceptional indulgence clouded by brief angers. At the queen's revolutionary trial in 1793, one of her servants made the preposterous claim that Louis XVI had ordered her to be consigned to her apartment for fifteen days for plotting the murder of the duc d'Orléans. Replying in her defence, Marie Antoinette said: 'It may be that my husband ordered me to stay in my apartment for fifteen days, but that was not the reason.'

Marie Antoinette's conduct, condoned by an apathetic king, gave rise to a campaign of vilification unprecedented in French history. All of France's ire and discontent seemed to concentrate on the frivolous young woman who had become known as 'the Austrian.' No royal mistress was ever exposed to the farrago of filth which the French read and believed about their queen. Even after her courageous death at the guillotine the pamphleteers would not let her memory rest, and dozens of editions of invented memoirs and forged letters appeared on the market. Perhaps attacks against Marie Antoinette were an expression of loathing for the French alliance with a former enemy, Austria. Perhaps they were a warped expression of disgust with the king's weakness. Certainly, they showed that the monarchy could now be openly discredited in the baldest terms.

The attacks began the same year as the marriage, over the queen's extravagance. It was true that she spent a great deal, that she bought diamond bracelets and earrings on credit, and that she had expensive whims, such as ordering red costumes with gold braid for the Fontainebleau musicians. It was also true that she surrounded herself with a small coterie whose common denominator was greed. She spent large sums in generous gestures toward her friends, such as paying 15,000 livres in gambling debts for the handsome Hungarian colonel Count Esterhazy. She obtained a pension of 30,000 livres for the comte de Vaudreuil because he owned lands in Santo Domingo and the war had cut off his income. The pamphlets had a point when they said that this was the first reign where it was not the king, but the queen, who had favourites, and that these favourites exploited her shamelessly. Two of the best known were the princesse de Lamballe and the comtesse de Polignac. In 1775, at a time when Turgot was desperately scraping for ways to reduce court expenses, Marie Antoinette revived the post of Superintendent of the Queen's Household and gave it to the Turin-born princesse de Lamballe with an income of 200,000 livres a year. Mercy d'Argenteau, the fretful Austrian ambassador who served as her watchbird at court, wrote of her 'very particular friendship' with the princesse. In 1778, the comtesse de Polignac, a beauty with deep blue eyes, curly shoulder-length hair, and an angelic expression, replaced the princesse de Lamballe (whose fainting spells and nervous fits were attributed by her doctor Saiffert to masturbation). No royal mistress ever exploited a king so thoroughly as the comtesse, who in four years accumulated an income of 500,000 livres a year. The queen gave her 400,000 livres to pay her debts and 800,000 livres for her daughter's dowry. Her husband Jules became the king's first equerry, with a large pension; in 1785 he was made inspector of the king's stud farm with 60,000 livres a year; in the same year he became director of the pony express; in 1782, having been given the county of Fenestrange to govern, he exchanged the office for 1,200,000 livres. Mercy d'Argenteau was impressed. The queen has 'a much stronger inclination for her than any of the preceding ones,' he wrote Maria Theresa. He deplored Marie Antoinette's public shows of affection toward the comtesse. 'Another mark of familiarity,' he wrote, 'which had unfortunate results, was to see the queen in the evening pass through crowded antechambers arm in arm with the comtesse de Polignac.' The comtesse was a fair-weather friend who fled to Vienna at the first sign of trouble, whereas the princesse de Lamballe returned in 1789 to be at the queen's side, with the result that her head found its way to the point of a pike. The queen's affection for the comtesse never wavered, and her letters after 1789 pulsate with a kind of desperate tenderness. 'As long as I have a heart it will exist to love you,' she writes, or again, 'Believe that, in spite of what I cannot write, you are engraved deeply in my heart.' (This was at a time when the queen's letters were being opened and she had to be circumspect.)

Finally, there was Fersen. Count Axel Fersen was a Swedish

nobleman who arrived at Versailles in 1774, at the age of seventeen. He was tall and blond, with a sombre Viking elegance, a quiet courtesy, and a reserved manliness that set him apart from the frothy, lace-handkerchief French courtiers. Thanks to his growing friendship with Marie Antoinette he was given a regiment and a pension of 20,000 livres a year. In 1779 he left the French court to become Rochambeau's aide-de-camp in the American war, amid persistent rumours that he had become the queen's lover. The Swedish ambassador, comte de Creutz, wrote to King Gustav III: 'I cannot help believing that she [Marie Antoinette] has a penchant for him; I have seen signs too sure to be doubted. Young Count Fersen's conduct has been admirable by its modesty and reserve and by his decision to go to America . . . the queen could not take her eyes off him the last days he was here; and when she looked at him her eyes were filled with tears . . . the duchess of Fitz-James told him: "What, sir, are you abandoning thus your conquest?" "If I had made one I would not abandon it," he replied.' Fersen returned to Versailles in 1783 and became the queen's confidant, often seeing her alone at the Petit Trianon. He never married. He was recalled to Sweden in 1784 but came back to Paris after the Revolution, in 1790, and helped organize the flight of the royal family to Varennes in 1791. The proof of intimacy historians have sought in their correspondence is disappointing. Marie Antoinette's twenty-eight coded letters to Fersen express a strong affection and sense of devotion, but they should be read in the light of the mawkish sentimentality that was part of her nature. 'When will we see one another quietly?' she asks in one letter, and in others writes, 'Goodbye, I am all yours' and 'I have only the time to say that I love you.' Fersen scratched out passages of her handwritten notes which might have been of a more intimate nature. The only passage in Ferson's diary which sheds light on this minor mystery is dated February 13, 1792: 'M[onday] 13 . . . went to see her, following my usual route! fear of nat[ional] guar[ds]; her apartment is splendid, did not see the king,' followed by two scratched-out words which have been speculatively deciphered as 'remained there,' meaning that he spent the night with the queen. Finally, whether or not Fersen had access to Marie Antoinette's bed is a problem for boudoir history. What matters is that he was a trustworthy and loyal northern knight whose devotion was entire and reciprocated.

Embroidering on the framework of Marie Antoinette's real

extravagances, her generosity with her favourites, and her *amitié amoureuse* with Fersen, the pamphleteers created an extraordinary legend. It was written that the queen slept in black sheets, lit her bedroom with 1,000 candles a day, and had a room at the Petit Trianon tapestried with diamonds. Such detractions were taken so seriously by the citizenry that deputies of the Estates General in 1789 asked to visit the celebrated diamond-studded room. According to the pamphlets, Marie Antoinette was both an incorrigible lesbian and an insatiable Messalina. Pamphlets with titles like 'The Uterine Furies of Marie Antoinette' described her alleged lovemaking with the 'comtesse Jules,' as Madame de Polignac had come to be known, and illustrations represented the queen in erotic positions. In 1777 a treasurer of the king's household was jailed for distributing a pamphlet entitled 'The Coquette and the Impotent One.' The Paris police chief, Gabriel de Sartine, said that 'if I started making arrests for the things people say, I would have to arrest all of Paris.' Marie Antoinette's most innocent deeds became transformed into saturnalias. A wish to see the dawn rise became a pagan love rite, and a kind word to a courtier became an admission of adultery. She could do no right. When she began to dress less extravagantly, the pamphleteers wrote that she was trying to ruin commerce.

She pretended to be indifferent to calumny and said that the Parisians were 'frogs who only know how to croak.' But she confided to her page, the comte de Tilly, that 'it hurts, when one has nothing to reproach oneself.' There was unfortunately always a skeleton of likelihood upon which the pamphleteers draped their falsehoods. Her well-known fondness for jewellery made her the victim of the murky 'affair of the necklace,' in 1785. On one level it was no more than an elaborate swindle in which the gullible cardinal de Rohan was made to believe that he should buy an expensive necklace for the queen. The necklace disappeared, and had not been paid for. Rohan and the adventuress who had put him up to it were arrested, but doubts lingered about Marie Antoinette's involvement. She wrote to her brother in August, 1785: 'The cardinal admitted having bought a diamond necklace in my name and having used my signature. He claims that he was taken in by a certain Madame Valois de la Mothe . . . it should be noted that the bill of sale is in the hand of the cardinal and that after each paragraph there is the word "approved" in the same hand as the signature: Marie Antoinette de France. It is believed that the signature is that of Valois de la Mothe

. . . no attempt was made to counterfeit my handwriting, for this one does not resemble it in any way, and I have never signed de France.' On another level, the affair became a pretext to attack and vilify the regime. There was a torrent of pamphlets about it. An abbot's Lenten sermon, which compared Louis XVI to Nero for his failure to take action in the affair, was tacked up in churches all over France. Cardinal de Rohan was tried by the Paris Parlement and acquitted, which was a way of implying the royal family's guilt. Public opinion became convinced that the queen had tried to obtain a diamond necklace without paying for it. The 'affair of the necklace,' which should have been a comedy by Beaumarchais, became a melodrama with Marie Antoinette as villainess.

It was not the calumnies about Marie Antoinette's private life, but her constant meddling in affairs of state, which did the most damage to the reign. She became the prow figure of the aristocratic reaction which sabotaged the king's attempts at reform, and also interfered in foreign affairs. In lobbying for Austria at the French court she was, after all, only following her mother's advice: 'Be a good German; do not be ashamed of the German blood that flows in your veins; be German even to the point of awkwardness.' In 1778, she tried to obtain French assistance when Austria declared war on Bohemia. She wrote to her mother in April that 'after having discussed the sorry state of affairs with Mercy, I summoned messieurs de Maurepas and Vergennes. I was peremptory and I think I impressed them, especially the latter. I was displeased by their reasoning, for they seek only to please the king and evade the issue. It is cruel to have to deal with hypocrites in so important a matter.' There was no French intervention in Bohemia. In 1784, Joseph II claimed, despite existing treaties, access to the sea over the Escaut River and possession of the Dutch city of Maestricht. France offered to mediate the dispute, but the Austrian chancellor Kaunitz asked the French Foreign Minister, Vergennes, to endorse Austrian claims, which would invalidate any mediation role. Marie Antoinette vehemently insisted that Austrian interests should be defended. She wrote to her brother on December 23, 1784: 'I spoke very clearly to the king about it, more than once . . . but as he is incapable of discussion I was unable to convince him that his minister was leading him on.' The minister, Vergennes, took the trouble to explain the French position to Marie Antoinette, who threatened to break off the Franco-Austrian alliance unless he changed his views. He firmly declined, and sent a memorandum to Joseph II. She accused him of working behind her back, and thereafter worked behind his, but death dislodged him before she could, in 1787.

With other ministers she was more successful. Shortly after she became queen, the duc d'Aiguillon, who with the abbé Terray and Maupéou had formed the 'triumvirate' under Louis XV which was responsible for the regime's recovery in its final years, was disgraced. Marie Antoinette took full credit for the move in a letter to Count Rosenberg: 'This departure is my doing—I had had enough. This evil man engaged in all sorts of calumnies and espionage . . . thus, I asked the king to remove him . . . we are also getting rid of M. de la Vrillère [Minister of the King's Household]. Although he is hard of hearing, he realized it was time to leave before the door was slammed in his face.' Her brother, who was glad enough to have her defending his interests in foreign affairs, rebuked her for her inter-ference in French internal matters. 'Why don't you mind your busi-ness instead of displacing ministers?' he wrote to her in 1776. 'Have you asked yourself by what right you are meddling in the govern-ment of the French?' And a year later he wrote: 'I find your head very light to be carrying a crown.'

Marie Antoinette delighted in childish displays of power. Count Esterhazy, a member of her coterie, was to be sent to Montmédy with his regiment. He considered this northern garrison 'the most unpleasant in France,' and complained to the queen, who said: 'Let me handle this, and you will hear for yourself what I will tell him [the comte de Saint-Germain, a crusty old soldier named Minister of War, who said he feared cabals more than cannonballs].' Esterhazy slipped into an adjoining drawing room while the minister was sent for. 'Well, sir,' Marie Antoinette told Saint-Germain, 'it is enough for me to take an interest in someone to have him persecuted. Why are you sending Esterhazy's regiment to Montmédy, which is a wretched garrison?' 'But madam,' replied Saint-Germain, 'the orders have been given. Can we displace an entire regiment to put another one in its place?' 'As you like,' said the queen, 'but I want Esterhazy to be content, and I will hold you to account.' She turned her back on him. The next day, Saint-Germain sent Esterhazy a list of vacant garrisons and asked him to take his pick.

Thus, ministers had to consider not only the merit of a decision, but whether it would please the queen. She could not tolerate the slightest vexation, and her hold over Louis XVI made her a dangerous foe. Her outbursts were frequent enough to hint at some nervous ailment. Once the comte de Saint-Germain presented the king with three names to fill a colonel's vacancy. Louis XVI consulted an adviser, the prince de Montbarey, who singled out one man, ignoring the fact that the queen was kindly disposed to one of the others. Marie Antoinette summoned Montbarey and berated him for half an hour for what she called a grave personal insult. 'Her agitation was so great,' wrote Montbarey, 'that when she slammed the gate of a railing around her bed it almost jumped off its hinges.'

Having seen nothing of France except for her initial trip from Vienna to Paris, surrounded by fawning favourites, preoccupied by her diversions, the hamlet, masked balls, faro, and her wardrobe, Marie Antoinette completely ignored the forces which were changing France under the reign of Louis XVI. She wielded great power, but her motives had always to do with details of court life, not the interests of the nation and the monarchy. She was against ministers who opposed her whims and supported those who were properly submissive. When she wanted to buy the castle of Saint-Cloud from the duc d'Orléans for 6 million livres, the Controller General, Charles-Alexandre de Calonne, tried to describe the state's financial distress. 'If Saint-Cloud is not mine,' she replied, 'I prohibit you from appearing before me and to be at Madame de Polignac's when I am there.' Her experience at the hands of public opinion made her hostile to the king's decision to seek the advice of the nation. In November, 1785, she wrote to Joseph II: 'What saddens me greatly is that the king announced that he would convene the Estates General within five years. There is on this point a great fermentation, so that the king felt he had to head off a direct request, and control events by taking measures himself. But he could prevent the inconveniences of those assemblies.' It never occurred to Marie Antoinette that she had contributed to making the convocation of the Estates General necessary by helping the forces of the feudal reaction discredit the policies of the one man with a complete plan of reform which might have saved the monarchy, Anne-Jacques-Robert Turgot.

Turgot was the model of the enlightened public servant. He had written five articles for the *Encyclopédie*, on Etymology, Existence, Expansibility, Fairs and Markets, and Foundations. As Intendant of Limoges, he had abolished the corvée in his province. He was an advocate of the physiocrat programme for the free circulation of grain. He shared the Encyclopedists' views of the church and the clergy. He was brilliant, hard-working, honest, and did not suffer cant—he had a library painted in *trompe-l'oeil* with the titles of imaginary books like The Art of Complicating Simple Things, and The True Utility of War.

After the death of Louis XV, when his nineteen-year-old successor was still numbed by the responsibilities which were suddenly his, one of the first persons to see him was the seventy-three-year-old Maurepas, the veteran courtier and politician who had served Louis XV until he was disgraced on the recommendation of Madame de Pompadour. Maurepas had long been naval secretary, and Louis XVI was fascinated by naval affairs. His courtliness, self-confidence, and experience impressed the king, who named him his principal adviser and minister without portfolio. Maurepas made his influence felt in two contradictory ways. He urged the king to dismiss the new tribunals created by Louis XV and Maupéou and bring back the old Parlements, which had so impeded the former reign. Maurepas was a traditionalist who felt there was something illicit about Maupéou's 1771 coup. Moreover, he had many personal friends among the families of the gown nobility which had been exiled. Finally, there was a strident public opinion campaign to re-establish the old Parlements. An incalculable number of pamphlets attacked Maupéou. The old Parlements were popular because they were credited with the banishment of the Jesuits and with blocking new taxes. They still posed as the defenders of the Third Estate against despotism, and it was not until later that they revealed their real function as the rear guard of the dissatisfied nobility. Louis XVI gave in to public opinion and to the advice of Maurepas and a court faction which supported the old Parlements. Maupéou and the other two members of Louis XV's triumvirate, the duc d'Aiguillon and the abbé Terray, were disgraced. When the judges and lawyers once again donned their red and black robes in November, 1774, they were acclaimed as heroes. 'The Paris mob rejoiced without knowing why,' wrote a courtier. Louis XVI nourished the illusion that the Paris Parlement would be, out of gratitude, meek and obedient. Parlement, however, presented itself as the victor in its long struggle against the crown, and protested the wording of the very decree which had brought it back to power. How could it be 're-created,' it asked, when it could not legally be dissolved? The familiar routine of remonstrances and beds of justice was resumed, with Parlement in its traditional fractious role.

At the same time that Maurepas was partly responsible for the return of Parlement, he also urged Turgot on a reluctant Louis XVI. The king objected that Turgot was an Encyclopedist, a physiocrat, and never went to church. He finally accepted him as Controller General in August and received him warmly. 'All I have told you is a bit confused,' declared Turgot after outlining his programme, 'because I still feel flustered.' 'I know you are shy,' said the king, 'but I also know you are firm and honest and that I could have made no better choice.' Seizing both his hands, he added: 'I give you my word of honour to enter into all your views and to always support you in the courageous positions you will have to take.'

Louis XVI had summoned to power a man who could bring the nation's institutions back into line with its social and economic needs, but he had also brought back the Parlements, which would resist Turgot's programme. He had swallowed together the poison and the antidote. Turgot proposed, in effect, a peaceful revolution. He wanted a fair tax based on property which the privileged orders would also have to pay. And he wanted a limited form of constitutional monarchy, based on local assemblies of landowners which would in turn elect a national assembly to advise the king. His first step was to decree the free circulation of grain, but the poor harvest of 1774 led to the so-called 'flour war,' of which he was the principal victim. In a short time his popularity waned. He had been hailed as the new Sully, but after the flour war he was accused of sacrificing the good of the people to his economic theories. In 1776, he presented Louis XVI with his next economic innovation, a series of six decrees. The three major ones called for the suppression of the corvée, guilds and masterships, and the Paris grain police; the other three involved reforms of markets and inspectors governing the sale of fish, meat, and tallow in Paris. There was immediate resistance to the measures. The Lord Privy Seal, Armand-Thomas de Miromesnil, an ally of the Parlement, defended the corvée, arguing that peasants who built roads had the satisfaction of using them. 'May the Lord Privy Seal allow me to believe,' Turgot replied, 'that the pleasure of walking on a well-paved road is no compensation for the labour of having paved it without pay.' Turgot regarded the corvée as double taxation, for it took the peasant's time, and it did not pay him for his work. He wanted the corvée replaced by salaried labour paid with the product of a special tax. Turgot's decree on the guilds ended the abuses of closed shops and constant jurisdictional quarrels and decreed a right-to-work law and free competition in crafts and trades. The eighteenth-century guilds were controlled by small groups of men whose 'bizarre, tyrannical, obscure codes were drawn up out of greed, and adopted out of ignorance,' Turgot wrote. The grain police enforced a forest of regulations which, had they been carried out to the letter, would have starved Paris. Turgot contracted with a grain merchant to supply Paris, and the contract continued to be enforced up to the Revolution. Parlement opposed the decrees on the corvée and the guilds. The jurists saw quite clearly that the question of whether French peasants should be assembled in unpaid road gangs to improve rural transportation begged the far more basic question of tax exemptions for the privileged classes. To abolish the corvée and levy a tax for public works which the nobility would also pay was to abolish the nobility's privilege. The guilds were defended as a link in the corporate state going from the family to the throne. The irony of Parlement's defence of the guilds was that it had also opposed their reform under Henri IV.

Louis XVI held a bed of justice at Versailles on March 12, 1775, to insist that Parlement register the six decrees. To mollify the gown nobility, he said: 'My intention is not to confuse the classes . . . if inconveniences arise from experience in certain of these dispositions . . . I will find the proper remedies.' On March 19, all the decrees were registered, but now the lobbies and special interest groups were out to destroy Turgot. His brusque disregard for cliques and favours had earned him many enemies at court. He once told a lady of high birth: 'You know, then, madam, that the reign of women is over,' to which she replied: 'But not the reign of impertinents.' Marie Antoinette's hatred of Turgot crystallized when he urged the recall of the bumbling French ambassador in London, the comte de Guines, who was one of the queen's protégés. Maurepas, who had been stung by the enmity of one powerful woman under Louis XV, had learned his lesson, and joined the queen in her efforts to rid the court of Turgot. In March, 1776, Turgot's only strong ally in the ministry resigned—Chrétien-Guillaume de Lamoignon de Males-herbes, Minister of the King's Household, who had defended the Encyclopedists under Louis XV as head librarian, and who would volunteer sixteen years later to defend Louis XVI before the Convention. (As he was sentenced to death, the revolutionary judge asked him how he was able to show such fortitude. 'Contempt for life,' said Malesherbes, 'and contempt for you.') In discussing Malesherbes' resignation with Louis XVI, Maurepas found a way to damage Turgot's credit. 'One of these men is leaving you,' he said, 'the other often threatens to leave you unless you follow all his suggestions. I regret to see that neither is attached to you.' Maurepas also criticized Turgot's accounts for 1775, which showed a deficit of 24 million livres. He decided to impose as successor to Malesherbes his own incompetent nephew, Amelot de Chaillou, knowing that the appointment would dishearten Turgot. At the same time, with customary impatience, Turgot had followed up his controversial six decrees with a project for a national assembly. The timing of this experiment in representative government, just when Louis XVI's confidence in his zealous minister was being shaken, amounted to political suicide. Louis XVI viewed the assembly as a threat to the institutions of the monarchy, and said that Turgot was 'all of a piece, even in the good he tries to accomplish. I can see that despotism is good for nothing, not even for forcing a great people to be happy.'

Feeling the ground trembling beneath him, Turgot on April 30 wrote the king a letter which served only to worsen his position. 'You are considered weak, sire,' he said, 'and there are times when I fear that this defect is not absent from your character . . . never forget, sire, that weakness put the head of Charles I [of England] on the chopping block.' He insisted on a public vote of confidence from the king, adding: 'Your silence has made me doubt whether you want me to remain in your service.' In May there were frontal attacks on Turgot: from Parlement, which presented new remonstrances asking that his decrees be voided because of the troubles that had resulted from their application; and from Marie Antoinette, whose plan was to have Turgot arrested and sent to the Bastille at the same time that she rewarded the incompetent comte de Guines with a ducal title. Turgot learned on May 10 that Maurepas' nephew Amelot would be appointed over his objections. His disgrace was a fait accompli. On May 12 Marie Antoinette demanded the ducal title for Guines. 'The queen's project,' wrote Mercy-Argenteau, 'was to demand of the king that Monsieur Turgot be exiled, even sent to the Bastille, on the same day the comte de Guines was declared a duke. . . . The strongest and most urgent arguments had to be made to curb the queen's anger, which has no other motives than the demands Turgot had made to have the comte de Guines recalled.'

The recall had taken place five months before. Marie Antoinette would have agreed with Talleyrand that revenge is a dish that is eaten cold. Turgot wrote a last letter to Louis XVI, in which he expressed the hope that time would not prove him right. The king did not answer and the two men never met again. In August of the following year the corvée was re-established, and so were the guilds. In retirement, Turgot's gout worsened. He used crutches, put yeast on his throbbing foot, and gave up coffee. On March 18, 1781, five years after his disgrace almost to the day, he died.

Turgot's twenty months in power were a brief remission in the *ancien régime*'s mortal illness. He diagnosed the deep economic malaise and the need for popular representation, and proposed remedies. But his programme met the same fate as the celebrated 'Turgot machine' which he had underwritten—it was an ice-breaking machine, a kind of floating pier with chains and blades designed to break up the ice floes that blocked winter navigation on the Seine. On paper it seemed practicable, but each time it was tested there was a snag, the blades broke or the pier came loose from its moorings and smashed against the ice.

Part of Turgot's failure came from his refusal to play the courtier or enlist the support of public opinion. Also, as an eighteenth-century preacher might have said, the heavens were against him. By enforcing free circulation of grain in a bad harvest year he lost his first major battle. Finally, the reactionary alliance of gown and sword nobility, supported by the queen and the king's closest adviser, was an enemy too formidable to resist. Louis XVI at first enthusiastically supported Turgot, and then jettisoned him under pressure. This was his typical pattern of behaviour throughout his reign: encouraging enlightened measures and then giving in to the court lobbies. Even his two most successful reforms, the suppression of torture and of serfdom, were at best compromises. Criminals under the *ancien régime* were automatically subjected to two forms of torture, or questions: the preparatory question, after arrest, which was intended to extract a confession; and the preliminary question, before execution, to make the sentenced man deliver his accomplices. When Louis XVI came to power, the two most common torture methods were water and the boot. They had been adopted as improvements over seventeenth-century techniques which too often led to the deaths of the suspects. The accused subjected to the water torture was seated on a stone stool with his hands tied behind him by two iron rings fixed to the wall. His feet were bound by two other rings fixed to the floor. One assistant held his nose while another poured a quantity of water, regulated by royal ordinance, from a hollow beef horn down his throat. In the boot torture, the legs of the accused were placed between planks which were tightened with ropes, and then wedges were hammered between the planks and the skin.

Louis XVI wanted to suppress both questions. In 1780 he successfully abolished the preparatory question (torture after arrest). But Parlement blocked his attempts in 1788 to abolish torture before execution. Parlementarians wrote the king memoranda listing the many advantages for the state of this form of torture. In 1779, Louis XVI abolished serfdom, but only on the royal domains, the properties he owned. He explained that he was too attached to property rights and too poor to reimburse the owners of serfs to extend the measure. He knew that this was the only way to get around Parlementary resistance. He was already pursuing the *politique du possible* of a weak regime.

XIII

THE SAGE OF PASSY

*The French Revolution was, 'in its immediate
cause, born of the financial crisis which was itself
caused by the debt contracted at the time of the
American Revolution.'*
—C. E. LABROUSSE, *The Crisis in the French
Economy at the End of the Ancien Régime*

*Benjamin Franklin was a nice old man,
Washed his face in a frying pan;
Combed his hair with a wagon wheel,
Died with a toothache in his heel.*
—CHILDREN'S RHYME

ON DECEMBER 3, 1776, the sixteen-gun sloop *Reprisal*
dropped anchor in Quiberon Bay and put ashore a cargo of
indigo and a grey-haired, elderly gentleman in a fur cap
who had been sorely tried by forty days of rough Atlantic seas and a
diet of tough salt beef and fowl. His title was Commissioner Plenipotentiary of the United States of North America. His name was
Benjamin Franklin, and his seventieth birthday was only a month
away. His mission was to obtain French aid. He represented an
insurgent government in open rebellion against a European monarchy, which no nation had yet been willing to recognize. The
insurgent army under George Washington faced the disheartening
winter of Valley Forge and the evacuation of Philadelphia. Washington was paralysed by Congress' inability to raise troops and
funds. His desertion rate was high. His officers were often untrained
or irresponsible. There was a shortage of that essential military
supply, gunpowder. A revolution's hopes rested on Doctor Franklin's rheumatic shoulders.

France at the time of Franklin's arrival resembled an ice-bound river. Beneath the frozen crust of absolutism ran the currents of a society in flux. Franklin saw a France from which the Jesuits had been banned, but where Freemasonry was welcome. The Philadelphia Mason, elected to the Lodge of the Nine Sisters in Paris, also saw that many of his fellow Masons were members of the liberal nobility or the clergy. He was to have another demonstration of the aristocracy's need for escapism from a musty court life when volunteers began to pester him for letters of recommendation to General Washington. For most of these young and restive warriors, like Lafayette, the futility of court life was as strong a motive as liberal political ideals. The French Foreign Minister Vergennes said that joining the insurgents was 'an escapade stirred up by idleness and boredom.'

Franklin's arrival contributed mightily to the spirit of change; for America provided the one ingredient which could give political meaning to all the disparate, unconnected signs of dissatisfaction with the *ancien régime*—the example of a people incorporating the ideals of the Enlightenment in a written constitution.

French enthusiasm for the American cause was not born with Franklin's arrival. The Philosophes had long admired the saga of the settlers. Here was a life which the writers of the Enlightenment could praise without reserve, a life of religion without clergy, reward for hard work, rustic simplicity, and a God who, instead of collecting taxes, tipped the horn of plenty. Prerevolutionary America became all that was virtuous, noble, and good. The various states, with their assemblies and elected governors, were hailed as models of republicanism. Montesquieu wrote that 'Monsieur Penn is a veritable Lycurgus.' Voltaire's chapter on Pennsylvania in his *Essai sur les Moeurs* described a happy people who needed neither army, judges, doctors, nor priests, but lived in a natural state of organized goodness and prosperous altruism.

Praising America became a way of criticizing the regime, and from 1760 to 1790 there were twenty-six books which exposed the inadequacies of the monarchy by describing the happy conditions of life in the New World. When the colonies rose up against the mother country, America became more than a distant utopia, it became an example to follow. Ideas that had been blurred and abstract took on a new urgency. Monarchic principles which had long remained unquestioned were tested by events. In 1775, George III recruited an expeditionary force of 55,000 men and asked friendly German princes for manpower. The Landgrave of Hesse-Cassel sent 12,000 men and the Duke of Brunswick contributed another 5,000. The delivery of soldiers from prince to prince and king to king was based on the idea that human beings are subjects to be disposed of at the ruler's whim. But the recruitment of mercenaries to fight the American insurgents created a furor. The Prince of Anspach's men refused to march. There was dissension in the ranks of royalty. Frederick II, in his only gesture of assistance to the American cause, prohibited the recruitment of Prussians and made mercenaries crossing his territory pay the *Viehzoll*, a customs duty usually reserved for livestock.

The fact that the people of a country could write a constitution to govern themselves made a profound impression on the French, who had no written constitution, and venerated the American text as a sort of catechism of freedom. Events in the American War of Independence had a contrapuntal effect in France. The Declaration of Independence was used by Mirabeau as a polemic against the French monarchy. Reflecting on 'that sublime manifesto,' he wondered whether, 'out of the thirty-two princes of the third race of our kings, at least two-thirds are not more to be blamed by their subjects than the English kings by their colonies?' American revolutionary terms, such as 'Convention' and 'Committee of Public Safety,' crossed the Atlantic to be used again after 1789. The spiritual fathers of the Paris national guards of 1789 are the Massachusetts minutemen of 1776. The American example was there to be invoked. As Robespierre told the Jacobins on January 11, 1792: 'We will fight until we are naked, like the Americans.' Just as there was no virtue like American virtue, there was no courage like American courage. Chamfort wrote that 'an American, having noticed six English soldiers separated from their corps, had the inconceivable boldness to charge them, wound two, disarm the others, and take them all to General Washington. The general asked him how he had mastered six men. "I surrounded them," he said.'

The most surprising aspect of the American example is that it was admired not only by those who were later to make the French Revolution but also by its victims, members of an exhausted society no longer conscious of its own interests. The new generation of a once-prestigious warrior caste, ill-used and disregarded since Louis XIV, sailed forth to die for the insurgents in a kind of last hurrah. This was also a chance for vengeance on an enemy who had

278

consistently defeated France in eighteenth-century warfare. Tales of farmers rising up with pitchforks against the Redcoats made French officers grip the pommels of their swords. Lafayette was not a hero of democracy. He was a member of a declining class which longed for some new cause; he was nineteen, and impetuous; his father had been killed by an English cannonball when he was two; he was unpopular at court (he was called a parvenu because he had married the rich daughter of the duc d'Ayen when he was fourteen and she was twelve); he seemed prophetic when he was merely overeager, and, as Talleyrand noted, 'There was nothing in him out of the ordinary.'

But there was such irresistible enthusiasm for the American cause that when Lafayette returned to Versailles in 1779 after fighting at Washington's side, Marie Antoinette asked him for news of 'our good republicans, our good Americans.' This enthusiasm was not shared by other European monarchs, who had no scores to settle with England and saw more or less clearly that if the British cause foundered in America the ripples would eventually reach their own courts. When the Austrian Emperor Joseph II visited Versailles incognito in 1777 and a lady asked him whether he was sympathetic to the insurgents he replied testily: 'Madam, it is my profession to be a royalist.' His mother, Maria Theresa, refused to receive the American envoy Arthur Lee and prohibited her Belgian subjects from trading with the Americans.

Catherine the Great's attitude was more ambiguous. She admitted that if she had colonies she would rather 'lose my head' than give them up. But she was a hard-headed pragmatist who saw that George III had made a mess of things, and she rejected a British request for Russian troops. She said that the very mention of the English king's name made her blood boil. In Prussia, Frederick II was careful not to provoke the English and affirmed his 'perfect neutrality.' He showed little interest in the American war and less understanding of its outcome, for he predicted that the colonies, after having won their independence, would ask England to take them back. Spain, with her own American empire in Louisiana and west of the Mississippi, was of two minds concerning the insurgents —she was France's ally and wanted to follow French policy insofar as war against Britain could win her back Gibraltar. But she also knew that an independent America would threaten her colonial holdings and her control over navigation on the Mississippi.

France was the only European power to support the insurgents and eventually sign a treaty of mutual assistance with them. The architect of that policy was Charles Gravier, comte de Vergennes, a career diplomat schooled in the courts of Constantinople, Stockholm and Lisbon, who was named Foreign Minister in 1774. The only flaw in his record was a misalliance, for even though he enjoyed one of the rare happy marriages at court, he lived in an age where immorality was condoned but marrying beneath one's station was not. He had married a lady of Franco-Greek ancestry named Anne Testa, the wife of a Constantinople doctor whom he met and seduced while ambassador to the Sublime Porte. When he was named ambassador to Sweden he was not allowed to take her along.

One of Vergennes' early dispatches about the American war shows that he was interested mainly in its potential for reducing Britain's power in Europe. 'The English,' he wrote on July 28, 1775, 'have inconsiderately embarked upon a war with their American colonies which from now on will cost them dearly . . . their weakening . . . will pave the way for the two crowns [France and Spain] to retake, and perhaps without striking a blow, that place of superiority both as to consideration and influence, which is always the reward of a wise and well-directed administration.'

The most vigorous lobbyist for the American cause was the playwright and secret agent Beaumarchais, a prototype of the eighteenth-century self-made man. The son of a watchmaker, he had, thanks to his wit, his pen, and his lack of scruples, become a celebrated figure. He had the distinction of being on one hand a secret agent trusted by two kings with confidential state matters and on the other a playwright who ridiculed the court in *The Marriage of Figaro*. His description of diplomacy was to 'spread spies, pension traitors, loosen seals, and intercept letters,' a good summary of his own activities. He had first served as an agent for Louis XV, who sent him to London to buy off the author of a pamphlet about Madame du Barry called 'The Secret Memoirs of a Prostitute.' His success led Louis XVI to use him, and he was asked while on a mission to London in 1775 to supply information about the Americans. Beaumarchais was no political thinker, but he saw the American war with his dramatist's imagination and became an outspoken partisan of the republican underdogs.

He confessed that he was 'wild about the Americans' and bombarded Vergennes with emphatic reports insisting that 'we must help the Americans.' While Vergennes in his replies tried to moderate the zeal of his fiery emissary, he used Beaumarchais' information as the basis for a confidential memorandum to Louis XVI. He said that France's interest lay in favouring the independence of the insurgents, who would be defeated by England unless they received assistance. Helping the insurgents would ruin British commerce in North America and strengthen France's position there. Like a good diplomat, Vergennes also weighed the disadvantages of helping America. He was a loyal monarchist who had no sympathy with any struggle for freedom against constituted authority, but he saw the American war as a local uprising taking place in a distant hemisphere. He was worried that the spirit of revolt might spread to France's Caribbean possessions. He did not even consider contagion in Europe. He concluded that the insurgents should be supported, without specifying the nature of the support.

Louis XVI showed little eagerness to give his backing to such a cause, but in August, 1775, he allowed Vergennes to send a soldier of fortune named the chevalier Achard de Bonvouloir as unofficial agent to America. Bonvouloir, posing as an Antwerp merchant, arrived in Philadelphia and met the five members of the recently formed Committee of Secret Correspondence (one of the five was Franklin). Writing in milk between the lines of commercial statements, he reported that he knew 'the most secret goings-on.' Bonvouloir was enthusiastic about the insurgents' resolution and achievements. He assured the Americans that they had nothing to fear from France, who was interested only in trade relations and sought no territorial gains in the hemisphere. The Americans asked Bonvouloir what help could be expected from France, and on the strength of his reply, appointed their first agent to a European court, Silas Deane.

From the first material gesture, the dispatch of an agent to America, French policy continued to move in the same slow direction, toward open support, even though a formal treaty was not signed until two and a half years later. This sluggishness can be ascribed to hesitations within the French government and to the military situation in America, for every defeat of the insurgents made the French more cautious. Beaumarchais kept pressing his case from London and wrote Vergennes in April, 1776: 'Will you not try to convince His Majesty that the little help they ask for will allow us to win a great victory without risking battle. . . .'

Louis XVI was not convinced. He had a king's intuitive aversion to a struggle for liberty, and years later he told his naval secretary, Bertrand de Molleville: 'I never think of the American affair without regrets; in those days my youth was taken advantage of and now we are suffering the consequence.' However, the king was incapable of imposing his own will. Vergennes submitted another memorandum supporting French intervention, which was debated by the principal cabinet ministers. Approval came from Maurepas, the First Minister, who agreed with the goal of weakening Britain, and from Sartine, the Secretary of the Navy, who anticipated a naval war which would allow him to expand his fleet. The comte de Saint-Germain, Secretary for War, was not eager to commit his army to such a remote expedition, however. Curiously enough, it was the most liberal of Louis XVI's ministers, the man responsible for the major reforms of the reign, Minister of Finance Turgot, who expressed the strongest opposition to French intervention. He argued that colonialism was a bankrupt doctrine and that all European nations would sooner or later lose their colonies. What did it matter then whether France helped the insurgents or not, for England would inevitably have to make concessions to her colonies? He warned that France could afford a war only at the expense of essential reforms. It would be guns or butter, and France's deepest interests lay in preserving peace and devoting her resources to her own people. Turgot, however, spoke with one foot already outside the ministry, thanks to a court cabal and Louis XVI's indecisiveness. He was disgraced in May, 1776, and Vergennes had a clear field.

In the light of events to come, Turgot's position seems prophetic and Vergennes' shortsighted. Vergennes saw the American War of Independence as a factor in the European balance of power. He was pursuing the limited objectives of classic French diplomacy, which were to prevent England from becoming too powerful and to avenge previous French humiliations. He failed to consider that no colony in history had ever before declared itself an independent state. He saw only that this would be a good opportunity to end the humiliation of the English supervision of Dunkirk. To Vergennes the Declaration of Independence was not a document of universal importance in direct contradiction to the principles of monarchy but a convenient weapon to weaken Britain. The possibility that the principles he was supporting in America might someday reach Europe never dawned on him. Although no advocate of freedom, this discreet apostle of French intervention did more for the American cause than either Lafayette or Rochambeau. He could not see the forces of history at work in the Anglo-American conflict and, mercifully, he died before these same forces spread to France.

France became America's de facto ally in June, when Beaumarchais received one million pounds from Louis XVI to purchase military supplies for the insurgents. Beaumarchais threw himself into this new adventure with customary dash. He founded the firm of Roderigue Hortalez and Company as a cover for his gunrunning. In August he received a second million from the Spanish government and a third million was raised from private supporters. By the end of 1776 he had loaded, after a number of picaresque adventures, some 200 field guns and other supplies aboard ships whose names changed with each trip to confuse British spies.

In July and August, 1776, the first two of the three men commissioned by Congress to treat with European courts arrived in Paris: Silas Deane, big and blond, the son of a Connecticut blacksmith who had done well at Yale, married Elizabeth Saltonstall, and prospered as a lawyer and merchant; and Arthur Lee, the pompous, neurotic Virginia patrician who was to knock at the door of the Spanish court for thirty months without success. When Deane asked Vergennes on July 17 for military equipment for 25,000 men (through an interpreter, for Vergennes spoke no English), the minister turned him down but suggested he get in touch with a merchant named Beaumarchais who might be able to help.

The presence of Deane and Lee in France went almost unnoticed, but Franklin's arrival was cataclysmic. 'The father of all the yankees,' as Carlyle called him, was not an envoy but an apparition. Franklin, in France, in 1776, entered that curious historical dimension where a man becomes the tangible expression of his time, and sums up in his own person the dimly perceived aspirations of an age. Franklin was the incarnation of the Enlightenment. He was a signer of the Declaration of Independence, who in his simplicity of manner and dress reminded the French of the Romans and the Greeks. He had 'that air of antiquity,' wrote the marquis de Ségur, 'which seemed suddenly to transport within our walls, in the midst of our soft and servile eighteenth-century civilization, the wise contemporaries of Plato or of the Republicans in the time of Cato and Fabius.' He was a scientist, and had carried his experiments much further than such other wizards of the Enlightenment as

Montesquieu, who had held a duck's head under water to see how long it took to die, or Voltaire, who liked to tinker in his laboratory at Ferney. Franklin embodied the programme of the Enlightenment, the scientific spirit, the belief in progress, the perfectibility of man, and the coming of a new political age. Turgot composed for him the famous Latin epigram: 'He ravished the thunder from the sky and the sceptre from tyrants.' Franklin's experiments with kites and lightning rods were famous in France. While priests denounced the irreverence of meddling with 'God's Arrows,' Condorcet called Franklin 'the modern Prometheus.' He was also the hero of the rising middle class. There was something reassuring about the elderly fellow with the benign, modest manner, who was not averse to honest gain and seemed to have invented the homely virtues of a conservative but mobile bourgeoisie.

News of his arrival spread with such alacrity that Vergennes, under pressure from the British ambassador, Lord Stormont, instructed the Paris Lieutenant of Police to prohibit conversations about him in cafés. Ambassadors reported the important event to their governments. As the Venetian envoy Mark Zeno wrote: 'Three reasons are given for Doctor Franklin's trip. The first is the desire to raise his children in France; the second, his intention to publish new works; finally, his need for rest because of advancing years and his wish to end his days here, far from civil strife and its bloody consequences . . . all these reasons, however founded, can be perfectly reconciled with the simultaneous accomplishment of secret negotiations with a French court . . . all of Europe is in suspense.'

Franklin's presence worried Lord Stormont, who wrote Whitehall eight days after his arrival: 'Some people think that either some private dissatisfaction or despair of success have brought him into this country. I cannot but suspect that he comes charged with a secret commission from Congress, and as he is a subtle artful man, and void of all truth, he will in that case use every means to decision . . . In a word, my lord, look upon him as a dangerous engine—I am very sorry that he did not meet with some English frigate by the way.'

The French did not care what reason had brought him to their shores. They adopted him. The *Gazette d'Amiens* tried to prove that he was of French origin, and wrote that 'the name Franquelin or Franklin is very common in Picardy.' Franklin learned to his surprise that his name had given birth to a movement. Joseph Bertier, the author of a 'Letter on Electricity,' wrote to him that 'I was a Franklinist without knowing it, and shall not fail to name the founder of my sect.' All of France intoned with Franklin's friend, the abbé Morellet: *'Le verre à la main, chantons notre Benjamin* (glass in hand, let us sing our Benjamin's praise).' The Commissioner Plenipotentiary good-naturedly informed his daughter, Sarah Bache, in June, 1779, that he was idolized. Franklin medallions for snuffboxes and rings were being marketed, 'and the numbers sold are incredible. These, with the pictures, busts, and prints (of which copies upon copies are spread everywhere) have made your father's face as well known as that of the moon, so that he durst not do anything that would oblige him to run away, as his phiz would discover him wherever he should venture to show it.' If we are to believe Marie Antoinette's maid, Madame Campan, Franklin's likeness even found its way to the base of a Sèvres chamber pot offered by Louis XVI to the duchesse de Polignac.

Perhaps most surprising was the universality of Franklin's appeal. His revolutionary principles appealed to the embryonic liberal minority, his literary and scientific reputation made him popular with the intellectual world, and his blend of simplicity and courtliness won him the aristocracy. He had more in common with 'the powdered heads of Europe' than he liked to admit. He lived like a lord, suffered from the gout like a lord, and bantered with ladies like a lord. He was a reassuring rebel. The courtiers who would one day place their heads in the lunette of the guillotine admired him as much as the commoners who would order their deaths. The duc de La Rochefoucauld translated the American Constitution for him. Marat submitted physics experiments to him. Madame de Forbach, dowager duchess of Deux-Ponts, gave him a crabtree walking stick with a gold head. A country lawyer named Robespierre sent a copy of his summation in a case involving a lightning rod to 'the most illustrious scholar in the universe.' And Doctor Guillotin, whose contribution to the Revolution was a painless method of execution, corresponded with Franklin about a plan to found a settlement on the Ohio River. Greuze used Franklin as a model for the father in his famous painting *L'Accordée du Village*. Madame du Deffand invited him to her salon, where he said little, since his French was not fluent, but successfully played the wise patriarch.

Franklin met Voltaire on several occasions and when the two elderly sages embraced, *à la française,* someone said that it was charming to see Solon embracing Sophocles. The good doctor was lionized. He wrote to a friend that he 'dined abroad six days in seven.' In the words of a police report dated three weeks after his arrival: 'Doctor Franklin, who lately arrived in this country from the English colonies, is very much run after, and feted, not only by his colleagues the scholars, but by all people who can get hold of him; for he is difficult to approach, and lives in a reserve which is supposed to be dictated by the government. This Quaker wears the full costume of his sect. He has an agreeable cast of features. Spectacles always on his eyes—but little hair—a fur cap is always on his head. He wears no powder, but is well kept. He dresses in very white linen and a brown coat. A cane is his only defence. If he sees our minister, he does so in the greatest secrecy, in Paris at night.'

Franklin remained in France nine years. He was the only American envoy who negotiated both the 1778 treaty with France, which gave America the aid she needed to win the war, and the 1783 treaty with England, which recognized American independence and conceded the former colonies' land claims. He was thus instrumental in two of the most important diplomatic victories ever won for America. He was also an agent of France's destiny, for when Louis XVI agreed to help the insurgents he depleted his own treasury and precipitated the financial chaos that was one of the immediate causes of the French Revolution; the king financed a demonstration in how to overthrow despotism, which was not lost on his own people. The final irony was the exchange of gifts, in which Franklin gave Louis XVI a morocco-bound copy of texts concerning the proposed constitution embossed with the royal seal, while Louis XVI gave Franklin his portrait encrusted with 408 diamonds. Franklin's enormous personal popularity made him a catalyst of the French Revolution, which hailed him as one of its heroes. Paradoxically, he had little sympathy with the French Revolution, nor did he realize, as D. H. Lawrence wrote, that 'in contriving money out of the court of France he was contriving the first steps of the overthrow of all Europe, France included.'

The man, whom a kind of secular hagiography has built up as a model of typically American virtue, is in fact one of the most complex and least representative of the founding fathers. The inspiring progress of his own life appears as though in a series of Norman Rockwell illustrations: the industrious printer's devil, the frugal manager of his own printing shop working in leather breeches, the resolute businessman who knew how to make an honest dollar, the civic leader who organized the Philadelphia fire department, the intrepid scientist who flew a kite in a thunderstorm, the temperate family man playing the harmonica (which he invented) for his children, the sincere but skilful diplomat who charmed the French court, and the tranquil, kindly gentleman in the fur cap reading the Good Book through his bifocals (another of his inventions). Franklin is all that, and much more, for he managed at one time or other in his life to lapse extravagantly from most of the thirteen virtues on his list (the last one, humility, cancels itself out as a magnificent conceit consisting in the imitation of Jesus and Socrates).

To complete the portrait, Franklin should also be described as an expatriate and a latecomer to the cause of American independence, a speculator guilty of grave conflicts of interest, a writer of smut, a man possessed by periods of apathy and a streak of pessimism, and a salacious old gentleman. He was not the perfect man of the Enlightenment the French considered him to be. He had little faith in mankind, which he considered 'very badly constructed.' He was not, as the French thought, a Quaker, and there was a bit of mild charlatanism in allowing that legend to persist. Nor was there anything Roman or Spartan about Franklin. He lived in a fine house in the rolling green village of Passy, in keeping with his ambassador's rank. He had nine servants and a wine cellar of over a thousand bottles.

The French saw in Franklin the embodiment of the American experience, while in fact he had lived in England since 1757 as agent for Pennsylvania, Massachusetts, Georgia, and New Jersey, and postmaster for the colonies. In twenty years, he had been home on only two brief visits. There was nothing plebeian about Franklin, who traced his own ancestry back to 1555. His suspicion of the popular mind was equal to his contempt for the 'groundless and absurd' European nobility. He said in 1788 that 'though there is a general dread of giving too much power to our governors, I think we are more in danger from too little obedience in the governed.' And his view of welfare laws was that they 'encourage idleness.'

He long hoped that the disputes between the colonies and England could be settled peacefully and without recourse to independence. Franklin's political thinking is utilitarian. If a monarchy is doing its job he is for it. He wrote in 1770: 'Let us therefore hold fast our loyalty to our king, who has the best disposition toward us and has a family interest in our prosperity.' He believed in peaceful change, and when he saw it was impossible, in 1775, he returned to America to become a somewhat tardy leader of the War of Independence.

The French liked to contrast the plain-speaking, truth-loving, honest, virtuous Franklin with the frivolous and corrupt court. But again they created a false image, for there were facets of Franklin which reflected the persiflage, bawdiness, and hypocrisy of the court. Franklin the writer showed a talent for literary hoaxes, and a style more reminiscent of Rabelais than any Greek or Roman sage. He praised the amorous talents of older women in his 'Advice to a Young Man on the Choice of his Mistress,' because 'there is no hazard of children, which irregularly produced may be attended with much inconvenience,' and because, 'as in the dark all cats are gray, the pleasure of corporeal enjoyment with an old woman is at least equal and frequently superior; every knack being, by practice, capable of improvement.' But this, after all, was the bawdy side of the Enlightenment, and Voltaire and Montesquieu wrote some salty passages too. They did not, however, share Franklin's heavy-handed penchant for scatological facetiousness. In 'A letter to the Academy of Brussels,' which had criticized his discoveries, he proposed that scientists should try to find a way to make discharges of wind as agreeable as perfume. 'Were it not for the odiously offensive smell accompanying such escape,' he wrote, 'polite people would probably be under no more restraint in discharging such wind in company than they are in spitting or in blowing their noses. . . .' Franklin argued that 'surely the liberty of ex-pressing one's sentiments is important to human happiness. Compared to this, he said, the science of the philosophers is 'scarcely worth a FART-HING.'

Far more serious than Franklin's hoaxes and off-colour amusements was the conflict of interest between his mission to France and his business interests in a British syndicate with vast land options in the American West. Before coming to France, Franklin had pretended to resign from the Vandalia syndicate, but he had a secret understanding with his London banker friend Thomas Walpole, who looked after his shares. The land claims would be validated only if England won the war, but there is no evidence that Franklin's mission was influenced or that his patriotism was tarnished by his private interests. However, he had to keep up a business correspondence with the enemy in wartime. Conflict of interest was not an eighteenth-century concept, but by modern standards of political ethics, Franklin was guilty of a grave impropriety. At best, he was leaving himself open to the temptation of treachery. He resisted, but his colleague Silas Deane, also associated in the Vandalia enterprise, was not so virtuous, and it is a matter of record that Deane and a Philadelphia land speculator named Samuel Wharton leaked news of the American treaty with France to promote their speculations on the New York stock exchange.

There was also in Franklin what Vergennes called his 'apathy' and what John Adams termed his 'dissipation.' The French Foreign Minister complained that despite his respect for Franklin 'I am nevertheless obliged to concede that his age and his love of tranquility produce an apathy incompatible with the affairs in his charge.' Adams, who had been sent to the Low Countries on a mission similar to Franklin's, expressed a New England puritan's contempt for a man who was sensitive to comfort and partial to pleasure. Franklin, he wrote his cousin Samuel on December 7, 1778, 'loves his ease, hates to offend, and seldom gives any opinion till obliged to do it. I know also . . . that he is overwhelmed . . . with answering visits from multitudes of people, chiefly from the vanity of having it to say that they have seen him. There is another thing which I am obliged to mention. There are so many private families, ladies and gentlemen, that he visits so often, and they are so fond of him, that he cannot well avoid it—and so much intercourse with Academicians, that all these things together keep his mind in a constant state of dissipation. . . . He is not only so indolent that business will be neglected, but you know that although he has as determined a soul as any man, yet it is his constant policy never to say yes or no decidedly but when he cannot avoid it.'

In the winter of his years, Franklin kept up a vigorous interest in the ladies, and no duty was too pressing to delay his rendezvous with his two most frequent muses, the sexagenarian widow Madame Helvétius, and the pretty wife of a treasury official, Madame Brillon de Jouy, who was forty years his junior. Madame Helvétius retained the delicate bone structure of her once-famous beauty and presided in haphazard fashion over a household of eighteen cats fed on the white meat of pheasants. She was faithful to the memory of her doctor-philosopher husband, and Franklin was no more successful in his advances than another of her admirers, the minister Turgot. He visited the suburban house of 'Our Lady of Auteuil' two or three times a week, and made it clear that 'if this lady likes to spend her

days with him, he would equally wish to spend his nights with her.'
But Madame Helvétius spurned his advances.

His flirtation with the gay, sprightly Madame Brillon was hardly
more substantial. Her friends criticized her habit of sitting in Franklin's lap. He asked her whether 'the most effectual way to get rid of
a certain temptation, is, as often as it returns, to comply with and
satisfy it. Pray instruct me how far I may venture to practise upon
this principle.' Franklin indulged his temptation no further than
playing chess with Madame Brillon when she was in her bath. 'Can
you forgive my indiscretion?' he wrote to her.

Franklin, for all his peccadillos, was the most effective envoy Congress sent to Europe, overcoming enormous difficulties. The only
constant factor of American foreign policy was the urgent need for
funds. The rest was improvisation. There was no president, no cabinet, and Franklin was his own secretary of state, writing most of his
own instructions. He went far beyond the framework of the treaty
plan drawn up by a committee under John Adams, which called for
a purely commercial agreement. Once in France, Franklin's correspondence with Congress was episodic. Dispatches took months to
arrive and had a way of being captured by the English on the high
seas—they bore the warning: 'To be sunk if in danger of falling into
the hands of the enemy.' Congress did not hear directly from Franklin for an entire year, from May, 1777, to May, 1778. One reason for
the high percentage of captured dispatches was Franklin's own gullibility. The usually shrewd appraiser of human nature had placed his
trust in his good friend Edward Bancroft, a Massachusetts-born doctor
and natural scientist who was England's most successful spy. Franklin used the treacherous doctor as a secretary and sponsored him for
confidential missions. Each week Dr. Bancroft would take his constitutional in the Tuileries garden, and, sauntering past a certain tree,
drop into the hole in its trunk a bottle with a string tied to its neck,
which contained his report in invisible ink, signed 'Edward Ed-
wards.' Thus many of Franklin's secrets, including the departure
date of ships carrying dispatches to America, found their way to
Lord North's desk in London. Franklin was warned by several
friends about the sievelike security of his office but took no notice.
The damage would have been much greater had it not been for
George III's suspicion of his own agents when they provided intelligence that did not agree with his preconceptions, and for Bancroft's
curious reticence in the performance of his duties. Bancroft seems to

have been an example of the double agent who becomes a split individual, with divided but genuine loyalties to each side.

Franklin might have better coped with his enemies if he could
have been preserved from his friends. The other American envoys to
Europe had, it seemed, been chosen on the basis of their irascibility,
dishonesty, and general uselessness. The Southern snob Ralph Izard
was sent to the court in Tuscany, which refused to receive him.
William Lee, Arthur's brother, suffered similar rebuffs in Vienna.
Stephen Sayre was a charlatan who hoped to enlist the support of
Catherine the Great by seducing her. Silas Deane was involved in
several questionable business deals and was accused of embezzlement
and stockjobbing. He was recalled by Congress in 1779 and became
so embittered by smear campaigns that he defected to England.
Franklin in a rather harsh letter compared him to Benedict Arnold.
Arthur Lee, stewing with envy in the dull and inhospitable Spanish
capital, spent much of his time making wild accusations against
both Deane and Franklin, whose patience finally wore so thin that
he warned his fellow plenipotentiary in April, 1778, that he was
showing signs of a mental disorder: 'I do not like to answer angry
letters,' Franklin wrote in reply to some typical Lee charges. 'I hate
disputes, I am old, cannot have long to live, have much to do, and
no time for altercation. If I have often received and borne your magis-
terial snubbings and rebukes without reply, ascribe it to the right
causes, my concern for the honour and success of our mission, which
would be hurt by quarrelling, my love of peace, my respect for your
qualities, and my pity of your sick mind, which is forever tormenting itself, with its jealousies, suspicions, and fancies that others mean
you ill, wrong you, or fail in respect to you. If you do not cure yourself of this temper it will lead to insanity.' But Lee was incurable,
and kept conspiring against Franklin, whom he wanted sent to
Vienna so that he could replace him at the French court, 'the great
wheel that moves them all.' Meanwhile, Lee's most noteworthy
achievement had been the loss of important papers to a British agent
during a trip to Prussia. Lee was recalled shortly after Deane.
An investigating committee with a delegate from each state questioned the envoys' usefulness because of 'suspicions and animosities
. . . highly prejudicial to the honour and interest of the United
States.' Franklin himself was more unanimously popular in France
than in his own country, where Lee's charges fell on some receptive
ears. But despite a motion for his recall, he was cleared by Congress.

Franklin was stung by the criticism and offered his resignation, which was turned down. He observed that 'if my enemies would have a little patience they may soon see me removed without giving themselves any trouble, as I am now seventy-five.'

The Paris mission was a heavy burden for a man of Franklin's age, suffering from gout, boils, and a skin disease. He was distracted from his main work of securing the treaty by a multitude of other tasks. 'Drive thy business or it will drive thee,' he had written, and in Paris he was driven. Every American with a problem appealed to him, whether it was a ship's captain with a mutiny on his hands, John Paul Jones in quest of a fleet (he got the *Bon Homme Richard*), or a privateer suffering cruel treatment in a British jail. Since there were nearly a hundred British prisoners aboard American ships in French harbours, Franklin proposed an exchange to Lord Stormont, who replied: 'The King's ambassador receives no applications from rebels, unless they come to implore His Majesty's mercy.' Franklin called the letter 'indecent' and sent it back for Stormont's 'more mature consideration.' He kept pressing the issue, and a partial exchange of prisoners was arranged in 1779.

More than a year elapsed between Franklin's arrival and the signing of the treaty, and there was little the harried emissary could do to accelerate French decision-making. He was no miracle-worker who could with a wave of his magic wand drastically alter the course of French policy. He was a sometimes gullible, often disorderly diplomat, and tended to disperse his energies. At the same time, he showed great talent for grasping the essence of a situation and working within it. He understood perfectly that Vergennes was not a wide-eyed crusader eager to help the American cause. Thus, he did not appeal to Vergennes' idealism or to his sympathy for a struggling people, but to the Foreign Minister's fear of England and the unique opportunity now at hand to crush her. Franklin's repeated theme to Vergennes, in many variations, was that if the French did not help the Americans win the war and 'if the English are suffered to recover that country, such an opportunity of effectual separation as the present may not occur again in the course of ages; and that the possession of those fertile and extensive regions, and that vast seacoast, will afford them so broad a basis for future greatness, by the rapid growth of their commerce and breed of seamen and soldiers, as will enable them to become the Terror of Europe, and to exercise with impunity that insolence which is so natural to their nation and which will increase enormously with the increase of their power.'

Vergennes was agreed on the principle of helping America for those very reasons, but he needed assurances that the insurgents were capable of winning the war. Franklin's offer of trade advantages did not sway him, for he believed that American trade, 'thrown open as it is to be henceforth to the avidity of all nations, will be for France a very petty consideration.' He made it clear from the start that he would not be rushed into a treaty. When Franklin, on January 5, 1777, held up the spectre of a defeated America and an all-powerful England and asked for eight manned and outfitted ships, Vergennes' reply was chilly: 'It is not by methods so under-handed and little in keeping with the dignity of a great power that war may be started,' he said. 'It is useless to precede time and events. They must, if they are to be taken advantage of, be waited for . . . His Majesty, unable to enter into the detail of the various American needs, will demonstrate his benevolence and good will with secret funds which will increase their credit and buying power.' Instead of his eight ships, Franklin obtained that year a gift of 2 million livres.

Franklin conspired to prod France into war with England, but failed. He felt that Franco-British relations had deteriorated to the point where the least snip would be enough to sever them. He saw possibilities in the sanctuary provided in French harbours for American privateers. Before leaving Philadelphia in the fall of 1776 he told the privateer Captain Wickes to bring a British prize into a French port to publicize France's clandestine assistance. Wickes captured the English mail packet *Swallow* and brought her back to Nantes. The action angered Parliament into authorizing English privateering but did not lead to war. Vergennes fended off Lord Stormont's almost daily protests as tactfully as he could. When the English ambassador complained about the presence of American envoys in France, Vergennes countered that England was harbour-ing the Corsican nationalist Paoli. For fourteen months Vergennes sparred with Stormont and avoided a break in diplomatic relations. On May 3, 1777, in another of Franklin's initiatives, the Irish privateer Gustavus Conyngham brought the British mail packet the *Prince of Orange* into Dunkirk. There was such a furor in England over the 'Dunkirk pirate' that Vergennes had to arrest Conyngham and his crew and return the packet to avoid war.

Aside from his experiments with privateers, Franklin was content to wait for the situation to ripen. While he could do little to influence Vergennes, he could refrain from vexing him. His virtue lay in maintaining the reserved behaviour of an officious emissary, basking quietly in his many-sided popularity, and in remaining in the minister's good graces. Franklin's way was, like Vergennes', oblique and inferential. One shudders to think what damage the bull-headed tactics of an Adams would have done to the American cause at this particular point. What American could have been more successful in Paris than Franklin the popular hero and Franklin the urbane and subtle diplomat? And yet it was no manœuvre of Franklin's that pushed Vergennes to action, but an item of news that arrived on November 30, 1777, when a carriage rumbled into the courtyard of the Passy retreat and a young Bostonian named Jonathan Loring Austin jumped out. 'Sir, is Philadelphia taken?' asked Franklin. 'It is, sir,' replied Austin, 'but, sir, I have greater news than that. General Burgoyne and his whole army are prisoners of war.'

Burgoyne's October 17 surrender at Saratoga was the turning point. Vergennes blew hot and cold according to American victories and defeats. Franklin's jest about Philadelphia taking Howe had fallen rather flat when Vergennes closed French ports to American privateers after learning of the defeat. But Saratoga was the decisive victory which closed this initial, picaresque period of secret aid, companies with cover names, nocturnal meetings, double agents, and ships laden with weapons and uniforms stealthily leaving French ports. It took only nine more weeks to sign the treaty which the French had delayed for over a year. Franklin's communiqué underlining the importance of the battle dispelled the last misgivings of Louis XVI. The treaty signed by the three American commissioners on February 6, 1778, in the Hôtel Coislin, Place de la Concorde, went far beyond Franklin's instructions. It was in effect a military alliance, since it agreed on joint military action should England hamper trade between France and America or break the peace with France. In case of war, the French king agreed to fight until America won her independence and promised to seek no conquests on the American continent. Franklin, co-author of the treaty with Vergennes, was pleased. He wrote to his friend Thomas Cushing on February 27 that 'the king has treated with us generously and magnanimously; taking no advantage of our present difficulties to exact terms which we would not willingly grant when established in prosperity and power,' Vergennes had asked for nothing. American independence, stripping England of one-third of her empire, afflicting her commerce and increasing her national debt, was to him reward enough.

On March 20, in a scene that illustrated the passing of an age, the Very Christian King, twenty-four-year-old, paunchy scion of an 800-year-old monarchy, received in Versailles' Hall of Mirrors the Freemason envoy of the world's youngest republic, a gouty seventy-two-year-old 'Quaker' with thinning grey hair. The major of the Hundred Swiss announced: 'The Ambassadors of the thirteen United Provinces.' The duc de Croÿ, who was present, recalled: 'The king, rising from his faldstool, adopted a noble stance. M. de Vergennes named M. Franklin, M. Deane, M. Lee, and two other Americans [William Lee and Ralph Izard]. The king was the first to speak and said: "Please assure Congress of my friendship. I hope that you will also say that I am very satisfied with your conduct during your stay in my kingdom. I hope this will all be for the good of both nations." M. Franklin very nobly thanked him in the name of his country and replied: "Your Majesty can count on the gratitude of Congress and its loyalty to its commitments." . . . Since I knew Franklin, I went up to him and said: "It is fitting that the man who discovered electricity should electrify both ends of the world." ' Reflecting on the meaning of the event, Croÿ wrote: 'What an example to substitute Franklin the insurgent, the leader of the insurgents, to the British ambassador, to recognize insurgents who were not even independent yet, to be the first to recognize them! And against a nation with whom we were not yet at war, and to whom we would declare war only because she was in difficulty; not to mention the risk of being the first to establish a power which was to become so formidable.'

For the first time in history, a European monarchy was treating a colony in revolt against its king as an equal. It lifted a group of insurgents with insurmountable military and financial problems to the dignity of a state and then proceeded to help solve those problems. France gave America men, ships, arms and funds. Eight thousand men left with Admiral Rochambeau in 1780, and Vergennes asked only that they be used judiciously. 'Being ready to undertake any task to assist America,' he wrote, 'they must not be sacrificed to temerity or frivolity.' Now that the treaty was signed, Franklin, who had written that 'he who goes a-borrowing goes a-sorrowing,' became America's most successful borrower. The urgent demands of war made Congress desperate. More than 60 million dollars in almost worthless paper money had been printed. Franklin had to borrow from Vergennes funds that were already spent. The exasperated ambassador finally wrote John Adams that he was 'quite sick of my Gibeonite office, that of drawing water for the whole congregation of Israel.' Franklin's repeated pleas for more money tried even the generous Vergennes' patience. The minister wrote him curtly on the last day of the year 1781: 'I shall not enter into an examination of the successive variations and increases of your demands on me for funds to meet your payments.'

The country destined to become the richest in the world was largely dependent on French aid. That the aid was decisive in America's victory is generally acknowledged. More important for France, however, was the drain of lend-lease on the king's treasury. The American Revolution prepared the French not only by the example of its struggle for freedom but by contributing to the financial chaos which paralysed the regime. Relieved of the burden of American aid, the *ancien régime* might have stumbled along a few years longer, and would at least have had the option of devoting its resources to reforms, as Turgot had urged.

Besides the enormous cost of naval and military expeditionary forces, estimated at between 250 and 300 million livres, the monarchy gave or lent the insurgents a total of 45 million livres between 1776 and 1783. Two contracts signed by Vergennes and Franklin, and ratified by Congress, stipulated that the war loans, which carried a 5 per cent interest and amounted to 38 million livres, would be repaid over a twelve-year period starting three years after peace with England, thus from 1786 to 1798. But in 1786, when the first payment was due, the emerging nation could not pay even the salaries of its ambassadors, much less the French loan. The lender was not demanding and the borrower was in good faith. There was no dunning by the one or shirking by the other. The loan was repaid in full, from 1790 to 1802, but not to the same regime which had made it.

The member of the king's cabinet who was most alarmed by the cost of the war and Vergennes' munificence was the Minister of Finance, Jacques Necker. Floating high-interest loans was Necker's classic expedient, and he was struck by the fact that France was at the same time making large low-interest loans to the Americans. Necker, like his predecessor, Turgot, realized that peace with England was the condition of internal reform. For the good of the state and his own ambitions, the folly of involvement in America must stop. Never a man to question the soundness of his own views, Necker began to intrigue behind Vergennes' back, and sent direct peace feelers to King George III. He favoured a very simple solution for a quick end to the conflict: the partition of America.

The go-betweens in Necker's attempt to jettison the American cause were Viscount Mountstuart, who was crossing Europe on his way to a diplomatic assignment in Turin, and whose father, Lord Bute, was a friend of George III; and Paul-Henri Mallet, a Swiss professor who had done the Grand Tour with Mountstuart in 1765 and was friendly with Necker. Mallet saw Necker in Paris in the spring of 1780 and reported to Mountstuart that the minister considered the American Revolution the only stumbling block to peace. Mallet proposed that one American province could be granted independence while the others would return to England, and Necker, although vague, seemed favourable.

George III still clung to hopes of total victory, however, and took a dim view of the Necker-Mountstuart contacts. The king's position was that England would only treat with France once she had stopped assisting the rebels. Mountstuart was told to cut off his secret dialogue with Necker.

On December 1, 1780, Necker tried another channel. He sent a secret letter to the English Prime Minister, Lord North. Acknowledging that he was not himself Prime Minister and that he wrote without authority to negotiate or treat, he took a man-to-man approach, saying: 'You desire peace. I wish it also.' He proposed a truce, with both sides keeping the territory held by their troops, another form of partition. George III, blind to the advantages that could be gained from divisions in the French cabinet, repeated his position: 'With France it [is] easily to be settled if she would desist from encouraging Rebellion and not add to her insults by wanting to affect independency which whether under its apparent name, or a truce, is the same in reality; till she gives up that view I do not see how peace can be a safe measure.' A précis of the king's remarks was sent to Necker, but the minister was prevented from pursuing his one-man foreign policy by his disgrace the following May. Vergennes knew Necker was undermining his policy, for he told him on one occasion: 'Peace is a fine thing, only you should propose the means of attaining it in an honourable manner.' Necker was divided between his oft-expressed liberal sentiments, his conviction that France's best interests lay in appeasement, and his inordinate ambition. His daughter, the 'mistress to an age,' Madame de Staël, quoted him as saying: 'Louis XVI was wrong to mix into the war between America and England, although the independence of the United States was desired by all generous spirits.'

Necker's backhanded partition proposal was the first of many attempts to subvert the American cause to European interests. European statesmen, most of whom had little faith in America's ever becoming a viable state, let alone a world power, continued to weigh the thirteen struggling colonies as an ingredient in the scales of continental power politics. Their policies, quite naturally, were based on the way events in America would affect Europe. America's ally, France, and France's ally, Spain, were ready to bargain off vital American interests against gains for themselves. No one viewed the American war as a privileged cause for which European powers should have been eager to sacrifice their own interests. Even the French, who had said they were not involved in a war of conquest, modified their position as victory approached.

It was, in George Canning's phrase, a case of 'every nation for itself and God for us all.' The tortuous manœuvres that led to the final treaty of 1783 between England and the allies provide a classic example of the rifts that develop between allies, of broken pledges, backstairs deals, secret understandings with the enemy, and of the enemy's attempts to exploit the allies' diverging aims. God, in this case, was on the side of the Americans, whose negotiators, like the neophyte in the poker game who asks 'how do you play this game,' took the pot. It was not, however, blind luck, but a shrewd appraisal of the power politics involved and a lack of scruples about double-crossing their allies and disregarding their own instructions which transformed the American diplomats from lambs being led to the slaughter into the kind of clear-eyed, sharp-clawed eagles which graced their own national emblem.

The credit goes mainly to John Adams and John Jay, who arrived in France in the fall of 1779 as replacements for the disgraced Silas Deane and Arthur Lee. Adams had been instructed, in a time of American military reversals, to negotiate a treaty with Great Britain, while Jay had left his post as president of the Continental Congress for a mission to Spain. Their prejudiced attitude towards their co-negotiator Franklin and their ally France was, paradoxically, to be one of the keys to their success. They were suspicious and envious of Franklin, and considered him an expatriate, too long steeped in the fleshpots of the French court and out of touch with his country's affairs. Adams called Franklin 'the old conjuror' and criticized his disorderliness and laziness. Jay mistrusted Franklin to the point of keeping vital stages of the negotiations from him. To both men, Franklin was tainted by the very fact that he had engineered the alliance with France and was bound by feelings of gratitude which they did not share. Franklin had personally pledged to Vergennes that America would make no separate peace with England. They had not.

Franklin was in fact the only one of the three who was genuinely fond of France, which he called 'the civilest nation on earth.' He found 'nothing wanting in the character of a Frenchman that belongs to that of an agreeable and worthy man.' By contrast, John Jay, the acrimonious descendant of French Huguenots victimized during the Edict of Nantes, the vigilant enemy of popism who had tried to limit the civil rights of Catholics in America, was a curious choice as envoy to the Catholic monarchies of France and Spain. As Adams observed: 'Mr. Jay likes Frenchmen as little as Mr. Lee and Mr. Izard did. He says they are not a moral people; they know not what it is; he don't like any Frenchman. The marquis de Lafayette is clever but he is a Frenchman.' Adams himself considered the attractions of Paris a diabolical lure. He wrote to his wife Abigail that 'there is everything here that can inform understanding or refine the taste, and indeed, one would think, that would purify the heart. Yet it must be remembered there is everything here, too, which can seduce, betray, deceive, deprave, corrupt, and debauch it.'

Moreover, there was a clash of temperaments between Adams and Vergennes; there could be no sympathy between the courtly, flexible diplomat, whose tools were subtlety and the lights and shades of language, and the bull-headed, sharp-tongued, peremptory New England puritan, who made a virtue of tactlessness. Adams' touchiness made him bluster to Vergennes that 'the United States of America are a great and powerful people, no matter what European statesmen may think of them.' Vergennes advised Adams that he would deal only with Franklin, the sole accredited envoy to the French court, and that Louis XVI could get along without Adams' advice. Discredited at Versailles, Adams left for Holland to squeeze a few florins out of tight-fisted Dutch bankers, while Jay languished in Madrid on an equally unpromising mission.

In 1781, with Franklin ailing and Adams and Jay out of France, Vergennes' steadfastness for the American cause wavered. He was war-weary and concerned by France's growing deficit. As he wrote to his ambassador to Spain, he had 'little faith' in America's ability to win. He favoured a plan to end the war quickly with the mediation of Austria and Russia. The plan, as expressed in a confidential memorandum drawn up by Vergennes in May, was nothing but a warmed-over version of Necker's partition. It called for a long truce which would lead to de facto recognition of American independence by the British. But Georgia and South Carolina would remain in British hands (the one was unpopulated and the other's heat was destructive to energetic effort, Vergennes reasoned). Vergennes backed the plan in spite of reports from his ambassador in Philadelphia, Anne-César, chevalier de la Luzerne, that the insurgents viewed it with horror and would fight alone rather than give up territory. There were flurries of diplomatic activity that year between the courts of Versailles, St. Petersburg, and Vienna, which was chosen as the site for the mediated negotiations, but the plan was doomed to failure. The British insisted that the Americans could not be represented at the negotiations, a condition unacceptable to Vergennes. Second, Vergennes summoned Adams to Paris in July to inform him of the mediation efforts. Adams' suspicions were confirmed that the European powers were trying 'to chicane the United States out of their independence.' He protested vigorously against any kind of truce or settlement on the basis of a status quo, or any negotiations where the Americans were not represented. Vergennes incorporated Adams' objections in his reply to the mediators.

As a final blow to mediation prospects, news of Cornwallis' surrender at Yorktown reached Europe in November. Yorktown bore out John Jay's belief that the best negotiator is a military victory. In England, the American victory had the repercussions of a natural disaster. The Prime Minister, Lord North, could only repeat: 'O God, it is all over,' and it was, for him—his government fell a few months later. Yorktown served to show George III that there was no alternative to negotiation, and gave the American envoys a strong hand. They were no longer the officious emissaries of a feeble republic ignored by most of Europe, pleading like paupers in foreign courts for a doubtful cause. They were the ambassadors of a nation which had defeated Europe's greatest power.

The American envoys needed a strong bargaining position to offset the private projects of their allies. Vergennes had already shown that he was ready to sacrifice basic American interests. More than that, through his persuasive ambassador in Philadelphia, la Luzerne, he was able to pressure Congress into placing peace negotiations under French control. The ruddy, ham-faced la Luzerne was a talented lobbyist who controlled a large block of votes in Congress and who used secret funds to bribe men like Tom Paine and Hugh Henry Brackenridge. La Luzerne had keys to the American ciphers. There were no secret dispatches to Congress where he was concerned. There are probably few examples in history of an ambassador who took such an active part in the domestic affairs of a country. Even so, la Luzerne was unable to make Congress reduce America's aspirations, or accept a truce, or give up its pretensions to western lands. However, he was able to influence Congress into voting new instructions to Adams, the peacemaker, in June, 1781, which pledged that America would make no separate peace with England. Adams was told 'to make the most confidential communications upon all subjects to the ministers of our generous ally, the king of France, to undertake nothing in the negotiations for peace or truce without their knowledge and concurrence, and to make them sensible how much we rely upon His Majesty's influence for their effectual support in everything that may be necessary to the present security or future prosperity of the United States of America.'

La Luzerne tried hard, but was unable to carry out Vergennes' instructions to have that 'arrogant, inflexible pedant' Adams recalled. Instead, he spurred the election of four more peace commissioners who, it was hoped, would temper Adams' mulishness. They were Jay, Franklin, Jefferson (who never took part in the negotiations), and Henry Laurens (who was captured en route and released only in time to sign the preliminary treaty). Translating Congress' June instructions into plain language meant that the peace commissioners would be puppets manipulated by Vergennes.

Moreover, Vergennes had succeeded in bringing Spain into the war, but at a high price. According to the secret Treaty of Aranjuez signed on April 12, 1779, France agreed not to make peace with England until Gibraltar was restored to Spain. Thanks to this treaty, the settlement of the war now depended on Spanish as well as American demands, and Vergennes time and again had to equivocate between the conflicting claims of his two allies.

Spain, for the security of her own vast American empire, wanted to keep the thirteen colonies east of the Mississippi, and on this fundamental issue Vergennes was willing to back Spanish claims. Finally, France herself had interests which conflicted with American goals, mainly concerning what James Lovell called 'the long struggle over cod and haddock.' France wanted to regain the Newfoundland fishing rights lost in the Seven Years' War, and exclude the Americans from fishing off those North Atlantic banks. It may in retrospect seem slightly absurd that what amounted to a world war was prolonged by a few boatloads of fish, but in those days fishing rights were considered an important part of a nation's policy. Vergennes' position was that with the Declaration of Independence, the Americans had forfeited the fishing rights they had enjoyed as English colonies. However, fishing rights remained an essential American demand.

With all these forces at play, Britain's best route to a low-priced peace clearly lay in dividing the allies, either by treating first with France and Spain, or by snatching a separate peace from America which would not hinge on French and Spanish demands. This is what William Fitzmaurice, Lord Shelburne, into whose nimble hands the negotiations fell when he became Prime Minister in July, 1782, was able to accomplish. In the months to come, Shelburne, Vergennes, the Spanish negotiator Count Aranda, and the American peace commissioners, seemed like players in a four-handed chess game where everyone was cheating.

It was John Jay who decided that America's basic interests would be lost unless the peace commissioners negotiated behind the backs of their French allies. In June, 1782, Parliament passed the Enabling Act, allowing George III to treat with the Americans. Shelburne sent his envoy, the Scottish merchant Richard Oswald, to talk to Franklin. Jay and his family arrived in Paris on June 23. On August 10, Jay and Franklin paid Vergennes a visit at Versailles which convinced the naturally suspicious Jay that the French minister intended 'to keep America in leading strings.' Vergennes told the Americans not to worry about the technicality of proclaiming America's independence before negotiations began, which to Jay was a crucial point. Vergennes did not support the American position in the quarrel with Spain over the northwest territory and the western boundary. Jay saw that France and Spain wanted a general peace which would limit the American gains. It was a toss-up between a satisfactory European peace at the expense of America, or meeting American demands at the expense of the allies. In his famous conversation with Franklin, Jay announced his intention to break his instructions. If there is any 'conflict with America's honour and dignity I would break them—like this,' he said, and flung his clay pipe into the fireplace. Jay lost no time in giving the English agents Oswald and Benjamin Vaughan broad hints that once an American treaty was signed, America would not support the demands of her allies. When Oswald asked him whether an America independent of England would also be independent of other nations Jay replied: 'We will take care of that.'

In the meantime, Vergennes was indulging in some private diplomacy of his own. Despite the charges of the American commissioners that he wanted to delay the peace, he seized on what looked like an opportunity for a quick settlement. The French naval hero De Grasse, captured in the spring of 1782, had been released in England. Lord Shelburne asked him to convey to Vergennes the terms of a suspiciously generous peace settlement which granted America independence and satisfied French and Spanish demands: France would regain her commercial counters in India, her lost Caribbean islands, her fishing rights, and her military control in Dunkirk; Spain could choose between the Balearic island of Minorca and Gibraltar.

The prospect of this feast whetted Vergennes' appetite to the point of sending a secret emissary to London to pursue De Grasse's conversation with Lord Shelburne. His trusted second-in-command, Gérard de Rayneval, reached London on September 7, travelling under the cover name of Monsieur Castel. Shelburne, who, although he claimed 'an unconquerable aversion to dealing with men' had few equals at it, renegued on the peace terms proposed to De Grasse but managed to charm Rayneval all the same with phrases like 'let us cease fighting one another and we will lay down the law to the rest of Europe.' He in turn sounded out Rayneval about French plans, and Vergennes' emissary said flatly: 'We do not want the Americans to share in the fisheries.' When it came to American boundaries, Rayneval was more discreet, but nonetheless suggested as a starting point a previous plan which could have deprived the thirteen states of lands north of the Ohio River.

Rayneval's mission was unofficial. His communication with Lord Shelburne was oral, and led to nothing. Nonetheless, it had been kept from the Americans. Jay found out about it and considered it proof of French treachery. His suspicions were fanned by British agents who gave him a copy of an intercepted dispatch from Barbé-Marbois, the secretary of the French embassy in Philadelphia, which said that France should make it clear that it did not support American claims on the fisheries.

Since he did not know the nature of the Rayneval mission, Jay exaggerated its importance. It was a counterprobe to an English proposal, not an offer of a secret treaty with England. There is no evidence that Vergennes ever considered a separate peace. Quite to the contrary, treating with the Americans strengthened his hand, for he could use American interests to threaten the British into meeting French and Spanish claims. By treating separately, he would lose the useful leverage of American demands, and his bargaining power would be seriously affected. Jay, however, believed on the basis of skimpy information that the American cause had been betrayed, and now worked towards a separate peace with England. His justification was that since France did not back all of America's views, she was no longer worthy of American confidence. Jay placed his trust not in his colleague Franklin or in his ally Vergennes, but in Lord Shelburne's private agent, Benjamin Vaughan, a young intellectual who had brought out an edition of Franklin's writing and who was perceptive enough to realize that a generous settlement with the Americans would lead to important trade advantages. Without informing either Franklin or the French court, Jay sent Vaughan to convince Lord Shelburne of the advantages of a secret deal with America. Although America would be faithful to her obligations to France, he said, 'it was a different thing to be guided by their or our construction of it.' Jay's construction was clearly to sign a treaty and then let the allies shift for themselves. The price to Shelburne, Jay continued, would be the fisheries, access to the Mississippi, and western lands. History judges the success of an initiative more often than its propriety. Jay violated his instructions and tricked his ally, and in so doing became the principal architect of the treaty which created America. He successfully prevented the French and Spanish from nibbling away at American claims, and he persuaded the British into making a more generous settlement than they had ever intended. Vaughan returned from his secret mission on September 27 and announced Shelburne's determination to make the peace.

From the moment of Vaughan's return to Paris to the signing of the preliminary treaty in which England forfeited her American empire, there lapsed only two months and three days. Both sides rushed the treaty through so that neither the French court nor the querulous English Parliament would learn of the secret talks. Franklin, who had because of poor health and old age lost the initiative to Jay, made a half-hearted effort to keep Vergennes informed, but Jay insisted that the French minister 'merited no such confidence.' Adams arrived from Holland on October 26, and the English sent Henry Strachey, Undersecretary of State in Home Affairs, who learned to consider Adams and Jay as 'the two greatest quibblers that I ever met.' Quibbling there was in plenty, but it led to a treaty signed on November 30 which conceded the principal demands of the Americans—the western lands, navigation on the Mississippi, and the freedom to fish in Newfoundland. Vergennes when he learned of the treaty said it 'exceeded all that I could have thought possible.' This was also the reaction in England, for it led to the downfall of the Shelburne government in February, 1783. A week before signing, Vergennes had written to Congress saying that he could no longer back some of the American peace commissioners' 'pretentious ambitions,' little knowing that his support had become academic. Even when Franklin sent Vergennes a copy of the preliminary treaty, he left out a secret article which was an incentive to Britain to conquer Florida from Spain—America agreed to give a British Florida a northern border ninety miles deeper than the one Spain enjoyed. Jay, usually so parsimonious with American territory, seemed in this case to be indulging in a private vengeance for his rebuffs at the Spanish court.

On December 15, Vergennes expressed his polite annoyance with the separate American agreements. 'I am at a loss, sir,' he wrote to Franklin, 'to explain your conduct and that of your colleagues on this occasion. You have concluded your preliminary articles without any communications between us, although the instructions from Congress prescribe that nothing shall be done without the participation of the king.' He found in 'the abrupt signing of the articles . . . little which could be agreeable to the king.' Vergennes completely misjudged the peace commissioners, whose action he attributed to inexperience. They 'acted with a precipitation which would be inexcusable if they had understood the consequences,' he wrote. He never realized that the Americans had outsmarted the three European courts which boasted the oldest diplomatic traditions, while performing the additional feat of remaining on friendly terms with the ally they had cozened. Franklin apologetically wrote to Vergennes that the Americans had indeed been 'guilty of neglecting a point of propriety' but hoped that the alliance would not crumble because of 'a single indiscretion of ours. And certainly the whole edifice sinks to the ground immediately if you refuse on that account to give us any further assistance . . . the English, I just now learn, flatter themselves they have already divided us. I hope this little misunderstanding will therefore be kept secret, and that they will find themselves totally mistaken.' By appealing to Vergennes' need to maintain a united allied front until he had pulled his own irons out of the fire, Franklin was able to obtain continued French financial aid. Indeed, the very ship which carried the preliminary articles to America under a British safe-conduct on December 30 also carried the first payment of a 6-million-livres French loan.

The separate American agreement scuttled French and Spanish positions. Without the leverage of American claims, the Spanish could no longer insist on Gibraltar, which remained in British hands. All France received in the final Treaty of Paris signed on September 3, 1783, was the Caribbean island of Tobago, a few commercial counters in India, a share in fishing rights, the islands of St. Pierre and Miquelon, and what Vergennes called his 'tip,' the end of British supervision in Dunkirk. For France it was a return to the pre-Seven-Years'-War status quo. The cost was the depletion of the French treasury and the potent example of a successful war of independence.

Franklin, the only American who had participated in both the treaty with the French and the treaty with the English, and who was more than any other man responsible for the image of America abroad, never understood the forces he had helped to spread, just as Vergennes never grasped that in recognizing the insurgents he was helping to create a new kind of society whose very existence threatened his own. None of Franklin's writings doubt the permanence of the monarchy. When he left France in July, 1785, he could not conceive that exactly four years later, the whole structure of the French society he had known would collapse. It did not occur to him that in assisting America, France was acting against her own long-range interests, for the option to weaken England did not offset the financial drain of the American war or the example of a nation which had given itself a constitutional form of government.

Back in Philadelphia, the octogenarian Franklin kept up with transatlantic events through his many correspondents. On July 12, 1787, the duc de la Rochefoucauld wrote to him that 'France, which you left talking zealously of liberty for other nations, now begins to think that a small portion of this same liberty will be a very good thing for herself.'

Franklin at first considered the turbulence in France a passing phase which would lead to greater happiness for all. In one of his cheerful analogies, he compared the French Revolution to wine, writing to a friend on October 24, 1788, that 'when the fermentation is over and the troubling parts [have] subsided, the wine will be fine and good and cheer the hearts of those who drink it.' He wanted to believe that the Revolution was no more than a French version of the Boston Tea Party, and that everything would work out for the best.

After the bloody events of 1789, he viewed the situation with a mixture of levity, continuing optimism, and concern. On November 13, 1789, he wrote to Jean Baptiste Le Roy: 'It is now more than a year since I have heard from my dear friend Le Roy. What can be the reason? Are you still living? Or have the mobs of Paris mistaken the head of a monopolizer of knowledge, for a monopolizer of corn, and paraded it about the streets on a pole? . . . Great part of the news we have had from Paris, for over a year past, has been very afflicting. I sincerely wish and pray it may all end well and happy, both for the king and the nation. The voice of Philosophy I apprehend can hardly be heard among those trumpets.'

The following year Franklin died, and was spared the beheading of the king whose diamond-encrusted portrait he had kept. He immediately became a hero of the Revolution. Mirabeau proposed three days of nation-wide mourning. Condorcet pronounced a long and windy eulogy to his fellow scientist and philosopher. The abbé Sieyès wrote a letter of condolence to Congress. All over France, there were demonstrations of revolutionary sympathy for the man who 'had wrested the thunder from the sky and the sceptre from the tyrants.' In Nantes, the first city to receive Franklin on his arrival in France in December, 1776, the printers held a funeral ceremony for him and vowed in honour of his memory that they would break their composing sticks before printing anything obscene, untruthful, or contrary to revolutionary principles.

XIV

THE FIRST REVOLUTION

*The Revolution was unleashed by those whom it
was to destroy, not by those who profited from it.*
—GEORGES LEFEBVRE, *Etudes sur la
Revolution Française*

THERE WAS, wrote the baron de Frénilly, an illusion of
stability, just as 'painted cardboard ramparts would protect
a city if the enemy mistook them for stone.' The generation
of thinkers—Voltaire, Montesquieu, Rousseau, Diderot—was being
replaced by a generation of orators—Danton, Robespierre, Camille
Desmoulins, the abbé Sieyès. Better communications and schools, an
excitable public opinion, a rising standard of living, a growing
administrative centralization, contributed to the diffusion of ideas
and gave the variegated French provinces a new sense of national
consciousness. Soon, political parties would formulate the demands
of the nation. Louis XVI congratulated the maréchal de Richelieu on
his good health and advanced age and said:

'You have seen three centuries.'

'Not quite, sire,' replied Richelieu, 'but three reigns.'

'Well, what did you think of them?'

'Sire, under Louis XIV, no one dared speak; under Louis XV they
spoke in a whisper; and under Your Majesty they speak out loud.'

The king and his ministers did not direct policy, they responded
to events. Ministers were either sceptics like Maurepas, Calonne and
Loménie de Brienne, intelligent opportunists like Necker, or men of
conviction defeated by vested interests, like Turgot. In the revolving-
door government of Louis XVI, there were sixteen Controllers
General and thirteen Ministers of War in fifteen years. The old
court was dying. Marie Antoinette scorned its usages. Versailles was

deserted in favour of the clubs, salons, and Freemason lodges of Paris or the adventure of the American war. While the liberal nobility espoused fashionable causes, the bulk of the aristocracy conducted a rearguard action for the preservation of its privileges. One of the keys to understanding the nobles is their pursuit of wealth. It made them exchange ideals with the bourgeoisie. Lords went into business and on the eve of the Revolution controlled an important share of industry (mines, textile works, foundries) and commerce (colonial companies, shipping). They married the daughters of the rich bourgeois. Meanwhile, the bourgeoisie aspired to the status symbols of the nobility. They overdressed to look like gentlemen, and carried swords. They painted coats of arms on their sedan chairs and built châteaux on country estates. They invested their wealth in offices and positions that would confer nobility, and gave their names an aristocratic fillip. Danton became d'Anton and reverted to the original spelling when he became a revolutionary orator. Derobespierre, as a young provincial lawyer, called himself de Robespierre.

Far from being bent on the destruction of the monarchy, the bourgeoisie was a rising class glad to accept the superiority of the aristocracy as long as it could attain it. It was not revolutionary, because its prosperity depended on a stable society, peaceful growth, and a developing economy. It was not equalitarian, because its own success had fostered a creed of personal competence akin to the feudal knight's ennobling valour. The bourgeoisie supported a society based on privileges as long as it continued to accept men who had singled themselves out through excellence, hard work, and thrift. The bourgeois even endorsed the notion that business is contemptible, since, whenever they could, they disguised their origins and passed themselves off as lords. Honours which washed away traces of bourgeois origins were known as 'churl-soap.' The bourgeoisie had its own laws of growth, based on personal initiative and free competition rather than the gift of birth and belief in God. It was a secular, dynamic class, which nonetheless was still dazzled by the aristocratic system and the glamour of privileges. The bourgeois wanted what the nobles had, but for different reasons. Extravagance and dissipation were to the nobility a natural condition of their birthright. The pursuit of pleasure and the refined elegance of Louis XV were the distractions of a class grown futile. To the bourgeois, pleasure and wealth were the consecration of success. A rich banker collected paintings and kept mistresses to show that he could afford them. A duke and peer pursued the same activities to fill his vacant hours.

So long as careers which conferred nobility remained available, the bourgeoisie was a dynamic but submissive element of the Third Estate (an inclusive term which embraced the humblest peasant as well as a banker who married his daughter to a duke). The favoured son of the bourgeoisie could buy a seat in Parlement, or a diocese, or a regiment. When d'Argenson was Minister of War under Louis XV, he preferred giving commissions to bourgeois who could afford to keep up a regiment. But under Louis XVI there was an almost total occlusion of the channels of social mobility as the caste of nobles reacted against change and sought to monopolize every form of power. When careers were closed off a growing sense of frustration seized the bourgeoisie. Its allegiance to the regime wavered. This disaffection was aggravated by the government's fiscal policies, which were leading it to bankruptcy. Financiers lost confidence in the regime. Since the bourgoisie's reasons for supporting the monarchy no longer existed, it gradually assumed an opposition role. A dynamic group, conscious of its abilities and eager for responsibilities, laid siege to a defensive aristocracy which had filled the moat, raised the drawbridge, and barricaded itself behind the crumbling ramparts of its privileges.

Under Louis XIV the foes of the feudal nobility had been the lawyers and jurists, who had formed the gown nobility and taken over positions of power. But when the Regent came to power in 1715, the feudal nobility was given a chance to govern and muffed it. After the failure of that experiment, there was a growing sense of kinship between sword and gown nobility. Their interests were identical: the maintenance of their privileges and the protection of their favoured place in society. The gown nobility had the weapon of the Parlements to wield against royal reforms. The feudal nobility also sat in Parlement and exerted considerable influence at court. Nothing could be more inaccurate than the picture of a weak aristocracy collapsing before the thrust of the Third Estate. The aristocracy was powerful and conservative, and under Louis XVI staged its own revolution against a liberal king.

Parlements were long able to disguise the narrow defence of their caste interests as popular victories over despotism. They also supported regional rights against the encroachment of central authority. In this manner, they built up solidarity among the nation's twelve

Parlements, so that moves taken by the Paris Parlement would immediately be echoed in the rest of France.

In 1789 there was a total of about 12,000 sword and gown noble families, or roughly 150,000 persons; there were in addition 100,000 persons who claimed certain noble privileges. But only 942 families were admitted at Versailles, under a ruling of Louis XV that barred from court families who could not trace their lineage to the fourteenth century. The nobility represented less than one per cent of the population and owned an estimated 25 per cent of the land. It became, like a guild, hostile to outsiders and jealous of its advantages. It succeeded in monopolizing careers in the magistrature, the army, and the church. As early as 1762 the Paris Parlement ruled that 'henceforth, to be admitted, candidates who do not have magistrates among their direct ancestors must justify their candidacy, with documents, by proving four degrees of nobility in the paternal line.' This was enough to make the Parlements a self-perpetuating oligarchy. In the church, half the bishops in 1730 were commoners. They were usually given the poorer dioceses, called 'muddy bishoprics.' In 1789, however, every one of the 118 bishops and 18 archbishops was a noble, as were 8,000 canons and several thousand monks.

In the army, the edict of 1781 restricted commissions to nobles with four degrees, except for men promoted through the ranks or graduates of military schools. In the navy ministers like Choiseul and Castries favoured 'blue' (noble) over 'red' officers. Thirty-four of the thirty-six ministers under Louis XVI were chosen from the ranks of the nobility. The sword nobility, like the duc d'Aiguillon and the marquis de Ségur, served side by side with the recent gown and clerical nobility, like the comte de Vergennes and archbishop Loménie de Brienne. Also, as the nobility laid claim to every important post, it insisted on a strict interpretation of its feudal land rights, at a time when the very foundations of feudal privileges were a growing target of criticism.

After Turgot's disgrace, Parlement consolidated the position of the aristocracy by voiding his basic reforms, the suppression of the guilds and the corvée. Louis XVI, faced with a full-scale depression at home, the expense of aid to the American insurgents, and what was probably the greediest court in the history of the monarchy, resorted, as the Regent had in 1718, to the services of a foreign miracle-worker. In June, 1777, he made the Swiss Protestant banker

Jacques Necker 'director-general' of finances in a country where Protestants normally did not enjoy even the basic rights of citizens. Necker was a large, florid man with a sonorous voice. He exuded self-confidence and self-importance, and once wrote: 'To my great surprise I seek in vain something to reproach myself for.' His adoring wife, a pastor's daughter whom Edward Gibbon had loved and lost, once read to the guests of her salon a description of her husband which compared him to a lion, an angel, a volcano, an Apollo, and a column of fire.

Necker was an enterprising international financier who, like Law, understood the power of credit and the methods of modern capitalism. He had left his native Geneva at the age of sixteen to work as a clerk in a Paris bank. He became chief clerk, and eventually, a partner. He met the right people (his wife was a tireless social climber) and used his political contacts for intelligent speculation. Thanks to contacts in the Foreign Ministry he was told in advance that a peace treaty would be signed with England to end the Seven Years' War, in 1763. One of the treaty's secret clauses was that debts to Canadians would be honoured. Necker bought up Canadian bonds, which because of the French colonial defeats were selling at 10 to 20 per cent of face value. He sent the bonds to London, where his collaborators arranged to have Canadians pose as their owners and ask for reimbursement at full value. The deal netted Necker close to 2 million pounds. Thanks to similar deals worked out with his political contacts, including wheat speculation between France and Switzerland, Necker amassed a fortune of 8 million pounds. His fortune made, he opened his own bank and professed to be a friend of enlightened thinkers. In 1773 he won the annual essay prize of the Académie Français on the subject 'Homage to Colbert.' His essay had been read personally to the Académie by his friend d'Alembert. It became clear that Necker, infatuated by his successes in banking and letters, wanted to play a part in government. He tried to discredit Turgot's policies with an 'Essay on the Legislation and Commerce of Grain,' which was published at the time of the flour war. Privately, Turgot said that Necker was 'a man who will always be odious to me.' He could not abide his bragging and posturing. Publicly, he thanked Necker for his essay, saying only: 'In your place I would have chosen a more tranquil moment.'

Necker was the first minister who not only acknowledged the power of public opinion, but tried to use it to his advantage. He called public opinion 'my infallible queen.' He had interests in the *Gazette Anglo-Française*, a sheet published in London, and after he had been presented to the king, the *Gazette* dutifully reported: 'He spoke to His Majesty with all the energy and all the sensibility of a heart acutely penetrated with the great obligations he was about to contract.' Necker lasted three years. He created the illusion of success because no new taxes were levied even though France was fighting England in the American war. As a foreigner, he was in no position to resist the looting of the treasury by the queen and her coterie, and the cutbacks he made in the king's household were more than offset by the special pensions that had to be granted to Madame Polignac and others. Necker's system was simply borrowing at high interest from his banker colleagues. He placated Parlement but increased the national debt. He broached some interesting reforms, which were rather like trying to repair broken windows when the roof is caving in. He reduced the number of General Farmers from sixty to forty and experimented with provincial assemblies in two provinces, Berri and Haute Guyenne. The assemblies had forty-eight members, one-third named by the king, two-thirds elected by land-owners; half were recruited from the privileged orders and half from the Third Estate, and the vote was by head, not by order. The assemblies awakened the provinces to political life and were a preliminary form of national representation.

In 1781, Necker confirmed his magician's reputation with his famous financial report to the public. State finances were traditionally a closely guarded secret. The treasury belonged to the king. He could spend as he liked, without accounting to his subjects. One of the most frequent of Parlement's protests was the right to examine finances. It was this right which Necker offered the public. He addressed himself 'proudly to public opinion, which the evil have in vain tried to stop or lacerate, and which, despite their efforts, follows in the wake of justice and truth.' The report increased Necker's popularity because the nation was grateful for his confidence and because he presented a rosy picture of the state's finances. According to his 116-page treatise, the current fiscal year showed an income of 264 million livres and expenses of 254 million livres, or a surplus of 10 million livres. Necker was a clever propagandist who used the technique of the big lie. Instead of shedding light on the murky financial situation, he led the public into a labyrinth of his own devising, carefully concealing the truth, which was a deficit for the year of 90 million livres. His growing popularity emboldened him to seek greater powers. He asked Louis XVI for the title of minister, control over the budgets of the war and naval ministries, and the extension of provincial assemblies to the rest of the nation. Louis XVI was not personally fond of Necker and followed the advice of his chief counsellor, Maurepas, to disgrace him. Necker went back to Switzerland, but returned to Paris in 1785 and married his daughter to a Swedish embassy attaché, baron de Staël-Holstein, while awaiting the crisis which would bring him back to power.

After two other ministers had lost their way in Necker's labyrinth, Louis XVI gave the pivotal post of Controller General to Charles-Alexandre de Calonne, who, like Turgot, had been recruited from the ranks of provincial Intendants. But there the resemblance ended, for Calonne was a cunning courtier who generously distributed pensions and gifts to stay in power, an elegant spendthrift so riddled with debts that when he was appointed he said with alarming candour: 'France's finances are in a deplorable state and I would never have accepted the responsibility if my own were not equally shaky.' His personal fortune improved during his ministry, and he was accused of irregularities, not without reason. Nevertheless, he made a courageous effort to foil the aristocratic reaction and impose a programme of reforms. He was, like Turgot, a victim of the court cabal.

Faced with a financial crisis, Calonne borrowed a page from Necker and gave the nation the illusion of prosperity. He levied no new taxes. In December, 1783, he borrowed 100 million livres at 10 per cent. In 1784, he borrowed another 125 million livres at 8 per cent. In 1785, he borrowed still another 80 million livres plus 40 million livres from various provinces and cities. There was a national debt of 783 million livres, and he created a sinking fund which he said would wipe it out by 1809. But for the sinking fund to work there had to be a budget surplus instead of a deficit. Calonne was besieged by courtiers, financiers, and 'accredited ladies.' He said that being Controller General was like being 'a tree covered with caterpillars, which those vile insects relinquish only after having gnawed it completely.' At the same time, his rule was permissive and he did not like to see influential courtiers go away empty-handed. He was famous for his gifts, and was said to have given the court painter, Madame Vigée-Lebrun, a box of pistachio nuts, each of which was wrapped in a 300-livre note. Calonne did not forget his own reward.

When a new contract with the General Farmers was signed, it was customary to give the Controller General a substantial gratuity. Turgot and Necker had refused it, but Calonne accepted. He was also involved in speculations through relatives and friends. In March, 1785, Louis XVI was persuaded to exchange scattered properties with an income of 200,000 livres a year, plus one million livres in cash, for the county of Sancerre, which returned 88,000 livres a year. Sancerre belonged to the baron d'Espagnac, a friend of Calonne's, and one of the properties he received from the king was snapped up by the Controller General—it was adjacent to one of Calonne's own properties, the comté d'Hannonville. In a similar deal, the husband of one of Calonne's nieces, the marquis de Fouquet, was able to exchange the viscounty of Auvillars for the far more valuable barony of Viviers.

In 1785, Necker resumed his literary career with a *Treatise on the Finances of France*. It was an oblique attack on Calonne, full of false figures and spurious arguments. Mirabeau called the book 'double nonsense.' Nonetheless, it rapidly sold 80,000 copies and made Calonne's position precarious. In August, 1786, Calonne presented Louis XVI with a memorandum urging a full financial reform. He said that loans from 1776 to 1786 totalled the frightening sum of 1,250 million livres and that the deficit was growing annually.

His proposals were a mixture of Necker and Turgot: a territorial tax, payable by all; elected provincial assemblies; the free circulation of grain; the suppression of the corvée, and the suppression of some indirect taxes. Calonne realized that submitting his programme to the ratification of Parlement would condemn it. But he balked at going directly to the people. Caught between the Parlement and the Estates General, Calonne revived a substitute used by Henri IV in the sixteenth century—the Assembly of Notables, a relatively small, hopefully manageable group of lords, prelates, provincial officials and members of Parlement. Even though an Assembly of Notables would normally support the views of the aristocratic reaction, Calonne believed he could control it and push through his programme. As soon as he had presented his plan to the king, other ministers began conspiring against him. The Lord Privy Seal, Miromesnil, who was a lobbyist for Parlement, wrote Louis XVI a confidential letter denouncing Calonne. The initial reaction of Louis XVI was always in favour of reform, however, and he scheduled the Assembly of Notables for January 24, 1787. It would have 144 members including 7 Princes of the Blood, 14 prelates, 36 lords, and 87 magistrates and provincial and local officials. Its opening was delayed by Calonne's collapse from overwork and Vergennes' sickness and death on February 13. It opened in a Versailles outbuilding on February 22, nearly a month late.

The delay had allowed enough time to launch a violent anti-Calonne campaign in Paris. A popular caricature showed Calonne as a monkey addressing a group of barnyard animals. 'Dear friends, I have gathered you here to ask you how you want to be eaten,' said the monkey. 'But we don't want to be eaten,' replied the animals. 'You are straying from the subject,' said the monkey. The notables were also likened to the idols of nations in Psalm 103: 'They have a mouth and speak not, they have eyes and see not.' They arrived in Versailles already humiliated by public raillery and in a nasty mood because Calonne had sent them the topics to be discussed only a few days beforehand. The assembly was divided into seven committees, each of which was chaired by a Prince of the Blood whom Calonne thought he could count on out of loyalty to the king and because he had helped to pay their debts. But all the royal princes opposed him except the king's youngest brother, the comte d'Artois.

Calonne's performance before the notables was candid and realistic. He placed before the nation's elite the choice of accepting a few modest sacrifices or tempting anarchy. He described the disastrous state of the nation's finances. The reforms might be costly to some of them, but would allow them to keep their rank and the bulk of their privileges. The notables interpreted Calonne's dramatic admissions as either a proof of his incompetence or as a series of lies intended to scare them, for they remembered Necker's reassuring statistics. They considered the new tax an unfair burden. They could not swallow the suppression of distinctions in the proposed provincial assemblies. The upper clergy was particularly ill-disposed to Calonne. Archbishop Dillon of Narbonne said: 'Monsieur Calonne intends to bleed France, and he is seeking the notables' advice on whether to bleed her in the foot, in the arm, or in the jugular vein.' When the committee chaired by the comte de Provence, the king's brother, rejected the provincial assemblies, the other committees were encouraged to do the same. The assembly approved the free circulation of grain and the replacement of the corvée by a cash tax but voted down the other, more important measure.

To justify his reforms, Calonne revealed the 112-million-livres deficit for the year's budget and showed how Necker had juggled the books in his 1781 report to show a surplus. Calonne met with the leaders of the upper clergy and offered to resign if his reforms were adopted, for opposition was thought to derive partly from a refusal to provide Calonne with a political victory which would keep him in power. He visited each of the seven committees personally to explain why reforms were urgent. When the notables recessed for a week at Easter, however, the attacks against him redoubled. Calonne had explained his reforms in a pamphlet intended to sway public opinion, and the notables could not forgive what they considered a breach of confidence and an impertinence. Miromesnil continued to chip away at his credit with the king, and Louis XVI's allegiance began to waver, as it had with Turgot—the king was seen on April 2, on the verge of tears, muttering to himself that he wished Vergennes was still alive because 'he would have gotten me out of this mess.' On April 5, Calonne forced a showdown and asked the king to choose between himself and his two most dogged enemies in the ministry, Miromesnil and the baron de Breteuil, Minister of the King's Household. Louis XVI promised to dismiss Miromesnil but not Breteuil, who was protected by the queen. Once again, Marie Antoinette's intervention was decisive, for when she learned that Calonne had tried to force the ouster of Breteuil she furiously attacked him. On April 8, Easter Sunday, both Calonne and Miromesnil were disgraced.

Calonne was so unpopular that he was burned in effigy in the streets of Paris. In August, 1787, the Paris Parlement opened criminal proceedings against him for irregularities in office, which Louis XVI quashed, realizing that the trial of Calonne would be the trial of the monarchy. Calonne fled to England, which seemed an admission of guilt, and died there in 1802. He had in his years of power amassed a collection of Van Dycks, Murillos, Ruysdaels, Titians, Veroneses, Tintorettos, Da Vincis, Giorgiones, Raphaels, Rubenses, Poussins, and Rembrandts, which were sold at auction.

Louis XVI still hoped that the Assembly of Notables would accept Calonne's programme, now that its author was gone. He pulled from the ranks of the notables one of the leaders of resistance to Calonne, Loménie de Brienne, archbishop of Toulouse. He was the last cardinal-minister of the *ancien régime*, a well-meaning but ineffectual caricature of the great predecessors he took for models, Richelieu and

Fleury. He was a deist, if not an atheist, and a friend of the Encyclo-pedists and the ladies, thanks to whom he had contracted a bother-some skin disease for which he was endlessly seeking remedies. He was a worldly and learned prelate, a man of charm, grace and erudition, proud of his collection of rare books. He later said of his sixteen months in power: 'I wanted to do good, I wanted it with good will, but my character was not made for storms and trouble; it was a relief to retire and my only regret is to have been mixed up in it.' Brienne was appointed minister on May 1 and reassured the assembly that he remained a notable at heart. He asked each of the seven committees to work out for themselves the amount of the regime's deficit, and they arrived at figures ranging from 133 to 145 million livres. For the first time they realized that the deficit was not a trick to relieve them of their privileges. But when Brienne proposed a limited tax, the notables accused him of slavishly imitat-ing Calonne. Six committees out of seven refused the new tax. Weary of the notables' obstruction, Brienne dismissed the assembly on May 25. But before it broke up, one of its members, the Parle-mentary President d'Aligre, said that the government measures deserved 'the most careful consideration.' Brienne was encouraged, thanks to this remark, to seek from the Paris Parlement what the Assembly of Notables had denied him.

Brienne sadly misjudged the temper of the Paris Parlement. He took his reforms to a body which was in open revolt against the crown. In 1787 the Paris Parlement had 144 members, to which were added 7 Princes of the Blood, 7 ecclesiastical peers, and 27 lay peers when it sat as a Court of Peers. Opposition to the monarchy was general, although it stemmed from several different and sometimes contradictory motives. Among the peers, for instance, the duc de Montmorency-Luxembourg wanted to protect the claims of the feudal aristocracy against ministerial despotism; the duc de la Roche-foucauld, translator of the American Constitution and friend of Lafayette, opposed the government out of liberal patriotism; other peers were angry with the economies carried out in the king's house-hold; and the duc d'Orléans, the king's cousin, opposed the govern-ment because of personal hatred of the royal family. This same complexity of motives was to be found among the gown nobility. The leader of Parlementary opposition was the short, fiery, council-lor Duval d'Epremesnil, of recent but wealthy nobility. His cele-brated wish to 'debourbonize France' makes him sound like a revolutionary. He was in reality a conservative, hostile to the Encyclopedists, devoutly Catholic, and fervently attached to aristocratic and Parlementary traditions. As the revolutionary figure Jacques-Pierre Brissot later said: 'He wanted to debourbonize France, but only so that Parlement could reign.' There were also a good many elderly magistrates, like Advocate General Séguier, who had systematically opposed the crown all their working lives and would never change. They were, in the words of the lawyer Beugnot, 'laborious athletes of the good old causes.' But there was also a liberal opposition, imbued with the example of the American Revolution and the ideas of the Enlightenment. Another leading orator, Adrien Jean-François Duport, wanted the regime's downfall and a constitutional government. While this mixed opposition to the king's programme was eloquent and clamorous, his cause was poorly defended by a few elderly peers and Princes of the Blood, a tongue-tied, simple-minded lot lacking gifted orators, Parlementary tacticians, or bold programmes. The king's brother, the comte d'Artois, drafted speeches which he planned to deliver at Parlementary sessions, but once there he was too shy to speak.

Brienne had imagined a new tax in the form of a stamp act, an unfortunate choice in view of the American war. Parlementary opposition had a field day denouncing the despotic tax which had led the thirteen colonies to seek their freedom. The real reason was that a tax on stamped paper would mainly affect bankers, commercial people, printers, and librarians, all of whom had lobbies at Parlement. Brienne wisely shelved the stamp act and presented Parlement with a tax on property-owners, which was easier to justify. The king's brother, the comte de Provence, who owned extensive real estate, said he would submit to the tax like any loyal subject. But Parlement voted down the tax and made the convocation of the Estates General a precondition to reforms. Brienne decided on a show of force. On August 15, police brought each member of Parlement a sealed letter exiling him to Troyes, where they were put in the former palace of the comte de Champagne.

The exile of Parlement was a test of its popularity. It was still the only channel of discontent, the only banner around which all forms of opposition could rally. There was considerable agitation in Paris. Sidewalk orators who spoke of revolution drew large crowds. Government notices were burned at the bottom of the big staircase at the Palace of Justice. There was talk of a march on Versailles, and mobs threw stones at the homes of government officials. The French guards were insulted and threatened by crowds and had to draw their swords. The Palace of Justice was evacuated and guarded. The Police Lieutenant ordered all clubs closed, even chess clubs. On September 20, Parlement was allowed by royal decree to return to Paris, which public opinion interpreted as a capitulation to agitation in the capital. The crown had submitted to the popular will.

Brienne now proposed a five-year tax and loan plan and promised to convene the Estates General within the next five years if it were accepted. The Estates General, an assembly of delegates from the kingdom's three orders, had first been mentioned by Lafayette at the Assembly of Notables, when, in his usual impetuous manner, he had thrown out the random idea of 'a really national assembly . . . the Estates General of the kingdom.' Thereafter, to embarrass the government, Parlement periodically called for them. The Estates General, a tradition originating in the fourteenth century, had not been summoned since 1614, and had in the entire history of the French monarchy met only twenty-five times. They were called in times of crisis, when the king needed popular support. They were not a democratic institution, but a technique to strengthen the absolutism of the French monarchy. In 1302, Philippe le Bel created the Estates General as a weapon in his struggle against the papacy, which was trying to affirm the omnipotence of the Holy See in temporal French affairs. By showing that the nation was behind him, he was able to unfetter the monarchy from the influence of Rome. Thereafter, the Estates General were summoned whenever the king needed support against some internal threat, such as the Templars, feudal lords, or Huguenots. After Louis XIII, and as a result of the long, monolithic reign of the Sun King, the Estates General were forgotten.

Now that the idea of the Estates General had been roused from 173 years of slumber, the liberal opposition was too impatient to wait five years and called for their immediate convocation. Mirabeau wrote that the nation could not survive sixty months of expediency. The Estates General seemed a miraculous panacea that would cure all the nation's ills.

Parlement continued to obstruct Brienne's programme, despite the promise of the Estates General. The magistrates met on November 19 in a seven-hour special session during which Louis XIV lost

THE LAST PROCESSION OF THE MONARCHY TO OPEN THE ESTATES GENERAL, MAY 4, 1789

THE ROYAL FAMILY AT THE TUILERIES, JUNE 20, 1792

MADAME DU BARRY ON THE WAY TO THE GUILLOTINE
By Gaildrau

his temper. When the duc d'Orléans questioned the legality of the king's presence at a session which was not a formal bed of justice, the king replied: 'It is legal because I want it to be.' Parlement refused to register Brienne's five-year tax and the following day d'Orléans was exiled and two Parlementary concillors were jailed.

In January, 1788, Parlement adopted the decree making Protestants full-fledged citizens. But Brienne realized that the court would continue to block all efforts to find a sound fiscal basis for the country. This was not the voice of the people but the voice of the landed gentry, of the tiny minority whose pocketbooks would be affected by new taxes. Brienne had the merit of facing the difficult choice between complete paralysis of the government or decisive action against Parlement. He staged the government's last coup against the aristocratic reaction. He secretly planned to suspend the thirteen Parlements and establish a plenary court which would in effect be a permanent Assembly of Notables. Its members would include Princes of the Blood, dukes and peers, ecclesiastical, military, and administrative officers, and 47 magistrates from the Paris Parlement. There would also be established in the provinces 47 bailiff's courts. Brienne's proposed coup was a bold experiment in federalism, and chroniclers of the period have said that even Louis XIV at the zenith of his power would not have attempted it.

The texts of the new laws were being secretly drawn up at the royal printing press, and an armed guard kept away the curious. But d'Epremesnil, the leader of the Parlementary opposition, learned of Brienne's plan, thanks to a double agent, and took preventive measures against it. The government texts were published on May 1, and on May 3 the Paris Parlement declared that under no condition could any members of the nation's thirteen Parlements be removed from office or stripped of their rights to judge the laws of the nation. They also vowed never to sit in any newly constituted body. Brienne ordered the arrest of d'Epremesnil and another Parlementary leader, Goislard de Montsabert, who sought refuge among their colleagues in the Palace of Justice.

Between ten and eleven on the night of May 5, the Palace of Justice was invested by a detachment of French guards commanded by the marquis d'Agoult, who was booed by the magistrates, and most particularly by the peers belonging to the military nobility. The duc de Luynes gibed that he was unfit to carry out the king's orders, having neglected to don his gorget. Confused by the clamour, d'Argoult retreated from the hall as a hundred voices shouted: 'We are all d'Epremesnil and Montsabert. You must arrest us all.' The following morning d'Agoult returned, and the wanted men gave themselves up after making speeches. They were imprisoned, and released September 15.

Most provincial Parlements joined the resistance. They said Brienne had violated the fundamental laws of the nation. Louis XVI held a bed of justice on May 8 to enforce the decrees, which royal commissioners duplicated in the provinces. Parlements were notified of their suspension for an indeterminate period. The Paris Parlement, usually the spearhead of resistance, had been shaken by the arrests of May 6, and meekly complied with the suspension. The burden of resistance passed by default to the provincial Parlements, which were no less imbued with their traditional role as the defenders of just laws, no less attached to their privileges, and no less hostile to change. The provincial Parlements, controlled by a coalition of sword and gown nobles, both landowners ready to defend their tax exemptions and feudal benefits in the name of high principles, were faithful only to their prejudices. They were far less influenced than the Versailles court and the Paris Parlement by the ideas of the Enlightenment. A Besançon Parlementarian wrote in February, 1789: 'I am tired of hearing that our ancestors were imbeciles unworthy of imitation; equality, uniformity, liberty, these are big words, but how can they be applied and reconciled with the monarchy . . .' By setting themselves up as guardians of the monarchy, the Parlements were in fact destroying measure after measure which might have allowed the monarchy to survive.

Several provincial Parlements openly flouted the king's suspension order and continued to meet. The government had recourse to its traditional weapon, the sealed letter. Soldiers distributed them to members of the most insolent Parlements—Toulouse, Besançon, Dijon, Metz, Rouen, Rennes, and Grenoble. Loménie de Brienne expected local uprisings, and said: 'I am ready for anything, even civil war.' In Grenoble there were incidents which fell short of civil war but proved that he was not ready.

The Grenoble riot, remembered as the 'Day of the Tiles,' was, in the words of the revolutionary orator Joseph Barnave, 'the first blood spilled for the Revolution.' It showed that the army, influenced by the writings of the Enlightenment and angry at being used to police rioting compatriots, could not be counted on in case of civil strife. It was the first serious example of the monarchy's impotence against the mob. It bared, behind Parlementary resistance, a growing popular opposition with very different goals, a mysterious popular will, still unled and disorganized, but eager to take to the streets. The immediate cause of the Grenoble riots was a conservative reaction against the exile of the provincial Parlement. But the riot was maintained and amplified by members of the Third Estate, whose interests were continuously thwarted by Parlement. A reactionary protest became transmuted into a popular protest. Parlementary exile served as the outlet for the manifestation of the popular will, the still inchoate aspirations of the Third Estate.

The duc de Clermont-Tonnere, Lieutenant-General of the province, made the mistake of ordering his men to deliver the thirty-six sealed letters on Saturday, June 7, a market day. When the first letters were served early that morning, agitators began to mingle with the street crowds. More than the popularity of Parlement was at stake; its exile was an economic issue. Parlement was a source of jobs and wealth in a city which was not a centre of trade or industry. Its suspension would make hundreds of lawyers and clerks idle. It was this legal fraternity which stood to lose the most, and whipped up the spirit of riot.

The Place aux Herbes, where the fishmongers, greengrocers, and butchers had their stalls, was crowded with peasants in town for the day. Bundles of cut wood lined the sidewalks and drovers waving switches led livestock through the streets. Agitators called for shops to close as a sign of protest. Groups began forming at street corners. Servants were told by their masters to join the mob. At noon, the rioters rang the bells of the Grenoble churches, and the word went out: 'The magistrates must be prevented from leaving!' Hundreds of men and women armed with pitchforks, axes, iron bars, and rocks marched from the marketplace to the five badly defended city gates, which they invested, closed, and nailed shut. A crowd whose leaders waved the keys to the city gates at the end of a stick paraded through the streets. Two hundred screeching women pushed into the courtyard of the First President of Parlement, Monsieur de Bérulle, whose coachmen were waiting for him to finish lunch. They cut his trunks away from the carriage roof and unbridled the horses. They informed the astonished jurist, who had not had the slightest intention of disobeying the king's order, that he would leave over their dead bodies.

Between noon and 1 P.M. the duc de Clermont-Tonnerre ordered two regiments, the Austrasie and the Royal la Marine, to patrol the city. The soldiers were given no cartridges and told not to use their bayonets. Clermont-Tonnerre's quarters were in a massive, rectangular, two-storey building with a sloping slate roof and thirty windows to a side. A grilled courtyard separated it from an alley which led to the rue Neuve and, a hundred yards further, the First President's house, which the mob had invested. Two companies of troops took up position in the alley and were soon confronted by a grumbling, seething crowd. Some rioters took to the roofs, others loosened cobblestones. At 2 P.M. a hail of roof tiles and cobblestones fell on the troops, and about thirty rioters attacked them head on. A lieutenant-colonel of the Austrasie regiment named de Boissieu was struck in the nape of the neck by a rock and severely wounded. The troops dispersed the crowd with a bayonet charge.

Stendhal, then a five-year-old boy named Henri Beyle, watched the riot from the window of his grandfather's apartment on the Place Grenette. First he saw a man go by and yell: 'I am rebelling, I am rebelling!' Then he saw 'a hatmaker, allegedly wounded in the back from a bayonet blow, and walking with great difficulty, held up by two men around whose shoulders he had thrown his arms. He was coatless and his shirt and trousers of nankeen or linen were covered with blood. I can see him still, the blood pouring from a wound in the small of his back, at about the same level as his navel. He had trouble reaching his room on the sixth floor of the Périer house. When he arrived he fell dead.' The sight of blood made the crowd savage. A four-man patrol of the Royal la Marine regiment led by a flag-bearing officer was surrounded and had to shoot its way out, killing one demonstrator and wounding another. A large crowd gathered in front of Clermont-Tonnerre's courtyard and again bombarded the troops with rocks and tiles. Clermont-Tonnerre himself came into the courtyard to tell the officers that under no circumstances were their men to fire. He tried to reason with the crowd but had to dodge flying rocks.

Meanwhile, attracted by the ringing churchbells, hundreds of peasants were trying to enter the city. Some arrived by river. Weavers from the faubourg of St. Joseph, led by a man beating the drum on a barrel, scaled ladders into a school courtyard and appropriated the pins and balls of a bowling game as weapons. A gang of fishwives attacked the bishopric. Clermont-Tonnerre's advisers wanted to take

action against the mob. One suggested arresting the magistrates, because 'by making them share the peril, they would be forced to try
to end it.' The marquis d'Ambert, colonel of the Royal la Marine,
could not understand why the riot was not severely repressed. When
his regiment was reprimanded for firing at the mob, he wrote to the
Secretary of War that 'the moderation of the troops went too far; it is
hard to believe that two regiments could be crushed without receiving
the order to defend themselves; of what use are we, I ask you? . . .
they want to punish my regiment for having fired two rifle shots—
they should have given us no cartridges, we would have defended
ourselves with the rocks that were thrown at us. . . .'

The officers of the Austrasie regiment, on the other hand, urged
Clermont-Tonnerre to capitulate and warned that they were not sure
of their men. They said that if he did not give the order of with-
drawal they would march their troops out of the city. As the comte
de Chambord, colonel of the Austrasie, later explained: 'The tocsin
was still ringing in all the parishes, and you could hear the bells of
country churches ringing in reply. The city was surrounded by peasants trying to force their way in, and two shots were fired at us. Men
were climbing over the ramparts. Monsieur le duc resolved . . . to
spare the blood of the king's subjects.' Clermont-Tonnerre asked to
talk to the leaders of the riot, who promised to pull back their men
if the troops were called off. As they talked, a separate group of
rioters found an underground passage that led into the garden of
Clermont-Tonnerre's house. Most of them made for the wine cellar.
The rest crowded into the courtyard and roughed up city officials
who tried to reason with them. For three hours the highest officials
of the province were subjected to the whims of drunken rioters who
looted Clermont-Tonnerre's apartment, and gave the duc some uncomfortable moments—at one point he was threatened with an axe.
The troops made no move to resist the mob.

The rioters insisted that the magistrates march in a triumphant
procession to the Palace of Justice. Clermont-Tonnerre sent emissaries to the house of the First President, only to find that far from
leading the riot he too was victim of it, an embarrassed and frightened prisoner of the mob. Clermont-Tonnerre asked him to find as
many magistrates as he could, have them put on their black robes,
and march them to the Palace of Justice. Twenty-four terrified magistrates were rounded up and marched through the city, more like
captives than conquerors. The First President, who had with great

pains refused a wreath of roses the mob wanted him to wear, led the procession. Rioters armed with pikes and wearing garlands kept the magistrates in orderly columns of two. They were followed by several hundred ruffians and the First President's carriage, which was decorated with a stuffed eagle stolen from Clermont-Tonnerre's natural history cabinet. Once inside the Palace of Justice the magistrates regained their composure and congratulated themselves for having put an end to the riot.

By nightfall the city was calm. The last trespassers of Clermont-Tonnerre's wine cellar weaved their way home. Two actors recited verses from Racine's *Iphigénie* under the First President's window. A few days later, the officers of the Royal la Marine, concerned with the regiment's unpopularity, gave 600 francs to the widow of the man their patrol had slain. The Austrasie regiment, which had refused to stop the rioters, was moved to Briançon as a disciplinary measure. No punitive measures were taken against the estimated 15,000 rioters. The victims were at least two dead and about forty wounded. On June 12, the Grenoble Parlement was able to slip unnoticed out of the city and into exile. The king's will was done.

The Grenoble riots were unusual in that the aristocracy and the Third Estate were allied against the monarchy. The Third Estate was still for the most part a body without a head, an amorphous majority of illiterate peasants who were devoted to the king and believed in plentiful harvests rather than freedom and equality. Their ambitions were limited to scraping together enough money to buy a small piece of land. All valets were not Figaros, and the ideas of the Enlightenment were slow in reaching the masses. Still, one result of the nationwide ferment caused by the aristocratic reaction, was the formation of a 'national' or 'patriots' party made up of Encyclopaedists like Condorcet (who was at the time writing an apologia of American institutions), lawyers (Lacretelle, Danton, Barnave), magistrates (Hérault de Sechelles), journalists (Brissot, who had in 1788 founded the anti-slavery society of Les Amis des Noirs), and liberal nobles (Lafayette, Mirabeau). The core of their programme was the immediate convocation of the Estates General and the drafting of a written constitution.

Some of these patriots approved of the royal reforms but nonetheless spurred on the aristocratic reaction because it was then the only vocal protest. Lafayette, although sympathetic to Brienne's programme, joined the opposition. He wrote to George Washington on

May 25, 1788: 'Despite their disadvantage the Parlements are champions whom it is necessary to thrust forward.' Other patriots seized on Parlementary resistance as an opportunity to further weaken and eventually overthrow the regime. The liberal magistrate Adrien Duport said of the government's May coup: 'They have opened a gold mine which will ruin them, but we will find the gold.'

The Grenoble riot of June, 1788, and the government's inability to repress it mark the point where events began to slip out of the monarchy's control. For the eleven months until the inaugural session of the Estates General on May 4, 1789, Louis XVI in his groping equivocation and sudden reversals resembled a fly buzzing around a room looking for an open window. The French Revolution is not a biological organism with a moment of birth and a span of life. It did not begin on this or that particular day. But it is useful to note, as astronomers note the death of stars whose light we still receive, that the monarchy stopped functioning in the second half of 1788. This was so clear that even ambassadors, the most circumspect of prophets, were predicting its downfall. The astute Austrian Mercy d'Argenteau wrote that 'the Revolution in the national spirit threatens some great change in the constitutional principle of the monarchy, and if the promised assembly of the Estates General takes place, it is more than likely that the royal authority will suffer attacks it cannot easily evade.' The Swedish ambassador de Staël-Holstein reported that 'the lack of consideration into which the king's ministers have made him fall has inspired his subjects with a courage founded on their belief in his weakness.' But it was not only the ministers who weakened the monarchy, it was the self-destructive behaviour of the very groups which could not survive a change of regime. Their mounting criticism of the king was like a family quarrel at the foot of Vesuvius, just as the volcano shows signs of erupting. The first two orders of the state, the aristocracy and the clergy, forced the monarchy into an isolation from which it could escape only by appealing to the nation.

Hundreds of pamphlets were published to discredit Brienne's plenary court, which was called, among other things, 'an Areopagus of robots.' Six dukes refused in a letter to the king to sit on the new court. Many lawyers were faithful to the Parlements and turned down attractive posts. The crown had misjudged the degree of loyalty the magistrates commanded. There had, after all, been other attempts to do away with Parlements, and those who were asked to replace them feared their eventual return and revenge. There was a tightly disciplined legal hierarchy which the Parlements continued to control after their suspension. The provincial reactionaries were particularly virulent. They had visions of a massive Paris bureaucracy, insensitive to local interests and traditions. The Parlement of Brittany wrote to the king on May 26: 'Sire, you are being misled by your ministers [Brienne and Chrétien-François de Lamoignon, the Lord Privy Seal responsible for drafting many of the new judicial measures], both of whom are criminals.' Louis XVI made a half-hearted attempt to punish refractory nobles. He deprived Lafayette of his command, the duc de Rohan-Chabot of a 10,000 livres pension, and the comte de Boisgelin of his sinecure as Master of the Royal Wardrobe. Others were told not to appear at court, which they had in any case long since stopped doing. The aristocratic reaction found an unexpected ally in the clergy, which met on May 5 for its quinquennial general assembly and refused to support the crown. Here again, although there were a great many speeches about God and the fundamental laws of the nation, the issue boiled down to the pocketbook.

The clergy felt threatened by a 1787 government order to inventory church property for tax purposes. Once the government evaluated the church's wealth it would be able to tax the clergy on a realistic basis. The clergy's jealously guarded right to make only voluntary gifts almost certainly would be suppressed. The inventory of the extensive church domains had hardly begun and would take years. In the meantime, the government asked for an 8-million-livres gift, over two years, in addition to the 8.5 million livres a year the clergy was already paying. Archbishop Brienne thought he could count on his many old cronies among the sixty-four prelates present. But short-term avarice rather than its long-term interests ruled the upper clergy. The attempt to squeeze a few million extra livres from the affluent church provoked such violent resistance that Brienne finally compromised on a gift of 1.8 million livres over two years. Bishops denounced the government demands as a sacrilege against God. They invited the clergy to join Parlementary opposition. Borrowing a page from Parlement, they sent remonstrances to Louis XVI on June 15, in which they urged him to restore the Parlements, apparently forgetting the latter's consistent anticlericalism and their part in banning the Jesuits from France. 'Our silence would be one of those crimes which the nation and posterity would never forgive,' the clergy sanctimoniously wrote. It also demanded that its tax immunity be confirmed, and again the crown gave in.

Thus, although the Parlements had been suspended, their members were able to prevent the plenary court from operating, turn the high clergy against the king, and create a climate of chronic insurrection in several provinces. In only two cities where Parlement had previously sat, Rouen and Toulouse, was the government able to set up the new bailiff's courts, and in both cases the success was due to the firmness of the local authorities. In cities where there had been no Parlement, the crown had no trouble; fifteen bailiff's courts were set up, for instance, in the territory which had once been the sole jurisdiction of the Paris Parlement—cities welcomed the new courts as a source of wealth and prestige and were relieved no longer to depend on the slow and corrupt Paris justice.

Brienne commissioned pamphlets praising the alliance between the monarch and the Third Estate. But there was a fundemental hypocrisy in his position. The Estates General had been mentioned often, and it was generally accepted that they would be called. Brienne, while pretending to favour their convocation, had warned Louis XVI to put the meeting off as long as possible. He foresaw that the three orders would quarrel and precipitate a grave crisis. He had evidently gone so far as to promise the king that the Estates General would never be held, but he was overtaken by events.

In August, 1788, one of Brienne's financial advisers disclosed that the state was on the verge of bankruptcy. There was in the state treasury the ridiculous sum of 400,000 livres, enough to keep the government solvent for roughly six hours. Brienne was astonished. He had been too absorbed by the Parlementary crises to supervise the treasury. He was labouring under the misapprehension that the 1788 budget was balanced. In fact, there was a deficit of 240 million livres. Brienne was desperate. He appropriated the savings of the Invalides Hospital, the Opera, and the Théâtre Français to meet current expenses.

On August 8, hoping to restore confidence in the regime, he announced that the Estates General would meet on May 1, 1789. It was the first time a specific date had been mentioned, and there was no turning back. The 'patriots' exulted, but the bankers were chary. Bankers are normally enemies of upheaval and allies of the regime in power, but this time the uncertainty of events and the indecisiveness of the government frightened them off. Brienne's announcement did not restore confidence, so he suggested that Necker be brought back into the government, much as a plumber is summoned to repair a burst pipe. Louis XVI and Marie Antoinette disliked the smug Protestant banker, but recognized that he was the only man proficient enough to make some sense out of the untidy state finances. At the same time, influential courtiers like Madame de Polignac and the comte d'Artois, anxious about the effect of a financial crisis on their personal incomes, began undermining Brienne. He sensed at cabinet meetings that 'the king no longer had his customary cordiality toward me.' On August 25, after a strained conversation with Marie Antoinette, it became clear that he had lost the royal family's confidence, and he traded his resignation for a cardinal's hat. Three weeks later, giving in to renewed court pressures, Louis XVI dismissed his courageous liberal Lord Privy Seal, Lamoignon, who received 400,000 francs and the promise that his eldest son would be made a duke. Lamoignon was found dead on May 23, 1789, nineteen days after the convocation of the Estates General, his shotgun beside him, a probable suicide.

No sooner had Brienne and Lamoignon departed than Louis XVI cancelled the judiciary reform and recalled the Parlements. In revoking his own programme, he gave the nation further assurances of his ineptitude. What was seen as a popular victory over despotism was in fact the triumph of the most backward social elements, for whom the Parlements were the mouthpiece.

Necker's recall as de facto Prime Minister created confidence in financial circles. He immediately obtained a loan of 75 million livres. The value of royal bonds rose 30 per cent between August 26 and August 31. Here was a banker whom other bankers could understand, an international capitalist who spoke the language of bonds, annuities, and compound interest. Furthermore, Necker, although or perhaps because he was not French, was tolerant of the new patriotic spirit. He had faith in the will of the nation and thought the Estates General would cleanse the political air.

On September 25 the Paris Parlement announced that the Estates General should follow the precedent of 1614, when they voted by order and each order deliberated separately. Under this system the Third Estate, representing 99 per cent of the nation, would have the same voting strength as the clergy or the nobility. With this disclosure of its reactionary bias, Parlement was completely discredited. The aristocratic reaction, from this moment, was overtaken by the national revolution. Parlement had resisted the crown and prevented the success of a monarchy-led peaceful renewal. It had first won popular support because it was the only outlet for opposition, but as it revealed that its fundamental motive was to embalm society rather than change it, it lost its popular appeal. It had served its purpose and was now discarded. As one 'patriot' put it: 'Once a poison has cured you, you break the bottle so it will not destroy you.'

Necker, when he summoned a second Assembly of Notables in November to rule on voting methods for the Estates General, made the same mistake as Calonne in thinking that the notables would sacrifice their interests. There might be a group of liberal nobles who admired Voltaire or had fought at Yorktown, but the majority was fastened to its privileges. The key issue was whether the Third Estate would have the same number of delegates as each of the other two orders or as both of them combined. The notables voted 114 to 32 against the double representation of the Third Estate and warned the king against any innovations which would make the Third Estate more powerful than the other two orders.

The king was faced with pressures from the notables but at the end of 1788 there were even stronger pressures from the Third Estate, which was finding its leaders, often defectors from the two other orders, disseminating its programme, and creating a growing awareness of political issues among the masses. Louis XVI, by the end of the year, had received an estimated 800 petitions calling for the double representation of the Third Estate. There were so many pamphlets published that the cost of printing doubled. Some sample titles: 'When the Cock Crows, Look Out for the Old Hens'; 'Plan for a National Alliance Between Monsieur Third Estate and Madame Nobility'; 'Magnificat of the Third Estate'; 'Requiem of the General Farmers.' The names of publishers and printers were disguised to escape censorship, so that one pamphlet called 'Diogenes and the Third Estate,' was published 'by Diogenes in his tub.' Revolutionary periodicals like *The People's Sentinel* began to appear. Patriots congregated in clubs like Adrien Duport's Society of Thirty, whose members met three times a week from 5 to 10 P.M. Discussion groups proliferated, cafés became political science seminars, and political programmes were drawn up by agricultural societies, Masonic lodges, and reading clubs. France was seized with the effervescence of a political campaign. One noteworthy feature of the political ferment was the large number of nobles who deserted Versailles for memberships in the clubs. Deprived of political power since the Regency, their minds had marinated in the juices of the Enlightenment for years. It cost nothing to talk about justice and liberty. As the marquis de Ségur wrote in his memoirs: 'We, the young French nobility, who had neither regret for the past nor anxiety for the future, stepped gaily on a carpet of flowers that concealed an abyss. Laughing critics of traditional forms, of the feudal pride and solemn manners of our fathers, everything that was established appeared cumbersome and ridiculous. The gravity of ancient doctrines weighed heavily. Voltaire's merry philosophy amused and guided us. Without really studying the thought of more serious writers, we admired it for its courage and resistance to arbitrary power. . . . Whatever the language of freedom, its valour pleased us; equality seemed convenient. It is pleasant to climb down when you can climb back up as soon as you like; we unthinkingly appreciated both our patrician advantages and the attraction of a plebeian philosophy. Even though our privileges and the vestiges of our former powers were crumbling beneath our steps, the little game pleased us. We saw the spectacle, not the danger . . . we applauded republican plays in our theatres, philosophical speeches in our academies, bold works by our writers.'

The liberal nobility was even willing to discuss giving up its privileges as long as it did not lose its prestige. On the day Mirabeau voted for the abolition of feudal rights he reminded his valet that he was still Monsieur le comte. Such men were hyphens between two forms of society. The curious mixture of nobles and revolutionaries which made up the patriots' party served to water down revolutionary doctrine and led to the recognition of what Condorcet called the 'legal prerogatives of the nobility.' Almost alone among the pamphleteers, the abbé Sieyès, who belonged to no club, refused to doff his hat to the nobility, and wrote: 'I will say frankly . . . that their greatest vice is that they tend to debase the great majority of citizens, and it is no small evil to debase men. It is not easy to conceive how anyone could have consented to seeing 25,700,000 men humiliated so that 300,000 could be ridiculously honoured.'

How many liberal nobles who adopted new ideas and acclaimed the Revolution imagined that their castles would be burned and that they would be lynched or guillotined? A typical example is the duc de Lauzun, who became citizen General Biron and was named commander in chief of the Revolutionary armies in Alsace and Vendée.

The Convention in 1793 accused him of being 'thanks to his inertia, a sort of enemy column,' and of having 'taken on the mask of patriotism to deceive the nation.' He was guillotined after the following exchange with the head of the revolutionary tribunal: 'What is your name?' 'Biron, cabbage, turnip, Biron, whatever you wish. It's all the same to me.' 'You are insolent!' 'And you talk too much. Get to the point. Guillotine me. That is all you have to say.'

For the time being however, there was a spirit of equalitarian euphoria that was expressed both through promises of friendship between the classes and through disrespect to people of quality. The people of Paris sang:

> Long live the Estates General,
> For the marquise and the fishwife
> Will be friends for life,
> And sit across the table
> To have a jolly gabble.
> Long live the Estates General.

But Sébastian Mercier the chronicler of Paris at the end of the *ancien régime*, said that 'formerly, when I entered a printer's shop the workers removed their hats. Today they are content to stare at you and snicker.' And the court painter, Madame Vigée-Lebrun, said that the peasants whom she crossed on a country road in 1788 'failed to remove their hats, and stared at us insolently; a few of them threatened us with their big sticks.'

Disrespect did not extend to the king. There were untapped reserves of esteem for Louis XVI. The overwhelming majority of political writers still considered reforms within the framework of the monarchy. Pierre-Louis Lacretelle, a leader of the patriots' party, wrote that 'the august monarchy is a part of our physical situation and our moral character; our wishes and principles do not tend to weaken it; we only want to regulate it to make it stronger.' Not a single one of the cahiers of grievances which the three orders presented at the Estates General called for the overthrow of the monarchy. Marie Antoinette was so sure that the alliance between the monarchy and the people was a fact that she said in January, 1789: 'I am the queen of the Third Estate.'

The scope of the patriots' campaign and the growing acceptance of liberal ideas were alarming to the conservative aristocracy which rightly viewed the Estates General as a menace to its survival. On

December 12 the comte d'Artois and the prince de Condé presented
Louis XVI with a memorandum in which they proposed to give up
their fiscal privileges if the Third Estate would renounce double
representation. This was little more than a frightened appeal to the
monarchy to save what still could be saved of the old order. 'The
state is in peril. . . .' the princes said. 'A revolution is being prepared
that will affect the foundation of government . . . soon property
rights will be attacked, the inequality of wealth will be presented as
an object of reform: already the suppression of feudal rights is being
proposed . . . is Your Majesty capable of sacrificing, of humiliating
his brave, ancient, and respectable nobility?'

Louis XVI had a clear choice before him. He could throw the
monarchy's already tarnished prestige on the side of the reactionary
aristocracy and repress a popular movement which cut across class
lines and had already gathered considerable momentum. Or he could
disavow the reaction, underwrite reform, and emerge as the sponsor
of a national movement of renewal. This is what Mirabeau was later
to urge in a secret message which tried to show that the Revolution
was a blessing in disguise. 'Compare the new state of affairs with
the old regime and there can be found reasons for consolation and
hope,' he wrote. 'Is it then nothing to be rid of the Parlements . . .
and the privileged orders? The idea of one class of citizens would
have pleased Richelieu: this even surface facilitates the exercise
of power. Several reigns of absolute government could not have
matched the achievement of this Revolution for the benefit of royal
authority.'

Louis XVI was not Richelieu, and was capable only of tempo-
rizing. Political survival demanded that the monarchy abandon the
two discredited privileged orders and forge a victorious alliance
with the Third Estate. This meant granting the Third Estate double
representation and vote by head, which would give them the same
voting strength as the aristocracy and clergy combined. But a nostalgic attachment to the privileged orders and fear of mob rule impeded Louis XVI. After long deliberations with his ministers and
equivocal advice from Necker, he agreed on December 27 to double
representation but refused to settle the key matter of vote by order
or by head. This was like La Fontaine's fable, in which a fox is given
milk to drink from a fluted vase. It made double representation meaningless. The number of delegates from the Third Estate would be
equal to the number of delegates from the other two orders. But its

voting strength would be the same as each of the other two orders. The Third Estate would naturally demand vote by head and quarrel with the privileged orders. Louis XVI was making a conflict between the orders inevitable. By evading the issue, he lost whatever control he had over events. His indecision was as irrevocable as an abdication.

XV

THE SECOND REVOLUTION

> *The debate about king, despotism, and the Constitution became secondary; it was now a war between the Third Estate and the two other orders.*
>
> —MALLET DU PAN

IN THE first four months of 1789, as the nation suffered from one of the worst winters of the century and the high price of bread made it a luxury instead of a staple, Frenchmen prepared their first national assembly in 171 years. The traditional method of consultation, the *cahiers de doléances* (notebooks of complaints), were being drafted by each of the three orders, just as they had been since the fifteenth century. In every town and village, men left their ploughs and shops, their cottages and manors, and gathered in the parish church to define the France they wanted. Sometimes it took only a few hours, sometimes weeks. Quill pens scratching on long sheets of foolscap listed the abuses of the regime, the changes that must be made, the interests that must be protected. Archbishops and parish priests, royal princes and tenant farmers, wealthy bourgeois and chimneysweeps, consigned to posterity their views of society. Men who could not write could at least be heard, and the cahiers apologized in footnotes that only those had signed who knew how. Others, for whom French was not yet the national tongue, wrote in their own. Cahiers in Italian arrived from Corsica, in German from Strasbourg, in Flemish from Flanders.

As in every political campaign there were parties, lobbies, influential men and special-interest groups who tried to impose their views. The mass media of the time were pamphlets and word of mouth. Masonic lodges were centres of liberal discussion and many revolutionary leaders belonged to the Grand Orient. There were pamphlets expressing pro-slavery views (the Committe for Saint-Dominique) and anti-slavery views (the Sociéte des Amis des Noirs). The duc d'Orléans, who was Grand Master of the Masons as well as the king's cousin, hired the radical abbé Sieyès to draft a pamphlet of instructions which was sent to the twenty-five electoral districts where he had manorial rights. There were many such model cahiers but few servile imitations. Not one of the duc d'Orléans' twenty-five districts adopted his proposal for legal divorce. The role of the pamphlets and the lobbies was similar to that of modern political parties during an election campaign. They presented the popular will with issues and alternatives, provoked discussion, and created political ferment.

The pamplets did have some influence, as identical paragraphs in different cahiers prove. But local interests were too strong and the opportunity for expression too rare for their verbatim adoption. There were cases when one man dictated a cahier—the physiocrat Dupont de Nemours practically wrote the Third Estate cahier for Nemours single-handed. There was also the opposite case—the Third Estate deputy for Aix-en-Provence, Serva, drafted a model cahier, but not one of his views was adopted by the district he represented. There were revolutionary examples, like the American War of Independence, which weighed heavily in subsequent events, but in the cahiers is not mentioned once.

Thus, the cahiers were the result of the free exchange of ideas rather than pressures. There was no attempt on the part of the crown to look over its subjects' shoulders. It would in any case have been quite impossible to control the deliberations of 50,000 parishes. The division of the cahiers by order ensured that the nobles and clergy would not browbeat the Third Estate. The first two orders drafted their cahiers at the district level. The Third Estate cahiers were drafted at the parish and village level and then edited into a single district cahier. A total of 615 cahiers accompanied the 1,139 delegates to Versailles in May, and 545 of these have been preserved. They are not almanacs of existing conditions, but an accurate expression of the national state of mind in 1789, an eighteenth-century opinion poll as valid as such soundings of the popular conscience can be. Many of the cahiers attest to their own good faith with preambles such as 'the advice and vote of all the inhabitants of the parish, without distinction, was sought and agreed on by simple majority.'

The most striking aspect of the cahiers is their moderation. This is not the voice of a people who will three years later commit the act of regicide. It is the voice of a people abused but not oppressed. People do not list such a wealth of grievances or demand fundamental changes when they are happy and prosperous. But if the monarchy had been tyrannical, its subjects would not have been asked to draft cahiers at all. The cahiers are a blend of prayers and prescriptions. Perhaps their moderation is a result of their having been written upon royal invitation. There was confidence in Louis XVI simply because he had convened the Estates General. Perhaps it reflected the vain hope that the thousand-year-old institution of the monarchy was still capable of renewal. It was, on the one hand, a return to the naive faith of previous centuries that abuses would be remedied 'if only the king knew.' It was also a crude distillation of the ideas of the Enlightenment, optimism, belief in progress, man's (and the monarchy's) perfectibility. But where is the republicanism of 1793? Where is the anticlericalism that was to lead to the confiscation of church property? Where is the fanatical belief in the virtues of the Revolution which was to justify the Terror?

There was, in the cahiers, not a single republican call to arms, not one denial of the monarchic principle. There was, instead, the co-existence of traditional beliefs with new and still unassimilated ideas, a dimly perceived, stammering attempt to reconcile the lessons of the Enlightenment with the divine right of kings. The cahiers almost always begin and end with an expression of loyalty to the king. The Third Estate of Carcassonne finds 'the origins of its happiness in that of its king and the stability of the monarchy.' The Third Estate of Calais begins its complaints, as do many other cahiers, with a reminder that 'the French government is a monarchy.' The archetypal figure of the king-magician who cures the ills of his subjects is recalled in the Third Estate cahier of Meaux, which 'attributes the greatness of its evils to remoteness from the presence of the monarch.'

But alongside the king there now appears another, still shadowy figure—the citizen. 'Our hearts are full of love and respect for the citizen king,' said one cahier. The implication is great. It expresses the will to secularize the monarchy, to displace the origin of the king's power from God to the nation. The right of the nation to temper absolute power replaces divine right. Thus, say the cahiers, the wording of the coronation oath should be changed to reflect the union of king and nation—it should include the promise to uphold the new, written constitution of France; the formula by which the king signs laws, *de par le roi* (by and of the king), should be changed to something on the order of 'by and of the king and the nation.' These modest demands are a footbridge from absolute to constitutional monarchy. Other attacks on absolutism were more practical. The nobles of Angers asked that the king receive a salary from the state like any public official, and other cahiers insisted that the vast royal domains had only been loaned to the monarchy by the nation.

The clergy, although it did not fare quite so well as the monarchy, was still defended by the majority of cahiers. The secularism of roughly one-third of the cahiers is based on the idea that the clergy should stop collecting tithes and give up its wealth and property. 'Since the clergy should not be attached to temporal things, it should be deprived of all its temporal holdings and continue to direct purely spiritual affairs,' is a typical statement.

A Third Estate cahier says that 'curates ought to be regarded as performing a public and a religious service useful to the state.' But the only overt irreverence came from the nobility. The Bourbonnais nobles, who did not like paying tithes, referred to the clergy as 'oppressive bloodsuckers.' The Vivarais nobility asked for the suppression of monastic orders: 'Their existence and opulence having become noxious to the state, may they be forbidden to receive novices . . . and may their property be employed for charitable purposes.'

Just as there was a reserve of devotion to the king, there was in the Third Estate still considerable reverence for the church, un-eroded by Voltaire and the other anticlerical writers of the century. The Paris Third Estate, for instance, wrote that 'religion is necessary for man because it instructs him in his childhood, represses his passions at all ages, upholds him in adversity, and consoles him in old age.' Criticism of the church was practical, not philosophical. People were shocked by the church's wealth and the upper clergy's display of luxury. But even on this point, of the 185 cahiers which specifically mentioned the problem of clerical property, only 21 called for its suppression, 60 asked for reforms, and 104 wanted the status quo. Thus, when the National Assembly, on November 2, 1789, voted to confiscate church property, it was acting against the mandate of the consulted majority.

The cahiers were at the same time an expression of the national will and of hundreds of particular wills, so that many of them stressed what separated them from the rest of the nation. The Lorraine wanted to remain 'a foreign province.' A Provence cahier stated that 'the king of France will be recognized in Provence only under the title of comte de Provence.' The Béarn asked: 'Up to what point is it in our interest to stop being Béarnais to become more or less French?' Navarre insisted on its ancient right to mint money. The clergy of Rouen called the king 'duke of Normandy.' The nobles of Roussillon insisted that offices and benefits in their province should go exclusively to Catalans. Such demands give the impression that the great achievement of the monarchy, national unity, had been superficial indeed. France still seemed an aggregation of independent provinces, a quilt of local prejudices and aspirations.

But there also ran through the cahiers a parallel current of understanding that the state could no longer function as a sum of special interests. The Carcassonne nobility said that France would be saved 'on the day it was no longer a collection of incoherent parts.' The cahier from Loury, near Orléans, said that 'as the subjects of the kingdom form a single people obeying the same master . . . it is essentially necessary that the Estates General decide on a single and unique code of laws for the entire kingdom.' The cahiers were drafted under the twin banners of preservation of local interests and the need for national unity.

Certain reforms were urged by all three orders. A written constitution, 'clear, precise, invariable, and containing the essence of the laws,' was a unanimous demand. Fiscal reform was a near-unanimous wish. The Third Estate called for the suppression of the most outrageous taxes and the institution of a land or income tax. Many cahiers of the first two orders renounced their fiscal privileges and favoured a general tax. When the idea of equality is expressed in the cahiers, it is usually in fiscal, not social terms. The Third Estate, said one typical cahier, 'does not seek absolute equality, all that it asks is that respect for the law and before the law should be equal for all.' This was not Rousseau's equality, it was the taxpayer's equality. The most curious request for equality came from the cahier of Castelferrus, which objected to social distinctions in death sentences. 'A noble guilty of a certain crime is beheaded,' it said, 'while a non-noble guilty of the same crime must hang from a gibbet; by this disposition alone it is established that some forms of death are infamous while others are not, that the noble belongs to a privileged class, while the commoner belongs to the debased class of citizens. (While there were privileged methods of execution, torture was democratic. Noble and commoner wore the same prison garb when tortured after arrest, so that there would be no favouritism, a measure to which the nobility strenuously objected.) The Third Estate did not aspire to equality. It continued to accept the corporate structure of the state, which attributed to each order a specific function. Thus the Third Estate of Agen 'envies the clergy only its privilege of offering God pure and sincere wishes for the conservation of the monarchy and the prosperity of the state; and the nobility that of watching over the defence of the nation.'

It was not the lessons of the Enlightenment, but the inadequacies of the regime that provoked demands like the unity of weights and measures, the abolition of internal customs, a unified currency, the foundation of a national bank, and a reform that would fuse the half-dozen different types of administrative units, such as *Pays d'Etat, Pays d'Election*, free cities, free provinces, and other unwieldy designations. Limitations on the monarchy were sought in areas where it had failed—thus, the Estates General should meet regularly, like a legislative body, and control fiscal measures, because the disorder of royal finances had pushed the nation to the edge of bankruptcy. Feudal and ecclesiastical courts should be done away with. The army should be reformed, since in recent years it had known defeat more often than victory—defence was thus seen for the first time as a national problem. The cahiers showed that the old absolutist idea of France as the monarch's personal property was no longer feasible. The monarchy had botched its job, a new management had to be brought in. The new management would work with the monarch, but had to look at the books. More than 200 cahiers asked that royal decisions and expenditures be made a matter of public record.

Just as equality was expressed in fiscal terms, freedom was demanded in terms of relief from the burden of archaic feudal practices. Freedom was the right to keep a dog or sell one's wine. 'The feudal regime has produced nothing but slaves,' wrote the Third Estate of Forcalquier. 'The branches of the tree have been chopped off, but the trunk still lives. The axe must be used to cut it down forever.'

Feudal privileges had once had a reason for being. There had been a time when only lords owned mills which peasants had to use against a fee in kind. Now they had their own mills but were still obliged to use the lord's, who refused to improve his facilities since he enjoyed a monopoly. The flour was coarse. One-sixth of the grain was lost. The lord's fee was extravagant, often every fourth bag of grain.

The peasant's crops were constantly threatened by the lord's favourite pastime—the hunt. There was a mystique surrounding the hunt which made its every detail sacred. To tamper with a hunt was a sacrilege, like insulting a priest. For the nobility, the first function of the land was not to be tilled, but to serve as a course over which men on horseback chased fleeing animals. Hunting privileges, against which there was no recourse, did more damage than all other feudal abuses combined. If there were pheasants or partridge on his land the peasant had to let it lie fallow so as not to disturb their nests. He had to plant thorny bushes which would serve as cover for game. He could not own dogs, which might distract or compete with the lord's hounds. Lords on a hunt killed all domestic animals which had the impertinence to get in their way. The lord, his pack of hounds, his huntsmen, and his guests would gallop through the peasants' fields like Attila and the Huns, ravaging his lands. A small landowner could not build fences or hedges, or interfere with the passage of game which ruined his ploughed fields. An Alençon cahier said that 'the only ones who profit from our land are stags, does, boars, and other beasts.' Tenant farmers were even worse off, for they could not weed or deforest the land they rented, and had to arrange the timing of each agricultural operation so that it would not interfere with a hunt. The hunt, it was repeatedly affirmed, was 'one of the worst scourges of agriculture.' A lesser but nonetheless annoying feudal privilege was the lords' dovecotes, whose large populations lived off the fields of tenant farmers.

When feudal lords had protected the inhabitants of their fiefs, it seemed natural for obeisance to be paid. Protection had become unnecessary, but obeisance continued. In Provence, peasants had to fall to their knees at the lord's passage. In Brittany, newlyweds had to jump over the cemetery wall for the lord's mirth. There were dozens of these obsolete customs, 'all indecent, absurd, and ridiculous . . . which recall the ancient tyranny of the lords and the servitude of the people he suppressed,' said the cahier of Ploermel. Sometimes the peasant forfeited his produce, as in the *abeillage* (the lord's right to a percentage of the honey that came from the peasant's hives); sometimes the right was a monopoly, like the *banvin* (the lord's exclusive right to sell wine for forty days after the vintage); sometimes it was a humiliation, such as the practice of carrying an egg in a carriage to present to the lord on certain occasions, or the *marquette* (a silver coin newlyweds gave the lord to keep him from exercising his traditional though now-legendary right to sleep with the bride). Many cahiers expressed in similar terms the wish of the Rennes Third Estate for 'the abolition . . . of these outrageous and extravagant usages.' Freedom was also expressed in terms of guarantees for classic civil liberties, the demand for a written constitution, and the right to participate in government.

In addition to these widely sought reforms there were dozens of particular suggestions. The Paris nobility called for the destruction of the Bastille, which Louis XVI was already planning. The Calais nobility wanted state prisons razed, 'those monuments to the abuse of power and the vengeance of ministers.' The royal habit of opening mail was denounced by the Agen Third Estate, which said: 'Let men so indelicate as to furtively extort family secrets be severely punished.' The cahiers brought out the absurdity of some local regulations. In Nemours it was forbidden to cut wheat with a sickle. In the Poitou it was illegal to make cider. Everyone wanted repeal of the hated salt tax (it was finally suppressed in 1790, only to return in 1806 under Napoleon). There was a general condemnation of the General Farmers. 'One cannot sympathize with the odious administration of the Farmers,' said a Besançon cahier, 'who are interested in profit and think themselves lost if they do not become rich. . . .' The programme of social improvements sought by the cahiers appears surprisingly up-to-date. They asked for right-to-work laws, pensions for widows and minors, workshops for beggars, family allowances, low-interest loans, civics courses, price controls, drug inspection, accident insurance, a tax on rouge, 'which destroys beauty,' and a tax on bachelors. Forty cahiers denounced capital punishment and many more called for the abolition of torture. The most radical demand came, surprisingly, from the Dax nobility, who affirmed that 'the law has an essential object, to try to place some landed property in the hands of every citizen, either by the partition of communal land, or by other means.'

The cahiers cannot be called revolutionary, for they do not anticipate or propose the overthrow of the monarchy. The word revolution is seldom used, and then only in rhetorical terms, as when a cahier from Paris-outside-the-walls says that 'a glorious revolution is being prepared . . . abuses of authority will no longer be possible.' The cahiers accept the process of orderly change within the framework of the monarchy and class differences. They are, however, essentially different from the cahiers of any previous Estates General in that a few extremely simple but powerful ideas have taken hold. Not revolutionary ideas, but simply an awareness of things as they are, just as a child looking in a mirror comes to realize that he is seeing his own image.

Under the influence of the pamphleteers, the Third Estate had after hundreds of years grasped that it was in fact the kingdom, or 99 per cent of it. As the Poitou Third Estate said: 'We know now what the Third Estate is; it is the nation less the nobility and the clergy, that is twenty-four million Frenchmen less a million, that is twenty-three/twenty-fourths of the kingdom.' The figures could be debated. The abbé Sieyès in his famous pamphlet ('What is the Third Estate? Everything. What has it been until now? Nothing. What does it aspire to be? Something.') said the clergy numbered 80,000 and the nobility 110,000 (a figure including only those nobles eligible to vote for the Second Estate, with three or more generations of nobility). One thing, however, was certain: the first two orders were a tiny minority. Having suddenly grown conscious of its size, the Third Estate was wondering how best to use it. One obvious way was to insist on a vote by head instead of by order, which is what the majority of Third Estate cahiers proceeded to do. If the first two orders insisted on separate deliberations and votes, said the Dijon Third Estate, a National Assembly would be formed 'despite the schism of the representatives of four or five hundred thousand individuals.' The Quimper Third Estate warned that if the privileged orders refused to accept the vote by head 'the French people alone would constitute the Estates General and would, with the king, be the nation.'

Another new idea that appeared in the cahiers was that of the general good. While the *ancien régime* had juggled particular interests with rules that were little more than a string of exceptions, so that every individual had by virtue of his geographic and social origin some special status, the cahiers occasionally saw beyond the corporate structure. Sometimes they were couched in the language of the Enlightenment, and talked of 'the dignity of man' and 'the happiness of the greatest number.' Such preoccupations, which seem innocent enough, would have been unthinkable only fifty years earlier. There was even an awareness of social problems outside France, and the clergy of Peronne criticized slavery and called Negroes 'our unfortunate brothers.'

Frenchmen of 1789 could be tolerant and humane in general matters and prejudiced when their own interests were affected. The clergy of Colmar warned of the proliferation of Jews, who, 'by their vexations, their graft, and their grasping duplicity, offer such pernicious examples,' and asked that only the eldest son in a Jewish family be allowed to marry. The cahier of Sougy-en-Beauce asked that Protestants be prohibited from holding public services that might 'shake the simplicity of our faith, or, one day, that of our children.'

Thus the cahiers were a mixture of traditional views and new ideas, of respect for the monarchy and exasperation with its shortcomings, of patient moderation and a new awareness of the strength of the people. A political programme based on their suggestions would have made France a constitutional monarchy. Class differences would have survived, although the aristocracy would have lost many of its privileges. The clergy would not have lost its property and the king would not have lost his life.

The 291 deputies of the clergy, 270 deputies of the nobility, and 578 deputies of the Third Estate (including 200 lawyers and 100 businessmen) met at Versailles as scheduled in May—Louis XVI had the French kings' atavistic fear of Paris and believed the deputies would be more tractable on his home territory. The reception of the Estates General by the king on May 2 and the procession through the streets of Versailles on May 4 are the closing ceremonies of the *ancien régime*. They were intended to show, by distinctions of costume and etiquette, the inherent differences among the three orders. Before a word had been said, before the Estates General had conducted their first meeting, it was already established that the Third Estate was an inferior order that should keep its aspirations modest. Louis XVI could not have grasped the significance of such ceremonial details, or he would not have left them up to subordinates like the Grand Master of Ceremonies, Dreux-Brézé, who in the absence of other instructions copied the procedure of 1614.

The chosen Assembly Hall was the Hôtel des Menus Plaisirs, a large warehouse near the palace where the decorations for royal balls and festivities were kept. Teams of carpenters and masons relayed one another to prepare chambers for the delegates. In the rush, two carpenters were killed and six were wounded, the first victims of the French Revolution. An initial blunder was made in the assignment of chambers for each order. The clergy and the nobility were given separate chambers for their deliberations, but the Third Estate, because it had twice as many delegates, was told to meet as an order in the same hall where the three orders met in joint session. Thus, the Third Estate physically occupied the main assembly hall by order of the king, and it was a simple matter to rename it the National Hall, and eventually to ask the two other orders to join them there and form a National Assembly.

Another mistake was to inflict upon the Third Estate costumes that made them look like the valets in boulevard comedies. While the clergy wore its ceremonial vestments, and the nobility wore capes with gold linings, hats with white plumes and turned-up brims à la Henri IV, lace jabots, and swords, the Third Estate was in black broadcloth, black stockings, a muslin cravat, and a black pointed velvet cap. There was such resistance to the cap that it was changed at the last minute for a three-cornered hat. 'Distinctions in clothes,' said one letter of complaint, 'can create the assumption that other distinctions will be granted in the presentation of the cahiers or the manner of counting the votes.' The Third Estate deputies, after months of pre-convention agitation, were oversensitive to any sign that they were being treated differently from the other orders.

'The noble,' one Third Estate deputy wrote, 'must be prepared to sit next to his cobbler without aversion, for the cobbler votes as he does, and is as important as he is.' The courtiers, however, found the members of the lower clergy and the Third Estate a source of immense amusement. The country priests with their dusty shoes and frayed cassocks, the farmers in their Sunday best, with their hair tied in a knot and their sweat-stained caps, were stared at like strange beasts when they visited Versailles, and the powdered courtiers in cloth-of-gold suits and embroidered jerkins snickered at the sight and wondered how they would ever be able to sit on the same benches with such bumpkins.

It was also fashionable at court to treat the Estates General as an amusement. The marquis de Ferrières, a noble deputy from the provinces, was surprised to find fashionable ladies 'seated at their dressing tables or buried in the softness of their boudoirs, and saying: "What a pretty thing a revolution is. Let us make a revolution!" '

On May 2, Louis XVI received the Estates General in his apartments by order; the clergy at 11 A.M. the nobility at 1 P.M., and the Third Estate at 4 P.M. He summoned the first two orders punctually to his cabinet, opening both panels of his door to admit them and showing considerable interest as the name of each delegate was called out. But he grew tired and fell behind on his schedule, so that the Third Estate was kept waiting three hours and was received in the king's bedroom, with only one panel of the door open, which was taken as yet another slight.

On the morning of May 4, in a chill wind, began a formal procession which was both the last of the old order and the first of the new. The procession marched through streets lined with troops presenting arms. Tapestries were hung from balconies. Leading the march through the streets of Versailles from Notre Dame to the church of Saint Louis, where mass and a sermon would be heard, were the last four kings of France: Louis XVI, resplendent in a gold-lined cape; his brothers, the comte de Provence and the comte d'Artois, who were to be restored to the throne in the nineteenth century as Louis XVIII and Charles X; and the son of the duc d'Orléans, who was to reign from 1830 to 1848 as Louis-Philippe I. At the tail end of the procession, behind the king's falconers with birds perched on their fists, behind the Franciscan friars in brown robes and the bishops in crimson, there marched a country lawyer in black broadcloth and three-cornered hat named Maximilien Marie Isidore Robespierre.

The agitated Master of Ceremonies, Dreux-Brézé, ran back and forth along the line of march to settle disputes of precedence. The upper clergy complained that it was marching in an indistinct group with the lower clergy; Dreux-Brézé placed an orchestra between them. Members of the Third Estate grumbled about having to carry processional candles. The king's cousin, the duc d'Orléans, who wanted to show he was a man of the people, left the other Princes of the Blood to march with the Third Estate, and Dreux-Brézé had to invoke the king's displeasure to persuade him to return to his own order.

In church, Third Estate deputies appropriated the front pews and the harassed Dreux-Brézé had to ask them to move back. A Breton deputy complained and Dreux-Brézé said: 'Sir, that was the order of 1614.' 'Sir, we are no longer in 1614,' the Breton deputy replied, 'and a good deal of water has gone under the bridge since then.'

In his sermon, Monsignor de la Fare, bishop of Nancy, tried to

347

sound reform-minded without forgetting the natural distinctions that separated the orders, so that in the end he pleased no one. The nobility was annoyed by the contrast he drew between court luxury and misery elsewhere and the reference to Marie Antoinette's hamlet as a 'puerile imitation of nature.' No one was sure what the bishop had in mind when he said that the first two orders would willingly give up their privileges. And the Third Estate was annoyed by the bishop's salutation: 'Sire, receive the homage of the clergy, the respect of the nobility, and the very humble supplication of the Third Estate.'

The mood of the Third Estate was not one of supplication, and it was the crown's grave mistake to hope that the Estates General of 1789 would be a carbon copy of the Estates General of 1614, in which the three orders had quarrelled for several weeks and then disbanded. For if, in 1614, the Third Estate had been made up of country bumpkins who waited obediently, cap in hand, for their cue to shout 'Long live the king,' this time it was the nation's elite: bankers, merchants, jurists, economists like Dupont de Nemours, scientists like the astronomer Bailly, journalists like Camille Desmoulins, Protestant pastors like Rabaut Saint-Etienne, and defectors from the privileged orders like the comte de Mirabeau and the abbé Sieyès. There was not a single peasant or workingman in this assembly of prosperous farmers and intelligent, educated, and articulate men who were soon to call themselves the nation. Louis XVI had, moreover, irritated them by condoning artificial distinctions of costume and seating, while giving them the powerful weapon of double representation.

The king wrote three drafts of his inaugural speech in his large, slanted hand. When he delivered it, from the golden throne in the Assembly Hall on May 5, with Marie Antoinette sitting at his side, he promised reforms while advising caution. In his high, whining voice he warned of 'the general anxiety and the exaggerated desire for innovation which risk taking hold of minds and will finally lead public opinion completely astray.' The Earl of Dorset, British ambassador, reported that 'His Majesty delivered his speech with great dignity, though he was interrupted in the course of it by the repeated acclamation of "*vive le roi*," accompanied by the clapping of hands.'

On May 6, the three orders began to meet in their respective chambers, and seemed, said the marquis de Ferrières, 'like separate armies in the presence of the enemy.' The first order of business was 'verification,' or checking each deputy's credentials. The Third Estate made this formality a test case to force common deliberations and the head vote which would give it control of the assembly. It asked that verification be carried out by the three orders in joint session. The nobility, aware that its salvation lay in preserving its distinctness as an order, voted on May 6 to verify only its own deputies. But the vote, 188 to 46 (not all voted), revealed the existence of a sizable minority of liberal nobles.

The Third Estate continued to disregard the first principle of the Estates General, division by order, and invited the two privileged orders to join it in a single assembly. After these initial gestures it was content to wait, like a large magnet ready to attract loose scraps from the other two orders, and took to calling itself the Commons.

The Commons began to find its leaders, settle into the practice of parliamentary debate, and form political groups. Feelers were regularly sent to the other orders, but there was no grand strategy. These men had come to Versailles with the cahiers as their only programme. They had no idea how long the Estates General would last or what it was supposed to accomplish. Many had rented rooms for three months only, thinking that everything would be over by then. For all three orders, May was a month of groping. The nobility rested on its fixed and defensive positions. 'Even in the Frankish forests, we deliberated by order,' they said. The marquis de Ferrières wrote to his wife on May 15: 'Our Estates General do nothing. We meet each morning at 9 and get out by 4:30 in the afternoon. The time passes in useless chatter, in shouting, in not listening to one another. Everyone wants to shine and make fine phrases . . . the French are not made to govern themselves.' Third Estate deputies held fruitless lobby conversations with the nobles, one of whom complained that the 'Commons' was too numerous. The Third Estate deputy replied that the privileged orders were grossly overrepresented. 'Sir,' asked the noble, 'in an army, should the general be counted merely as one man?' Jacques Antoine Creuzé-Latouche, a Third Estate deputy who kept a diary, was annoyed by the nobility's arrogance. 'The nobility speaks with emphasis about the blood they have spilled for the fatherland,' he wrote, 'but we have made them stop their boasting by asking whether what the Third Estate spilled was water.'

As positions hardened, the Estates General resembled the opening of a siege. The nobility waited behind the ramparts of its traditions.

The Third Estate dug its trenches and placed its troops, and the combatants eyed each other warily, probing and exploring without opening fire. The clergy, faithful to its role as peacemaker, acted as referee, and tried to reconcile the second and third orders. But the spectators were becoming impatient. Arthur Young, when he visited the Estates General, was shocked to see the public roaming at will over the Assembly Hall, and applauding. There was no trace of parliamentary discipline. Everyone spoke at once amid shouts from the gallery. It was more like an open fruit and vegetable market than a parliamentary assembly. For an Englishman accustomed to his own experienced and orderly bicameral legislature, the fledgling French efforts seemed like utter chaos. There was immense popular interest in the Estates General. The marquis de Ferrières observed that 'there are women who never miss a session, who stay there five and six hours at a time . . . have they no husbands or children?' Unofficial Estates General met on every Paris street corner. Parisians consumed huge quantities of daily pamphlets and newspapers written in a style more polemic than informative. 'The cats and the rats got together to correct abuses and draft a constitution,' said one. 'At first there were eight cats and six rats, but the rats said: "Sirs, you are more powerful than we are, let us at least be eight against eight." The cats bowed to the logic of this remark, but when the Assembly was formed with a like number of cats and rats, the cats said: "Sirs, we must deliberate by order; consequently we will deliberate in our own chambers." The cats retired and said—"Since rats taste good, and we have been eating them for centuries, we must continue eating them always." '

Since the nobility was maintaining its discipline as an order, the leaders of the Third Estate began working on the clergy, which had shown itself deeply divided when it voted 134 to 114 against joining the Commons. In keeping with its role as arbiter, the clergy suggested that commissioners from all three orders be named to confer on the problem of verification. At the same time, a number of bishops asked Louis XVI to break the deadlock. The king proposed a compromise solution which the nobility vetoed on June 5.

Five days later, the Third Estate acted. 'We must end this long period of idleness,' said the abbé Sieyès. He proposed that the Third Estate summon the other two orders to join them, and take a roll call which would rule absentees out of the Assembly. The motion was adopted and the roll call began on June 12. At the same time, repeated entreaties were made to the clergy. Mirabeau asked them to defect 'in the name of the God of peace.' Robespierre, still a young lawyer, told the clergy that 'if you are so impatient to relieve the people, come and join the friends of the people . . . take up once again the modesty of your origins and dismiss the proud lackeys who escort you. . . .' On June 13, the magnet drew three parish priests from the Poitou, the first fissure in the defences of the two privileged orders.

That evening, Bailly, the president of the Commons, boasted about the defecting priests to the Lord Privy Seal, Barentin. 'Allow me to congratulate you on the important conquest you have made,' said Barentin with heavy sarcasm. 'Sir, you may think it insignificant,' replied Bailly, 'but let me say this, and do not forget it, these will be followed by many others.' Nine more priests did in fact rally to the Commons in the next two days, but there was still not a single defector from the liberal nobility. On June 17, after toying with various names, such as 'Assembly of known and verified representatives of the French nation,' the Third Estate, plus the sprinkling of defecting clergy, adopted the name of National Assembly by a vote of 491 to 89. One-sixth of those voting rejected the unilateral decision, while the other two orders were not consulted, but were simply presented with the fait accompli of a body which claimed to represent the nation.

On June 19, the clergy voted to join the Third Estate, and its president, the cardinal de la Rochefoucauld, alarmed by the disintegration of his order, asked Louis XVI to intervene. At the same time, forty-six nobles asked the king to dissolve the Estates General because of the illegal actions of the Third Estate. Louis XVI decided on a show of firmness and announced a royal session of the Estates General on June 23. In the meantime, he ordered, the salle des Menus Plaisirs would be closed to allow workmen to prepare for his visit. Locking the Assembly was a convenient way to prevent fresh defections.

Early on June 20, the Master of Ceremonies, Dreux-Brézé, notified the presidents of the three orders by letter that 'the necessity of not interrupting the urgent task of the workers will not allow the access of the assembly halls to anyone.' Bailly, president of the Third Estate, who had scheduled a meeting for that day, replied immediately that he had 'received no order from the king about the royal session, or about the suspension of the Assembly, and my duty is to attend the one I have scheduled for this morning at eight.' The royal lockout was seen by the Third Estate as a mark of contempt for their order and as evidence that Louis XVI was siding with the privileged orders and planning to dissolve the Assembly. Arriving at the Menus Plaisirs, Bailly found it guarded. The National Assembly, Mirabeau later wrote to his constituents, 'was made to look like an unlawful assembly.'

A friendly guards lieutenant opened the iron gate so that secretaries could retrieve their documents, but worriedly told them not to linger. The assembly benches had been removed and the courtyard was full of soldiers. More and more deputies were milling outside, wondering how to reply to this affront. It was Doctor Joseph-Ignace Guillotin, the man who was later to propose a heavy blade dropped between two grooved uprights as the most humanitarian form of execution for enemies of the people, who suggested that the Assembly repair to a nearby indoor tennis court, large enough to accommodate them all.

If June 20 is, as some historians like to say, the beginning of a volcanic eruption, then the black-walled Versailles tennis court is its crater. The court where Louis XIV had often played was a curious site for a public forum, with its waist-high net strung from wall to wall, its musty closeness which evoked the perspiration of princes, and its blue ceiling decorated with gold fleur-de-lys. In David's famous painting, arms are outstretched in solemn vows, priests are embracing members of the Third Estate, hats are joyously waved, and in a corner lies a pile of tennis rackets and balls. There were no tables or desks, so Bailly stood on a door which had been placed over two barrels, and asked those present to 'swear never to separate and to meet whenever circumstances demand it, until the kingdom's Constitution is firmly established on a solid foundation.'

The tennis-court oath was the first act of defiance to the king, for its effect was to refuse in advance the demands Louis XVI was expected to make. The Assembly's vow meant that it would not disband, even if ordered to do so by the king. Five hundred and seventy-seven deputies signed the oath—only one refused, a man named Martin Dauch from Castelnaudary, who said he could not vow to carry out a programme which the king had not ratified.

The duc des Cars, an old-guard aristocrat, had gone to the tennis court to discover, in his words, 'what diabolical machinations were being hatched there.' He reported what he had seen to the king's

LOUIS XVI WEARING
THE PHRYGIAN
BONNET

Photo: Bibliothèque Nationale

PHILIPPE D'ORLÉANS—
PHILIPPE ÉGALITÉ—
WHO VOTED FOR
THE KING'S DEATH

Photo: Bibliothèque Nationale

THE HEAD OF LOUIS XVI DISPLAYED TO THE POPULACE,
JANUARY 21, 1793

Photo: Bibliothèque Nationale

brother and leader of the aristocratic reaction, the comte d'Artois, and together they hastened to the king's side and urged the immediate dissolution of the Estates General. But Necker was there, wrote des Cars, and 'that damned Genevois opposed everything. He had the gall to assure me that the intentions of the tennis-court oath are pure and that the Commons are devoted to the king.'

The royal session of June 23 was the *ancien régime's* last bed of justice. Louis XVI came to curb, as he and his predecessors had often done, a balky Parlement. That the procedure would this time be different did not apparently cross his mind. His speech was a blend of honey and hemlock which pledged reforms while warning against disobedience. 'Never did a king do so much for a nation,' he told the Assembly. To break the deadlock, he suggested that each order verify its membership separately, with contested cases arbitrated by all three orders and the king. Matters of 'general interest' would be discussed in joint session, but the traditional rights of each order would be preserved. The Assembly was promised fiscal equality, the people's right to consent to taxes, freedom of the press and of the individual, and provincial assembles. But, added Louis XVI, 'if you abandon me in this noble endeavour, I will accomplish the good of my people alone. I order you to separate immediately and to return tomorrow morning to the halls to which your orders have been assigned, and to resume your deliberations.' The king departed, followed by the nobility and part of the clergy. The Third Estate, already in a combative mood after the tennis-court oath, and further irritated by the monarch's paternalistic and peremptory tone, refused to budge. 'Sir, you heard the king's order,' pleaded the harassed marquis de Dreux-Brézé to Bailly, who replied: 'I do not think that the nation assembled can receive such an order.' Mirabeau shouted his famous words: 'Only the force of bayonets can make us leave our seats,' which, as Bailly pointed out in his memoirs, was little more than windy rhetoric, for no one had mentioned the use of force. To Bailly, it was a juridical, not a military problem: should the Assembly, bound by its oath, heed the king's order? The general sentiment was voiced by the abbé Sieyès when he said: 'You are today what you were yesterday.'

Louis XVI toyed with the idea of evicting the defiant Assembly by force, but finally gave in to the entreaties of a few liberal nobles, including Lafayette, and said: '*Foutre,* let them stay, then.' Two days later, forty-seven members of the nobility joined the Assembly, and on June 27 Louis XVI reversed his previous attitude, and urged the two privileged orders to join the Third Estate. In his letter to the nobility, he said that his personal safety depended on it. A symptomatic reaction came from the marquis de Saint-Simon. 'The king says his life is in danger,' he cried. 'Let us race to the castle and form a rampart with our bodies.' The brave but doltish nobility was always far readier to sacrifice its blood than use its head. The privileged orders had been outmanœuvred by the clever bourgeois of the Third Estate and were now irrevocably split. Louis XVI, in asking the orders to meet jointly, was buying time. He was advancing troops on Paris which he hoped would give him enough strength to dissolve the Assembly.

The First Revolution had opposed the aristocrats and the king, and had led Louis XVI to summon the Estates General as a countermove against a threatening reactionary caste. The Second Revolution saw the Third Estate lay siege to the privileged orders and finally assimilate them, despite the king's efforts to maintain the traditional balance. This second, juridical phase of the conflict was over on June 27, when Louis XVI capitulated to the Assembly. The Third Revolution, pitting the nation against the king, was about to begin.

XVI

THE THIRD REVOLUTION

> *I wonder whether the initial error of contemporary*
> *France does not go back to the execution of Louis*
> *XVI.*
> —RAYMOND POINCARÉ

> *The Revolution could not forgive the monarchy—*
> *the monarchy: 'that usurpation,' that 'eternal crime'*
> *subjecting an entire people to a single man, that out-*
> *rage which, according to Saint-Just, 'even the blind-*
> *ness of an entire people could not excuse.' To forgive*
> *Louis XVI and grant him extenuating circumstances*
> *was to justify foreign intervention, invasion, civil*
> *war. To forgive the king was to condemn the nation.*
> —ALBERT SOBOUL, *Le Procès de Louis XVI*

THE ESTATES General and the National Assembly, meeting in 1789, never once conceived of tampering with the
monarchy or the monarch. The Convention, formed in
September, 1792, abolished the monarchy in its initial decree and,
shortly after, voted the king's death. This change in attitude, from
the unthinkable to the necessary, constituted the *ancien régime's*
death scene, played out over a period of less than four years. In that
relatively short time, France's absolute ruler and centre of authority
became an impotent victim of the mob. The protective incense with
which the monarchy surrounded itself evaporated. The king before
1789 was a prestigious figure who dwelt in an awe-inspiring palace
where adoring subjects came to watch him crack a soft-boiled egg,
which was considered a soul-satisfying lifetime memory. The king
after 1789 was exposed as a mortal who could suffer in his flesh, feel
pain, lose blood. He and his family now had to be vilified as extrava-

gantly as they had been honoured. Louis XVI, though no tyrant himself, had to do penance for all the sins of the monarchy. The French king had disregarded Paris and built Versailles—he had to be dragged back to the capital. The king wore a crown—he was made to put on a Phrygian bonnet. For every honour attached to his person there had to be a compensating humiliation. Some of the accusations made in the trial of Marie Antoinette seem like a grotesque attempt to match the level of past splendour with a like level of vileness. Thus, the queen was accused of teaching her eight-year-old son to masturbate and committing incest with him when they shared the same cell in the Temple prison.

The deterioration was gradual, a result both of Louis XVI's behaviour and the growing radicalism of the revolutionary leadership. The Estates General had been summoned by the king to debate the nation's needs. It was a collaboration between the monarch and the three orders, whose cahiers were drafted in terms of invariable respect. The erosion of respect for royalty began with the formation of the National Assembly, which refused to abide by the ruling of the royal session on June 23. But more important than this initial act of disobedience was the conflict between two concepts of the nation: the nation as the people (which, as the abbé Sieyès pointed out, was in effect the Third Estate), or the nation as the personal property of a divine-right monarch, who was the origin of the law and recognized no national will other than his own. This conflict came into the open on June 23 and continued until the violence of July 14, when a few thousand Parisians, proclaiming themselves the people, took control of the capital. The attack on the Bastille is incidental to the central fact that royal authority in the city was replaced by a 'permanent committee' selected from Paris districts, an executive body named by the people, which treated as an equal with the king.

The events of July 14 did not, however, damage the king's personal prestige. The people continued to believe in an alliance with the monarchy against the privileged orders. Parisians did not consider the king an obstacle to the Revolution, but an asset who should be brought in more direct contact with it. Thus, Louis XVI was 'persuaded' to return permanently to his capital in October.

In five months, France's growing pains had been greater than in the previous five centuries. Louis XVI settled into the Tuileries with the remains of his court, which still enforced the *lever* and the *grandes et petites entrées* as visible signs that nothing was changed (like the widow of a cavalry officer who polishes his boots daily). The National Assembly pursued its task of drafting the country's first written constitution. A popular child's board game of the period, called 'Revolution,' begins with the attack on the Bastille (throw a double six to cross the drawbridge in one move) and ends with the king's acceptance of the 1791 constitution. Many thought that the Revolution, like the game, was over at this point. And it might have been, if the king had accepted the role of constitutional monarch. But Louis XVI was an evolutionary discard, like one of the early species of animals that became extinct. He had a generous heart, vigorously applied reforms, and opposed the aristocratic reaction. But he clung to the absolutist concept of the state as embodied in his person.

Louis XVI had two options. He could make the transition to constitutional monarchy and form an alliance with the powerful conservative wing of the National Assembly to limit the scope of the Revolution. (Suspicion of the common man ran deep enough among the bourgeois who represented the Third Estate to make a constitutional monarchy feasible.) Or he could revert to the traditional bonds that tied the monarchs of Europe, and defend his concept of legitimacy by seeking foreign intervention. Louis XVI chose to feign adhesion to the Revolution while secretly relying on the solidarity of European monarchs to help him subvert it. As early as October, 1789, he wrote to his cousin Charles IV of Spain: 'I have chosen Your Majesty, as head of the second [Bourbon] branch, to depose in your hands the solemn protest that I make against all the acts contrary to royal authority, which were torn from me by force since July 15 of this year. I beg Your Majesty to keep this protest secret until the occasion when its publication could become necessary.'

It was in large part Louis XVI's own ambivalence that destroyed the mystique of the monarchy. The increasingly violent Paris press found the king's equivocation a convenient target. Pamphleteers wrote wild articles about reactionary plots and émigré armies, and linked the king to these movements. They had little evidence, but their guesswork was partly right. The king became what the Paris penny press accused him of being. Thus, in April, 1791, national guards prevented the royal family from leaving the Tuileries to spend the day in Saint-Cloud because of rumours that the trip was part of a plot to flee France. It was not, but his detention in the palace on that day convinced Louis XVI that he was a prisoner of the mob and must escape; the attempt was made two months later. Its failure, with the ludicrous capture of the royal family at Varennes, gravely deteriorated his position. Here was proof that Louis XVI considered himself safer among the enemies of France than in his own country. The bond between king and nation was publicly severed at Varennes.

The king's position worsened as France approached war with Europe. It was only after a coalition army had invaded France that an organized campaign for Louis' overthrow began in Paris. The opposition between king and nation was complete. A friendly word for the king was enough to make one suspected of treason. Louis XVI and his family represented the enemy inside the walls. An attack on the monarchy became proof of patriotism. The August, 1792, invasion of the Tuileries was just such a burst of patriotic fervour. It was while the palace was being looted that papers were discovered proving Louis' collusion with the enemy. To a besieged nation, overrun by the Duke of Brunswick's troops, living in a state of patriotic overstimulation, the issue was clear: Louis XVI must be tried as a criminal. His trial and conviction were necessary for political reasons; they would unite France against the invader. They would also allow the extremist revolutionary leaders of the Montagne party, who had clamoured loudest for the king's head, to defeat the moderate Gironde party, and usher in the real democratic revolution.

But beyond political considerations, the king's execution was the essential revolutionary act. Without it, there was no authentic revolution, merely a more or less radical reform programme. Regicide, the leaders of the Revolution knew, was much more than a reply to the threat of invasion. It was the final scene in the drama of a dying society, the auto-da-fé which would permit the passage from one world to another. The death of the king, the Conventionnel Saint-Just predicted, would 'astonish cold posterity.' For the first time in 800 years, no one would say: 'The king is dead; long live the king.' The execution brought about a profound change in the French sensibility. The absence of protest, the public silence with which the event was met, proved that the Revolution was accomplished. Buried with Louis' decapitated body was the mystique of the Very Christian King, anointed by God, healer of the scrofulous, incarnation of the state, link in an unbroken and eternal dynastic chain. Twenty-three years later, the monarchy was restored, but it was a synthetic product that could not last. Divine-right monarchy in France was permanently laid to rest on January 21, 1793.

Thus, the so-called monarchic era of the Revolution may be seen as the gradual but certain progression of Louis XVI towards the scaffold, which we can retrace by stopping before each of its stations.

First Station: The Bastille on July 14, 1789

France in the last days of June, 1789, gave the illusion of being a nation blessed with such political maturity that it had absorbed a revolution without bloodshed or the intervention of the people. Louis XVI had generously agreed to allow the elected delegates of the three orders to form a National Assembly which replaced royal absolutism. A new age had dawned. The enlightenment was made flesh.

On June 25, however, Louis XVI wrote to the maréchal de Broglie: 'Monsieur le maréchal, I need someone near me on whose loyalty I can count and who knows how to command troops. I will not try to conceal the fact that the situation is rather critical, but I count on your zeal and attachment to me. Please come to Versailles as soon as you can.' Having lost his political leadership, Louis XVI turned to the army. At the same time as the letter to Broglie, orders were sent to move 20,000 troops into the Paris region over a ten-day period. It was clear that the king could not count on his own French guards, who detested their commanding officer, displayed open sympathies with the Revolution, and complained of having to carry out police duties against the population. On June 30, 4,000 Parisians marched on the Abbaye prison to free ten French guards who had been jailed for refusing to obey orders.

As the king ringed Paris with uncontaminated troops, the 407 electors of Paris (the men who had picked the Third Estate Paris deputies) began marshalling their own forces against a possible military coup. On July 1, Jean-Paul Marat warned in his newspaper L'Ami du Peuple that the king's ministers were preparing to dissolve the Assembly by unleashing a civil war. On July 8, on the marquis de Mirabeau's initiative, the National Assembly asked the king to withdraw his troops. 'Your Majesty does not need them,' Mirabeau said. 'Eh! Why should a monarch adored by twenty-five-million Frenchmen rush in a few thousand foreigners around his throne?' (a reference to the high percentage of German mercenaries in the regiments bivouacking in the capital). The king's reply on July 11 was that the troops were needed to maintain order, and that if the National Assembly feared disturbances it should move to some more remote headquarters, such as Soissons or Compiègne. On the same day, Louis XVI replaced the popular Necker, who disagreed with the policy of troop reinforcements, and named as his principal minister the baron de Breteuil, whose lack of sympathy with the aims of the Revolution was well known. The maréchal de Broglie was named Minister of War.

News of Necker's disgrace, which spread through the capital on July 12, ignited the popular revolt. The journalist Camille Des-moulins, standing on a café table in the Palais Royal and waving a pistol, called to arms. As an expression of mourning for Necker, crowds closed the theatres, which in those days had a 5 p.m. curtain. The busts of Necker and Philippe d'Orléans were removed from the Curtius wax museum and paraded through the streets. French guards joined the demonstrators. At 8 p.m. the Royal-Allemand regiment, commanded by the prince de Lambesc, tried to force the crowds out of the Place Louis XV (today's Place de la Concorde), but demonstrators took refuge on the Tuileries terrace, from which they bombarded the loyal troops with cobblestones and bricks. Future revolutionary leaders were later to brag that they received their baptism of fire on that day: Marat claimed he led a charge against the king's men at the Pont Royal and Danton was said to be the chief agitator in the Odéon neighbourhood, where his statue stands today. Already, on July 12, Paris was in total confusion, and respectable burghers locked themselves up in their homes and left the city to the mob, which began taking its vengeance on symbols of abuse, just as the nineteenth-century Luddites would someday expend their hatred of the industrial revolution on machines. The crowd burned down some of the General Farmers' custom gates and looted Saint-Lazare prison, thinking it was a grain depot.

On July 13, the Paris districts formed a 'permanent committee' (the first version of the Commune), which called upon each district to provide 200 armed men. The search for weapons began. The newly formed Paris militia broke into a firearms museum on the Place Louis XV and took, among other weapons, a sword that had belonged to Henri IV and a small cannon inlaid with silver which the king of Siam had given to Louis XIV. The rumour spread that there were 32,000 rifles at the Invalides. The Invalides governor,

Monsieur de Sombreuil, received a deputation from the districts asking for the rifles and passed the request on to the baron de Besenval, Lieutenant-General of the Swiss guards, who later wrote in his memoirs: 'Versailles, in this cruel situation, had forgotten me, and was determined to regard 3,000 mutinous men as nothing more than an unlawful assembly, and the Revolution as a riot.'

Besenval told the men of the districts that he could not turn the rifles over without an order from Versailles. On the night of the 13th he assigned twenty men to remove the hammers from the rifles in the Invalides cellar, but they were sympathetic to the districts and worked with purposeful slowness. At 5 A.M. a wild-eyed Parisian barged in on the sleeping Besenval to warn him that all Paris was on the march, but the baron seemed resigned to the flow of events. The district militia, returning to the Invalides later in the morning and encountering no resistance, distributed the rifles. They needed ammunition, and knew that 30,000 pounds of gunpowder had been transferred from the Arsenal to the cellars of the Bastille.

The Bastille was built under Charles V in 1370 to defend one of the entrances to Paris. It was a massive stone quadrangle with eight towers as high as seven-storey buildings, and a complicated system of multiple courtyards, drawbridges, and moats, which made it virtually impregnable to attack. In the seventeenth century, having outlived its military use, Richelieu made it a state prison for men and women sentenced outside the courts, in sealed letters signed by the king. Even then the Bastille was the object of popular sarcasm, and a poet wrote in 1662:

> What's the use of this old wall in the water?
> Is it an aqueduct, a cellar,
> Or a reservoir for frogs?

The Bastille's aspect changed when it became a prison. One of the towers was named Freedom Tower because the prisoners who resided there could wander at will in the fortress' courtyards. A huge clock held up by figures representing chained prisoners was erected between two inside towers. Shops and barracks for the army pensioners who guarded the prison were built, and the prison governor planted a vegetable garden atop one of the ramparts. The Bastille could accommodate forty-two prisoners without doubling up. In the reign of Louis XVI it was never crowded. From 1774 to 1789 there was a total of 240 prisoners, or an average of 16 a year.

Typical prisoners were an abbot who had sold tickets for a non-existent lottery, a counterfeiter who had forged Sardinian banknotes, a maid who had stolen diamonds from her mistress, sorcerers, Jansenists, heretic priests, and critics of the regime, such as a minor civil servant jailed for two years after he was overheard saying: 'How are we to live since the king takes everything and weighs us down with taxes . . . he eats the child in the mother's womb; he is unworthy of ruling.'

Treatment in the Bastille was better than in other prisons. There were fewer prisoners, and some were nobly-born. Women of condition were allowed to have their toilet articles and receive visits from their hairdresser, dressmaker, and upholsterer. Prison authorities went to considerable trouble to grant the special needs of their guests. A man who complained that a weak bladder prevented him from drinking red wine was given white. Those who could afford it had catered meals brought to their cells. Servants accompanied their masters into seclusion and prisoners who were planning a long stay had their furniture sent for. The governor often invited prisoners to his table, like a ship's captain. A brief incarceration was a guarantee of success for a writer. As Chamfort wrote: 'Good Heavens! No news from the Bastille and my rent is due at any moment.'

Louis XVI rarely signed a sealed letter, and the government began to consider the Bastille an expensive, unnecessary piece of real estate that was also the butt of popular discontent. In 1784 an architect was asked to draw up plans for its destruction and replacement with a spacious square dominated by a statue of Louis XVI, the base of which would be cast from the melted chains and locks of the prison.

Popular legends made the Bastille the symbol of arbitrary power. It was, it is true, a prison where people were sent without knowing why or for how long, on a simple order of the king, without due process. The Bastille faithfully mirrored both the lack of justice of the old order and its habit of making everyone an exception to the rule—prisoners were victims of the arbitrary but were reasonably well treated and unexpectedly released; there were both abuses and indulgences. The awesome appearance of this medieval fortress in the centre of Paris and the secrecy that surrounded its administration contributed to the rumours. Prisoners arrived in curtained carriages, and when they alighted the guards in the courtyard had to face the wall. One mysterious seventeenth-century prisoner was the man in

the iron mask, who in fact wore a velvet mask to conceal his identity
—he was probably a minister of the duke of Mantua named Mattioli.
More recent prisoners of note, such as Voltaire, helped publicize
the Bastille. Sensational accounts of life in the fortress by former
prisoners were published shortly before 1789 and propagated the
legends. The diary of Latude, a man arrested in a complicated plot
to blackmail Madame de Pompadour, told of underground dungeons, bad food, and harsh treatment. He explained how he made
friends with ten rats in his cell and had them eating bread out of
his hand. When he ran out of ink, he said, he wrote with his blood.
One of his typical complaints was for more varied food, because the
meat was tough, the butter was rancid, the pigs' feet were gristly,
the pastry was underdone, the wine was sour, and his delicate stomach
could not tolerate eggs, artichokes, or spinach.

On July 14, 1789, the Bastille is commanded by forty-nine-year-old
Bernard René Jourdan, marquis de Launey, who in twelve years as
the prison's governor has been given an undeserved reputation as a
villainous brute. In reality, de Launey is half-crazed with fear and
anxiety. For weeks he has been requesting reinforcements for the
eighty-two army pensioners guarding the fortress. 'Who is going to
attack the Bastille?' he is asked. However, thirty-two Swiss soldiers,
a sergeant, and a lieutenant are sent to him on July 7. De Launey
is expecting trouble and has taken precautions. He has repaired the
drawbridges and boarded up the windows with thick planks. He has
placed his fifteen eight-pounders on the towers and his three field
cannons in the courtyard, aimed at the entrance gate. He has un-
loaded six wagons of scrap iron at the top of the towers, to fling at
assailants as in a medieval siege. He has posted his men on the outside ramparts, but on the 12th he orders them to pull back to the
inner courtyards.

The crowd marching towards the Bastille in search of gunpowder
is alarmed by the sight of the cannons pointing from the towers. A
delegation is received by de Launey and asks him for assurances
that he will not harm the crowd. De Launey orders the cannons
withdrawn from the towers. The mob, watching from the street,
sees the cannons pulled back and thinks they are being loaded. Since
it has had no news from its delegates, it thinks they are being held
as hostages. A second delegation is sent, which, as it enters, meets
the first delegation just finishing lunch. De Launey offers to show

them that the cannons have been withdrawn, but the delegations escalate their demands and ask that he turn over the Bastille to the people to avoid spilling blood. De Launey refuses the ultimatum and the delegates are jeered by the crowd as they leave the fortress. Waiting has made the crowd restless and increased its size. Its purpose imperceptibly shifts from the quest for gunpowder to an assault on the fortress. Shouts of 'Down with the Bastille' and 'We want the Bastille' begin to be heard. Different groups goad each other to action. Two men climb onto the roof of a perfumer's shop which leans against the prison's undefended outer rampart and jump to the outside courtyard. They are followed by others with axes and maces who sever the drawbridge chains attached to the counterbalance weights. The drawbridge crashes down, killing one demonstrator too close to the moat, and wounding another. The gates are hacked open and the mob stream into the outer courtyard.

Who fired first? Each side accuses the other. The mob in the courtyard shouts 'down with the bridges' leading into the fortress. Soon there is firing from both sides, from the soldiers in the crenels on either side of the gate and from the mob in the courtyard and on rooftops near the fortress. The bulk of the mob does not realize that the drawbridge has been lowered by some of its own members. They think de Launey has lured them into the courtyard and then fired on them. The myth of de Launey's 'betrayal' is the main reason for his subsequent massacre.

The Swiss guards have pierced two holes in the raised second drawbridge through which they fire rampart guns. The controlled firing of the Swiss holds the mob in check. Repeated attempts to approach the drawbridge are repulsed by the defenders' salvos. The demonstrators pull two wagonloads of hay into the courtyard and set fire to them, advancing behind the smoke screen. Meanwhile, two other delegations have been sent to reach an agreement with de Launey but when he sees men waving white handkerchiefs in the courtyard he fires at them, suspecting a trick. So far, the Bastille attack is a stalemate.

At about 3:30 P.M., two organized columns of troops arrive at the Bastille to reinforce the mob. The first is led by a French guard named Hulin, who had been director of the queen's laundry in Saint-Denis, and is made up of some sixty guards dragging four cannons and a mortar taken from the Invalides that morning, and three or four hundred armed civilians. Another column of armed civilians is led by a second lieutenant named Elie, one of the rare army officers to have been promoted in the field. The disconnected efforts of an undisciplined rabble now become, thanks to these two leaders and the presence of the guards and the cannon, an organized siege. Cannons are brought into firing position against the towers but are unable to dent the thick stone walls. The obvious strategy is to fire at the Bastille's wooden drawbridge but the burning wagons of hay with which the demonstrators have littered the courtyard block the line of fire. A team of volunteers pulls the wagons out of the way under heavy fire and loses two men. Two cannons (including the one given to Louis XIV by the king of Siam) are dismounted from their carriages to fit them through the outside gate, and are set up in the courtyard.

At the sight of the cannon the army pensioners defending the Bastille plead with de Launey to capitulate. De Launey orders his men on the towers to wave white handkerchiefs, but the mob disregards them and keeps firing, shouting 'down with the bridges.' De Launey scribbles a note that says: 'We have twenty thousand-weights of gunpowder, we will blow up the garrison and the whole neighbourhood unless you accept our capitulation. From the Bastille, 5 P.M., July 14, 1789, Launey.' He hands the note to the Swiss guards officer, who pokes it through one of the holes in the drawbridge. The assailants see a piece of paper being waved and find a long plank that reaches across the moat. Several men stand on one end of the plank to weigh it down while a cobbler named Bézier advances over the empty moat, slips, and falls, fracturing an elbow. A second man ventures onto the plank and is able to snatch de Launey's note. The message is handed to Hulin, who reads it aloud, but the mob shouts 'no capitulation.' Giving in to the renewed entreaties of the army pensioners, de Launey hands the key to the small drawbridge to a corporal, and moments later it is lowered.

One of the first demonstrators to enter the Bastille is J. B. Humbert, a watchmaker. He accosts a Swiss soldier and orders, 'Put down your weapon.' The Swiss turns to the crowd and says: 'Gentlemen, you may rest assured that I did not fire.' 'How dare you claim you didn't fire,' replies Humbert, 'your mouth is still black from biting cartridges.' Humbert finds another Swiss in a dungeon, who pleads: 'Comrade, do not kill me. I am of the Third Estate and I will defend you to my last drop of blood. I had to serve, but I did not fire.'

The mob disarms the soldiers, and throws the prison archives out of a window. It sets about freeing the prisoners, but is astonished to find that they number only seven: four forgers guilty of passing bad letters of exchange in banks; the comte de Solages, jailed on request of his family, and accused of incest 'and other atrocious crimes'; and two madmen, a Frenchman named Tavernier and an Irishman named Whyte, who thinks he is Julius Caesar and who, with his emaciated face and waist-length beard, personifies the victim of injustice perishing in some forgotten dungeon. A thorough search of the premises uncovers parts of an old printing press and ancient armours which are later exhibited as instruments of torture.

The crowd of about one thousand has suffered roughly ninety dead and sixty wounded, and among the defenders there is one dead army pensioner and three wounded. The casualty rate is lower than that of Paris street riots that April. The crowd's vengeance focuses on de Launey, who is severely manhandled as Elie and Hulin attempt to bring him to city hall alive. Arriving at city hall, de Launey is stabbed with bayonets and an unemployed cook cuts his head off.

That evening the vicomte de Noailles arrives at Versailles and tells the National Assembly that the Bastille has fallen to the Paris districts. A delegation leaves for the palace to inform the king, but Louis XVI is deaf to the event's meaning. He tells the delegation that 'my heart is torn by your account of the troubles in Paris but I cannot believe they have been caused by the orders given to the troops.' He does not realize that aside from the Swiss, he can no longer count on his troops, and that the French guards fought on the side of the besiegers. In 1827, the comte de la Rochefoucauld wrote that his father, the comte de Liancourt, had awakened Louis XVI during the night of the 14th and 15th to tell him the news. 'But is it a revolt?' asked the king. 'No, sire, it is a revolution,' came the famous but probably apocryphal reply, for Louis XVI had already been informed of the day's events.

It would be unjust to accuse Louis XVI too harshly of misjudging the significance of July 14, for the Bastille's emergence as the primordial symbol of the French Revolution is a triumph of myth over fact. The Bastille was far from the medieval torture chamber it was made out to be. And on July 14, it was not stormed, it capitulated—the drawbridge was lowered from the inside. Finally, it has little to do with the struggle for freedom, since it contained only seven prisoners, two of whom had to be transferred to the Charenton lunatic asylum, and much more to do with the phenomenon of mob violence. It was only after the fall of the Bastille that the argument that revolutions must be violent began to be heard. 'Nations must have victims,' said Mirabeau after the fact. And Barnave, after the murder of two municipal officials, asked: 'Was their blood so pure that we should regret spilling it?' The theoreticians of a violent revolution were influenced by the events of July 14, rather than the other way around. Once the Revolution became violent, there arose the doctrine that it had to be.

There were far bloodier and more meaningful incidents during the Revolution, but somehow none had the evocative power of the fall of the Bastille. Foreign ambassadors were quick to appreciate the importance of the first example of mob rule. The Austrian ambassador wrote to Vienna: 'The city of Paris has assumed the role of king.' The Russian ambassador reported: 'The fall of the state prison was the first triumph of this stormy liberty.' On July 31, Gouverneur Morris wrote to George Washington that the king's authority had been completely destroyed.

All over Europe, the fall of the Bastille was seized upon as the emblem of the Revolution. There were plays about it in England and Ireland, books about it in Holland, engravings of it in Germany. The Saint Petersburg *Gazette* of August 7, 1789, wrote: 'The hand trembles with horror in relating events that can only be attributed to contempt for one's duty towards the sovereign and towards humanity.' Carlyle said that compared to the Bastille, the siege of Troy was nothing.

The Bastille is one of those monuments that, like archaeological ruins, increases in fame after its destruction. This task was entrusted to the patriot Palloy on July 16. It was more than a blow for liberty, it was a public works project that kept 500 men employed for six months at wages of 45 sous a day. Palloy was as much a businessman as a patriot, and he sold miniature models of the fortress made from its stones, as well as medals, inkwells, and paperweights made from the locks and chains, and fans and playing cards made from prison registers. He sent officials in each of France's eighty-three departments 'several fragments of a crust three or four inches thick which was formed on the vaults of the dungeons by the breaths of the prisoners.' On February 6, 1790, the demolition work was finished. A decree on June 19, 1790, conferred the dignity of 'victor of the

Bastille' on 954 citizens who 'took up arms to shake off the yoke of slavery and make their country free.' A grateful nation gave them the right to bear arms and a special uniform with a small tower embroidered on the left sleeve.

Second Station: The submission of Louis XVI to the people of Paris on July 17, 1789

On July 16, the king's youngest brother, the comte d'Artois, flees to Holland with his wife and his mistress. On the same day, the Earl of Dorset, British ambassador to Paris, reports to his government that 'a troop of armed ciizens numbering no less than 50,000 men will leave for Versailles to bring the sovereign back to the capital, by force if necessary.' Force is not necessary, for the king resolves to go to Paris and consecrate the end of the *ancien régime*. He fears he will be murdered on the way or held as a hostage, and he names his remaining brother, the comte de Provence, Lieutenant General of the Kingdom, with full powers during his absence. At the Chaillot gate, Jean-Sylvain Bailly, the new mayor of Paris, receives the king with this felicitous phrase: 'Henri IV had reconquered his people, here the people has reconquered the king.' The crowd is in a festive mood and hearty cheers reassure Louis XVI as he proceeds to city hall, but as commentators note, there are more cries of 'Long live the nation' than 'Long live the king.' Bailly offers the king a red, white, and blue cockade—red and blue are the colours of Paris and white the colour of the Bourbon monarchy. Louis XVI pins the new national emblem on his hat and mumbles a few half-hearted remarks: 'I am very satisfied . . . you can always count on my love for the people.' The king appears at the balcony of city hall wearing his cockade and is acclaimed. He returns to Versailles the same evening. On July 19, Thomas Jefferson, an eyewitness, writes to John Jay that the king had 'made apologies such as no sovereign ever made and no people ever received.'

Third Station: On August 4, 1789, in a calculated fever of generosity, the National Assembly buries the ancien régime but becomes divided and gives the king reason to resist its measures

After July 14, the provinces copied Paris. Towns and cities formed people's committees, raised armed militias, and stormed local Bastilles.

The peasantry, a fourth estate unpresented in the National Assembly, reacted to the confusion with a mixture of opportunism and irrationality. They saw their chance to liquidate feudal abuses by direct action, and demanded that the lords turn over the charters and registers on which feudal claims were based. When a lord was stubborn, his castle was sometimes burned and he himself was lynched or subjected to lesser indignities, such as being dumped onto a heap of manure. But coupled with this Jacquerie was the terrible shiver that rippled through the land under the name of the Great Fear. The essentially conservative French peasant could not conceive that disorder did not have its legions, and in their absence he invented gangs of brigands that were about to descend on him like a flight of locusts to ravage all he had. The bandits were coming—they were raising clouds of dust on the horizon—they were in the next village. The peasants, armed and prepared for the confrontation, but finding no bandits, sought more tangible foes in the castles and abbeys of the privileged orders.

The disturbing news from the provinces gave the National Assembly its first difficult choice: repression of disorder, which meant establishing an authoritarian regime remarkably similar to the one it was intended to replace; or, as Mirabeau put it, 'giving the people a down payment on happiness, and tempering their anxiety through prompt enjoyment of the benefits of freedom.'

The down payment was made when the Assembly met at 8 P.M. on August 4 for a night session which had been cleverly masterminded by some of its bourgeois leaders. The trouble in the countryside was directed mainly against feudal abuses. A distinction could be established between forms of personal bondage, such as serfdom, and income-producing privileges, which could be abolished outright, and suppression of the second could be promised against suitable indemnity. Such a solution would both gratify popular aspirations and protect property-owners.

This was the heart of the programme presented by the vicomte de Noailles, a penniless younger son for whom generosity was inexpensive, who interrupted a speech by the Assembly president on the need to restore public order. Noailles said that to restore order the causes of disorder must disappear. He proposed an income tax to be paid by all citizens without exception; suppression of personal bondage such as the corvée and serfdom; and the end of feudal property rights, against compensation. The duc d'Aiguillon, one of the largest landowners in France and a leading member of the liberal nobility, spoke after Noailles and said that 'this insurrection [of the peasants], however damnable, can find its excuse in vexations.' He seconded Noailles' plan. A thunder of applause greeted the generous proposals of these two great lords. A kind of delirium swept the two privileged orders, whose members fought for the floor so that they could be the first to relinquish their privileges. The bishop of Uzès said he wished he owned lands so that 'I could make a sacrifice and return them to those who are living on them.' This orgy of abnegation lasted until two in the morning, and covered such disparate vexations as the lord's right to keep dovecotes and the clergy's fee for saying mass. The principal traditions of the *ancien régime* were, with the rhetoric suitable to a funeral oration, buried.

To a conservative member of the Assembly, viewing the scene with profound distaste, 'the Assembly was like a troop of drunkards in a warehouse of precious antiques, breaking whatever they could lay their hands on.' Most regional and personal privileges, the honeycomb of exceptions and special customs which had made France impossible to administer, were jettisoned. The Assembly enacted what amounted to an eighteenth-century civil rights programme, not for a minority but for a discriminated-against nation: equal job opportunities, equal justice, suppression of the tithes and other abusive taxes, and the end of personal, local, and provincial privileges which were the framework of the *ancien régime*. As the marquis de Ferrières, a liberal noble, put it: 'In one night was achieved the unity which twelve centuries, the same religion, the same language, and the same customs had not been able to accomplish.' In a final burst of euphoria, at 2 A.M. on August 5, the Assembly proclaimed Louis XVI 'restorer of French freedom.'

There are no gifts in politics, and the 'sacrifices' of August 4 were also eminently practical. Assembly leaders had sought primarily to quell the uprisings in the provinces while protecting property rights. Even so, the morning after, there was a rude awakening. Members of the privileged orders, like hung-over carousers, muttered about the folly of the night before.

On August 5, Louis XVI wrote to the archbishop of Arles: 'I will never consent to despoil my nobility and my clergy.' The Assembly was more cautious when it came to putting the fine feelings of August 4 down on paper. It was evident in the decrees of August 5 and 11 that their principal concern was the protection of property rights. Feudal taxes would continue to be levied until compensation was settled. The peasants of a given fief were held jointly responsible for settling the matter of compensation with the lord. Forty years of ownership were declared sufficient to qualify for the compensation of feudal rights, a measure favourable to the recent bourgeois acquirers of large domains. Thus, the principle of feudalism was banished, but its practical effects persisted. The Assembly decree began with the phrase: 'The National Assembly completely destroys the feudal regime,' and continued with multiple provisions which ensured that no member of the privileged orders would be out of pocket.

The abolition of feudalism was followed by what the historian Alphonse Aulard has called 'the *ancien régime*'s death certificate,' the Declaration of Human Rights. It is summed up in its first article: 'Men are born and remain free and equal in their rights, social distinctions can be founded only upon common utility.' France was no longer the property of a monarch. Obedience was owed to law, not to a king or his agents. A man could not be arbitrarily arrested or summarily judged. The accused was innocent until proven guilty (whereas the systematic use of torture under the *ancien régime* to extort a confession presumed him guilty until proven innocent).

Even though the decree abolishing feudal privileges and the Declaration of the Rights of Man and the Citizen were compromise measures enacted by an Assembly controlled by the bourgeoisie (civil rights, for instance, were still denied to Protestants, actors, and Jews, which led Camille Desmoulins to say that it was 'the height of absurdity' that to prove you were a citizen, 'you also had to prove you had a foreskin'), they were dramatic enough to provoke a split in the Assembly and encourage the passive resistance of Louis XVI.

A conservative party, called Monarchiens, formed in the Assembly and advocated restoring executive power to the king as the only way to prevent the nation's disintegration. The Monarchiens wanted separation of powers and an upper house, like the House of Lords in England. The radical wing of the Assembly was against two chambers and wanted to further weaken the king's power by depriving him of his veto on legislative decisions. In Paris, the districts adopted a decision that 'the veto belongs not to a single man but to twenty-five million citizens.'

But Louis XVI, finding himself supported by what his agents told him was a controlling portion of the Assembly, found arguments and excuses to keep from ratifying the Assembly's August measures, thereby provoking the second major popular intervention of the Revolution.

Fourth Station: On October 5 and 6, 1789,
the monarchs' lives are endangered for the first
time as the mob invades Versailles and forces
the royal family to move to Paris

After the reciprocal philanthropy of the night of August 4, in which the clergy offered to give up the nobility's hunting privileges while the nobility urged the abolition of tithes, the National Assembly entered a period of muted conflict with the king. On September 10, the proposal for a second chamber was overwhelmingly defeated. On the following day the Assembly granted the king a suspensive veto for a minimum period of four years. The majority for this vote was rounded up by parliamentary leaders who had been promised that in return Louis XVI would ratify the August 4 reforms. When the king failed to live up to his part of the bargain, and continued to find pretexts for not signing them, both he and the moderate leaders of the Assembly were discredited.

Under the suspensive veto, Assembly decrees were sent to Louis XVI to be signed either 'the king consents and will execute' (keeping up the pretence that he still held executive power) or 'the king will examine,' which amounted to a veto. But with the exception of the veto, the Assembly gradually dismantled royal authority. On September 22, it knocked away the cornerstone of the whole absolutist edifice, the claim that the king's will had force of law. 'There is in France no authority superior to the law,' it said. 'The king reigns by virtue of the law, and only by virtue of the law can he demand obedience.'

There was, parallel to the parliamentary action which was quietly gelding the monarchy, a high-pitched permanent level of popular excitement maintained by the heady mixture of freedom and power. In the Paris districts, elections were held on the flimsiest pretext. As soon as more than five persons gathered they formed an assembly and elected a president and secretary. The lesson of the Bastille—that the common man could force change—was applied at the local level. When the parish priest of Saint-Jacques la Boucherie refused to give a free burial mass to a carpenter killed in an accident, the people of the district forced their way into his church and bodily led him to the cemetery. The people were still religious, but they were also patriotic. Patrotism, which usually meant popular agitation, was fanned by the proliferation of pamphlets and newspapers, which printed the slogans the crowd recited.

One idea often repeated in the revolutionary press was that in Versailles Louis XVI was prey to the evil intrigues of the aristocrats, while in Paris he would be in the midst of his own good people, protected from plots and cabals. The belief that the monarch and the people were allies against the malevolent privileged classes still prevailed, even though none of the king's actions since July 14 justified it. The presence of Louis XVI in Paris began to be seen, just as a year before the Estates General had been seen, as the only solution for the people's ills. For Paris was in a paradoxical condition of political euphoria and economic distress. The flight of people and capital (200,000 passports had been delivered between July 14 and September 10) had slowed the economy and made unemployment soar. On August 29, 400 servants whose masters had fled held a protest rally in the Palais Royal. The 1789 harvest was good, but the distribution of grain was impeded by events, and in Paris there was a bread shortage. There were long bread lines, and during the month of September, armed guards had to be posted in front of bakeries sixteen out of thirty days.

In a typical conversation, a member of the Paris Commune named Dussaulx told the General Farmer Augeart: 'This business will only be settled once the king is in the Tuileries; it was a great mistake on July 16 not to have kept him there; a king should live in his capital.'

'You are right, but who can force the king to change his residence?'

'When it is for the general good, he should be forced, and it will come to that.'

The implementation of the Revolution was stalled by the royal veto, and the capital was threatened by famine. The vacillations of the National Assembly were an invitation for further mass action.

Louis XVI, whose French guards have been transferred to Paris and exposed to the revolutionary virus, has asked for reinforcements of loyal troops. Transferred from Douai, the 1,050 men and officers of the Flanders regiment arrive in Versailles on October 1 with orders to protect the royal family. A banquet in honour of its officers is held that evening on the deep stage of the Versailles opera house.

Two hundred and six guests at the horseshoe table cheer as the duc de Villeroi, captain of the first guards company, toasts the king, the queen, and the dauphin. At the end of each toast the regimental trumpets sound the charge.

Louis XVI and Marie Antoinette pay the banquet a brief visit, and the officers raise their swords, vow to die defending them, and intone the song: 'O Richard, O my king, the universe is abandoning you.'

Accounts of the banquet appear in the Paris revolutionary press on October 3. It had been a fairly innocent affair. Some guards officers had too much to drink and expressed their devotion to the monarch in overexuberant terms. But with repeated telling, new and lurid details are added, until the banquet becomes a reactionary orgy during which the king and queen watched drunken officers trample the red, white, and blue cockade. The guards banquet had much the same effect as the cry 'to the Bastille'—it galvanized crowds into action.

On October 5, beneath a pouring rain, a bizarre procession leaves Paris and hikes ten miles to Versailles to ask the king for bread. It is led by a twenty-five-year-old, sallow-faced, consumptive clerk named Maillard, and is made up mainly of women, who grow increasingly excitable as the march progresses. The object of their ire is another woman, Marie Antoinette. Trooping down Versailles' avenue de Paris at 6 P.M., the drenched, mud-spattered women, brandishing pikes and halberds, shaking fists, straddling cannons, are heard shouting: 'We want to cut off her head . . . tear out her heart . . . fricassee her liver . . . make ribbons out of her guts.'

Despite the bad weather, the king has been hunting in Châtillon forest and returns in the afternoon to learn that the crowd is on its way. It could have been stopped by blowing up a wooden bridge at Sèvres, which Louis XIV had kept from being rebuilt in stone in view of just such an emergency. Versailles is as vulnerable as the Bastille was inaccessible. It has always been open to visitors. The gates in front of the marble courtyard are locked, and doors which have not been closed for years groan on their hinges. A guards detachment lines up in front of the gate. The crowd masses across from the guards and shouts for 'bread at six sous a pound.' A militiaman scuffles with a sentinel and stabs him. A guards officer on horseback, the marquis de Savonnières, charges the militiaman and is stopped by a rifle bullet in the arm. The guards charge the crowd with bayonets and disperse it. The crowd decides to bivouac near the palace for the night and sends a delegation of women to see the king. Speaking for the delegation, a seventeen-year-old girl named Louison Chabry tells the king they have come for bread. The king promises them wagonloads of flour. The girl asks to kiss the king's hand, and he replies that she deserves better than that and busses her on both cheeks. Returning to the crowd, the delegation is received by cries of 'string them up,' because they have not got the king's promise in writing. They go back, and Louis XVI scribbles a note promising flour.

The hostility to the royal family, and the rioting at the gate lead Saint-Priest, the Minister of the King's Household, to urge flight. But Necker, who is also on hand, argues that flight would be abdication. Louis XVI repeats, as though to himself: 'A fugitive king! A fugitive king!' Thoughts of flight are ended by the arrival of Lafayette, general of the national guard, a salaried militia which he formed on June 18, at the head of 20,000 men. Lafayette sees the king shortly before midnight and promises 'on my own head' that his troops will enforce order. The promise is not kept. The next morning, in the queen's bedroom, the clock with the tiny organ that plays the refrain of the children's song *'Il pleut, il pleut bergère,'* strikes six. The queen hears the approaching murmur of crowds, who have found an unlocked gate, broken past the guards and are scurrying across the courtyard. Her two ladies-in-waiting open the door of her apartment leading into the formal dining room and see a single blood-spattered guard fighting off assailants armed with axes, pikes, and iron bars, who is yelling 'save the queen.' The ladies-in-waiting lock the door and hurriedly dress the queen, who flees to the king's apartment, where she finds a distraught Louis XVI holding the four-year-old dauphin, wrapped in a blanket.

As the king and queen hide like malefactors in the secret corridors of Versailles, the crowd is quieted on the promise that it will be shown Louis XVI. He is brought out on the balcony of the marble courtyard like a trophy but is too upset to speak to the crowd, which clamours for the queen. Lafayette tells Marie Antoinette: 'Well then, Madam, come with me.' 'What,' replies the queen, 'alone on the balcony? Haven't you seen the gestures they are making?' 'Yes, Madam, let us go,' says Lafayette. He steps out on the balcony with her and kisses her hand. A rifle is lifted and aimed at the queen, but not fired. The crowd yells: 'To Paris—to Paris.' Louis XVI gives in. He reappears on the balcony and tells the armed citizens who a few moments earlier were stalking him through his own palace: 'My friends. I will go to Paris with my wife and children. I entrust what I hold most precious to the love of my good and faithful subjects.'

A few hours later, the king is squeezed into a carriage with the queen, his two children, his sister, and the children's governess. He is part of a motley procession of wagons of flour covered with leaves, national guards with loaves of bread stuck on the points of their bayonets, women armed with long poles and poplar branches, General Lafayette prancing alongside the royal carriage, and the heads of two decapitated guards mounted on pikes. 'It looked like a walking forest through which shone the iron of pikes and rifle barrels,' said an eyewitness. Again, as on July 17, the mayor, Bailly, is waiting at the city gate, this time with the keys to the city in a gold dish. The royal carriage makes its slow way toward the Tuileries, where no king has resided since the minority of Louis XV, and the people joyously proclaim that they have brought back 'the baker, the baker's wife, and the baker's apprentice.' In the October 7 issue of *The Friend of the People,* Jean-Paul Marat editorializes: 'It is a feast for good Parisians to finally possess their king: his presence is sure to bring about some fast changes; the poor people will no longer starve. But this happiness would vanish like a dream if we did not make sure that the royal family would stay among us until the Constitution is completely fulfilled. *The Friend of the People* shares the joy of its dear fellow citizens, while intending to keep up its vigil.'

The prevailing view among patriots, however, is that the Revolution is over. *'Consummatum est,'* writes Camille Desmoulins, 'all is consummated, the king is in the Louvre; the National Assembly is in the Tuileries [it had followed the king to Paris on October 18 and settled into the only building near the palace large enough to seat its 800 members, a riding stable built to teach young Louis XV how to sit a horse].... We can say to the National Assembly: "Now you have no more enemies." '

What had actually been consummated was the July 14 technique of mass riot as a political weapon. When the Revolution stalled, mass action started it up again. Violence became accepted as the most effective midwife of change. After July 14, Louis XVI moved his troop reinforcements out of Paris. After October 6, he signed the Assembly's decrees. There is a direct link between the 'spontaneous' riots of July 14 and October 6 and the sacrificial theories held by the leaders of the Terror that the Revolution must necessarily be founded on bloodletting.

Fifth Station: On April 18, 1791, Louis XVI
is prevented from leaving the Tuileries
for a day's outing at Saint-Cloud

Louis XVI's émigré brother, the comte d'Artois, has formed a shadow cabinet and announced that his programme is to free the royal family and incite a royal counterrevolution in the provinces.

The Assembly has voted the civil constitution of the clergy in July, 1790, and Louis XVI has ratified it, although it is opposed by the majority of French priests. The pope has condemned the measure, which calls for the election of priests and bishops by the people, and the clergy is split between those who have signed it and those who remain faithful to Rome, and are called 'refractories.'

In view of his ratification, Louis XVI wonders whether he should carry out his Easter obligations. Bishop de Bonnal of Clermont advises Louis XVI to abstain from any public observance. To hear mass said by a priest who has signed the constitution would be scandalous. To attend the offices of a refractory priest would be dangerous. The bishop advises Louis XVI not to take holy communion, for 'His Majesty can only wash away in the eyes of God his contribution to this Revolution with a large number of deserving works.'

On Palm Sunday, Louis XVI nonetheless summons the refractory cardinal de Montmorency to say a private mass at the Tuileries. A national guardsman named Andouin denounces the service to the Club des Cordeliers, an embryonic political party founded by the lawyer Georges-Jacques Danton, the journalist Camille Desmoulins, and the physicist Jean-Paul Marat. In posters widely distributed through Paris, the club charges that the king 'is authorizing disobedience and revolt.'

On Easter Sunday, April 18, the royal family prepares to leave for Saint-Cloud, perhaps again to hear a mass said by a refractory priest. A crowd made up mainly of national guardsmen gathers outside the Tuileries and blocks the king's carriage. The national guard, a bourgeois militia commanded by the popular General Lafayette, is a loosely disciplined corps whose members keep their uniforms and weapons at home and are summoned when needed. Lafayette orders the crowd to let the king's carriage through but national guardsmen seize the horses' bridles. The king is kept waiting in the courtyard for one hour and a half as Lafayette harangues his men. 'You are behaving like enemies of the Constitution,' he says. 'In obstructing the king's will, you are making him seem like a prisoner and voiding all the decrees he has sanctioned.' The crowd's insults reach the king's ears, and he grumbles that 'it would be surprising that after having given freedom to the nation I were not free myself.' But he does not insist. He gets out of his carriage, saying: 'They do not want me to leave? It is not possible to leave? Well, then, I will remain.'

The day's lesson is twofold. The disobedience of the national guard proves that it cannot be counted on to defend constitutional monarchy, which, lacking troops, is exposed as a fragile thing, at the mercy of the first street riot. While Louis XVI, seeing his freedom of movement curtailed, decides that his only hope is escape. A coded letter dated April 20 from Marie Antoinette to the former Austrian ambassador to Paris, Mercy d'Argenteau, says: 'What has just taken place confirms us in our plans . . . our position is terrible! We must absolutely flee in the coming month.'

Sixth Station: Refusing to remain a prisoner
of the mob, Louis XVI flees Paris with his
family on June 20, 1791, but is captured
and brought back

Allusions to the king's plan to flee with the help of the Austrian Emperor and royalist agents had been made as early as December, 1790, in Jean-Paul Marat's *Ami du Peuple*. Popular fears of an émigré royal family were revived in February, 1791, when Louis XVI's two pious maiden aunts, the daughters of Louis XV, left for Rome, where they could find solace in proximity to the pope. 'We must keep these nuns hostage,' Marat warned, 'and be on triple alert about the rest of the family.' The 'nuns' were arrested twice on their way to the border, and only a special order of the Assembly got them safely into Italy. Their departure sparked discussion of a law prohibiting emigration. Rumours of the king's impending flight grew more frequent. Such a rumour was probably at the origin of the crowd's obstruction on April 18. It was in any case this obstruc-

tion that confirmed the royal family's plan. Louis XVI's public behaviour after the April 18 incident was exemplary. He swore to
uphold the Constitution. He sent a diplomatic note to the monarchs
of Europe explaining his unconditional adherence to the Revolution
(while at the same time sending them private messages to pay no
heed to his public announcements).

A passport signed by the Minister of Foreign Affairs, de Mont-
morin, valid for a month, has been made out in June to the baroness
de Korff, a German lady of condition on her way to Frankfurt with
her two children, a valet, a lady-in-waiting, and three other servants.
The valet is Louis XVI, the lady-in-waiting is Marie Antoinette, the
maid is the king's sister Madame Elizabeth, the two children are the
king's son and daughter, and the baroness is the children's governess, the duchesse de Tourzel. The king's plan is to reach the
royalist general the marquis de Bouillé in Metz, rally loyal troops,
and dissolve the National Assembly. Far from the nightmare world
of Paris and its mob rule, he hopes to reign again.

Bouillé has posted 723 men in five detachments along the king's
route, to protect him in case of trouble. The troops are said to be
guarding the passage of a carriage full of gold to pay the soldiers at
the front. But there are also 600 armed men guarding the Tuileries,
under Lafayette's command, to keep the king from escaping. Senti-
nels are posted in the courtyard, on the terraces, and in front of the
royal apartments. Toward 11 P.M., however, there is a moment, after
the public retiring of the king in front of the few remaining
courtiers, when the guards are accustomed to seeing members of the
household leave the palace for the night. Louis XVI, with his passion
for minutiae, has compared in his notebook the distances of the
various Paris exits. Outside the Tuileries, Axel de Fersen, the
Swedish nobleman whose devotion to Marie Antoinette has led him
to organize the escape, is waiting in a carriage, disguised as a coachman. Marie Antoinette is undressed as usual by her ladies-in-waiting.
Once the lights are out she puts on a grey silk dress, a black hat, and
a veil. In his apartment, Louis XVI dons a dark frock coat and a hat
with a round crown. The king and the queen reach the carriage
separately. The children, the governess and the king's sister are
already there. The queen is half an hour late. The carriage reaches
the Saint-Martin gate, already behind schedule. There, a green and
white coach drawn by six horses and specially built for the trip is

waiting—it is upholstered in white Utrecht velvet and contains two chamber pots and canteens for food and wine.

The royal family is riding eastward into the night, toward Metz and safety. But at the first relay in the chalky plain of Champagne, Louis XVI is surprised to find the road deserted. His coach is two hours late. Fearing a mishap and not daring to attract too much attention, the friendly troops have withdrawn. Louis XVI is in good spirits, however, and already dreaming of conquering France at the head of loyal troops. 'Now I have finally left the city of Paris where I had to drink so many bitter cups,' he says. 'You may be sure that once my arse is in the saddle I will be a very different man from the one you have seen until now.' The passengers of the green and white coach are careful not to show themselves in towns. Once Louis XVI stops by the the side of the road to pass water behind a barn. At the village of Sainte-Menehould, the postmaster, Jean-Baptiste Drouet, recognizes the king. He has served seven years in the dragoons and seen him at parades. Also, the jowly, large-nosed face in the coach matches the portrait on the assignat in his pocket. Drouet gallops cross-country to cut off the coach. On the night of the 21st, after crossing the Argonne forest, the royal family arrives at the small town of Varennes, where the last relay is waiting at the Great Monarch hotel. Varennes is divided by the Aire River, and the coach stops on the opposite bank from the hotel, where Drouet, who has finally caught up, spots it. Drouet enters an inn, asks the owner 'Are you a patriot?' and is taken to see a grocer named Saucé, who has been elected prosecutor of the town. Saucé seals off the bridge, and when the coach drives up to the barricade, asks to see the passenger's papers. Under the pretext that the baroness de Korff's passport is not signed by the president of the Assembly, they are taken to Saucé's house, where Drouet compares his assignat with the king's profile. In the midst of an argument about the passengers' identity, Marie Antoinette loses her composure and says: 'If you think this man is your king you should at least show him some respect.' Saucé remembers that a judge Destez, who knows the king by sight, is stopping in Varennes. The man is awakened and led in. He falls to his knees and says: 'Ah, Sire.' Louis XVI says: 'Well, I am your king, and this is the queen and the royal family.'

Louis XVI, still hoping to continue his trip, tries to be ingratiating towards the grocer Saucé and his wife. He asks about conditions in the town, whether there are political clubs, whether the parish priest has signed the constitution for the clergy. He confides that he is not planning to go abroad, but just wants to briefly visit Montmédy to see some members of the Assembly. But the longer he waits the more critical his position becomes. News of the king's presence has caused a crowd of more than 10,000 to gather. A delegation of townspeople urges the king to return to Paris. Loyalist officers ready to free the king by force are dissuaded by the personal risks to the royal family. At seven the next morning, a courier brings a National Assembly decree suspending the king. Marie Antoinette crumples the decree into a ball, flings it to the ground, and says: 'The insolents.' Louis XVI pretends he is asleep.

The royal family is brought back to Paris with 6,000 armed men, during a humiliating and precarious four-day trip. Outside Sainte-Menehould, the comte de Dampierre waits by the side of the road to salute the king. He is the archetypal provincial nobleman of the old order, and behaves as though the Revolution has not taken place. He continues to enforce rigidly his feudal privileges and is not a favourite of the local peasantry. He is on horseback, wearing a grey cape, a braided hat, boots, and displaying his cross of the order of Saint Louis. He is carrying a rifle and two pistols are stuck in his belt. When the king's carriage passes he presents arms and then rides alongside it, reminding the king that he is related by marriage to one of his former ministers, the comte de Ségur. He insists, in spite of warnings, on riding next to the carriage until a group of peasants forces him off the road. He fires a rifle shot into the air and shouts 'Long live the king.' He gallops off across a field, with peasants and national guardsmen in pursuit. His horse slips in a ditch and throws him, but he is up and running until a bullet in the back stops him. Peasants armed with knives and pitchforks repeatedly plunge them into his body. Louis XVI inquires about the disturbance and is told: 'It's nothing, it's a man being killed.'

At Epernay, three National Assembly deputies who have come from Paris to meet the procession question the king about his escape. 'No, sirs,' he insists, 'I was not trying to leave, I declare it, it is true.' The deputies crowd into the coach with the royal family, practically sitting in the laps of the queen and the king's sister. One of them, Jerome Pétion, a fatuous, self-important man destined to become mayor of Paris that November, imagines that Madame Elizabeth, the king's sister, is leaning against him with languorous abandon. He regrets that his official position does not allow him to take advantage of the situation. Pétion is surprised that none of the women remember their 'needs' during the long day's carriage ride. He approves of the simplicity of Louis XVI, who personally unbuttons the dauphin's trousers and holds a silver goblet for him. When they stop for the night, the king invites the deputies to his table, but they fear that such familiarity will compromise them with the people and demur on the grounds of urgent correspondence.

It is clear that Louis XVI and his family are returning to Paris as traitors, not as monarchs. The crowd is more rabid than ever. Men shake their fists at the carriage and call Marie Antoinette a whore. When she puts the dauphin up to the window, they say: 'She can show us her brat as much as she wants, we know it isn't his.' Only the presence of the three deputies prevents the crowd from overturning the coach. The royal family reaches Paris on Saturday, June 25, at 8 P.M. The streets are lined with silent, hostile crowds. Posters warn that 'Whoever applauds the king will be beaten. Whoever insults him will be hanged.' When the coach rumbles on to the cobblestones of the Tuileries courtyard the guards refuse to present arms. The king and queen return to the Tuileries as though to a prison from which they had tried to escape. The palace, like a besieged fortress, is surrounded by the tents of soldiers, whose rowdy laughter reaches the king's windows. Sentries are posted in courtyards and on rooftops. Passageways linking the royal apartments are walled up. The door of Marie Antoinette's room must remain open, and one of General Lafayette's aides-de-camp chaperones her at night. The queen has a curtained bed placed in front of her own for privacy.

The National Assembly ratifies the decree suspending the king on June 25 pending the results of an investigation, but is alarmed by the breadth and turbulence of popular demonstrations. The conservative majority considers that there is a triple threat in revoking Louis XVI for his escape attempt: it would provide foreign powers with a pretext to invade France; it would create the problem of naming a regent; and it would further weaken a government already challenged by mob rule. Thus, Louis XVI is absolved of personal responsibility so that he may be maintained on the throne. On July 15, the investigating commission rules that he is innocent, that he was 'kidnapped.' The burden of guilt conveniently falls on the marquis de Bouillé, who has fled France and sent the Assembly a threatening note: 'You will answer to all kings for the king and his family's safety. If a single hair on their heads is touched, not a single stone in Paris will be left standing one on top of the other. I will lead the foreign armies there, I know the way.'

Even though the king has been saved from deposition despite his rash escape attempt, Varennes is a dividing line. Before Varennes, Louis XVI ruled, if no longer by divine right, at least in the name of some legal or constitutional principle. He was, perhaps, no longer 'king of France,' but he was still 'king of the French people.' But after Varennes, he remained on the throne at the convenience of the National Assembly, which kept him there for pragmatic reasons. Whether the king remained on the throne or not was no longer a question of right, divine or otherwise, but a question of political expediency. Louis XVI found himself completely swallowed and digested by the Revolution, and became nothing more than a factor in the nature of its outcome. Also, before his flight, there was still a deep reserve of popular attachment to the person of the king and the institution of the monarchy. Varennes created the image of a cowardly, treacherous king, ready to desert his people and make pacts with the nation's enemies. Faith in the necessity of the monarchy was badly shaken. During the king's absence there had been no disturbances. Things had gone on as usual. Varennes made the monarchy dispensable.

Seventh Station: On June 20, 1792, the mob invades the Tuileries and the king is forced to wear the Phrygian bonnet, symbol of the Revolution

The émigrés who have raised an army at Coblentz under the command of the king's brother, the comte de Provence, consider Louis XVI a captive of the Revolution and refer to him as 'king log' and to Marie Antoinette as 'the democrat.' But Louis XVI is not yet completely hamstrung. He still names ministers and ambassadors. He vetoes measures against the émigrés and loyalist priests, exclaiming with petulance: 'I do what others want often enough to allow me for once to do what I want.'

A popular demonstration is planned for the double anniversary of June 20: it is the anniversary of the tennis-court oath of June 20, 1789, the first act of defiance to the monarchy; and of the king's flight to Varennes, June 20, 1791, the failure of which made the king a hostage of the nation. On the morning of the 20th, the crowd pushes into the Tuileries Palace, and Marie Antoinette, hearing the sound of axes against doors, hides in a narrow passageway, behind a door concealed in a wood panel. Since it is impossible to restrain the crowd, which is shouting 'down with Mr. Veto,' and brandishing nooses and calves' hearts stuck on the points of pikes, Louis XVI agrees to receive 'his people' in the palace. Several grenadiers stand in front of the king with swords drawn, but sheathe them at his request. A member of the king's entourage says: 'Citizens, recognize your king—respect him—the law demands it. We will perish before we tolerate the least violence upon his person.'

A butcher named Legendre says: 'Listen to us, sir. You must listen to us . . . you are perfidious. You have always betrayed us, you are betraying us now. But beware, we have had enough. The people are tired of being your plaything.' The crowd demands that Louis XVI revoke his veto. He replies calmly: 'This is neither the time nor the place.' A municipal guard named Mouchet pulls a red Phrygian bonnet over the king's large head and another demonstrator hands him a glass of wine. 'It's poisoned,' someone shouts. 'In that case I will die without having signed the decrees,' says the king. A grenadier in the king's guard says: 'They have tried to frighten Your Majesty.' 'Touch my heart,' replies Louis XVI, 'and see if it is beating any faster than usual.'

Jerome Pétion, the mayor of Paris, arrives out of breath, and says: 'Sire, I have just learned the situation you are in.' 'That is highly surprising,' says Louis XVI, 'since the situation has already lasted two hours.' Pétion tries unsuccessfully to disperse the crowd. 'If you stay longer,' he says, 'you will give your enemies the chance to poison your respectable intentions.' He sends someone for the Legislative Assembly bell so that he can ring it to maintain silence. The king's serenity seems to impress the mob. To further take the edge off the demonstration, Louis XVI turns it into a guided tour by ordering the royal apartments opened for the crowd's visit. National guardsmen in red bonnets and fishwives in stained dresses file through the king's bedroom, commenting on the royal standard of living: 'Is that fat Veto's bed?' 'It's nothing like ours, is it?' They surprise Marie Antoinette in her dressing room, at her desk with her son at her side. Someone puts a Phrygian bonnet over her powdered head. She removes it and gives it to her son.

The crowd leaves peacefully. The warning to the tyrant has been turned into a sightseeing expedition. Louis-Jacob Hébert, the most

virulent of the revolutionary pamphleteers, who under the pseudonym of Père Duchesne usually refers to Louis XVI as 'that drunken
pig' or 'Capet-capon,' writes that he went to the Tuileries on June 20
and told Louis: 'Don't let your wife wear the trousers. That's all we
ask. Is that too much to ask in exchange for the thirty million we are
paying you?' (The king was now paid an annual allowance voted by
the Assembly.)

But Louis XVI has held to his veto and reports of his courage
rekindle his popularity. The real meaning of the day, however, is
that with the crowd's intrusion, the palace has lost the prestige of
inviolability. Respect is based on distance, and Parisians made themselves the king's familiars. From an object of worship, Louis XVI
became an object of curiosity, and finally, an object of contempt and
loathing. As Pierre-Louis Roederer, one of the king's aides, remarked after June 20: 'The steps of the palace seemed now at the
same level as the cobblestones of the Paris streets.'

*Eighth Station: On August 10, 1792, insurgents
attack the Tuileries Palace and massacre the Swiss
guards. The royal family is saved by seeking asylum
in the Legislative Assembly, but the monarchy
is overthrown*

Since April, France has been at war with Austria, a war destined
to involve all of Europe and continue intermittently until 1815.
Louis XVI's brother, the comte de Provence, has proclaimed himself
Regent in Coblentz, formed a cabinet, and placed his émigré army
at the service of Austria. Louis XVI, after the Varennes fiasco, has
based his hopes on foreign intervention. He favours the war with
Austria in the hope that the revolutionary armies will be defeated
and he will be restored. His declaration of war on his brother-in-
law, the Austrian Emperor Leopold II, is intended to hasten anarchy
in France. The Revolution has forced upon him a terrible dilemma:
to save his throne he must secretly seek the help of those with whom
his country is at war. Loyalty to the old order requires treason to the
new. Louis XVI, referring to himself in the third person, writes to
Leopold II after Varennes: 'The pretence of his remaining authority
being useless to accomplish good and prevent evil, the king resolved
to make one last attempt to recover his freedom and rally those
Frenchmen who truly wished the good of their country. But his

enemies and the factions made his plan fail and he is now under arrest and a prisoner in Paris. The king has resolved to let Europe know the condition he is in, and in confiding his troubles to his brother-in-law, he does not doubt that every measure dictated by his generous heart will be taken to help the king and the French kingdom.'

Although Louis XVI has managed to keep his collusion with the enemy secret, the possibility that a king could be an enemy rather than a saviour of the people is settling into the popular consciousness. The flight to Varennes and the abject return journey have exposed the royal family's true sentiments. Louis' use of the veto has also made him seem a foe of the Revolution. No one is clamouring yet for the king's overthrow, but some pamphleteers suggest that he be replaced by a regent.

On May 29, the royal guard of 1,800 men is dismissed as an economy measure and its commander, the duc de Cossé-Brissac, is court-martialled. On June 8, the Assembly decrees the formation of a camp of 8,000 National Guardsmen, or Federates, intended as a patriotic elite of volunteers from all over France, whose mission is to protect the capital in case of an enemy attack or a royalist coup. Their presence, it is hoped, will bolster morale.

As the ragged, turbulent Federates begin to arrive in Paris, Marie Antoinette places her hopes in the manifesto which the Duke of Brunswick, commander in chief of the Austrian armies, has promised to address to the French nation. She believes that a stern admonition from a foreign general will suffice to shield the royal family from the popular will, and writes to Fersen on July 24: 'Tell M. de Mercy [the former Austrian ambassador to Versailles] that the king and queen are in the greatest danger, that a delay of a single day can cause incalculable damage, that the manifesto must be immediately drafted, that we await it with extreme impatience, for it will necessarily rally a great many people around the king and guarantee his safety, and that otherwise no one can tell what will happen in the next 24 hours. The troop of assassins grows constantly.'

The Federates who make the strongest impression on the Paris populace are the Marseillais, who have heeded with Latin exuberance the call of the Commune for '600 men who know how to die.' After a final harangue from the mayor of Marseilles, who tells them to 'go make the tyrant, who sits on a throne he no longer deserves, tremble,' and after a twenty-seven-day march, here they are finally in the streets of the capital, stirring the crowds with their rousing battle hymn, which promises that *'le jour de gloire est arrivé.'* To the Jacobin Chaumette, 'they had come to save France . . . and seemed to be bringing the thunder to strike down tyranny.' To the moderate Thiébault, they were 'an irruption of brigands, five hundred mad dogs, three-quarters of them drunkards, sloppily dressed, almost all in red bonnets . . . stumbling from cabaret to cabaret.'

On August 1, the day after the Marseillais' flamboyant entrance into Paris, the Brunswick manifesto is published. Brunswick threatens to burn Paris and summarily execute all the national guards if Louis XVI and his family are not freed at once. The result of the manifesto, far from saving the royal family, hastens its fall, for Louis XVI cannot dissociate himself from the ultimatum. Now, for the first time, there are demands for his overthrow. The 2,900 Federates already in Paris are beginning to exert a political role under the influence of the Jacobin Club. They have formed a secret political directorate and their programme is the king's disgrace. Their agents lobby in the Assembly and chastise the moderate Gironde party as 'hermaphroditic' for its efforts to maintain order. Political initiative is slipping from the Assembly and into the hands of the Federates and the forty-eight Paris 'sections,' one of which decreed on July 31 that it no longer recognizes Louis XVI as king.

The Assembly voids the decree on August 4, but cannot void the growing public agitation. The most incredible rumours circulate: that Louis XVI is having built an enormous guillotine with thirty blades, the quicker to liquidate revolutionary leaders, and that each point of the Tuileries grill work is destined to be decorated with the head of a patriot. The Federates and the Paris districts believe the king is about to either launch a counterrevolutionary coup or try to escape. Lafayette has in fact urged him to escape, but he has declined, preferring to wait in Paris for the liberating army of the Duke of Brunswick.

The August 10 insurrection is the most carefully plotted of the three great revolutionary riots. July 14 was a confused search for weapons and ammunition, which became, through the dynamics of mob action, a successful but unplanned attack on the Bastille. The October riots were partly organized and partly spontaneous, but also went far beyond their original goal. A protest conducted mainly by women against the scarcity of bread turned into a demand for the

king's return to Paris. In both cases there were unproven charges of
secret conspiracies and fortunes spent to manipulate crowds; no
leaders could be discovered. The peculiar character of the August
insurrection is that it is untainted by rumours of conspiracy, precisely because it was openly organized by known leaders whose aims
were clear. The event and the date had been so well publicized in
Paris that on August 10 only 300 of its 750 members had the temerity
to attend the Assembly meeting. Louis XVI himself, usually the last
person to know of any development, was expecting trouble and had
brought his regiment of 900 Swiss guards from their suburban
barracks and ordered them to bivouac around the palace.

The headquarters of the insurrection is the church of the Enfants-
Trouvés, where the wealthy brewer Antoine-Joseph Santerre commands one of the forty-eight Paris sections. Santerre is an aristocrat
of the Revolution, a baron of hops and riots, a veteran of July 14
who has been named secretary of the 'Victors of the Bastille' organization. He is a popular figure, as generous with his beer as he is with
his rabble-rousing harangues. He has given the Assembly an ultimatum: they have until August 9 at midnight to reach a decision
concerning Louis XVI. On the night of August 9, the Marseille and
Breton Federates are incorporated into the Paris sections, and Santerre asks each section to elect three commissioners, who invest the
Hôtel de Ville as the representatives of revolutionary authority,
while Mayor Pétion is placed under guard.

At the Tuileries, 200 armed courtiers who have vowed to defend
the royal family take up positions in the palace. The commander of
the national guard, Mandat de Grancey, has positioned his 2,600
men in the Tuileries gardens and courtyards. But they are short of
gunpowder. Some have only enough to fire one round. Mandat goes
to the Hôtel de Ville, only to be arrested by the Communards, who
have managed to obtain a copy of his order telling the guards to fire
from behind on crowds marching on the Tuileries. Mandat is
ordered to be transferred to the Abbaye prison, but is murdered on
the way. Santerre's plan of attack is for two sections, one coming
from the right bank and one from the left, to meet behind the palace,
at the Carousel arch. The left bank section finds the Pont-Neuf
defended by a guards battalion armed with cannon, which agrees to
withdraw. It crosses the bridge as dawn breaks, arriving at the
Carousel shortly after six. Horse guards occupying the Carousel fall
back without resisting. Moisson, leader of the Marseille Federates in

the left bank section, sees the guards' cannons in the palace courtyard pointing at them and fears he has been lured into a trap. For two hours, the left bank section waits uneasily in the Carousel for Santerre and his columns to arrive.

Inside the palace, La Chesnaye, who has succeeded Mandat as commander-in-chief of the guards, says his men are grumbling about the presence of armed irregulars. Marie Antoinette, whom the prospect of the monarchy's last stand seems to have brightened, says: 'I can answer for all the men who are here. They will march in front, behind, in the ranks, wherever you like. They are reliable, and ready for anything.'

As Santerre's columns reach the Carousel (he has been delayed by a section chief who refuses to march), Pierre-Louis Roederer, an adviser to Louis XVI, inspects the guards' positions in the Tuileries gardens. A gunner asks: 'Sir, will we be obliged to fire upon our brothers?' 'You are here only to guard this door and prevent its access,' Roederer replies. 'You will fire only if fired upon, and anyone who takes a shot at you will no longer qualify as your brother.' 'And if they do fire, where will you be?' asks another gunner, who removes the powder and lighted wick from his cannon, throws the wick on the ground, and stamps it out. Roederer sees the Paris section troops gathering in the Carousel, and sees the fraternization between the Federates and loyal troops.

Roederer finds Louis XVI in his study, sitting vacant-eyed, his hands on his knees. 'You have not five minutes to lose,' he tells the king. 'There is no safety for you except in the Assembly—there are not enough men left to defend the palace.'

'But I did not see so very many people in the Carousel,' says the king.

'Sire, there are twelve cannons and immense crowds arriving from the faubourgs.'

Marie Antoinette and Madame Elizabeth have entered the study with a lace merchant and court furnisher named Gerdret, who echoes Roederer's alarm.

'Be silent, Monsieur Gerdret,' Marie Antoinette says sharply. 'You are in no position to raise your voice here. One who has done wrong should not give the impression that he is trying to repair it. Be silent, sir. . . .' Turning to Roederer, the queen says: 'But, sir, we have strong defences.'

'Madam, all Paris is on the march,' says Roederer, who is losing

389

his patience and tells the king: 'Sire, time is running out; this is not a supplication we have brought before you; it is not advice we have taken the liberty to offer; there is no other choice—we beg permission to drag you off.'

Louis XVI gives in, but Madame Elizabeth asks Roederer whether he accepts responsibility for the king's life. 'Yes, madam, as on my own,' he replies, 'I will walk immediately ahead of him.' Marie Antoinette is seething at the indignity of asking the very authority which has reduced the powers of the monarchy for asylum. She had hoped that her 200 diehard followers and the loyal Swiss could win a decisive victory for the monarchy. She says she would rather be nailed to a palace wall than go to the Assembly, but the shouts of the Federates have become audible, and she reluctantly follows the king and the dauphin between two rows of guards for a walk of several hundred yards through the garden to the Manège, a refurbished riding academy where the Assembly is sitting.

They make a forlorn procession, walking ankle-deep in dead leaves, with Marie Antoinette wearing a simple white bonnet to cover her hair, which has turned grey in the last eight months. 'There are a great many leaves,' Louis XVI remarks, 'they are falling early this year.' The seven-year-old dauphin is having a fine time kicking leaves at his parents. The king changes hats with the guard on his right. The surprised and frightened guard removes the king's white-plumed hat and puts it under his arm. The royal family reaches the Manège at ten. A grenadier picks up the dauphin and seats him on one of the secretaries' desks. 'I have come here to avoid a great crime,' the king tells the Assembly. 'I do not think I could be safer anywhere than among you, sirs.' 'You may count on the firmness of the National Assembly,' president Vergniaud replies. 'Its members have sworn to die to uphold the rights of the people and constitutional authority.' The king and his family are asked to wait in the small loggia behind the president's bench, normally used by journalists who record the deliberations in a kind of shorthand.

Roederer believes that by removing the king from the Tuileries he has defused the insurrection. What would be the point of attacking an empty palace? In addition, the National Guards have defected to the Paris sections. Their cannons are now turned against the Tuileries. There are still troops defending the palace, however: Marie Antoinette's guard of nobles, and the Hundred-Swiss, a regiment commanded by the marquis de Maillardoz, whose motto is:

> My soul to God,
> My life to the king,
> My heart to the ladies,
> And my honour to keep.

An officer of the Hundred-Swiss, Louis de Saint-Venant, had recently written to his family: 'The odds are ten to one that he [the king] will be assassinated soon . . . yesterday we decided unanimously that if the king was a victim of a misfortune . . . we would be dishonoured if there were not at least 600 red uniforms lying on the steps of the Tuileries.' Each Swiss has fifteen rounds of ammunition in his pockets and sixty more in his cartridge-pouch. At 9 A.M. they are ordered to evacuate the courtyard and take position inside the palace, where their shakos and blood-red jackets show between the columns and behind open windows. The porter of the central courtyard, seeing it emptied of troops, opens the gate to the insurgents. The Marseillais wave their red bonnets and shout that the Swiss will be well treated if they lay down their arms. An Alsatian Federate named Westermann harangues them in German. Several Swiss throw their weapons out the window and go over to the insurgents. But as the deserting Swiss cross the courtyard arm in arm with insurgents, a shot is fired from the head of a stairway.

In the Manège, Roederer hears the crack of muskets and the cries of wounded men and realizes that his efforts to head off the battle have failed. A salvo from a gallery where many of the queen's nobles are stationed kills Moisson, the leader of the Marseille Federates. The Swiss captain Durler charges into the courtyard with 200 men, routs the Federates, and captures four cannon. He pursues the Federates into the Carousel, but reinforcements are streaming in from the faubourgs and Durler is forced to fall back to the palace. Repeatedly, the disciplined and accurate fire of the Swiss repulses the disorderly charges of the popular army, until the courtyard is littered with bodies. But the Swiss are running out of ammunition. At 11, a Swiss officer manages to reach the Assembly building and see the king, who tells him: 'Lay down your arms, I do not want such brave men to perish.' The king's scribbled order is handed to the marquis de Maillardoz: 'The king orders the Swiss to lay down their arms instantly and return to their barracks.' The barracks have been burned down by an insurgent leader named Fournier the American, who brags that for want of paper, he started the fire with Assignats.

In the panic that follows, some Swiss are able to retreat through the Tuileries garden and find refuge in the Assembly. Some of the queen's nobles, disguised as servants, escape through secret Tuileries tunnels. But the bulk of the Swiss cannot escape, so they stand and fight, and in that stifling August noon they offer themselves as sacrifices to the last day of the monarchy. The monument in Lucerne erected to the memory of the Swiss mercenaries who died on August 10 lists the names of exactly 600 soldiers and 26 officers. Eye-witnesses testify to the savagery of the Federates on that day. Mathieu Dumas saw young men in the place Vendôme throw heads in the air and catch them on the point of pikes, and women throw themselves on the bodies of the Swiss like hyenas. Napoleon, then a young artillery captain, said that on none of his own battlefields was he ever seized by such an overwhelming impression of carnage as in the Tuileries on August 10.

The insurgents occupy the royal apartments, throw Marie Antoinette's books out of windows, pierce mattresses and quilts and send the feathers flying. Several thieves are summarily executed, and the jewellery and gold found in the palace are presented to the Assembly. Documents proving that Louis XVI supports the invasion army threatening France have also been found. On the same day, the revolutionary Commune is proclaimed and the royal family is arrested. The moderate voices of the Assembly, asking that the royal family be transferred to the Luxembourg Palace, are silenced by the victorious Commune. On August 13, Louis XVI, Marie Antoinette, the dauphin, Madame Royale, and Madame Elizabeth are jailed in the Temple, a fortress built by the society of Templars and converted to a prison after the Order's persecution and disbandment in the fourteenth century. On the same day the guillotine is installed on the place du Carousel, and begins its work of painless decapitation eight days later, on three royalist agents.

The Paris sections (forty-two out of forty-eight had taken part in the August 10 battle) and the Federates had swept the Tuileries Palace clean, not only of the royal family, but of the liberal nobility which had sought to stabilize constitutional monarchy. Lafayette himself, the 'hero of Two Worlds,' the idol of the Paris crowds, fled to Belgium after an abortive attempt to raise an army to march on the capital. August 10 also doomed the Assembly, which had in the opinion of its radical wing and the insurrectional Commune temporized too long. It was replaced by a new political body, the National Convention.

Ninth Station: The betrayal of Louis XVI
by a member of the royal family

If Louis XVI represents the blood sacrifice which the new order claimed from the old, his cousin, the duc d'Orléans, represents the attempt to survive the old order by betraying his family and his class. D'Orléans donned the Phrygian bonnet with such eagerness that he voted for the death of the king to demonstrate his patriotic zeal. He tried to live, like a salamander, amid the fires of the Revolution.

His was the collateral branch of the Bourbon crown. He was, like Louis XVI, a direct descendant of the dynasty's founder, Henri IV. The Orléans were thus the closest figures to the crown after the king's own children, and there arose among them a tradition of rivalry and muted hostility to the monarch and support of opponents to the king. It was always possible that an Orléans would succeed an impotent king, and wary monarchs encouraged their vices to keep them at bay from state affairs. Thus, the Orléans could count among their family traits excessive hedonism, occasional liberalism, and a curious function as the crown's disloyal opposition.

Louis-Philippe-Joseph I (duc d'Orléans and, later, Philippe Egalité), who was seven years the senior of Louis XVI, resembled him physically, with the same fullness of figure and the same Roman nose. But he was like a flawed cast of the same mould, with a red, blotchy complexion that hinted at some skin disease, and the small shifty eyes of a fox. He was the wealthiest and most prestigious figure in France after the king. Thanks to his inherited *apanages* (tax-free gifts from the kings to their brothers), his land holdings totalled 9,209 square miles, or 5 per cent of the total territory of France. He owned most of several provinces. His income, which wavered in the vicinity of 6 and 7 million livres a year, was, respectively, three and seven times greater than the incomes of the king's two brothers, the comte de Provence and the comte d'Artois. This kingdom within a kingdom was administered by a committee of twenty and hundreds of notaries, inspectors, treasurers and accountants. D'Orléans lived with a splendour suitable to his rank in the

Palais Royal, attended by forty-five servants, and he came to represent, since the king was at Versailles, a kind of second monarch for the Parisians.

Because of his betrayal of the crown to which he owed his wealth and position, Philippe d'Orléans has, like a Judas, been held responsible over the years for a fantastic repertory of crimes. Talleyrand said he was 'the pail into which all the garbage of the Revolution was thrown.' It was said that this 'Jacobin Caliban' bribed assassins to murder Louis XVI and plotted to poison the queen; that he was responsible for the capture of the Bastille and all the subsequent popular uprisings; that he bribed a whore to give his brother-in-law a fatal venereal disease; and many other even more preposterous charges.

D'Orléans' record is bad enough without artificial blackening. But it is the record of a cynical, opportunistic, and weak man, not of a determined conspirator capable of overthrowing regimes and murdering rulers. D'Orléans' modest ambition was not to rule but to survive, and even in this he failed. From the record of his life emerges a man who realized that traditional values were bankrupt and yet wanted to keep his wealth and privileges, who was pushed from one expediency to the next into the front ranks of the Revolution, not because he loved the people or believed in liberty, but because he had come to hate the royal family and did not want to share its fate. The comte de la Marck, who knew him well, said that the mainspring of his character was 'a feeling of hatred and vindictiveness [towards the royal family] which dominated his personality with a fanaticism unique in his makeup.' He had no faith in the Revolution, and when the Estates General met in May, 1789, he bet 100 louis that they would separate without even having abolished sealed letters.

He had nothing of the Republican, and would in an earlier age have made a perfect courtier, one of those futile young men so lacking in resources that missing a pleasure is reason for despair, so eager for amusement that a trifle delights them. He was a steady customer of Madame Brissaud's fashionable brothel. Once, according to the report of a police spy, he sought out the favours of a Mademoiselle Durancy, who refused to renew the experience because 'the prince was extremely crude in his lovemaking, lacking all delicacy and swearing like a cart-driver . . . everything in him announces a debauched and libertine nature.'

He earned a reputation for supercilious wit. One of his sallies, about an ageing duchess who had stooped to recruting lovers among the bourgeoisie, was: 'For a bourgeois, a duchess is never over thirty.' Asked what he thought of low necklines, he said: 'I find the fashion most fetching. There is nothing so stylish as nudity.' He had, with the younger brother of Louis XVI, the comte d'Artois, divided the women at court into seven categories: beautiful, pretty, passable, ugly, awful, infamous, and abominable.

In 1769, Philippe married the sixteen-year-old daughter of the duc de Penthièvre, a descendant of the comte de Toulouse, bastard son of Louis XIV. The Sun King's generosity to his illegitimate off-spring had made the Penthièvre family almost as rich as the d'Orléans. Philippe at first probed marriage possibilities gingerly, for the duc de Penthièvre had a son and heir, the prince de Lamballe. But when he learned that an operation had made the prince sterile (rumour said Philippe had 'infected' the young man with a Miss David, who played walk-on parts at the Opera), the match was sealed over the protests of Louis XV himself, who knew that Philippe would be wealthier than his own children. The bride and groom were such close relatives (the thin blood of the Bourbons flowed through them both) that a papal dispensation was required for the wedding. Philippe was clearly marrying to increase his wealth and position, and showed little interest in his teenage bride, save eventually to sire three sons and two daughters. The tradition at marriages of Blood Princes in which the groom offers thirteen gold pieces to symbolize the purchase of the bride seemed particu-larly apt.

Philippe's life of diligent futility continued. He spent hours on card tricks and juggling lessons, and introduced in Paris (where gambling was illegal) a dice game called Kreps. He had a series of mistresses, one of whom, Madame de Genlis, became governess of his children. He preferred the Palais Royal to Versailles, where he was in the shadow of the royal family. In 1771, the comte de Clermont, Grand Master of the Masons, died. Philippe accepted his succession and received a sword decorated with his and the Masons' coat of arms. Freemasonry, an English import, was popular with the liberal nobility, and the rosters of the various lodges listed some of the most famous names in France. There is no doubt that Masonic lodges were culture mediums for new ideas and meeting places for men of different social backgrounds. But Philippe's role was largely honorific. The dilettantism which infected everything he did made him an indifferent Grand Master. As he later wrote: 'At a time when no one could foresee our Revolution, I had joined the Freemasons, who offered a sort of image of equality, as I had joined the Parlements, who offered a sort of image of liberty. I have long since given up the ghost for the reality.'

Philippe took an increasingly divergent path from the crown, but there was no open break until 1777, when he sought glory on the high seas. He joined the fleet of Admiral Count d'Orvilliers in the summer of 1778, and was given command of an eight-gun frigate named the *Saint-Esprit*. But after the first engagement there were reports that he had turned tail at the sight of the English fleet. In Paris, songs to the effect that Philippe had better restrict his naval manoeuvres to the pond in the Tuileries garden became popular. Louis XVI let him know that it would be unwise to pursue a naval career, and revived for him the obsolete army rank of Colonel-General of the Hussars. Philippe's failure made him openly hostile to the court. On his rare visits to Versailles, said one courtier, he seemed 'like an enemy searching for victims.' In 1779 he suffered another humiliation when he was refused permission to join Admiral Rochambeau's expedition to the United States. Marie Antoinette told him, to spare him 'the severe form of a letter from the king,' to stay in France.

From a naval career, Philippe turned to property speculation. He lived in and owned the Palais Royal, built in 1629 for the cardinal de Richelieu, and eventually inherited by the Orléans family. He surrounded part of the spacious gardens with three arcaded new wings, modelled on Saint Mark's Square in Venice, and rented apartments and shops. It was an enormously successful venture. The Palais Royal became the most fashionable residential section of Paris as well as the centre of Parisian life. The gardens, formerly open only to the aristocracy, became accessible to all. A wooden gallery squaring the three new wings had partitions for shops and was dubbed 'the Tartar's camp.' There were bath houses, restaurants, club houses, dressmakers, hairdressers, a cutlery store (where Charlotte Corday bought the knife to stab Marat), and two famous cafés, the Foy and the Gaveau. Daily entertainment was provided by a circus, concert halls, and a fireworks display. Philippe ruled benevolently over a colourful, animated, and socially mixed crowd of pleasure-seekers who turned the garden into a daily carnival. He became a famous and popular figure, the only prince Parisians saw regularly.

On the eve of the Revolution, the Palais Royal was the best thermometer of political fever in Paris. The cafés became annexes of the Estates General and orators stood on tables to shout out the principles of a new society. The English traveller Arthur Young was astonished when he visited the Palais Royal on June 9, 1789, by the 'singular spectacle' of speakers damning the monarchy before wildly enthusiastic crowds. 'I am surprised that the ministry should permit such nests of sedition and hotbeds of revolt,' he wrote.

Philippe's hostility to the crown became public during the battle between Louis XVI and the Paris Parlement in 1787. The king called a bed of justice on November 19 to force Parlement to ratify a series of government loans. But the usual procedure for a bed of justice, with its involved ceremonial and absence of debate, was not followed. Members of Parlement were allowed to speak, but not to vote. After the debate, Louis XVI ordered the ratification of his decree. Philippe rose and stuttered out a protest, astonishing Parlement, as he was notorious for his shyness and seldom took the floor. 'If the king is holding a Parlementary session,' he said, 'the voices must be gathered and counted; if this is a bed of justice he is imposing silence upon us.' The king was too taken aback to reply. 'Sire,' continued d'Orléans, 'allow me to lay at your feet my protest against the illegality of your orders.' 'It is legal because I want it to be legal,' blurted out the king to his cousin, and left the hall.

It was the first example in French history of a royal prince publicly siding with the king's opponents and questioning the legality of his decisions. As Talleyrand pointed out: 'There had been royal princes who, weapon in hand, resisted the power of a king; but none had ever attempted to place constitutional limits on a king's authority.' Philippe confided to his friend Brissot that he had acted out of spite rather than concern for the nation's welfare. 'Do not think I protested to serve a people I despise and an order to which I am indifferent,' he said. 'I was simply indignant that any man could treat me with such insolence.' 'And so,' writes turgid Carlyle, Philippe 'has cut his court-moorings, shall we say? And we will now sail and drift, fast enough, toward chaos? Thou foolish d'Orléans; Equality that art to be! Is royalty grown a mere wooded scarecrow; whereon thou, pert scald-headed crow, mayest alight at pleasure and peck?'

At 6 P.M. on the day after Philippe's outburst, the baron de Breteuil, a minister who specialized in passing on bad news because of his compassionate manner, handed him a sealed letter exiling him to his property of Villers-Cotterets, fifty miles from Paris. The comte de la Marck said that Philippe was 'grief-stricken at being exiled . . . he was like a child deprived of his toys.' Exile confirmed Philippe as the court renegade. He could not forgive the king for what he considered an unpardonable slight toward a person of his rank.

When Philippe was allowed to return to Paris in the spring of 1788, the capital was seething with the ferment of anticipation. Cafés were crowded with men hotly discussing the Estates General. The Masonic lodges were hearths of political agitation. Philippe was in the eye of the hurricane, the Palais Royal. Paid agents informed him daily about movements and conversations in the capital. He knew its mood better than anyone at Versailles. In October, on the recommendation of fellow Masons, Philippe hired as secretary a disgruntled artillery officer named Choderlos de Laclos, best-known as the author of a corrosive novel, *Les Liaisons Dangereuses*. Laclos became known as Philippe's 'black angel.' There were deep currents of sympathy between the two men, who both had unlimited faith in the corruptibility of human nature. After Laclos' arrival, the Palais Royal became a sort of ministry of propaganda for radical ideas. It was Laclos who overcame Philippe's rocklike apathy and helped draft a widely distributed and markedly liberal model *cahier de doléance*. It was Laclos who generated the idea of *Orléanism* as an alternative to the monarchy. To Philippe, the Estates General were a means of vengeance on Louis XVI for having exiled him. 'I don't care a hang what the Estates General are going to do,' he said. 'I only want to be a part of it for the moment when they discuss individual liberty, so that I can add my voice in favour of a law which will ensure that when I want to sleep at Raincy I will not be sent to Villers-Cotterets and that on the day I feel like leaving for London, Rome or Peking, nothing will prevent me.'

On April 26 and 27, crowds from the working-class faubourg Saint-Antoine district, angered by the alleged remarks of a wall-paper manufacturer named Réveillon that 'a worker can live on fifteen sous a day,' marched to the Seine shouting 'hang the rich' and 'bread for two sous.' They hanged Réveillon in effigy, and he asked for army protection. On April 28 the riots had grown to a full-scale workers' revolt. Between 5,000 and 10,000 men milled outside

Réveillon's home and factory, which had been turned into a fortress by 350 French guards. There were horse races at Vincennes that afternoon, and the carriages of the aristocracy had to cross the faubourg Saint-Antoine to reach the racecourse.

Demonstrators blocked the carriages, letting them pass only once the passengers had shouted: 'Long live the Third Estate.' Carriages bearing the duc d'Orléans' coat of arms, however, were applauded. When Philippe drove by he was cheered as 'the only true friend of the people.' He alighted from his carriage and told the crowd: 'Keep calm, my friends, keep calm, we are close to happiness.' He was applauded again when he distributed the coins in his purse, which led passengers in another carriage to remark: 'D'Orléans is reviewing his troops.' That afternoon, the duchess d'Orléans, returning from Vincennes in her own carriage, insisted on passing in front of the crowd and demanded that the guards let her through a barricade which blocked a street in front of the Réveillon factory. The crowd broke through the barrier. Troop reinforcements arrived and, in breaking up the riot, killed some 300 demonstrators and lost twelve of their own men. Some demonstrators were found dead in Réveillon's cellar, having mistaken bottles of varnish for more palatable beverages.

The Réveillon uprising marks the first attempt to explain the Revolution in terms of an Orléanist conspiracy. No evidence involving Philippe was found, but he was popularly believed to have paid the workers to riot. Thereafter, on every day of violence, from the capture of the Bastille to the invasion of the Tuileries in August, 1792, someone repeated the accusation that Philippe d'Orléans was pulling the strings, and manipulating thousands of rioters thanks to his paid agents. Actually, Philippe's temperament inclined him more to adapt himself to events than to control them. The marquis de Mirabeau, who kept urging him to use his popularity to assume a more active role in events, was disgusted by his apathy and finally wrote him off as 'a eunuch who has the desire without the potency.'

Philippe's eagerness to parade as a friend of the people kept the rumours of conspiracy alive. At the Estates General procession of May 3, he took his place with the Third Estate, although he was dressed in the costume of the nobility. The Master of Ceremonies whispered a few words in his ear and he moved ahead to join his own order, still refusing to march in the front line with the other Princes of the Blood. The crowd cheered him. When Louis XVI made his inaugural speech on the following day, Philippe sat with the deputies from his jurisdiction instead of with his order. The king summoned him and said: 'I am astonished not to see the First Prince of the Blood by my side. It seems that in these circumstances it is your duty not to abandon the king. Why secede from the other princes?' 'Sire,' replied Philippe, 'my birth gives me the right to be at Your Majesty's side at any time, but I think that at this moment I must place myself with the jurisdiction which sent me here.'

A popular hero had been manufactured thanks to a few simple exercises in image-building. Philippe was applauded whenever he appeared in public, and the Palais Royal was in a constant uproar. He was one of the forty-seven nobles who defected from their order on June 25 and joined the National Assembly. Proof of his popularity came when he was elected president of the Assembly by 533 votes out of 869, but he turned down his first chance to wield real power. He did not even become the spokesman for the liberal nobility. Paralysed by timidity, he was unable to deliver the speeches prepared for him by Laclos.

At the National Assembly session of August 4, when the vicomte de Noailles urged that the nobility abandon its privileges, one of the deputies remarked that the evening would probably cost Philippe a million and a half livres a year. 'Is that all?' he asked. 'In that case I am not worried. It is the end of all this . . . we will have to see.'

Responsibility for the October riots at Versailles was also attributed to Philippe. Belief in his covert involvement was so widespread that a playing card showing him as the king of spades was publicly sold (the spade card suit is called *pique* in French, a word which also means pike, and the designation was a reference to the rumour that Philippe had distributed 600 pikes on the day before the march on Versailles). A prosecutor investigating his role in the riots heard 388 witnesses and ruled that there was evidence to indict Philippe. But he was overruled by an Assembly committee whose chairman, Chabroud, was dubbed 'the whitewasher.' Even though he had been absolved, the inquiry left Philippe under a cloud. Lafayette, who was personally convinced of his guilt, told him to leave for England 'in your own interest, for no one is so compromised as you are.' Louis XVI found a mission for him, which involved ferreting out the degree of English involvement in French affairs. Philippe told his cousin he would 'try to discover in London the authors of the troubles.' He left in October with the faithful Laclos and one of his mistresses, Madame de Buffon, and his voluntary self-exile has been interpreted by some historians as evidence of his guilt.

But Mirabeau, who was trying to build up Philippe as an alternative to Louis XVI, was furious that he had left because he felt that no legitimate charge could be made against him. This view is confirmed by Pierre-Louis Roederer, an official close to Louis XVI who survived the Revolution to serve Napoleon, to whom he said: 'Mirabeau always said that too much importance had been given the duc d'Orléans in the events of October 5 and 6. I knew him personally and I believe that if there was an Orléans conspiracy he was not a part of it. He never said a single word to indicate it.'

Philippe was allowed to return to France in July, 1790, and was named Admiral of France, an empty title since there was no fleet. After a meeting with Philippe arranged by the Secretary of the Navy, Bertrand de Molleville, Louis XVI said: 'He is returning to the fold and intends to do whatever he can to repair the evil committed in his name and in which he may have had less of a part than we believe.'

It was too late for Philippe to return to the fold. He was stigmatized as an enemy of the crown. The rare times he attended court, he was insulted, and on one occasion, spat on. The marquis de Ferrières wrote that the sight of Philippe at court 'inspired a feeling of such horror that the women turned their backs on him and the men stared at him with contempt. Everyone believed he had come to lend his hand to some new crime.'

At the same time, Philippe was increasingly committed to the Revolution. The only way for someone of his background to prove his loyalty to the movement was to be more revolutionary than the revolutionaries. Thus, in November, 1790, he joined the Jacobin Club, which claimed revolutionary infallibility. He was discussed by its members as a possible regent, but insisted that he wanted to remain 'a simple citizen.' He tried to cast off the onus of his social position by telling the club that he was not his father's son, and had been sired by a coachman named Lefranc. In 1792 he sent his daughter Adélaide to the safety of England, and the tone of his correspondence with her shows the forced fervour of someone who knew his letters were opened and read. After the August 10, 1792, attack on the Tuileries and the massacre of the Swiss guards, he wrote that it was 'an abominable plot formed against our liberty,' by the king and queen. One of the victims of the September, 1792, massacres was the princess de Lamballe, Philippe's sister-in-law and a loyal friend of Marie Antoinette who had returned from the safety of exile to be near the queen. She wore a ring which contained a strand of the queen's hair, with the words 'misfortune has whitened them.' Her severed head on a pike was brought by the mob under Philippe's window at the Palais Royal. He came to the window and saluted it.

To mark the end of class privileges, the Paris Commune officially gave Philippe the family name of Egalité and renamed the Palais Royal the Garden of the Revolution. In a ceremony at the Hôtel de Ville, Philippe said: 'Citizens, with extreme gratitude I accept for myself and my children the name the Paris Commune has given me; none could be chosen that better reflects my feelings and opinions.' After the ceremony he ran into an acquaintance to whom he confided: 'What could I do? I had come to plead for my daughter who had been declared an émigré and I had to sacrifice my distaste for this burlesque name to that overwhelming interest.' As further proof of his revolutionary zeal, he posted a placard on his door announcing that anyone in his employment who called him by his title would be fined 5 sous, the proceeds going to the wives of soldier-citizens at the front.

In September, the Convention replaced the Legislative Assembly, and Philippe was elected last on the list of representatives from Paris. Lepeletier de Saint-Fargeau, who had been president of the Assembly, gave Philippe this bit of political advice: 'Anyone with an income of 400,000 livres should either be in Coblentz [with the émigrés] or on the summit of the Mountain [the radical wing of the Convention].' Thus, Philippe sat with the Jacobins like Robespierre, Marat, and Saint-Just. Since he almost never spoke, but automatically stood to vote with the extremists of the Mountain, the journalist-deputy Camille Desmoulins called him 'a sitting and standing Robespierre.'

He placed his great fortune at the service of the Revolution. In 1810, Napoleon was shown several cartons of d'Orléans' papers, and saw that they included a number of receipts for financial contributions to revolutionary leaders. 'This proves that the duc d'Orléans was not an evil man,' the emperor said. 'He was only the instrument of agitators, who compromised him to extract money from him, and it seems that once they began there was no limit to their demands.'

Napoleon ordered the papers, so compromising to so many historic figures, to be burned.

But if he was not an evil man, nor was he a courageous one. When Louis XVI went on trial for conspiracy against the state in December, 1793, Philippe promised his three sons that he would refuse to take part in the votes on the king's guilt and sentence. He pledged that 'nothing will make me vote against Louis XVI.' He would not have been alone, for twenty-seven members of the Convention abstained 'for personal reasons.' One had the courage to say he was not voting because he believed in the inviolability of the monarch. Others said they were not competent to try a criminal case, or that they had not attended the entire trial. Orléans, as a relative of the accused, had the best reason of all.

On the morning of January 15, when the first vote was to take place, two Conventionnels named Merlin and Treilhard came to see Philippe at the Garden of the Revolution. Abstaining, they argued, would be interpreted as a disapproval of the trial. A motion to banish Philippe and the rest of the Bourbon family was due for debate after the trial. If he was absent for the vote on Louis XVI, the Convention would doubt his loyalty to the nation and he would damage his own position. Philippe followed them to the Convention hall.

Here were two Bourbon princes, both descendants of Henri IV and Louis XIV, signatories of one another's marriage contracts, one of whom was in line to succeed to the other's crown; Louis XVI was also the godfather of Philippe's oldest son. Their lives were interwoven, but in the Convention hall, one was in the dock while the other, squinting through his lorgnette, was a member of the jury.

When Philippe's turn came, he voted for his cousin's death. Afterwards he explained lamely to his English mistress, Grace Dalrymple Elliott: 'I do not own myself. I obey what surrounds me.' Two days later, Philippe attended the execution of Louis XVI. He had tried to exorcize guilt by association by denying compassion by association. But he too became the victim of a member of his family. His twenty-two-year-old son the duc de Chartres had fled France and joined the émigré army, and letters to his father in which he accused the Convention of pushing France into 'an abyss' were intercepted and led to Philippe's demise.

On April 8, 1793, he was having dinner with a friend, M. de Monville, when news was brought that he was under arrest. He complained bitterly to his host that he had done everything in his power to prove his patriotism. Monville was squeezing half a lemon over a fried sole and said: 'They have obtained all they wanted from you . . . and now they are doing to you what I am doing to this lemon,' which he proceeded to fling into the fireplace, adding 'Eat your sole while it is hot.'

Philippe was jailed in a fort in Marseilles with his two younger sons, and refused to believe that anything could seriously be held against him. His record as a patriot, his conduct during the king's trial, his abdication of dynastic rights, the many favours he had done for some of the most rabid members of the Convention, seemed like sufficient collateral for survival. He remained optimistic, and told his sons that he was the victim of a judicial error. In November he was taken to Paris and jailed in the Conciergerie. He slept in the same trestle bed Marie Antoinette had used for seventy-six days before going to the guillotine on October 15. His valet shared his room. On the fifth day, he was brought to the same grand-chamber of Parlement where in 1787 he had led the resistance to the king. He heard the revolutionary tribunal (which had been created with the help of his own vote) list charges of treason with the kind of determined bad faith which made someone call it 'the only tribunal which delivered death sentences for misdemeanours.'

He heard the death sentence pronounced by the Jacobin judges whose fanaticism he had tried so desperately to adopt, and said: 'Since you were bent on having me perish, you might at least have found more plausible pretexts.'

On November 6, the day of his execution, he ate oysters, two chops, and downed two-thirds of a bottle of Bordeaux. He dressed carefully, in suede trousers, a white waistcoat, a green dress coat, and polished black boots. His hair was powdered and curled as though he were going to court. His tumbril stopped in front of the Palais Royal, which bore a sign that said NATIONAL PROPERTY. He shouted one short, obscene word. On the scaffold, the executioners wanted to remove his boots, but he said: 'Leave that, it is a waste of time, it is far easier to remove the boots of a corpse. Hurry up.'

Tenth Station: The trial and execution of Louis XVI

On September 21, 1792, the new political executive publishes its first decree: 'The National Convention decrees unanimously that royalty is abolished in France.' Government proclamations are now to be dated 'Year I of the Republic.' Louis Capet, as he is now called, reads Tacitus in the Temple prison while a legislative committee studies his case to decide whether there are grounds for his indictment. Louis gives his eight-year-old son history and geography lessons, and Marie Antoinette does embroidery. Madame Royale, Louis' fifteen-year-old daughter, complains that the municipal guards use the familiar *tu* form in addressing her. There is also a pipe-smoking guard who makes a point of blowing smoke in Louis' face. Graffiti predicting 'the tyrant's' decapitation mark courtyard walls, and rocks are thrown at the king from a window during his stroll one day.

The Convention is in no hurry to try the king. It realizes, as Danton has observed, that 'to try him is to kill him.' But on November 20, a locksmith named François Gamain, in whom the king has placed his trust, shows members of the Convention an iron safe he built for the king in a secret compartment in the Tuileries palace. As his reward, Gamain is named to the commission charged with removing royalist inscriptions from monuments. The 625 documents found in the safe force the Convention's hand. They prove that Louis XVI has been corresponding with the émigrés, negotiating with Austria, paying agents like Mirabeau to subvert patriots, and that, far from resigning himself to the Revolution, he has been plotting its dawnfall and his own restoration.

The trial opens on December 11, over two different sets of objections: moderates in the Gironde object to the trial because they fear that the king's almost cerain death will precipitate the dictatorship of the triumvirate, as the leaders of the 'Mountain'—Marat, Robespierre, and Danton—are called. Robespierre himself objects that Louis XVI cannot be tried because he has already been condemned by the people. 'To propose to put Louis XVI on trial, in whatever manner,' he says, 'is to retrograde towards royal and constitutional despotism; it is a counterrevolutionary idea which puts the Revolution itself in question . . . the people does not judge like a court of justice, it does not sell sentences, it unleashes thunder; it does not condemn kings, it plunges them into void.'

Louis XVI is charged with conspiracy against the state. Thanks to the disclosures of Gamain, the king's guilt is manifest. But because his life depends on a jury of 749 Conventionnels, who are judging him against a backdrop of party and leadership struggles, the procedure seems like a cross between a secular inquisition, a mock trial, and a political convention. Louis XVI appears on the opening day in the oval salle de Manège, where the Conventionnels occupy benches according to their political affiliation, and where fashionable ladies sit in a loggia decorated with tricolour ribbons, nibbling oranges and sipping cordials. The president of the Convention, Bertrand Barère, a thirty-eight-year-old lawyer and admirer of Rousseau (he has arranged to have a pension paid to Jean-Jacques' widow), intones: 'Louis, the French nation accuses you,' and reads the long indictment. The king denies everything and obtains a four-day suspension to choose his lawyers and prepare his defence.

One of his lawyers is Malesherbes, who as head of the king's library under Louis XV had protected writers like Rousseau from the bookburners. Malesherbes is seventy-two, and has volunteered to defend Louis XVI after a lawyer younger than himself begged off for reasons of age. 'Your sacrifice is all the greater,' the king tells him, 'because you are exposing your own life even though you cannot save mine.' The other two lawyers are Raymond de Sèze and François-Denis Tronchet. At his first meeting with the king, de Sèze expresses surprise at his great calm. 'Is not misfortune man's best master?' asks the king.

The four-day interruption gives the Gironde time to plan its tactics to try and stop the trial. The Girondist deputy Buzot links the trial of Louis XVI to the fate of all the Bourbons, and particularly Philippe d'Orléans. Buzot argues that Louis XVI cannot be tried unless the Convention votes the banishment of all Bourbons. 'You have immolated him to public safety,' he says, 'you owe to this same safety the banishment of all his family . . . I ask that Philippe and his sons carry outside the Republic the misfortune of having been born near the throne . . . the misfortune of bearing a name that can only serve to rally the seditious or the emissaries of foreign powers.' The Convention votes the banishment but agrees to suspend its application until after the trial.

On December 26, Louis XVI interrupts a game of Siam (a form of lawn bowling) to testify in his own defence. He arrives at the Manège with a four-day beard, for he is no longer allowed to keep a razor, and he looks twice his thirty-eight years, sallow-faced, pouchy-eyed, his slovenly appearance an admission not of guilt but of defeat. He makes a pitiful defendant, lamely repeating 'I know nothing about that' when he is shown incriminating documents, refusing to recognize letters in his own handwriting, foolishly argu-

ing that he ignored the secret compartment's existence. At the end
of his testimony, Louis tells the Convention members most of
whom have defiantly refused to remove their hats while he spoke:
'I declare that my conscience reproaches me nothing and that those
who have spoken in my defence have said only the truth.' From a
back bench on the Montagne comes a shout: 'To hear him speak,
you would think he was innocent.' It is Philippe d'Orléans.

It is time for de Sèze to deliver his summing-up. He reminds the
Convention that the man in the dock is the same man who convened
the Estates General in 1789 and whom the Assembly, on the historic
night of August 4, called 'the restorer of French freedom.' De Sèze
is no spellbinder, he does not command the epic verb that might
move men sensitive to rhetoric. His manner is matter-of-fact, dry,
precise but uninspired. Louis XVI needs a Danton or a Vergniaud
(with his 'bronze voice') but the great orators on this day are his
judges, not his lawyers.

The vote on the verdict and sentence is broken up into four questions and begins on January 15. Various measures of intimidation
let the Conventionnels know that there is only one correct way to
vote. Marat browbeats the Convention into adopting a public ballot,
so that those who might have wanted to save the king must decide
whether they want to take the risk of being publicly identified. The
mood of the Convention is also influenced by the daily diatribes of
the revolutionary press. 'How long and complicated it is to cut off
a tyrant's head,' complains the père Duchesne, who refers to Louis
XVI as 'that snoring rhinoceros,' and 'that pig it cost us so much
to fatten.' Marat's *L'Ami du Peuple* reports the trial in a similar
vein, giving the impression that public opinion is impatiently thirst-
ing for the king's blood. Finally, after the revelations of the king's
secret documents, taking his defence leaves Conventionnels open to
charges of bribe-taking and corruption. Louis XVI's generosity with
secret funds has been proven, and ugly rumours stigmatize Conventionnels who dare to favour leniency.

Voting begins at noon on the first question: 'Is Louis Capet, king
of the French, guilty of conspiring against public freedom and
against the safety of the state? Yes or No.' Of the 749 members of
the Convention, 31 are absent and 27 abstain. All the others vote in
the affirmative. There are rumours of disapproval when d'Orléans,
voting with the Paris delegation, affirms his cousin's guilt. The
second question, voted on the same day, is: 'Should the judgment

passed on Louis be submitted for ratification by the people gathered in primary assemblies?' There may still be a majority of Frenchmen who deplore regicide, so that ratification by popular assemblies is in effect a device to save the king. Louis XVI is so sure that the vote on assemblies will be in his favour that he has already drafted a statement which is to be sent to the assemblies when they meet. Only 287 deputies vote for ratification. The Convention mistrusts the popular will and refuses to let the final decision be removed from its control.

After the second vote, Pierre-Louis Manuel, the Procurator General of the Paris Commune, who will later be guillotined for his efforts, tries to have a mistrial declared on the grounds that Philippe d'Orléans is taking part in it. 'Citizens,' he says, 'I recognize legislators here; but I have . . . never seen judges, for judges are as cold as the law, judges do not murmur, they do not exchange insults. This Convention never was a Tribunal; if it had been one, it would not have witnessed the closest relative of the accused lack the conscience and modesty to declare himself incompetent to judge.'

But the Convention disregards Manuel and proceeds to the third question: 'What sentence has Louis, the king of the French, incurred?' The vote on sentencing is on the Convention's order of the day for January 16, but other matters must be discussed first. While crowds chant 'to the guillotine' and workers from the faubourgs armed with cudgels and pikes wait outside to make sure justice is done, the Convention rules on salaries for army quartermasters and discusses an offer from a Dutch businessman to buy the abbey of Honnecourt. The Convention's purview extends to matters great and small, legislative and judicial.

It is only when the dark of a winter night has fallen on the salle de Manège and torches are lit and throw moving shadows on its bare walls that the secretary begins calling the roll in his flat voice. Danton interrupts him to ask whether this decree is to be adopted by a simple majority. A Breton Conventionnel named Lanjuinais notes that under penal law juries must agree on a sentence by a three-fourths majority. This matter is penal, he argues, and the Convention is acting as a jury. 'You have rejected all the required forms of justice and humanity,' he tells the Convention, 'such as a secret ballot, which is the only way to guarantee a vote without constraint. We seem here to be deliberating in a free Convention, while in reality we are threatened by guns and knives of sedition . . . it is in the name of justice and humanity that I ask for a three-fourths majority which is necessary for judges.' But this attempt to save Louis XVI fails like the others, and the Convention rules that the sentence will be adopted by simple majority.

The vote continues through the night and into the pale morning of the next day. The first voter is Jean-Baptiste Mailhe, a lawyer from the Haute-Garonne. When he asks for a death sentence with a reprieve, the cry 'Who bribed you?' comes from the benches of the Montagne. Of the 749 Conventionnels, 23 are absent and 5 abstain. This leaves 721 voting, and a required absolute majority of 361. Many views are expressed. There is the syllogistic reasoning of Maribon-Montaut, who says: 'When I open the penal code, I read that treason and conspiracy are punishable by death; Louis is guilty of conspiracy. I also read in the Declaration of the Rights of Man that the law is equal for all, whether it protects or whether it punishes. I condemn the tyrant to death.' There is the surgeon Bodin's plea for mercy, based on the argument that 'liberty cannot be founded on a holocaust.' To the Conventionnels who express compassion for the king, Robespierre replies with glacial logic: 'I do not recognize a humanity which massacres the people and forgives despots.' There are Conventionnels like Dufriche-Valaze who vote for a reprieve because they are against capital punishment and Conventionnels like Jean-Paul Marat, so impatient for Louis XVI's head that they demand 'death within twenty-four hours.' Ladies in the loggia keep score by making pinpricks on cards as one by one, the Conventionnels stride up to the platform to determine the king's fate.

When his turn comes, Philippe d'Orléans removes a piece of paper from his pocket, steps up to the platform, and reads: 'Preoccupied only by my duty, convinced that all those who have threatened or will threaten the sovereignty of the people deserve death . . . I vote for death.'

When the total is added, two deputies have voted to put the king in irons, 286 for imprisonment or banishment, 46 for the death sentence with reprieve, and 26 for the death sentence to be followed by a debate or reprieve. The number of those voting unconditionally for death is 361, the exact figure of the absolute majority. One vote less and the king's life might still have been saved.

Renewed efforts to save Louis XVI are made when the fourth question is debated on January 19: 'Should there be a reprieve in the sentence of Louis Capet? Yes or No.' Buzot again tries to link the king's fate to the rest of the Bourbon family. 'Let us banish

Orléans and his sons and tomorrow all disagreement between us will cease,' he says. 'I conclude that there should be an interval between the verdict and the execution and that during this interval, all pretenders to the throne should be banished, all these men who cannot love liberty and equality, all these men who can only be the tools of foreign powers. . . .' Condorcet, the philosopher, mathematician, and apostle of progress, proposes the abolition of capital punishment. Brissot, the leader of the Gironde, uses the practical argument of reaction abroad. 'If Louis is executed,' he says, 'we must this moment declare war on England, Holland, and Spain, on all the tyrants of Europe, for war will inevitably come from them.' There are 690 voting, and 380 vote against a reprieve.

On January 21, Charles-Henri Sanson, the chief executioner, the same man who supervised the quartering of the would-be regicide Damiens thirty-four years earlier, dons a black frockcoat and a high hat with a round crown and proceeds with his two assistants in leather aprons to the place de la Révolution (today's place de la Concorde), which is fortified against sedition by 20,000 troops. At 10.15 A.M., after hearing mass in his room in the Temple, Louis XVI arrives in a closed carriage, with the republican general Santerre. The king is wearing grey trousers and stockings, a pinked silk waistcoat, and a brown coat. As the executioner Sanson later reported, 'When he got out of the carriage for the execution we told him he had to take off his coat. He objected and said we could execute him as he was. We said that was impossible and he took off his coat himself. He also objected when we wanted to tie his hands, but finally agreed when the person who accompanied him [his confessor] told him it was a final sacrifice. Then he asked whether the drums would continue to beat. We said we did not know and that was the truth. He stepped up on the scaffold and wanted to plunge ahead as though to speak. We told him that was impossible and he allowed himself to be led to the place where he was tied and he cried out: "My people, I die an innocent man." '

The king is laid on his stomach on a long wicker basket at the same level as the guillotine's lunette, into which his head is placed. The diagonal blade drops, his head falls into the basket below it, and Sanson picks it out, holding it by the hair to show the crowd. There is a rush towards the scaffold. Men dip handkerchiefs and bits of paper in the king's blood. Others fight over locks of his hair and the buttons of his shirt. Five government witnesses accompany the body to Saint Margaret cemetery and watch the burial. 'The corpse was whole,' says the report, 'the head being separated from the trunk. We remarked that the hair in the back of the head had been cut off, and that the corpse had no tie, no coat, and no shoes.' Sanson later wrote letters to the editor in revolutionary newspapers, denying any part in the sale of the king's belongings. In 1795, after forty-three years of faithful service, he asked the Paris Commune for permission to retire, explaining that he suffered from nephritis. His son Henri succeeded him.

BIBLIOGRAPHY AND NOTES

The *Journal de la Terre et Seigneurie de Vouhet* (Bibliothèque Nationale) gives an idea of the cost of living in 1700: a sheep was sold for 3 livres, a steer for 40 livres, postage for two letters cost 10 sous, a servant was paid 20 or 30 livres a year, and the room and board in a good hotel cost about 60 livres a month.

INTRODUCTION

On autopsies of members of the royal family, the following account is taken from the *Mémoires* of the duc de Luynes (1735–1758), Firmin-Didot edition (Paris, 1860): 'The body [Marie Thérèse, wife of the dauphin, who died at the age of twenty on July 23, 1746] was washed with eau de vie; the cranium was opened; there was a white liquid in the brain. The body was opened from the throat to the hips; the heart was removed; it was found to be slightly withered; it was opened and embalmed and placed in a lead heart . . . the stomach was opened and the entrails were removed and washed with spirit of wine, embalmed and placed in a lead bucket . . . the bucket was placed in a walnut box, covered with black velvet and a cross of silver moire attached by two rows of silver nails . . . the faculty found all the organs healthy. The body was washed with spirits and embalmed.'

The remark attributed to Fontenelle is quoted by the marquis de Ségur in *Au Couchant de la Monarchie* (Paris, 1910).

On the various schools of French historians, read the essay entitled 'French historians for and against the Revolution' in Peter Geyl's *Encounters in History* (Cleveland, 1961) and Alfred Cobban's *Historians and the Causes of the French Revolution* and *The Myth of the French Revolution* (London, 1955).

The Michelet quotation is from the first volume of his *Histoire de la Révolution Française* (Paris, 1879).

On sealed letters, see Frantz Funck-Brentano, *Les Lettres de Cachet sous l'Ancien Régime* (Paris, 1925). They are described in Trevoux' *ancien régime* dictionary as 'an order of the king contained in a simple letter closed with his seal and countersigned by a secretary of state.' I have been able to find no example of *lettres de cachet en blanc*, or sealed letters with the victim's name left blank, which ministers were widely believed to give their mistresses, like gift certificates.

Pierre Gaxotte, *Le Siècle de Louis XV* (Paris, 1933).

THE EIGHTH SACRAMENT

Rivarol, *De l'Universalité de la Langue Française* (Paris, 1930). 'An equality which did not exist,' quoted in the *Guide Noir de Versailles* (Tchou, Paris, 1966).

Michel Suriano quoted by Marcel Marion in his *Dictionnaire des Institutions de la France au XVIIème et XVIIIème Siècles* (Paris, 1923).

For population figures, see John Lough, *An Introduction to 18th Century France* (London, 1960).

On Peter the Great's visit to France, see Saint-Simon, *Mémoires* (Pleiade edition, 7 vols.).

Louis XIV on the subjection of a monarch, see *Mémoires de Louis XIV*. (Plon, 1933—collection *Les Meilleurs Ecrivains Politiques*). The Sun King's memoirs, a manual on the art of reigning, were dictated to secretaries with marginal notes in his own hand, and intended for the dauphin. They were kept for the years 1661, 1662, 1666, 1667, and 1668.

'As evil as a prince may be' quoted by Georges Pagès in *La Monarchie d'Ancien Régime* (Paris, 1952).

Dubois on absolutism quoted by Amedée Vialay in *Les Cahiers de Doléance du Tiers Etat* (Paris, 1911).

On the Franks, see Frantz Funck Brentano, *Les Origines* (Paris, 1928).

On Clovis and his baptism, see Georges Tessier, *Le Baptême de Clovis* (Paris, 1965).

King called Sergeant of God, see Frantz Funck-Brentano, *Ce Qu'était un Roi de France* (Paris, 1909).

On King's ability to heal, see Marc Bolch, *Les Rois Thaumaturges* (Paris, 1924).

On Salic law, see Jean de Pange, *Le Roi Très Chretien* (Paris, 1948).

On the emergence of the Capetians and the formation of France, see Pagès and Charles Benoist, *La Monarchie Française* (Paris, 1935).

On the monarch's various methods of acquiring land, see Paul Viollet, *Le Roi et Ses Ministres* (Paris, 1912).

On feudalism, see Frantz Funck-Brentano, *Le Moyen Age* (Paris, 1922).

On the three orders and the alliance of the king and the Third Estate, see R. Jaliffier, *Histoire des Etats Généraux* (Paris, 1885).

On administrative confusion and special privileges, see Albert Babeau, *La Ville sous l'Ancien Régime* (Paris, 1884), *Le Village sous l'Ancien Régime* (Paris, 1882) and *La Vie Rurale sous l'Ancien Régime* (Paris, 1885).

On the guilds, see Gaxotte, *Le Siècle de Louis XV*.

On the makeup of the nobility, see the marquis de Bouillé, *Mémoires* (Paris, 1859); A Goodwin, *The European Nobility in the 18th Century* (London, 1953); F. L. Ford, *Robe and Sword* (Cambridge, 1953).

On feudal privileges, see Frantz Funck-Brentano, *L'Ancien Régime* (Paris, 1926) and Charles Kunstler's *La Vie Quotidienne* books, *sous Louis XIV* (Paris, 1948); *sous la Régence* (Paris, 1960); *sous Louis XV* (Paris, 1953); and *sous Louis XVI* (Paris, 1950).

Talleyrand quotation from *Mémoires du Prince de Talleyrand* (Paris, 1891).

On the alliance of feudal and gown nobility, see F. L. Ford's *Robe and Sword*.

Noailles quote, see Henri Carré, *La Noblesse de France et l'Opinion Publique au Dix-huitième Siècle* (Paris, 1920).

John Moore quote from *A View of Society and Manners in France, Switzerland, and Germany* (London, 1779; 2 vols.).

Von Vizine quoted by the marquis de Ségur, *Au Couchant de la Monarchie*.

Chancellor Sillery quote by the duc de Levis-Mirepoix in *Le Roi N'est Mort Qu'une Fois* (Paris, 1966).

On the various French kings see Marie-Madeleine Martin, *Le Roi de France* (Paris, 1963), and the duc de Levis-Mirepoix, *Le Roi N'est Mort Qu'une Fois*.

On the way the monarchy became a hereditary, divine-right institution, see Montlosier, *De la Monarchie Française* (Paris, 1814).

THE SUN KING

Tore the nipples of his wet nurse, see Philippe Erlanger, *Louis XIV* (Paris, 1965).

Mazarin made him sleep in threadbare sheets, translated Latin, spent morning on close-stool, see Georges Mongrédien, *Louis XIV* (Paris, 1963).

Size of intestines, ate with fingers, height, read books, changed suits, hated Sodomites, doffed hat, granddaughter's miscarriage, see Saint-Simon, *Mémoires*.

Cost of Versailles, See Erlanger.

On Montespan, see *Archives de la Bastille*, Ravaisson edition (Paris, 1866–73; 7 vols.).

On Madame de Maintenon, see biographies by Marcel Langlois (Paris, 1932), and Gonzague Truc's introduction to her *Letters* (Paris, 1921).

On Louis XIV's doctors, see Mongrédien.

On king's love of praise, see Saint-Simon.

On flattery, see Jacques Levron, *Les Courtisans* (Paris, 1961).

Richelieu's programme, see duc de Levis-Mirepoix, *Le Roi N'est Mort Qu'une Fois.*

On visit of Versailles gardens, see *Manière de Montrer les Jardins de Versailles* (Wittman-Plon, 1951).

On the police, see Pierre Clément, *La Police sous Louis XIV* (Paris, 1866). On the Black Cabinet, see Saint-Simon.

On censorship and thought control, see Pagès.

On the sycophancy of writers, see Mongrédien.

On Louis XIV's interest in administration, see *Mémoires Historiques et Politiques* (Truettel et Wurtz, 1806).

Quotation of Louis XIV to his brother in Pierre Goubert, *Louis XIV et Vingt Millions de Français* (Paris, 1966).

On the humbling of his ministers, see Pagès.

On Colbert, see C. W. Cole, *Colbert and a Century of French Mercantilism* (1939); on Vauban, see Daniel Halévy, *Vauban* (1926); on Louvois, see Erlanger, *Louis XIV.*

On the move to Versailles, see Saint-Simon and J. Vatout, *Palais de Versailles* (Paris, 1837).

On aversion of kings to Paris, see H. Monin, *L'Etat de Paris en 1789* (Paris, 1837).

On visitors to Versailles, see Marie-Madeleine Martin, *Le Roi de France.*

On court of Louis XIV, see *Journal de Dangeau* (Paris, 1854–1860); *Mémoires de Saint-Simon*; Madame de Sevigné, *Lettres* (Paris, 1843); Jacques Levron, *Les Courtisans* (Paris, 1961); and *La Vie Quotidienne à Versailles* (Paris, 1962); and Charles Kunstler, *La Vie Quotidienne sous Louis XIV.*

On profiteering at court, see Mongrédien.

On venality of offices, see Marcel Marion, *Dictionnaire des Institutions.*

Desmarets quoted in Saint-Simon.

La Bruyère quoted in Jacques Levron, *La Vie Quotidienne à Versailles.*

Primi-Visconti quoted from *Mémoires sur la Cour de Louis XIV* (Paris, 1909).

Four servants to bring a glass of wine, see Hyppolite Taine, *Les Origines de la France Contemporaine* (Paris, 1876–1894).

Louis XIV's salad days, see Erlanger.

On king's marriage to Madame de Maintenon, see Saint-Simon.

Dauphin summoning his mistress and Monsieur rubbing holy medals, see Princesse Palatine, *Lettres* (Paris, 1962).

On king's religious policies, see Erlanger; Goubert; Latreille et Delaruelle, *Histoire du Catholicisme en France* (Paris, 1946); on violence done to Protestants and Franklin hearing sermon, see Paul Hazard, *La Crise de Conscience Européenne* (Paris, 1935).

On political consequences of religious policies, see Goubert.

For sermon Louis XIV heard as a child, see Cardinal de Retz, *Mémoires* (Paris, 1817).

Louis XIV quotation on the kings of France from his *Mémoires*. Louis XIV's foreign policy, see Goubert.

On subsidies and the war against Holland, see Louis XIV's *Mémoires*.

Voltaire quote from *Le Siècle de Louis XIV* (Paris, 1930; Œuvres Complètes).

International incidents provoked by Louis XIV, see Erlanger and Goubert.

On policy of reunions, see Lavisse, *Histoire de France* (Paris, 1911); and Goubert.

On War of Spanish Succession, see Lavisse; Goubert; W. H. Lewis, *The Sunset of the Splendid Century* (New York, 1963); and Jacques Boulenger, *The Seventeenth Century in France* (London, 1920).

On Louis XIV in defeat and the battle of Denain, see maréchal de Villars, *Mémoires* (Paris, 1819).

On diffusion of French arts and letters, see Louis Réau, *L'Europe Française au Siècles des Lumières* (Paris, 1938).

On new thought under Louis XIV, see Paul Hazard, *La Crise de Conscience Européenne* (Paris, 1963).

On Fénelon's influence, see Kingsley Martin, *French Liberal Thought in the 18th Century* (London, 1929).

On the development of the rococo, see Fiske Kimball, *The Creation of the Rococo* (Philadelphia, 1943).

On financial chaos at the end of Louis XIV's reign, see Goubert; and Erlanger.

Sorbonne professor Villemain is quoted by Aimé Cherest in *La Chute de l'Ancien Régime* (Paris, 1884–1886).

THE EIGHT-YEAR CENTURY

On the death of Louis XIV, see *Journal des Anthoine,* E. Dumont, ed. (Paris, 1880); and Saint-Simon, *Mémoires.*

On Louis XIV's opinion of the Regent, see Saint-Simon.

On the king's will, see *Mémoires Historiques et Politiques* (Treuttel et Wortz, Paris, 1806).

On the king's dying words to the Regent, see *Journal des Anthoine.*

On the Regent's coup, see Saint-Simon; and W. H. Lewis, *The Sunset of the Splendid Century* (New York, 1963).

On Louis XV's first bed of justice, see Charles Kunstler, *La Vie Quotidienne sous la Régence* (Paris, 1960).

On Regent's words to Parlement, see Jules Flammermont, *Remonstrances du Parlement de Paris* (Paris, 1888; 3 vols.).

On origins of Parlement, see Marcel Marion, *Dictionnaire des Institutions;* Flammermont; and F. L. Ford, *Robe and Sword.*

Barbier quotation from *Journal Historique et Anecdotique de la Régence et du Siècle de Louis XV* (Paris, 1866; 8 vols.).

On Intendant of Paris ordering pigeons curtailed, see Barbier.

On Regent's restoration of the right of remonstrance and subsequent measures against Parlement, see *Mémoires du Chevalier de Piossens* (Amsterdam, 1749).

On opposition of Parlements to reforms, see Henri Carré, *La Fin des Parlements* (Paris, 1912).

On Regent's initial reforms, see A. Jobez, *La France sous Louis XV* (Paris, 1864–1873).

On English alliance, see Jean-Louis Aujol, *Cardinal Dubois, Ministre de la Paix* (Paris, 1948).

On the Regency councils and the ineptitude of the nobility, see Saint-Simon.

'Fear not events sinister,' quoted by Philippe Erlanger, *Le Régent* (Paris, 1938).

On the Regent, see *Lettres de la Princesse Palatine* (Paris, 1962); Maurice Soulié, *Autour du Régent* (Paris, 1933); André Ransan, *Vie Privée du Régent* (Paris, 1938); Saint-Simon.

On Regent and censorship, see Philippe Erlanger.

On Voltaire and the police spy, see Jean Buvat, *Journal de la Régence* (Paris, 1865).

On style and debauchery of Regency, see M. de Lescure, *Les Maîtresses du Régent* (Paris, 1852); M. Capefigue, *La Comtesse de Parabère et le Palais Royal* (Paris, 1863); Mathieu Marais, *Journal et Mémoires* (Paris, 1863; 4 vols.); Saint-Simon.

'Devils abroad and saints at home,' see Saint-Simon.

Opera balls, muslin dresses, pencilled veins, see M. de Lescure.

Painting and Furniture, see Kunstler.

Madame de Pramenoux, see Mathieu Marias; Mademoiselle de Blois, see Palatine Princess; Monsieur de Gacé, princess of Würtemburg, and abbess of Montbuisson, see Kunstler and M. de Lescure.

On roués and Regent's orgies, see Ransan; Lescure; Soulié.

On Regent's diplomatic code, see Lescure.

On action taken against royal bastards, see Saint-Simon.

D'Argenson quoted in *Mémoires du Marquis René-Louis d'Argenson*, ed Rathry (Paris, 1859–67; 9 vols.).

On Cardinal Dubois, see Jobez; Erlanger; Aujol; Mongez, *La Vie Privée du Cardinal Dubois* (Paris, 1789); and Saint-Simon.

On Dubois' mission to Holland, see C. Aubertin, *L'Esprit Publique au XVIIIème Siècle* (Paris, 1889).

On the Cellamare conspiracy, see Saint-Simon; W. H. Lewis.

On religious issues and Jansenism, see Jobez; Erlanger.

Quotation about Caligula, see the Princesse Palatine.

On public debt after Louis XIV, see Germain Martin, *Histoire Economique et Financière* (Paris, 1920).

On the chamber of justice, see Kunstler.

On the Regent's diamond, see Saint-Simon.

On first mention of Law by duc de Noailles, see René Trintzius, *John Law et la Naissance du Dirigisme* (Paris, 1950).

On Law's projects, life, publicity campaign, colonial company, and speculation, see P. A. Cochut, *Law et Son Système* (Paris, 1863).

On fallacies of Law's system, see E. Levasseur, *Recherches Historiques sur le Système de Law* (Paris, 1854).

On the rue Quincampoix, see Kunstler; Mathieu Marais; Barbier.

On Law throwing money out of the window, see Jean Buvat.

On the Horn case, see Barbier.

On the duc de la Force, see Henri Carré, *La Noblesse de France et l'Opinion Publique au Dix-Huitième Siècle* (Paris, 1920).

On Law's reforms and efforts to keep his system alive, see Trintzius.

On the bank closing and the Regent's words to Monsieur le Duc, see Buvat.

On Law's flight and Regent's attitude, see Saint-Simon.

On the return to previous policies and the recall of Law's notes, see Gerard Walter's introduction to Edgar Faure's *La Disgrâce de Turgot* (Paris, 1961).

On Regent's death, see Erlanger.

THE PLAGUE OF MARSEILLES

On the Viceroy of Sardinia's dream, see National Archives, Cagliari.

On the spread of the plague through Marseilles, the attitude of the church, municipal officials, doctors, relations with other cities, remedies, Bishop Belzunce, measures against the epidemic, its spread through the rest of the province, its subsiding, see Paul Gaffarel et le marquis de Duranty, *La Peste à Marseilles* (Paris, 1911).

On deaths aboard ship, use of convicts, government assistance, controversies among doctors, see Shelby T. McCloy, *Government Assistance in Eighteenth-Century France* (Durham, 1946).

On the maréchal de Villars and Intendant Lebret and their correspondence, see Albert Babeau, *Le Maréchal de Villars, Gouverneur de Provence* (Paris, 1892).

On death totals, see McCloy and Babeau.

On the costume worn by doctors, see Edward J. Lovell, *The Eve of the French Revolution* (1892).

On the plague and various theories of contagion, see L. Fabian Hirst, *The Conquest of the Plague* (London, 1953).

THE FRAGILE ESSENCE

On origins of court, see Jacques Levrons, *Les Courtisans* (Paris, 1961).

On Agnes Sorel, see Brantôme, *Vie des Dames Galantes* (Paris, 1863).

On the court under Louis XIV, see Henri Brocher, *Le Rang et l'Etiquette sous l'Ancien Régime* (Paris, 1934); Saint-Simon; and the marquis de Dangeau, *Journal*.

On the contradictions in court etiquette, see Marcel Marion, *Dictionnaire des Institutions*.

On the duchesse de Bracciano fainting, see Henri Brocher; on advice of elderly courtier and four servants to give king a glass of water, see Hippolyte Taine, *Origines de la France Contemporaine.*

On the king's napkin, see Louis Ducros, *La Société Française au Dix-huitième Siècle* (Paris, 1926).

On size of nobility, see Marcel Marion.

On the Louis XV style and the rococo, see Fiske Kimball, *The Creation of the Rococo* (Philadelphia, 1943); Jean Starobinski, *L'Invention de la Liberté* (Paris, 1964); Mario Praz, *Psychology and Evolution of Interior Decoration* (Paris, 1964); and Lavisse, *Histoire de France* (Paris, 1911).

On Madame de Pompadour's theatre and the tickets of admission, see Jacques Levron, *La Vie Quotidienne à Versailles* (Paris, 1962).

On the erotic Bouchers, see Seymour O. Simches, *Le Romantisme et le Gout Esthétique au Dix-huitième Siècle* (Paris, 1964).

On the fishwives of Les Halles and queens giving birth in public, see Charles Kunstler, *La Vie Quotidienne sous Louis XV* (Paris, 1953).

On Louis XV and the General Farmer's wife, see Comte Dufort de Cheverny, *Mémoires* (Plon, 1909).

On the police reports for Louis XV, see *Rapports des Inspecteurs de Police au Roi* published and annotated by Camille Piton (Paris, 1906).

On Louis XV's desire for privacy, see Jacques Levron.

On the king's private suppers, see the duc de Croÿ, *Journal Inédit,* ed. vicomte de Grouchy and P. Cottin (Paris, 1960–1907; 4 vols.).

Quotations from *Angola* are from the collection *Conteurs Licentieux du Dix-huitième Siècle.*

Chamfort quotation from *Maximes et Pensées* (Paris, 1963).

Talleyrand quotation from *Mémoires du Prince de Talleyrand* (Paris, 1891).

'I allow you everything but princes and valets,' see Sénac de Meilhan, *Du Gouvernement, des Mœurs, et des Conditions en France Avant la Révolution* (Paris, 1862).

On Lauzun and estranged wife, see Taine.

On the man of good company and household affairs, see Alfred Leroy, *Histoire des Rois de France* (Paris, 1956).

On the young woman who did not cry at the theatre, and the husband who could not make a fool of himself, see Chamfort.

On prince de Ligne and Catherine the Great, see baroness d'Oberkirch, *Mémoires* (Paris, 1853; 2 vols.).

On Richelieu's expertise at gallantry, see Louis Ducros; on his speech at the Académie, see Chamfort; on the four unopened love notes, see Edmond et Jules de Goncourt, *La Femme au Dix-huitième Siècle* (Paris, 1890).

Prince de Léon anecdote, see *Chroniques de l'Oeil-de-Bœuf*.

Hussars anecdote, see d'Argenson, *Mémoires*.

On Maurepas being governed by his wife, see Sénac de Meilhan.

On fashion, cosmetics, hair styles, beauty masks, and balls, see Edmond et Jules de Goncourt.

On Madame de Pompadour as a patroness of the arts, see Pierre de Nolhac, *Louis XV et Madame de Pompadour* (Paris, 1903); and Jacques Levron, *Secrète Madame de Pompadour* (Paris, 1965).

On the literary salons, see Roger Picard, *Les Salons Littéraires et la Société Française* (Paris, 1943).

Fricassee of chicken anecdote, see Casanova, *Mémoires* (Paris, 1826–1838).

On the dauphin's boredom, see duc de Luynes, *Mémoires* (Firmin-Didot, 1860; 17 vols.).

Tantrum of Louis XV, see d'Argenson, *Mémoires*.

On duels, see Henri Carré, *La Noblesse de France et l'Opinion Publique au Dix-huitième Siècle* (Paris, 1920).

On criticism at court under Louis XV, see A. Jobez, *La France sous Louis XV* (Paris, 1864–1873).

On luxury of Louis XV's court, see Charles Kunstler, *La Vie Quotidienne sous Louis XV*.

On luxury of households and Rousseau knocked down, see Henri Carré.

On prince de Condé's pet monkey, see A. Goodwin, *The European Nobility in the Eighteenth Century* (1953).

On expenditures of Madame de Pompadour, see J. A. Le Roi, *Curiosités Historiques sur Louis XIII, Louis XIV, et Louis XV* (Paris, 1864).

Chevalier de Lorenzi anecdote, see Gaston Maugras, *Le Duc de Lauzun et la Cour Intime de Louis XV* (Paris, 1895–1896).

On Choiseul's exile, see Gaston Maugras, *Le Duc de Lauzun et la Cour de Marie-Antoinette* (Paris, 1895–1896).

On court under Madame du Barry, see prince de Montbarey, *Mémoires* (Paris, 1826).

On changes at court under Louis XVI, see Jacques Levron.

On Louis XVI style, see Guillaume Janneau, *L'Epoque Louis XVI* (Paris, 1966).

On *à la grecque* style, see Horace Walpole, *Letters* (London, 1937; 9 vols.).

On brocaded waistcoats, see baroness d'Oberkirch, *Mémoirs*.

On women's fashions, see Henri d'Alméras, *Marie-Antoinette et les Pamphlets Royalistes et Révolutionnaires* (Paris, 1907).

On Marie-Antoinette at court, see Charles Kunstler, *La Vie Quotidienne sous Louis XVI;* baroness d'Oberkirch, *Mémoires;* Gerard Walter, *Marie-Antoinette* (Paris, 1948).

Six days a week the court seemed a private society, see Sénac de Meilhan.

Queen and her page, see comte de Tilly, *Mémoires* (Paris, 1929; 2 vols.).

Ostentation of court under Louis XVI, see Kunstler.

Roland's presentation, see Madame Roland, *Mémoires*.

THE WELL-BELOVED

'Things will last as long as I do,' see Madame Campan, *Mémoires sur la Vie de Marie-Antoinette,* ed F. Barriere (Paris, 1876).

Madame de Pompadour tried to amuse the king, see G. du Fresne de Beaucourt, *Le Caractère de Louis XV* (Paris, 1887).

Description of Louis XV as a child, see Princesse Palatine, *Lettres*.

Dubois letter to Doge, see Aujol, *Cardinal Dubois, Ministre de la Paix*.

Story of cats, see marquis de Calvière, *Journal*, quoted by Goncourt brothers in volume I of *Portraits Intimes* (Paris, 1857–1858).

Darboulin anecdote quoted by Dufort de Cheverny, *Mémoires* (Plon, Paris, 1909).

Frederick II letter to Voltaire; see Jean Albert-Sorel, *Le Declin de la Monarchie* (Paris, 1945).

Cough with scent of pinewood, Villars anecdote, see duc de Luynes, *Mémoires*.

Sent equerry to look for graves, see Madame du Hausset, *Mémoires* (Paris, 1824).

King's cowardice when knifed, see the *Mémoires du Duc de Choiseul* (Paris, 1824).

Duc de Liancourt on the king's fear, see Mouffle d'Angerville, *La Vie Privée de Louis XV* (Paris, 1921).

Approved conflicting accounts, see duc de Luynes, who writes that in

1749, the Minister of War, d'Argenson, brought accounts of military expenses totalling 52 million livres, while the accounts of the Controller General Machault for the same expenses totalled 48 million livres. The king signed both with *'vu—bon,'* and Luynes added: 'the more one knows the king the more one is afflicted that he will not listen to both sides and reach a decision.'

King on his minister's merchandise, see Pierre Gaxotte, *Le Siècle de Louis XV* (Paris, 1933).

Marriage arranged with Infanta, see Saint-Simon, *Mémoires*.

'Arracheurs de Palissades,' see Mathieu Marais, *Journal et Mémoires* (Paris, 1863); also see on duchesse de Retz touching the king.

On Monsieur le Duc, see Saint-Simon; A Jobez, *La France sous Louis XV*; Gaxotte, *Le Siècle de Louis XV*.

On list of princesses, see original report by Fleuridu de Morville on exhibit at French History Museum at the Hôtel de Soubise, Paris.

On the marriage of Louis XV, see Pierre de Nolhac, *Louis XV et Marie Leczinska* (Paris, 1908).

On Spanish anger, see Kunstler, *La Vie Quotidienne sous Louis XV*.

Queen's births a great assurance for the kingdom, see duc de Luynes.

Disgrace of Monsieur le Duc, see *Mémoires du President Hénault* (Paris, 1855).

On Fleury, see Gaxotte and Jobez.

Common sense for fine wit, see J. Aubertin, *L'Esprit Publique au Dix-huitième Siècle* (Paris, 1889).

Mont Pagnotte and War of Austrian Succession, see Gaxotte.

On Mailly-Nesle sisters, see d'Argenson and duc de Luynes, *Mémoires*.

On Madame de Pompadour, see Pierre de Nolhac, *Louis XV et Madame de Pompadour* and *Madame de Pompadour et la Politique;* and Jacques Levron, *Secrète Madame de Pompadour*.

On Pompadour's cold-bloodedness, see Madame du Hausset; and *Mémoires du Duc de Choiseul*.

On the Deer Park, see E. Welvert, *La Vie Secrète de Louis XV* (Paris, 1910); and Joseph Valynseele, *Les Enfants Naturels de Louis XV* (Paris, 1953).

Homages to Pompadour's dog, see Abbé de Bernis, *Mémoires* (Paris, 1878).

Silhouette anecdote, see *Mélanges de Boisjourdain* (Paris, 1807).

On Maurepas' disgrace, see d'Argenson, *Mémoires*.

On d'Argenson's disgrace, see de Nolhac, *Madame de Pompadour et le Politique*.

On Choiseul and Pompadour, see *Mémoires du Duc de Choiseul*.

On Bernis and Pompadour, see Abbé de Bernis, *Mémoires*.

On Kaunitz, see Madame du Hausset.

On the reversal of alliances, see de Nolhac, *Madame de Pompadour et la Politique*.

On the banishment of the Jesuits, see Henri Carré, *La France sous Louis XV* (Paris, 1891); Gaxotte; Edmond Soreau, *La Chute de l'Ancien Régime* (Paris, 1937); and Jean Albert-Sorel.

On Choiseul and du Barry, see Gatson Maugras, *La Disgrâce du Duc et de la Duchesse de Choiseul* (Paris, 1903).

Prince de Ligne quote on Jesuits, see Louis Nicolardot, *Les Cours et Les Salons au 18ème Siècle* (Paris, 1879).

On Pompadour's ill health, see Madame du Hausset.

On Pompadour's death and Lord Hertford's comment, see Nancy Mitford, *Madame de Pompadour* (New York, 1953).

Sensual enjoyment of a new sort, and successor of Ste. Foix, see A. Fauchié-Magnan, *Les du Barry* (Paris, 1934).

Letter of Louis XV to Choiseul, see Lucien Perey, *La Fin du Dix-huitième Siècle* (Paris, 1891).

Du Barry's expenses, see J. A. Le Roi, *Curiosités Historiques sur Louis XIII, Louis XIV, et Louis XV* (Paris, 1864).

Louis XV on Parlements, see Madame Campan.

On struggle with Parlements, see Henri Carré; Pierre Gaxotte; and Lavisse, *Histoire de France* (Paris, 1911).

On Maupéou's report to Parlement, see the marquis de Ségur, *Au Couchant de la Monarchie*.

On king's popularity in Le Havre and unpopularity in Paris, see duc de Luynes.

On king as well-hated, see d'Argenson.

On death of Louis XV, see Edmond Jaloux, *Louis XV, le Roi et le Malade* (Paris, 1936); Mouffle d'Angerville, *La Vie Privée de Louis XV* (Paris, 1921), Madame Campan, and the duc de Croÿ.

DAMIENS

On Grimm's conversation with Diderot, see *Correspondence Littéraire, Philosophique et Critique;* M. Tourneux, ed. (Paris, 1877–1882; 16 vols.).

On Madame Campan's dinner, see her *Mémoires*.

An attempted murder, torture, and execution, see duc de Croÿ, *Mémoires,* and André Bouton et Dr. André Adnis, *Damiens* (Paris, 1955).

On Landsmath, see Madame Campan.

On Damiens' trial, see *Pièces Originales et Procédures du Procès Fait à Robert François Damiens, Tant à la Prévôté de l'Hôtel Qu'en la Cour du Parlement* (Paris, Pierre-Guillaume Simon).

On Casanova and Count Tiretta de Trevise, see Casanova's *Mémoires* (Paris, 1826–1838).

THE KING'S SECRET

On French foreign policy, see Pierre Muret, *La Préponderance Anglaise* (Paris, 1937); Philippe Sagnac, *La Fin de l'Ancien Régime et la Révolution Américaine* (Paris, 1947); and Jean Albert-Sorel, *Le Declin de la Monarchie* (Paris, 1945).

On Louis XV's instructions to ambassadors and print showing him whipped, see Henri Carré, *La France sous Louis XV* (Paris, 1891).

On maréchal de Saxe quotation, see Jean Albert-Sorel.

Louis XV on Frederick II, see Madame du Hausset.

On France's colonial policy, see Edmond Preclin and Victor-L. Tapié, *Le Dix-huitième Siècle* (Paris, 1952).

The cipher pad used by Louis XV is on exhibit at the French History Museum in the Hôtel de Soubise, Paris.

On Jarrelle's Black Cabinet, see Dufort de Cheverny, *Mémoires*.

On the secret diplomacy, see *Correspondence Secrète du Duc de Broglie avec Louis XV (1756–1774)*, Didier Ozanam et Michel Antoine, eds. (Société de l'Histoire de France); and the duc de Broglie, *Le Secret du Roi* (Paris, 1888).

Quesnay would not dine with the head of the Black Cabinet, see Louis Ducros, *La Société Française au Dix-huitième Siècle* (Paris, 1926).

On the Chevalier d'Eon, see Octave Homberg, *La Carrière Militaire du Chevalier d'Eon* (Paris, 1900); and Octave Homberg et Fernand Jousselin, *Un Aventurier au Dix-huitième Siècle* (Paris, 1904).

FONTENOY

On Soubise's letter at Rossbach, see Jean Albert-Sorel, *Le Declin de la Monarchie*.

On Prince Louis' cowardice, see A. Goodwin, *European Nobility*.

On duc d'Ayen hiding, see Henri Carré, *La Noblesse de France et l'Opinion Publique*.

On Saint-Germain at Rossbach, see Aubertin, *L'Esprit Publique au Dix-huitième Siècle*.

On deterioration of the Maison du Roi, see Léon Mention, *L'Armée de l'Ancien Régime* (Paris, 1909).

On the sale of commissions, see Louis Tuetey, *Les Officiers sous l'Ancien Régime* (Paris, 1908).

On Guibert's reforms, see Jean Egret, *La Prérévolution Française* (Paris, 1962).

On Saint-Germain's reforms, see Mention and Tuetey.

On Frederick II finding lavender water, see Henri Carré.

On officer taking bass viola to the front, see E. G. Léonard, *l'Armée et Ses Problèmes au Dix-huitième Siècle* (Paris 1942).

On Broglie blackfacing camp followers, see Mention.

On duc des Cars to marquis de Castries, see Henri Carré.

On signs in public gardens, see Mention.

On siege of Prague anecdotes, see E. G. Léonard.

On Maurice de Saxe, see Maurice de la Fuÿe, *Fontenoy* (Paris, 1945); and General Camon, *Le Maréchal de Saxe* (Paris, 1934).

Worthy Paris bourgeois quote, see Chamfort.

On changes in miltary tactics, see J. Colin, *Les Campagnes du Maréchal de Saxe* (Paris, 1901–1906).

On the choice of Fontenoy as the battle site, see *Relation de la Bataille de Fontenoy* (Paris, 1745).

On positions and size of armies, see J. Colin.

On king's eagerness to go to Fontenoy, see Voltaire, *Précis du Siècle de Louis XV*.

Cumberland confident of victory, minister of Sardinia, elector of Cologne, see the duc de Broglie, *La Journée de Fontenoy* (Navarre, 1897).

Accounts of battle, see J. Colin; General Camon de la Fuÿe; duc de Broglie.

Incident of firing first and quotation about Saxe pursuing enemies, see marquis de Valfons, *Souvenirs*.

On deserters at the bridge, French vivacity, king writing to queen on drumhead, see d'Argenson, *Mémoires*.

On Irish recovering flag and Saxe order to touch uniforms with breastplates, see duc de Luynes, *Mémoires*.

Letter of Cumberland to Louis XV, see Archives, Ministère de la Guerre.

On maréchal de Saxe's epitaph, see duc de Luynes, *Mémoires*.

On doctors giving Saxe few months to live, Campbell's head blown off, Saxe saying English not so easy to digest, official version of guards brigade retreat, Biron changed horses three times anecdote, Saxe's anger, Dutch cowardice, see J. Colin.

On British advance through ravine, marquis de Wignacourt and cavalry heroism, see duc de Broglie.

Saxe's letter to princess Hostein, see de la Fuÿe.

Napoleon was a Frenchman by accident because the treaty which made Corsica French was signed in 1768, a year before his birth in Ajaccio.

THE PEN AND THE CROWN

On the change in the writer's condition, see John Lough, *An Introduction to Eighteenth-Century France* (London, 1960).

On Racine's career, see Raymond Picard, *La Carrière de Jean Racine* (Paris, 1956); René Bady, *Portrait de Racine* (Paris, 1940); Gonzague Truc, *Racine* (Paris, 1926); and Pierre Moreau, *Racine, l'Homme et l'Œuvre* (Paris, 1943).

On Madame de Sévigné's tears, see her *Lettres* (Paris, 1843).

General studies on Voltaire, see Gustave Lanson, *Voltaire* (Paris, 1906); André Maurois, *Voltaire* (Paris, 1935); Raymond Naves, *Voltaire, l'Œuvre, l'Homme* (Paris, 1942); and Jean Orieux, *Voltaire* (Paris, 1966).

On Voltaire's childhood, see Henri Beaune, *Voltaire au Collège, Sa Famille, Ses Etudes, Ses Premiers Amis* (Paris, 1867).

On his relations with the marquise du Châtelet and Madame Denis, see Gilbert Pignet, *Monsieur de Voltaire et la Vérité sur Sa Vie Amoureuse* (Paris, 1938).

On Voltaire and Frederick II, see Pierre Gaxotte, *Frederic II;* and Henri Bellugon, *Voltaire et Frederic II au Temps de la Marquise du Châtelet* (Paris, 1963).

On Voltaire's income and money-making schemes, see Jacques Donvez, *De Quoi Vivait Voltaire* (Paris, 1949).

On Voltaire and the Philosophes, see Raymond Naves, *Voltaire et l'Encyclopédie* (Paris, 1938).

On Voltaire's letters to Madame Denis, see *Voltaire's Correspondence*, Theodore Besterman, ed. (Geneva, 1955).

On Voltaire and religion, see René Pomeau, *La Religion de Voltaire* (Paris, 1956).

On Voltaire at Ferney, see Fernand Causey, *Voltaire, Seigneur de Village* (Paris, 1912).

On Voltaire's triumph and death, see Arsène Houssaye, *Le Roi Voltaire* (Paris, 1853).

On letter of Swiss friend to Rousseau, see F. Rocquain, *L'Esprit Révolutionnaire avant la Révolution* (Paris, 1878).

On Almanac of Authors, and duc d'Orléans quotation, see John Lough.

On Racine and Saint-Cyr, see *Madame de Maintenon et la Maison Royale de Saint-Cyr* (T. Lavalée, Paris, 1862).

On the Calas Affair, see Marc Chassaigne, *L'Affaire Calas* (Paris, 1929).

On the *Encyclopédie*, see John Morley, *Diderot and the Encyclopedistes* (London, 1878).

On Malesherbes, see John M. S. Allison, *Malesherbes, Defender and Reformer of the French Monarchy* (New Haven, 1938).

On Elie Fréron, see François Cornou, *Trente Ans de Lutte Contre Voltaire et les Philosophes* (Paris, 1922).

On Marie-Thérèse Geoffrin and the literary salons, see Roger Picard, *Les Salons Littéraires et la Société Française* (Paris, 1943).

On Louis XVI reading *The Marriage of Figaro,* see Madame Campan, *Mémoires.*

On the 'Figaro Affair' see Felix Gaiffe, *Beaumarchais et le Mariage de Figaro* (Paris, 1939).

On Necker's faith in public opinion, see Lavaquerie, *Necker, le Fourrier de la Révolution* (Paris, 1933).

On Madame de Pompadour giving up her garden, see, d'Argenson, *Mémoires.*

On General Maillebois' recall, see F. Rocquain, *L'Esprit Révolutionnaire Avant le Révolution* (Paris, 1873).

On Machault seeing the monarchy in its grave, see Aubertin, *L'Esprit Publique au Dix-huitième Siècle.*

Police reports on criticism, see Frantz Funck-Brentano, *Les Nouvellistes* (Paris, 1923).

On clandestine tracts, see Ira O. Wade, *Clandestine Organization and Diffusion of Philosophic Ideas in France from 1700 to 1750* (New York, 1938).

On the upper clergy and the split with the lower clergy, see Abbé Sicard, *Ancien Clergé de France* (Paris, 1912).

On the antireligion aims of the Philosophes, see Paul Hazard, *La Pensée.*

Européenne au XVIIIème Siècle (Paris, 1963); Daniel Mornet, *Les Origines Intellectuelles de la Révolution Française* (Paris, 1932); and Kingsley Martin, *French Liberal Thought in the Eighteenth Century* (London, (1929).

On Christ as a clumsy juggler, see Bachaumont, *Mémoires Secrets* (Paris, 1859).

Philosophes in Académie Française, numerous editions of their works, see Daniel Mornet.

On studies of contents of libraries, see Pierre Gaxotte, *Le Siècle de Louis XV*.

On Freemasonry, see Gaston Martin, *La Franc-Maconnerie Française* (Paris, 1926); and Bernard Faÿ, *La Franc-Maconnerie et la Révolution Intellectuelle au Dix-huitième Siècle* (Paris, 1961).

On Rousseau's admiration of England, see Paul Hazard, *La Crise de Conscience Européenne* (Paris, 1935).

On Voltaire's belief in a good field, see Charles Morazé, *La France Bourgeoise* (Paris, 1946).

On influence of Philosophes, see Gottschalk, *Philippe Sagnac and the Causes of the French Revolution, Journal of Modern History (1948)*.

On influence of Rousseau, see Gordon MacNeil, *The Cult of Rousseau and the French Revolution* (New York, 1945).

Rousseau on the stages of democracy, see Lavisse, *Histoire de France*.

Rousseau and his letter on music, see F. Rocquain.

On cosmopolitanism, see Réau, *L'Europe Française au Siècle des Lumières* (Paris, 1938); and René Pomeau, *L'Europe des Lumières* (Paris, 1965).

On patriotism and nationalism, see P. Desjardins, *French Patriotism in the Nineteenth Century* (Paris, 1923); and A. Aulard, *Le Patriotisme Français de la Renaissance à la Révolution* (in *Etudes sur la Révolution*).

On the prince de Ligne, see his *Mémoires* (Paris, 1880).

Marquise de Crécy quoted in Sénac de Meilhan, *Du Gouvernement, des Mœurs, et des Conditions en France Avant la Révolution* (Paris, 1862).

Robespierre quoted in Paul Hazard, *La Pensée Européenne au XVIIIème Siècle* (Paris, 1963).

THE PARADOX OF PROSPERITY

On preoccupation with bread, see George Rude, *The Crowd in the French Revolution* (Oxford, 1959).

On bread riots, the price of bread, placards and criticism, see Siméon-Prosper Hardy, *Mes Loisirs* (Paris, 1912); and d'Argenson, *Mémoires*.

On winter of 1709 and chronic threat of famine, see Shelby T. McCloy, *Government Assistance in Eighteenth-Century France* (Durham, 1946).

Arthur Young, see *Travels During the Years 1787, 1788, and 1789 Undertaken More Particularly with a View of Ascertaining the Cultivation, Wealth, Resources and National Prosperity of the Kingdom of France* (London, 1794; 2 vols.).

On land deeds, see J. Loutchisky, *L'Etat des Classes Agricoles en France à la Veille de la Révolution* (Paris, 1911).

Laurence Sterne, see *A Sentimental Journey Through France and Italy* (Paris, 1934).

Tobias Smollett, Lady Wortley Montagu, and Sir Philip Thicknesse quoted in Constantia Maxwell, *The English Traveller in France* (Paris, 1932).

On wealth of cities and certain provinces, see François de la Rochefoucauld, *Voyages (1781-1783)*; Edmond Soreau, *La Chute de l'Ancien Régime* (Paris, 1937); Pierre Gaxotte, *Le Siècle de Louis XIV;* and Paul Ardascheff, *Les Intendants de Province sous Louis XVI* (Paris, 1909).

Description of day-to-day life, see E. G. Léonard, *Mon Village sous l'Ancien Régime, d'Après les Mémoires d'un Paysan* (Paris, 1941).

On general signs of prosperity, see Marcel Marion, *Histoire Financière de la France* (Paris, 1914-1928).

On the economic cycle of the *ancien régime,* see C. E. Labrousse, *La Crise de l'Economie Française à la Fin de l'Ancien Régime et au Debut de la Révolution* (Paris, 1943).

Carraciolo on starvation and indigestion, quoted by Louis Ducros, *La Société Française au Dix-huitième Siècle.*

On grain policy, see Shelby T. McCloy and Edgar Faure, *La Disgrâce de Turgot* (Paris, 1961).

On the famine compact and the flour war, see Edgar Faure, and Douglas Dakni, *Turgot and the Ancien Régime* (London, 1939).

On taxes and Pontchartrain's remark to Lord Portland, see Marcel Marion, *Les Impots Directs sous l'Ancien Régime.*

On the collection of taxes, see Jean Vilain, *Le Recouvrement des Impots Directs sous l'Ancien Régime,* Marcel Riviere, ed.

On Machault and the twentieth, see Charles Gomel, *Les Causes Financières de la Révolution Française* (Paris, 1892).

On clergy's taxes, see abbé Sicard, *Ancien Clergé de France.*

On indirect taxes and the General Farm, see George T. Matthews, *The Royal General Farms in Eighteenth Century France* (New York, 1958).

On ostentation of General Farmers, see Edgar Faure, *La Disgrâce de Turgot.*

On weights and measures, internal duties, and inspection of goods, see Charles Gomel.

On notion of budget, see Charles Gomel.

Abbé Terray to syndic of Languedoc, and Joly de Fleury's annuities, see Edgar Faure.

On cost of king's household, see Shelby T. McCloy and Marcel Marion.

Louis XV on theft, see Charles Gomel.

On Loménie de Brienne's reforms, see Jean Egret, *La Pré-Révolution Française* (Paris, 1962).

On the depression at the end of the *ancien régime,* see Georges Lefebvre, *Etudes sur la Révolution Française* (Paris, 1954); and C. E. Labrousse.

On the economic aspects of the feudal reaction, see Frederick Braesch, *1789, L'Année Cruciale;* and Hubert Methivier, *L'Ancien Régime* (Paris, 1961).

On the crisis of 1788, see Shelby T. McCloy; Paul Ardascheff; and C. E. Labrousse.

LOUIS THE BEHEADED

Alexis de Tocqueville, see *L'Ancien Régime et la Révolution* (Paris, 1952).

On Louis XVI's reforms, see Ernest Semichon, *Les Reformes sous Louis XVI* (Paris, 1876).

New language in official pronouncement, see Paul Ardascheff, *Les Intendants de Province sous Louis XVI* (Paris, 1909).

Mania for the hunt, see Louis Nicolardot, *Le Journal de Louis XVI* (Paris, 1873).

On coronation, see G. M. Tracy, *Les Bourbons.*

On king's wish to resign, see Allison, *Malesherbes* (New Haven, 1938).

'Change this drunkard for me,' see Emile Dard, *La Chute de la Royauté* (Paris, 1949).

On king's strength and physical appearance, see the marquis de Ségur, *Au Couchant de la Monarchie.*

On king's pastimes, see Alfred Leroy, *Louis XVI.*

On king's diary, see Nicolardot.

On arranged marriage, see Gérard Walter, *Marie-Antoinette* (Paris, 1948).

On the abbé de Vermond, see Pierre Lafue, *Louis XVI* (Paris, 1942).

On Marie-Antoinette's appearance, see the comte de Tilly, *Mémoires;* Madame Campan and the baroness Oberkirch, *Mémoires;* and Madame Vigée-Lebrun, *Souvenirs, Charpentier,* ed. (2 vols.).

On queen's trip to Paris, see Siméon-Prosper Hardy, *Mes Loisirs.*

On public drunkenness of Louis XVI, see abbé de Véri, *Journal,* J. de Witte, ed. (Paris, 1929).

On nonconsummation of Louis XVI's marriage, see Jean Torlais, *Louis XVI A-t-il Eté Opéré?* (Paris, 1938); and Dr. Paul Delaunay, *Le Monde Médical Parisien au Dix-huitième Siècle* (Paris, 1906).

Marie-Antoinette letter 'there is considerable change,' quoted by Jean Torlais.

Comte d'Aranda quoted by Gérard Walter.

Pamphlet on king's impotence quoted by Henri d'Almeras, *Marie-Antoinette et les Pamphlets Royalistes et Révolutionnaires* (Paris, 1907).

Joseph II letter 'Marie-Antoinette does not carry out,' quoted by Torlais.

On Louis XVI as young man and dauphin, see M. de la Fuÿe, *Louis XVI* (Paris, 1943).

Marie-Antoinette letter 'I live in the most essential happiness,' quoted by Jacques Arnna, *Le Double Visage de Marie-Antoinette.*

Joseph II letter 'as you know,' quoted by Jean Torlais.

Maria Theresa letter 'what my daughter tells me,' quoted by Gerard Walter.

Maria Theresa letter 'she thinks the king,' quoted by Alfred Leroy, *Historie des Rois de France* (Paris, 1956).

Marie-Antoinette letter 'my tastes are not,' see *Lettres de Marie-Antoinette,* eds. Maxime de la Rocheterie et le marquis de Beaucourt, (Société de l'Histoire de France, Paris, 1895).

On pamphlets against the queen, and friendships with Lamballe and Polignac, see Henri d'Almeras.

On princesse de Lamballe's fainting spells, see comte de Tilly, *Mémoires.*

On favours granted by Marie-Antoinette, see Gérard Walter and Pierre Lafue.

On letters to Polignac, see *Lettres de Marie-Antoinette.*

On Fersen and exchange of letters with him, see Henri Vallotton, *Marie-Antoinette et Fersen* (Paris, 1952).

On stories that circulated about the queen, see H. Fleischmann, *Libelles Contre Marie-Antoinette* (Paris, 1910).

On the queen's necklace, see André Castelot, *Marie Antoinette* (Paris, 1953).

Mother's advice, see *Lettres de Marie-Antoinette*.

Marie Antoinette letters 'after having discussed,' and 'I spoke very clearly,' quoted by Jacques Arnna.

Marie Antoinette letter on d'Aiguillon, see *Lettres de Marie-Antoinette*.

Joseph II letter 'why don't you mind your business,' quoted by Henri Vallotton.

Esterhazy incident quoted by marquis de Ségur, *Au Couchant de la Monarchie*.

Montbarey incident, see prince de Montbarey, *Mémoires* (Paris, 1826).

Marie-Antoinette buying Saint-Cloud, see Robert Lacour-Gayet, *Calonne* (Paris, 1963).

Marie-Antoinette letter 'what saddens me greatly,' see *Lettres de Marie-Antoinette*.

On Turgot, his programme and downfall, see Edgar Faure, *La Disgâce de Turgot* (Paris, 1961); Douglas Dakin, *Turgot and the Ancien Régime* (London, 1939); and C. J. Gignoux, *Turgot* (Paris, 1945).

On Louis XVI appointing Maurepas and recalling the Parlements, see Henri Carré, *La Fin des Parlements;* and Ernest Lavisse, *Histoire de France* (Paris, 1911).

On Malesherbes, see Allison.

On the suppression of serfs and the Question, see Ernest Semichon, *Les Réformes sous Louis XVI*.

THE SAGE OF PASSY

On Franklin's arrival in France, see Edward E. Hall and Edward E. Hall, Jr., *Franklin in France* (Roberts Brothers, Boston, 1887).

On Vergennes and joining the insurgents, see Charles de Chambrun, *A l'Ecole d'un Diplomate—Vergennes* (Paris, 1944).

Franklin on toleration, see *Collected Writings,* Smyth ed. (10 vols.).

On French admiration of America, see *Franklin in France;* Paul Hazard, *La Pensée Européenne au Dix-huitième Siècle* (Paris, 1963); and Alphonse Aulard, *Etudes sur la Révolution Française*.

On Lafayette, see André Maurois' biography.

On attitudes of other European monarchies towards America, see Richard B. Morris, *The Peacemakers* (New York, 1965).

On Vergennes' dispatch 'the English have inconsiderately,' see John J. Meng, *Vergennes, European Phases of His American Diplomacy* (Paris, 1932).

On Beaumarchais' support, see Georges Lemaître, *Beaumarchais* (Paris, 1949).

On Vergennes' correspondence with Beaumarchais, report to cabinet and Louis XVI, Bonvouloir mission, and reaction of French cabinet, see Charles de Chambrun.

On Franklin's popularity in France, see *Franklin in France* and biographies by Smith; Bernard Faÿ (Paris, 1930); and Carl Van Doren (New York, 1946).

On *Gazette d'Amiens* considering Franklin French, see John J. Meng.

On Venetian ambassador's quotation, see *Rapports des Ambassadeurs Italiens à la Cour de France* (Société de l'Histoire de France).

All Franklin quotations are from the Smyth edition of his *Collected Writings*.

Quotations on 'Advice to a Young Man on the Choice of his Mistress' and 'Letter to the Academy of Brussels,' are from *Curious and Facetious Letters of Benjamin Franklin,* printed for private circulation (200 copies, 1898).

On Franklin and foreign policy, see G. Stourzh, *Benjamin Franklin and American Foreign Policy* (Chicago, 1954).

On Franklin's Parisian life, tractations with Vergennes, diplomatic moves, arguments with other envoys, and conclusion of the treaty with France, see *Franklin in France;* and biographies of Smyth; Van Doren; and Faÿ.

On Bancroft's spying, see S. F. Bemis, 'The British Secret Service and the Franco-American Alliance,' *American Historical Review* (XIX, 1924).

On Franklin's land speculations and Silas Deane's deals, see *Western Lands in the American Revolution* (New York, 1937); and Jack M. Sosin, *Whitehall and the Wilderness* (1961).

Letter from John to Samuel Adams, see *Adams Family Papers.*

On Madame Helvétius, see Antoine Guillois, *Le Salon de Madame Helvétius* (Paris, 1894).

Sparring between Vergennes and Lord Stormont, see Charles de Chambrun.

On Franklin's reception at Versailles, see duc de Croÿ, *Journal Inédit.*

On French aid to America, see Alphonse Aulard, *La Dette Américaine Envers la France* (*Etudes sur la Révolution Française*).

On Necker's contacts with England, see R. B. Morris, *The Peacemakers*.

On the treaty with England, Jay's attempts for a separate peace, Vergennes' contacts with Shelburne, de la Luzerne's influence, the partition attempts, and the final treaty, see Richard B. Morris, *The Peacemakers*.

On Vergennes' notes about the treaty and his 'tip,' see Charles de Chambrun.

On Franklin funeral in Nantes, see Archives Municipales, Nantes.

THE FIRST REVOLUTION

Frénilly quotation, see baron de Frénilly, *Souvenirs* (Paris, 1908).

Richelieu quotation, see Pierre Lafue, *Louis XVI* (Paris, 1943).

On bourgeoisie, Parlement in 1560 defined the bourgeois as 'good citizens, inhabitants of cities, officers of the king, merchants, those living from their income, and others.'

On bourgeoisie as a class, see Marcel Marion, *Dictionnaire des Institutions*.

On aspirations of bourgeoisie and falling away from the monarchy, see Elinor G. Barber, *The Bourgeoisie in Eighteenth-Century France* (Princeton, 1955).

On the formation of a bourgeois philosophy, see Joseph Aynard, *La Bourgeoisie Française* (Paris, 1934).

On the rise of the bourgeoisie, see Charles Morazé, *Les Bourgeois Conquérants* (Paris, 1957).

On alliance of sword and gown nobility, see F. L. Ford, *Robe and Sword* (Cambridge, 1953).

On number of nobles, land ownership, and takeover of various careers, see Hubert Méthivier, *L'Ancien Régime* (Paris, 1961).

On Necker, see E. Chapuisat, *Necker* (Paris, 1938); Lavaquerie, *Necker, le Fourier de la Révolution* (Paris, 1933); Pierre Joly, *Necker* (Paris, 1952).

On Necker's secret deals, see René Stourm, *Les Finances de l'Ancien Régime et la Révolution* (Paris, 1885).

On Necker and public opinion, see Louis Ducros, *La Société Française au Dix-huitième Siècle* (Paris, 1926).

On Calonne, see Robert Lacour-Gayet, *Calonne* (Paris, 1963); and Pierre Joly, *Calonne* (Paris, 1950).

On the Assembly of Notables, see Jean Egret, *La Pré-Révolution Française* (Paris, 1962).

On Brienne, Parlement's resistance, the 1788 coup, and the makeup of the opposition, see Jean Egret.

On the day of the tiles, see Champollion-Figeac, *Chroniques Dauphinoises* (1880, 2 vols.); *La Journée des Tuiles, par un Vieux Bibliophile Dauphinois* (Recueil Chapuis); Jean Egret, *Le Parlement du Dauphiné et les Affaires Publiques dans la Deuxième Moitié du Dix-huitième Siècle* (Paris, 1942); and Stendhal, *La Vie de Henry Brulard* (Paris, 1913).

On ambassadors' predictions of revolution, see Charles Gomel, *Les Causes Financières de la Révolution Française* (Paris, 1892–1893).

On unrest in Paris and the clergy's opposition, see Jean Egret, *La Pré-Révolution Française*.

On bankruptcy of 1788, see baron de Besenval, *Mémoires* (Paris, 1805–1806).

On Brienne's disgrace and the recall of Necker, see Jean Egret.

Duc de Lauzun quotation from his *Mémoires,* Jonquières, ed. (Paris, 1928).

On Estates General, see R. Jallifier, *Histoire des Etats Generaux* (Paris, 1885).

On memoir of princes and Louis XVI's indecision, see Jean Egret.

On lack of respect, see Sébastien Mercier, *Tableau de Paris* (Amsterdam, 1783–1789); and Taine, *Origines de la France Contemporaine.*

On the Estates General song, see Louis Dollot, *La Question des Privilèges dans la Deuxième Moitié du Dix-huitième Siècle* (Paris, 1941).

THE SECOND REVOLUTION

On the drafting of the cahiers, see Beatrice Fry Hyslop, *A Guide to the General Cahiers of 1789* (New York, 1936).

On the contents of the cahiers, see Beatrice Fry Hyslop, *A Guide to the General Cahiers of 1789*; and *French Nationalism According to the Cahiers of 1789* (New York, 1934); Edmé Champion, *La France d'Après les Cahiers de 1789* (Paris, 1897); Amédée Vialay, *Les Cahiers du Tiers Etat* (Paris, 1911); and *Les Français Ont la Parole,* cahiers des Etats Generaux présentés par Pierre Goubert et Michel Denis (Paris, 1964).

On feudal rights and abuses, see Marcel Marion, *Dictionnaire des Institutions;* Henri Carré, *La Noblesse de France et l'Opinion Publique;* Louis Dollot, *La Question des Privilèges dans la Deuxième Moitié du Dix-huitième Siécle* (Paris, 1941); and Albert Babeau, *Le Village sous l'Ancien Régime.*

On the meeting of the Estates General, see Georges Lefebvre, *Recueil de Documents Relatifs aux Séances des Etats Généraux de 1789* (Paris, 1962); and J. Michaud, *Les Etats Généraux et le 14 Juillet, 1789* (Paris, 1960).

On the conflict between the three orders in May and June, see A. Soboul, *1789—l'An Un de la Liberté* (Paris, 1950); Etienne Dumont, *Souvenirs sur Mirabeau* (Paris, 1832); Jacques-Antoine Creuze-Latouche, *Journal d'un Constituant* (Paris, 1946); Gaultier de Biauzat, *Sa Vie et Correspondence* (Paris, 1890); and marquis de Ferrières, *Journal* (Paris, 1799).

On the Serment du Jeu de Paume, see Armand Brette, *Le Serment du Jeu de Paume* (Paris, 1893); Charles Vatel, *Notice Historique sur la Salle du Jeu de Paume* (Paris, 1883); and Bailly, *Mémoires* (Paris, 1804).

THE THIRD REVOLUTION

On the Bastille, see *Archives de la Bastille,* Ravaisson, ed. (1866–1873, 7 vols.); Latude, *Mémoires.*

On capture of Bastille, see Jacques Godechot, *La Prise de la Bastille* (Paris, 1965); H. Monin, *L'Etat de Paris en 1789* (Paris, 1889); Georges Rude, *The Crowd in the French Revolution* (Oxford, 1959); G. Martin, *14 Juillet, 1789* (Paris, 1939); and J. Durieux, *Quelques Vainqueurs de la Bastille* (Paris, 1925).

On first to enter Bastille, see *Journée de Jean-Baptiste Humbert* (Paris, 1789), and *Récit des Assiégés,* Archives de la Guerre, Vincennes ('Mémoires Historiques').

On Russian reaction, see M. Strange, *La Révolution Française et la Société Russe* (Moscow, 1961).

On king in Paris on July 16, see Frantz Funck-Brentano, *Scènes et Tableaux de la Révolution* (Paris, 1934); Georges Lefebvre, *La Grande Peur de 1789* (Paris, 1932); and E. Charavay, *Le Lendemain de la Prise de la Bastille (La Révolution Française,* vol IX; Paris, 1885).

On the October days, see Jules Mazé, *Les Journées d'Octobre* (Paris, 1939); and A. Mathiez, *Etude Critique sur les Journées des 5 et 6 Octobre, 1789* (Paris, 1899).

On Louis XVI prevented from leaving the Tuileries, see A. Mathiez, *Les Grandes Journées de la Constituante* (Paris, 1913); and Funck-Brentano, *Scènes et Tableaux.*

On the flight of Varennes, see André Castelot, *La Tragédie de Varennes* (Paris, 1954); duchesse de Tourzel, *Mémoires,* (Paris, 1883); Pétion, *Mémoires* (Paris, 1866); and Georges Lefebvre, *Etudes sur le Révolution Française* (Paris, 1954).

King puts on Phrygian bonnet, see Georges Rude, *The Crowd in the French Revolution*; Mathiez; Funck-Brentano.

On invasion of Tuileries and slaughter of Swiss guards, see Marie-Madeleine Martin, *Histoire de l'Unité Française* (Paris, 1948); J. G. Alger, *Paris in 1789–1794* (London, 1902); P. Thureau-Dangin, *Paris, Capitale de la Révolution Française* (Paris, 1872); Pierre-Louis Roederer, *Chronique de Cinquante Jours* (Paris, 1832); Albert Mathiez, *Le 10 Août* (Paris, 1931).

On d'Orléans wealth, see Beatrice Hyslop, *L'Apanage de Philippe d'Orléans* (Paris, 1965).

On the complete list of his titles, see Montjoie, *La Conspiration d'Orléans* (Paris, 1796).

On charges against him, see Montjoie, Montrey, *Les Orléans Devant l'Histoire* (Paris, 1887); and Le Corbeiller, *Le Léopard de la Révolution* (Paris, 1938).

Mirabeau opinions, see *Correspondence du Comte de la Marck et du Marquis de Mirabeau*.

Sénac de Meilhan quotation, see *Le Gouvernement, les Moeurs, et les Conditions en France Avant la Révolution* (Paris, 1862).

On d'Orléans' youth, life as a courtier, wit, bets, callousness, and marriage, see Amédée Britsch, *La Jeunesse de Philippe Egalité* (Paris, 1926).

On Philippe's Parlementary opposition, and explanation to Brissot, see André Castelot, *Philippe Egalité, le Prince Rouge* (Paris, 1950).

On comte de Pons' opinion, see Amédée Britsch.

On Laclos, see Emile Dard, *Choderlos de Laclos* (Paris, 1905).

On d'Orléans' contempt for Estates General, see G. du Boscq de Beaumont et M. Bernoz, *La Famille d'Orléans Pendant la Révolution*.

On leniency towards tenants and model cahier, see Beatrice Hyslop.

On Réveillon riots, see Jacques Godechot, *La Prise de la Bastille* (Paris, 1965).

On Estates General procession, see Georges Lefebvre, *Recueil de Documents Relatifs aux Séances des Etats Généraux de 1789*.

On remarks at August 4 session of assembly, see André Castelot.

On Roederer quotation, see *Mémoires du Duc de Rovigo*.

On October riots and d'Orléans' part, see Edmond Seligman, *La Justice Pendant la Révolution*.

On accepting name of Égalité, and behaviour in Convention, see André Castelot.

On Orléans' subsidies to revolutionary leaders, see *Mémoires du Duc de Rovigo* (Paris, 1823).

On members of the Convention who abstained, see E. Belhomme, *Les Régicides* (Paris, 1893).

On arrest and execution of d'Orléans, see André Castelot.

On trial and execution of Louis XVI, see *Le Procès de Louis XVI,* presenté par A. Soboul (Paris, 1966); Arthur Conte, *Sire, Ils Ont Voté la Mort* (Paris, 1966); A. Caille, *Un des Juges de Louis XVI.*

On life in the Temple, see *Mémoire Ecrit par Marie-Therese Charlotte de France sur la Captivité des Princes et Princesses et de Ses Parents* (Paris, 1892).

Index